Recipes to Attract and Feed

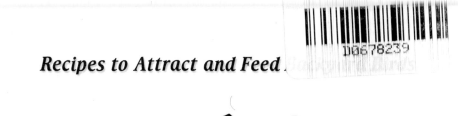

Cooking
for the Birds

Includes 26 Fun-to-Make Recipes

by Adele Porter

Adventure Publications, Inc.
Cambridge, MN

DEDICATION

This book is dedicated to Elizabeth, Byron and Rachael. Wamlati!

ACKNOWLEDGEMENTS

My sincere thanks to the countless volunteers who have contributed their time, energies and field data to breeding bird atlases, bird counts and other citizen science projects. The collaborative efforts of volunteers and wildlife professionals across North America, as well as globally important migratory wintering areas, provide vital information to the life histories and population status of birds. These resources have been imperative in the writing of the *Wild About* series of bird books.

Carrol Henderson, Supervisor, Minnesota DNR Nongame Wildlife Program: Thank you for reviewing the book and sharing your knowledge of North American birds. Your input has been invaluable.

Friends, the neighborhood gang, and the teachers and students who shared their ideas and support: Thank you for your incredible enthusiasm and imaginative input.

Helen and John Scuffham's Garden, Helen's Gourd Creations: Thank you for providing/preparing the incredible gourds for the feeders and for sharing your creative talents.

Cover and book design by Jonathan Norberg

Illustrations by Anna Kaiser

Photo credits by photographer and page number:
Front cover photos: Baltimore Oriole by Alan Stankevitz
Back cover photos: Krunchy Kabobs, Banana Split and Double-dipped Cone by Alan Stankevitz
Alan Stankevitz: 10 (sunflower chips), 11 (safflower), 28, 30, 32, 34, 36 (Eggshell Salad, Summer Tanager), 38, 40, 42, 44 (Irresistible Insects, Brown Creeper), 46, 48 (Krunchy Kabobs, Summer Tanager), 50, 52, 54, 56, 58, 60, 62, 64, 66, 68, 70, 74, 76, 78, 80 (Brown Creeper), 84 (Summer Tanager) **Stan Tekiela:** 36 (House Wren), 60 (American Black Duck), 72 (Red-headed Woodpecker), 80 (American Black Duck), 83 (Red-headed Woodpecker)

Copyright 2010 by Adele Porter
Published by Adventure Publications, Inc.
820 Cleveland Street South
Cambridge, MN 55008
1-800-678-7006
www.adventurepublications.net
All rights reserved
Printed in China
ISBN: 978-1-59193-262-8

Cooking
for the Birds

Table of Contents

RECIPES

Wild About Cooking for the Birds

If you are wild about birds, then *Cooking for the Birds* will guide you in planning, preparing and hosting a backyard banquet for the birds. Designed for the entire family (ages 5–105), the 26 easy recipes in this book provide a banquet of nutritious food choices for a wide variety of backyard birds—from robins, woodpeckers and hummingbirds to chickadees and more! Once your buffet is served, sit back and enjoy the festivities. Contribute the information about the birds in your backyard, school yard or urban setting to a citizen science project that works toward the stewardship of our limited natural resources.

How To Use This Book

Backyard bird feeding is like hosting a dinner party for wildlife. There are several stages involved in planning and implementing the whole affair. These stages are described in the following sections.

Set the Table for Success with an understanding of the foods birds eat, how food preferences vary by bird species and how a bird's nutritional needs vary according to season.

Cooking Basics will help you learn the basic ingredients of bird feeding.

Arrange the Dining Room with the help of tips for creating a backyard or urban habitat that attracts and meets the needs of wildlife. Then, create your banquet guest list from the seating chart.

Invite the Guests: Prepare the Menu by reviewing this list of the 75 most common North American backyard birds. This list is arranged by bird family and identifies the foods that each species is most attracted to in a feeder setting. It also identifies the region of the United States where the birds are most likely to inhabit. From this list you can plan your banquet menu by selecting the bird species you desire to attract and then preparing a recipe that matches the ingredients, or you can simply whip up a favorite recipe and prepare for guests to arrive.

Recipe Review provides a sample recipe to help you know what to expect.

Kids in the Kitchen features handy advice and safety tips for cooking when kids are in the kitchen.

Teaming Up: Citizen Science and Environmental Awareness are important, so once your banquet is served, find a comfortable seat and put on your citizen-science hat. You can be a part of ongoing science by contributing your bird information to a project sponsored by Wild About Science, the National Audubon Society, the Cornell Lab of Ornithology and more.

Chef Notes at the end of this book are yours to fill in. You can keep track of the birds that are attracted to particular recipes, note changes you've made to a recipe, and create your own recipes from the ingredients list. Put your creativity to work and journal, sketch, keep a checklist of birds and more.

Cooking for the Birds blends kitchen and backyard science into a banquet of fun for wildlife enthusiasts of all ages. Let the feast begin!

Set the Table for Success

Bird feeding is both a craft and a science. It can be as simple as setting out a sock feeder of thistle seeds and watching finches and chickadees feast. It may be as involved as understanding bird biology and the life histories of different species and then setting up feeders to attract specific birds in each season. This involves a full menu: insects for wrens, warblers and creepers; suet for nuthatches and woodpeckers; fruit for mockingbirds, orioles, cardinals and robins; acorns and other nuts scattered on the ground for Wild Turkeys and jays; and nectar for hummingbirds.

Bird feeding does not provide for a bird's total nutritional needs, but it supplements their diet of foods gained from the natural environment. This can be helpful during harsh winters. Black-capped Chickadees have been found to gain just over 20% of their overall nutrition from feeders. By setting up feeders and landscaping with plants that host natural food sources for wildlife, your yard can be an important part of providing for the basic needs of wildlife.

Seasonal Favorites

Each season provides an opportunity to set out food items that are suited to the specific needs of birds. For instance, neotropical migratory birds often feed on fruit in their South American winter homes, and when they come north to nest in North America they take advantage of the summer increase in mineral and protein-packed insects to fuel their chicks' fast growth.

WINTER: Birds that overwinter in the northern United States require high-calorie foods to produce enough heat to survive and to gain as many calories as possible while expending the least amount of energy. Fats and carbohydrates in the form of suet and nuts are on the winter menu along with calorie-laden sunflower and safflower seeds. Offering shelled nuts and seeds will also save birds the effort of opening the seeds.

SPRING/FALL: Fueling Migration The migratory movements of birds are triggered by changes in the length of daylight. During migration, birds produce additional hormones, allowing them to store energy in extra fat deposits; this energy is needed to fuel migratory flight. Migration is also the time of year when the widest variety of bird species pass through many areas. Provide a wide variety of food types and sizes at all habitat levels to attract these migrating birds.

In the spring, provide warblers with mealworms, and set out fruit, jelly, and nectar for orioles, catbirds and robins, along with the regular menu of seeds and nuts. Set out nectar and jelly feeders by May 1st in regions where birds are moving through on spring migration.

In the fall, set out high-calorie foods like nectar, suet and protein-rich items such as mealworms. Studies have indicated that feeding birds during migration has not been found to delay their normal departure schedules.

SUMMER: Nesting and Raising Young Feeding a nest full of young birds requires parents to spend their energy in searching, capturing and delivering food. The fast growth of young birds is fueled by large amounts of protein. Setting out mealworms along with the regular fare provides a ready source of protein for bird parents and their ravenous fledglings. Setting out eggshells offers female birds a source of replacement for the calcium that their body used to produce a clutch of eggs.

Providing suet and peanut butter on warm summer days can be a sticky situation for birds. The melted mixture can stick to and affect a bird's feathers, and consequently their eggs and young. Replacing suet and peanut butter with shelled, unshelled peanuts and peanut hearts provides a variety of pea-nutty treats for birds during the summer.

Cooking Basics

The recipes in this cookbook call for ingredients common to bird feeding and cater to a wide variety of birds. Careful attention has been given to include only ingredients that are healthy for birds to ingest. The recipes have been built around these base ingredients so you can select a bird species you would like to attract, pair the food it eats with a recipe and then serve the resulting food in an appropriate type of feeder placed at the habitat level where the bird lives.

Get to know the ingredients and the recipes will be as easy as A, B, C.

SUET

Suet is lard/fat generally from beef, deer or other wild game. Suet can be served up as it is straight from the host animal or as it comes packaged from your local butcher. Chickadees will pick the rib cage of a deer carcass clean making for a ready-made bird feeder.

Suet can also be warmed and melted into a softer composition more easily managed for working into recipes. Caution is necessary when melting suet as it can flame at too high of a temperature; **this is a task for adults only**.

Although suet can be provided and eaten by birds in all seasons, it can become rancid during periods of warm weather. Consider substituting peanuts and peanut hearts during warm months of the year.

SUET BASE RECIPE

5 lbs of ground suet (ask your local meat department personnel to grind the suet for you)

Place half of the suet in a heavy pan over low heat*. For the purposes of this recipe, low is considered 2 in a heat range of 1–10. Stir the suet occasionally until it is in a semi-clear and liquid form. This generally takes about 15 minutes. Remove from the heat.

To remove any fibers, pour the suet through a fine wire mesh strainer into an 8 inch by 8 inch baking dish or like sized plastic container with a lid for storing. Place the strained suet in the refrigerator until it is no longer clear and has hardened.

From this suet base, a wide variety of ingredients can be added to attract specific species of birds: seeds, nuts, dried fruit (fruity suet), peanut butter (pea-nutty suet), cornmeal, oatmeal and even dried mealworms for extra protein. For the best results, prepare with a ratio of two parts suet to one part extra ingredients.

CORNMEAL

Cornmeal is finely ground corn used in baking quick breads, as coatings for meats and vegetables and in stuffing. Many birds are attracted to and benefit from the nutrients in cornmeal. Cornmeal is used as a substitute for white flour (wheat) in the recipes of this book. Some birds do not have the ability to digest white flour and it has little nutritional value for birds.

BLACK OIL SUNFLOWER SEEDS

Black oil sunflowers are commercially grown for pressing into sunflower oil. They are thin-shelled and easy for birds to hull. This is one of the most popular seeds at backyard feeders, attracting some 40 species of birds, including chickadees, goldfinches and titmice.

STRIPED SUNFLOWER SEEDS

Larger than black oil sunflower seeds and with less oil content, striped sunflower seeds are commercially grown for uses other than oil. This includes the sunflower snacks that we eat! Cardinals, grosbeaks, Purple Finches and nuthatches are just a few of the many birds that eat striped sunflowers.

SUNFLOWER SEED CHIPS

Sunflower seed chips are eaten by smaller birds like chickadees, titmice, White-throated Sparrows and American Goldfinches. There are no hulls to clean up and very little seed is wasted.

NYJER SEED

American Goldfinches are late nesters that take advantage of wild thistle seed to feed their young. Nyjer thistle is a commercial seed grown in India and Ethiopia for use in bird feeding. The seeds are very small and fine—just right for the small bills of finches, siskins, redpolls and even Indigo Buntings.

SAFFLOWER

Safflower is a plant that produces a flower head with seeds that are commercially grown for cooking oil. The seeds are eaten by Northern Cardinals, chickadees, doves and many other birds, but not by squirrels!

PROSO MILLET

White Proso millet is the small seed of the grass *Panicum miliaceum*. Millet is rich in B vitamins, calcium, potassium and zinc. It's popular with doves, finches, sparrows and juncos.

CRACKED & SHELLED CORN

Corn is high in carbohydrates, which fuel metabolism and make for a ready source of energy. Many birds eat corn, whether as meal, cracked, or shelled, including jays, doves, juncos, sparrows, blackbirds, Red-headed and Red-bellied Woodpeckers, Ring-necked Pheasants, Wild Turkeys, Northern Bobwhite, Mallards and Common Ravens.

PEANUTS

Peanuts are a powerhouse of protein, minerals and vitamins B and E, and are a favorite of jays, woodpeckers, nuthatches, titmice and chickadees. Peanut hearts and chips are preferred by the smaller bird species.

TREE NUTS

Acorns, hickory nuts, hazelnuts and other tree nuts provide essential protein and oils to forest birds like Wild Turkeys, jays and woodpeckers.

DRIED FRUIT

Birds that eat fruit all year take advantage of wild berries dried on the vine or plant. Backyard birds especially like raisins, cranberries and other fruit plumped by soaking in orange juice; these include bluebirds, robins, mockingbirds, cardinals, catbirds, thrashers, White-crowned Sparrows and tanagers.

Arrange the Dining Room

In a bird's-eye view the natural world is a dining room and your yard is one part of the larger landscape. One of North America's most common birds, the

American Robin, requires about one-half of an acre to as much as 2 acres for its breeding territory. Your yard or common area may not be this large, but when you consider the big picture of neighboring yards and public areas, the needs of robins and many other birds and wildlife can be met. Providing year-round food, water and shelter with a variety of plants, ground covers and trees will attract a variety of birds in all seasons.

Rooftop Garden

- Invite birds to your yard by providing shelter and a place to nest and raise their young. Build and set out bird nesting and roosting structures, and provide nesting materials in the spring. Consider leaving older trees with hollow cavities or those with the potential for birds to excavate cavities. Many species of wildlife depend on older trees. Leave stumps for stump feeders, too.

- Landscape your yard with fruit-bearing trees and shrubs, and flowering plants with blooms spread throughout the growing season. A diversity of plantings in your yard will attract an equally diverse array of wildlife.

- Birds have adapted to eating foods at different levels of a habitat. Making a range of foods available at all habitat levels will attract a wide variety of birds to your backyard dining room.

- Include the sound of moving or dripping water. Provide a source of clean water all year. Refreshing the water in a bird bath at least once per week will keep algal growth in check and mosquito larvae from developing. There are bird water heaters available for use in northern areas during winter months.

Cedar Waxwing

- Keep the food fresh. Rancid or moldy food is unhealthy for birds. Clean your feeders with a solution of one part bleach to nine parts water several times per year.

- Arrange hanging feeders in stations of 3–5 feeders, but don't put too many feeders close together. Overcrowding can create unhealthy conditions.

- Set bird feeders in predator-free areas with some open space where birds can cue in on any movement of a predator. Some birds, like those that spend their time foraging for food on the ground, feel comfortable with a brush pile near a ground feeding station where they can find immediate cover. Keep cats indoors.

- Life exchanges for life in a continuous cycle. Your backyard is a part of this energy chain. While songbirds are feasting at your backyard banquet, they may become a meal for a Sharp-shinned Hawk or a Cooper's Hawk. These small, slender-bodied woodland hawks maneuver around trees with their short, rounded wings and long tails. Both species are gray above and light below with reddish bars. They have red eyes and long, yellow legs.

Cooper's Hawk

- To discourage hawks from dining on the smaller birds at your feeders, discontinue filling the feeders for a few weeks. The smaller birds will find food in natural areas with more cover and the hawk will move to another area. Resume feeding when the pattern has been broken and backyard birds are no longer an á la carte item for hawks.

- The stewardship of natural resources extends to our shared and individual home outdoor spaces. Pesticides and herbicides applied to lawns and gardens find their way through the food chain and can adversely affect wildlife at all levels. Children playing in these environments are exposed as well. Healthy lawn-care alternatives are available and used successfully in some North American communities including Madison, Wisconsin, where the community nonprofit organization Greater Madison Healthy Lawn Team, Inc. works for a healthy and safe community—one lawn at a time.

- Be consistent. Be patient. Birds may start to show up in as little as a few days or it may take a season or two for some bird species to arrive. However long it takes, it is sure to be well worth the wait!

Preparing foods that meet the needs of a specific bird species is the first step. Placing the foods in the proper feeder and at the level in the environment of the bird's natural niche is the next step. This backyard setting provides a sample of the variety of feeders and levels of habitat that birds often use.

1. Apple/Orange feeder
2. Buddy bird feeder
3. Ground feeder
4. Bird bath
5. Jelly feeder
6. Mealworm feeder
7. Nectar feeder
8. Platform feeder
9. Screen feeder
10. Stump feeder
11. Suet feeder
12. Tray feeder
13. Sock thistle feeder

Invite the Guests: Prepare the Menu

Planning a backyard banquet requires a guest list and a menu. Decide on which guests to invite by identifying the birds that inhabit your region of North America. The 75 common North American backyard and waterside birds in this list are arranged taxonomically, by bird family, and are identified as occurring in the Northern US (N), the South (S), the East (E), the West (W), or a combination (E/W). For the purposes of this book, the Mississippi River is the dividing line between east and west, and the 40th parallel north divides north and south.

It's easy to prepare the menu for your guests if you know their food preferences. Each bird species has adapted to eat certain foods; some eat only insects or fruit or seeds, and others eat a variety of foods. Only the foods a bird species commonly eats at a backyard feeder or waterside park are included in this list. You can also use this as a checklist for recording the birds that come to dine at your school, urban or backyard buffet. To learn more about the bird species in your region, check out the *Wild About* bird book for your state or region, or visit www.adeleporter.com.

Birds & Their Family	Seeds & Nuts	Fruit	Insects	Suet	Sap	Nectar
Anseriformes: Swans, Geese, Ducks						
Canada Goose (E/W)*	🐦					
Wood Duck (E/W)*	🐦					
Mallard (E/W)*	🐦					
American Black Duck (E/W)*	🐦					
Galliformes: Pheasants, Grouse, Quails, Turkeys						
Ring-necked Pheasant (E/W)	🐦	🐦	🐦			
Northern Bobwhite (N/E)	🐦	🐦	🐦			
Wild Turkey (E/W)	🐦	🐦	🐦			
Columbiformes: Pigeons & Doves						
Rock Pigeon (E/W)	🐦					
Mourning Dove (E/W)	🐦					

Birds & Their Family	Seeds & Nuts	Fruit	Insects	Suet	Sap	Nectar
Apodiformes: Swifts & Hummingbirds						
Ruby-throated Hummingbird (E)			●		●	●
Anna's Hummingbird (W)						●
Rufous Hummingbird (W)						●
Black-chinned Hummingbird (W)						●
Piciformes: Woodpeckers & Allies						
Red-headed Woodpecker (E/W)	●	●	●	●		
Red-bellied Woodpecker (E)	●	●	●	●		
Yellow-bellied Sapsucker (E/W)	●	●	●	●	●	●
Downy Woodpecker (E/W)	●	●	●	●		●
Hairy Woodpecker (E/W)	●	●	●	●		●
Northern Flicker (E/W)		●	●	●		
Pileated Woodpecker (E)			●	●		
Passiformes: Perching Birds						
Gray Jay (N)	●	●	●	●	●	
Steller's Jay (W)	●	●	●			
Blue Jay (E/W)	●	●	●	●		
Western Scrub Jay (W)	●	●	●			
Black-billed Magpie (W)	●		●	●		
Purple Martin (E/W)			EGGSHELLS ONLY			
Carolina Chickadee (E)	●	●	●	●		
Black-capped Chickadee (E/W)	●	●	●	●		
Mountain Chickadee (W)	●	●	●			
Boreal Chickadee (N)		●		●		
Tufted Titmouse (E)	●		●	●		
Bushtit (W)			●			

* Found only near waterside parks

Birds & Their Family	Seeds & Nuts	Fruit	Insects	Suet	Sap	Nectar
Red-breasted Nuthatch (E/W)	✓	✓	✓	✓	✓	
White-breasted Nuthatch (E/W)	✓	✓	✓	✓	✓	
Brown Creeper (N)			✓	✓		✓
Carolina Wren (E)			✓	✓		
House Wren (E)			✓			
Golden-crowned Kinglet (N)	✓		✓			
Ruby-crowned Kinglet (N/W)	✓		✓	✓		
Western Bluebird (W)			✓			
Eastern Bluebird (E)			✓			
American Robin (E/W)	✓	✓	✓			
Gray Catbird (E/W)	✓	✓	✓	✓		
Northern Mockingbird (E/W)	✓	✓	✓	✓		
Brown Thrasher (E)	✓	✓	✓	✓		
Bohemian Waxwing (W)		✓	✓			
Cedar Waxwing (E)		✓	✓			
Yellow-rumped Warbler (E/W)			✓	✓		
Ovenbird (E)			✓			
Spotted Towhee (W)	✓	✓	✓			
Eastern Towhee (E)	✓	✓	✓	✓		✓
Chipping Sparrow (E/W)	✓		✓			
Fox Sparrow (E/W)	✓	✓	✓			
Song Sparrow (E/W)	✓		✓			
White-throated Sparrow (E)	✓	✓	✓			
White-crowned Sparrow (E/W)	✓		✓			
Golden-crowned Sparrow (W)	✓		✓			
Dark-eyed Junco (E/W)	✓		✓			
Summer Tanager (E/W)	✓	✓	✓			✓
Scarlet Tanager (S)		✓	✓	✓		

Birds & Their Family	Seeds & Nuts	Fruit	Insects	Suet	Sap	Nectar
Northern Cardinal (E/W)	✓	✓	✓			
Black-headed Grosbeak (W)	✓	✓	✓			
Rose-breasted Grosbeak (E)	✓	✓				
Indigo Bunting (E/W)	✓		✓			
Bullock's Oriole (W)	✓	✓	✓	✓		✓
Baltimore Oriole (E)	✓	✓	✓	✓		✓
Pine Grosbeak (W)	✓		✓	✓		
Purple Finch (E/W)	✓		✓			
Cassin's Finch (W)	✓					
House Finch (E/W)	✓	✓	✓			
Common Redpoll (E/W)			✓	✓		
Pine Siskin (E/W)	✓					
Lesser Goldfinch (W)	✓					
American Goldfinch (E/W)	✓					
Evening Grosbeak (E/W)	✓		✓			

* Found only near waterside parks

Recipe Review

The 26 recipes in *Cooking for the Birds* are presented in an easy-to-follow format that provides recipe directions, helpful hints, guest list possibilities, birding background and ideas on how to present the completed recipes to your backyard guests. Get to know the recipe layout and you will be wild about cooking for the birds!

Notes
Interesting natural history information, bird watching and bird feeding tips, recipe ideas and ideas on landscaping with natural plant foods.

NOTES

Celebrate the birds in your backyard with a cake. How many candles do birds have on their bird-day cake? For most birds, the first six months are the most perilous. In perching birds (Passerines), once the young have survived their first six months, they may have one, two, three, or as many as six birthdays. There are exceptional individual birds, however, like an American Robin that lived nearly 14 years!

Attracts
Look to this space for four featured species that may come to eat this completed food recipe.

| ATTRACTS: | White-breasted Nuthatch | Northern Cardinal | Downy Woodpecker | Evening Grosbeak |

Ingredients
The base ingredients of the recipe.

Tools
A list of items required to prepare the recipe that are outside of standard cooking equipment. Basic kitchen supplies (bowl, spoon, etc.) are not included in the list.

Happy Bird-day Cake

Illustration
This demonstrates the type of feeder appropriate for serving the recipe and a species of bird that may be attracted to it.

INGREDIENTS

1 cup oatmeal, coarsely ground in food processor
¼ cup cornmeal
½ teaspoon baking powder
1 tablespoon thistle seed
1 tablespoon sunflower chips
1 egg
½ cup milk or water, warmed
2 tablespoons melted suet
⅓ cup Raisin-berry Relish (page 62), or raisins and cranberries
Toppings: peanut butter, nuts, seeds, carrot sticks and pumpkin seeds

TOOLS

Muffin tin and liners
Food processor

DIRECTIONS

STEP 1:
Preheat the oven to 350°F. Line a muffin tin with paper liners. Set aside.

STEP 2:
Combine the coarsely ground oatmeal, cornmeal, baking powder, seeds and sunflower chips in a medium mixing bowl. Make a well in the center.

STEP 3:
Whip the egg in a separate bowl. Add the warmed milk or water, melted suet and then the Raisin-berry Relish.

STEP 4:
Pour the egg mixture into the well in the center of the oatmeal-nut mixture. Stir until ingredients are combined, but do not overmix.

STEP 5:
Bake for 20 minutes or until lightly browned and a toothpick inserted in the center comes out clean. Cool. Frost with peanut butter and decorate with seeds, nuts and dried mealworms. Top with a carrot candle with a pumpkin-seed flame.

TIP
This recipe can be divided into individual cake tins, baked and then frozen until needed.

ALSO ATTRACTS: Black-headed Grosbeak; Hairy Woodpecker; Blue Jay; Northern Mockingbird; Gray Catbird

Directions
Each recipe is written in three to five easy steps.

Time
Most recipes require 30–40 minutes or less to prepare.

Tip
Includes hints on the use of the recipes, interesting bird science, ways to deter other wildlife like squirrels and more!

Also Attracts
A sampling of even more bird species that may come to eat this completed recipe.

Recipe Options

Use this chart to determine which recipes to make for certain species, or to determine which birds might be attracted to a recipe you'd like to make.

Species	Appli-licious Crumble Pie	Banana Split	Coconut Café	Double-dipped Cone	Eggshell Salad	Festive Ornaments	Gobbler Goulash	Happy 3ird-day Cake	Irresistible Insects	Jelly Deli
American Black Duck (E/W)*										
American Goldfinch (E/W)										
American Robin (E/W)	✓								✓	
Anna's Hummingbird (W)										
Baltimore Oriole (E)	✓								✓	
Black-billed Magpie (W)		✓							✓	
Black-capped Chickadee (E/W)			✓	✓		✓		✓		
Black-chinned Hummingbird (W)										
Black-headed Grosbeak (W)										
Blue Jay (E/W)	✓			✓	✓	✓	✓		✓	
Bohemian Waxwing (W)										
Boreal Chickadee (N)			✓							
Brown Creeper (N)								✓		
Brown Thrasher (E)										
Bullock's Oriole (W)										
Bushtit (W)								✓		
Canada Goose (E/W)*										
Carolina Chickadee (E)			✓		✓					
Carolina Wren (E)				✓				✓		
Cassin's Finch (W)										
Cedar Waxwing (E)										
Chipping Sparrow (E/W)							✓	✓		
Common Redpoll (E/W)										
Dark-eyed Junco (E/W)				✓						
Downy Woodpecker (E/W)		✓		✓		✓		✓		
Eastern Bluebird (E)		✓		✓				✓		
Eastern Towhee (E)		✓				✓			✓	
Evening Grosbeak (E/W)						✓		✓		
Fox Sparrow (E/W)										
Golden-crowned Kinglet (N)								✓		
Golden-crowned Sparrow (W)			✓							
Gray Catbird (E/W)	✓					✓	✓			
Gray Jay (N)	✓					✓			✓	
Hairy Woodpecker (E/W)		✓	✓			✓	✓	✓		
House Finch (E/W)			✓							
House Wren (E)				✓						
Indigo Bunting (E/W)								✓		
Lesser Goldfinch (W)										
Mallard (E/W)*										
Mountain Chickadee (W)		✓	✓		✓			✓		

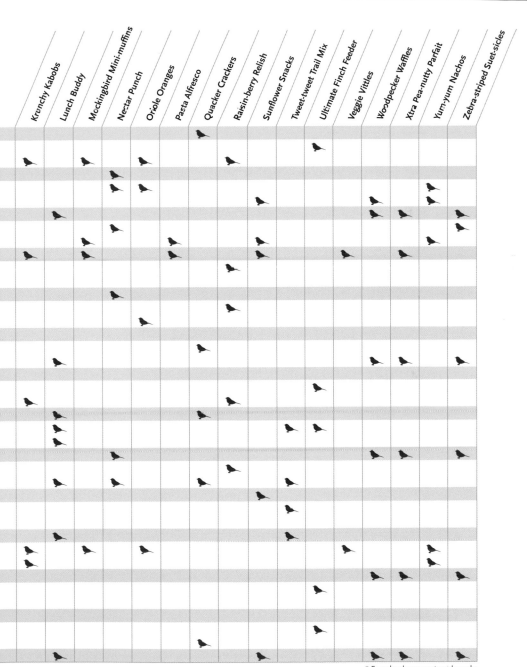

Krunchy Kabobs | Lunch Buddy | Mockingbird Mini-muffins | Nectar Punch | Oriole Oranges | Pasta Alfresco | Quacker Crackers | Raisin-berry Relish | Sunflower Snacks | Tweet-tweet Trail Mix | Ultimate Finch Feeder | Veggie Vittles | Woodpecker Waffles | Xtra Pea-nutty Parfait | Yum-yum Nachos | Zebra-striped Suet-sicles

* Found only near waterside parks

	Appl-icious Crumble Pie	Banana Split	Coconut Café	Double-dipped Cone	Eggshell Salad	Festive Ornaments	Gobbler Goulash	Happy Bird-day Cake	Irresistible Insects	Jelly Deli
Mourning Dove (E/W)	✓					✓				
Northern Bobwhite (N/E)	✓					✓				
Northern Cardinal (E/W)			✓	✓			✓			
Northern Flicker (E/W)		✓								
Northern Mockingbird (E/W)	✓				✓			✓	✓	
Ovenbird (E)				✓	✓			✓		
Pileated Woodpecker (E)					✓					
Pine Grosbeak (W)		✓								
Pine Siskin (E/W)										
Purple Finch (E/W)										
Purple Martin (E/W)					✓					
Red-bellied Woodpecker (E)	✓	✓			✓					
Red-breasted Nuthatch (E/W)		✓	✓	✓						
Red-headed Woodpecker (E/W)		✓			✓					
Ring-necked Pheasant (E/W)							✓			
Rock Pigeon (E/W)			✓				✓			
Rose-breasted Grosbeak (E)		✓								
Ruby-crowned Kinglet (N/W)								✓		
Ruby-throated Hummingbird (E)										
Rufous Hummingbird (W)										
Scarlet Tanager (E)				✓						
Song Sparrow (E/W)										
Spotted Towhee (W)	✓		✓							
Steller's Jay (W)				✓						
Summer Tanager (S)					✓				✓	
Tufted Titmouse (E)		✓	✓		✓					
Western Bluebird (W)								✓		
Western Scrub Jay (W)				✓						
White-breasted Nuthatch (E/W)		✓	✓	✓		✓		✓	✓	
White-crowned Sparrow (E/W)										
White-throated Sparrow (E)		✓								
Wild Turkey (E/W)							✓			
Wood Duck (E/W)*							✓			
Yellow-bellied Sapsucker (E/W)	✓	✓			✓				✓	
Yellow-rumped Warbler (E/W)		✓						✓		

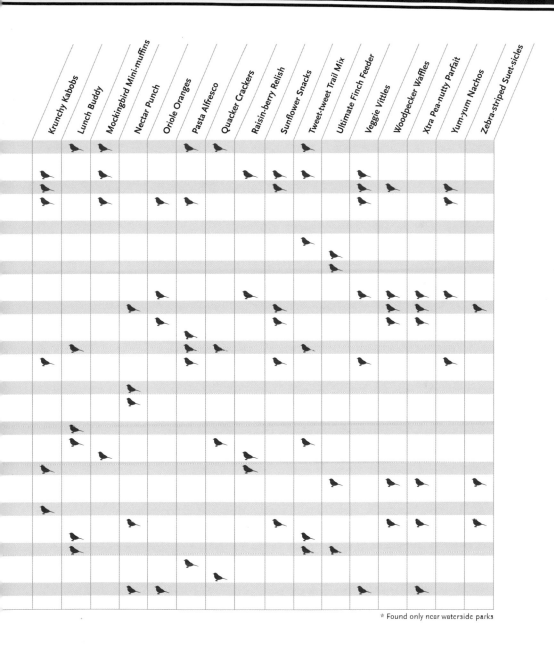

* Found only near waterside parks

Kids in the Kitchen

Cooking with your child is a fun way to spend time together while building essential life-long skills. The recipes in this cookbook are intended for adults and for children, with the premise that parents know best the unique capabilities of their child and what constitutes a safe level of engagement.

For kids, cooking in a kitchen can be a lot like doing a fun science experiment in a chemistry lab. It's fascinating to mix ingredients and see the reaction. Your goal is to make sure that the reactions occur as planned, so here are a few simple tips to make certain that kitchen science remains fun and safe.

- Read the directions thoroughly before starting. Modeling this essential rule of cooking will prepare your child for any steps that require your absolute supervision.

- When the recipe calls for the use of a knife, electrical appliance and/or heat, an adult should be in charge.

- Remind your young assistant to keep electrical cords and appliances away from contact with water.

- Keep any loose clothing, jewelry or hair away from moving parts and heat. Tie back long hair and remove jewelry. Roll up your sleeves, put on an apron and get ready to safely cook!

Hint: Cooking can bring on hunger for kids. Provide them with kid-sized portions of fruit, vegetables and nuts in a separate part of the kitchen from the ingredients being used to cook for the birds. Explain that the food they are cooking is not for people, even though some of the ingredients are familiar.

Teaming Up: Citizen Science and Environmental Awareness

With birds feasting at your banquet, it's time for action. You can contribute your backyard bird data to ongoing wildlife research by participating in the following citizen science projects. You can make a difference toward the stewardship of natural resources!

Birds for Kids	www.birdsforkids.com
Christmas/Holiday Bird Count	www.audubon.org/bird/cbc/index.html
Great Backyard Bird Count	www.birdsource.org/gbbcApps/kids
Journey North	www.learner.org/jnorth
Project Feeder Watch	www.birds.cornell.edu/pfw/
Project Pigeon Watch	www.birds.cornell.edu/pigeonwatch
Wild About Science	www.wildaboutscience.net

Cooking for the Birds is a part of the **Wild About Science** series that inspires curiosity, discovery and learning about natural history and resource stewardship.

Be a part of the ongoing *Cooking for the Birds* project by submitting your bird feeding data to the collective data pool on the **Wild About Science** website. You can enter your information about the birds attracted to a single food group or to each recipe. The collective data will be posted and then utilized for updating *Cooking for the Birds*. There is also a place to submit bird-healthy recipe revisions created for specific regions of North America and revisions according to the seasonal needs of bird species. Send in your photos of birds feasting on the recipes for others to enjoy. Photos may be considered for the next printing of *Cooking for the Birds*. You can even vote for your backyard birds' favorite recipes. **Get Wild About Science!**

female Baltimore Oriole

NOTES

The American Robins in your yard eat more than worms; they love apples! Last summer, a bold male robin came regularly to my backyard to eat chopped apples followed by a second course of grapes. He topped his afternoon snack by cooling off in the water sprinkler. Whip up this appl-icious crumble pie and prepare for hungry robins, catbirds, cardinals, doves, orioles and more!

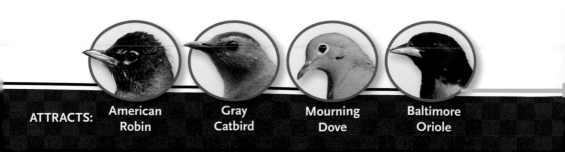

ATTRACTS: | American Robin | Gray Catbird | Mourning Dove | Baltimore Oriole

Appl-icious Crumble Pie

INGREDIENTS
Half an apple
1 cup cornmeal
1 tablespoon thistle seed
1 tablespoon millet seed
1 tablespoon sunflower chips
½ cup suet base
½ cup grape jelly

TOOLS
Mini-pie pan

DIRECTIONS

STEP 1:
Slice the apple into thin wedges and then cut them in half. Set aside for later. Combine cornmeal, thistle, millet and sunflower chips with the suet base in a mixing bowl. Use your hands to work into a crumble. If the mixture is too stiff, simply warm it in the microwave. Press the mixture into the sides and bottom of a mini-pie pan. Place pie shell in the refrigerator. Cool until hard.

STEP 2:
Place the jelly in a small saucepan over low heat. Stir until melted. Remove from heat. Pour the melted jelly into the cooled pie shell, filling it half full.

STEP 3:
Arrange the apple slices in a circle. Chill in a refrigerator for several hours or overnight. Optional garnish: Crumble extra crust mixture on the top and place a cherry in the middle.

STEP 4:
To release the pie from the pan, turn it over and tap the bottom. If the pie does not come out, place the very bottom of the pie pan in a sink of shallow warm water for 30 seconds and then try again. The pie may be served in the pan, also.

TIP
To serve your guests, place the pie in a backyard location away from cats and squirrels. Serve the pie near an oriole nectar feeder and attract Baltimore Orioles too!

ALSO ATTRACTS: Spotted Towhee; Northern Mockingbird; Gray and Blue Jays; Yellow-bellied Sapsucker; Red-bellied Woodpecker; Bullock's Oriole

female and male Eastern Bluebirds

NOTES

Just as dessert is only one part of a meal, the food eaten by backyard birds is only a supplement to their full energy requirements. Research indicates that just over 20% of the winter energy needs of chickadees are gained from food sources at bird feeding stations. Fill the water glasses (bird baths) all year, too. Birds fulfill their water needs from direct sources like puddles and bird feeders and from indirect sources such as the moisture content in foods and from respiration. Mourning Doves must visit a water source at least once per day. Bring on the feast!

ATTRACTS: Yellow-rumped Warbler   Eastern Bluebird   White-breasted Nuthatch   Northern Flicker

Banana Split

INGREDIENTS

1 peeled banana
Two small scoops of suet base,
    suet-fruit combo, or nutty suet
Half an orange, peeled and
    cut into pieces
Handful of grapes, halved
2 cherries
Shelled peanuts or other seeds
1 crushed eggshell
¼ cup of grape jelly
Live mealworms (optional—but the warblers and bluebirds would say required!)

TOOLS

Ice cream scoop
Banana split dish or
    recycled container

DIRECTIONS

STEP 1:

Slice the banana in half lengthwise and place both halves in a dish that can be kept outside. (Secondhand stores often have banana split dishes for sale, or be creative and recycle a leftover container.)

STEP 2:

Place two scoops of suet base between the banana halves. (Hint: Warm the scoop in hot water to allow it to scoop and release the suet more easily.)

STEP 3:

Heat the jelly until it is melted. Drizzle the jelly over the mounds of suet.

STEP 4:

Place the fruit pieces, nuts and seeds around the suet. During winter in northern regions, substitute peanuts and other nuts and seeds for the fruit.

STEP 5:

Sprinkle the crushed eggshell and squirmy mealworms on top.

TIP

Place the banana split on a tree stump or another elevated stand near tree branches (but not accessible to roaming cats and squirrels) in the spring and fall when warblers are migrating. Eastern Bluebirds will eat from this protein-packed meal during the summer nesting season.

ALSO ATTRACTS: Black-billed Magpie; Tufted Titmouse; Red-breasted Nuthatch; Eastern Towhee; Yellow-bellied Sapsucker; Downy, Hairy, Red-bellied and Red-headed Woodpeckers; Mountain Chickadee

White-breasted Nuthatch

NOTES

Bird feeders can be made of many natural items—gourds, hollowed tree stumps and limbs, and even coconuts. While some birds are eating the seeds inside the coconut feeder, other birds pull the fibers from the outer shell for nesting materials. This feeder can be made with either half of a coconut or, as in the directions, with the full coconut for a feeder with a roof.

ATTRACTS: Black-capped Chickadee | Rose-breasted Grosbeak | House Finch | Red-breasted Nuthatch

Coconut Café

INGREDIENTS
1 Coconut

TOOLS
Drill
Woodworking saw
3 lengths of twine
Screw-eye (optional)

DIRECTIONS

STEP 1:

This project works best with an assistant to help hold the coconut. Drill 3 holes in the base of the coconut. Drain the coconut water into a glass. You can drink it or save for other use.

STEP 2:

Hold the coconut upright. Use the saw to cut straight down from the top of the coconut, as if cutting in half from top to bottom—but only cut halfway down, to the center of the coconut.

STEP 3:

Turn the coconut on its side. Starting at the top, cut halfway down, meeting the first cut in the center of the coconut.

STEP 4:

Clean the coconut meat out of the bottom half of the coconut. Set aside to eat or for later use.

STEP 5:

Thread the twine through one hole and make a knot on the end inside the coconut. Repeat this with the other 2 lengths of twine, and then tie their ends together. Option: Screw a screw-eye into the top of the coconut and loop a length of twine through it for hanging the coconut feeder.

TIP

Fill the coconut feeder with Tweet-tweet Trail Mix (page 66) or with suet base, fruity suet, or Xtra Pea-nutty Parfait (page 74). Hang this snazzy feeder in your yard and watch for birds to take their turns snacking at the Coconut Café.

ALSO ATTRACTS: Spotted Towhee; Rock Pigeon; Northern Cardinal; White-throated and Golden-crowned Sparrows; Pine Grosbeak; White Breasted Nuthatch

NOTES

Seeds come packaged in very unique ways. Pine tree seeds are protected inside of pine cones. When a mature cone is exposed to heat, the individual sections spread open and the seeds eventually fall to the forest floor. Birds like Pine Siskins, and White-winged and Red Crossbills have bills uniquely shaped to remove and eat seeds from an opened pine cone. Make this recipe and watch for a variety of bird species to dip into a delicious snack right before your eyes.

ATTRACTS: Black-capped Chickadee | Tufted Titmouse | Hairy Woodpecker | White-breasted Nuthatch

Double-dipped Cone

INGREDIENTS
Pine cones
Suet
Seeds, any combination
Peanut butter

TOOLS
String or yarn

DIRECTIONS

STEP 1:
Explore an area with pine trees and collect a few pine cones. Take time to enjoy the smell of pine needles underfoot and the activity of wildlife.

STEP 2:
Tie a 12-inch length of string or yarn under the top layer of scales on the pine cone, just under the stem.

STEP 3:
Melt suet on low heat in a heavy saucepan or double boiler. Hold onto the string and dip the cone into the melted suet. If the suet is not deep enough for dipping, pour suet over the cone with a long-handled spoon. (Hint: Place wax paper on a countertop to catch any drips.)

STEP 4:
Immediately sprinkle seeds of your choice over the dipped cone. Let the cone cool on the waxed paper. To speed the cooling process, put the dipped cone in the refrigerator.

STEP 5:
Heat the peanut butter in a microwave until it is melted. This will only take about 3 ten-second intervals. Immediately dip the cone into, or drizzle the melted peanut butter over, the cooled cone. Hang the cones outside and wait for hungry birds to dip in.

ALSO ATTRACTS: Boreal, Carolina and Mountain Chickadees;
Downy Woodpecker; Red-breasted Nuthatch

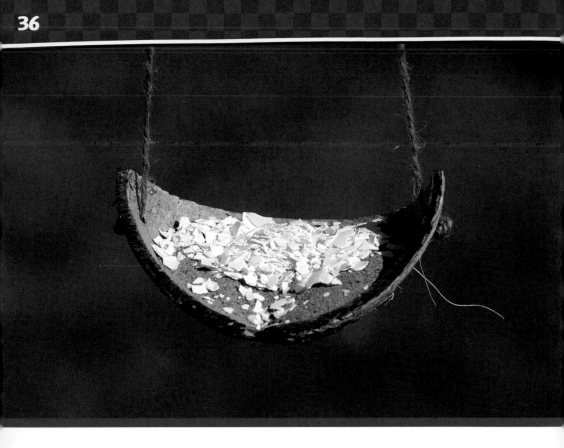

NOTES

The eggshells of birds are made of minerals, including calcium in the form of calcite crystals. Some bird parents eat the eggshells soon after the chicks hatch. This keeps the nest tidy, helps to keep predators from the nest and, in an adult female bird, replaces the calcium her body used to produce a clutch of eggs. Birds also need grit to aid in breaking down food. Eggshells and snail shells are eaten for both the calcium and the grit by birds like House Wrens. Set out eggshells in the spring and summer and watch the eggs-traordinary visits of busy backyard birds. At least 57 species of North American birds consume eggshells.

ATTRACTS: House Wren   Dark-eyed Junco   Purple Martin   Summer Tanager

Eggshell Salad

INGREDIENTS
2–6 eggs
Quarter of a coconut shell,
  leftover from making
  Coconut Café (page 32)

TOOLS
3 foot-long ½-inch-diameter
  wood dowel
Hot glue or other glue
Drill

DIRECTIONS

STEP 1:
Preheat oven to 275°F. Boil the eggs in a medium pan of water for seven minutes. Remove the eggs from the water with a slotted spoon and cool.

STEP 2:
Peel the eggs, keeping the shells to one side for the birds.

STEP 3:
Heat the eggshells in the oven for 15–20 minutes. This will rid the shells of any harmful bacteria. Cool. Crush the eggshells to the size of dry oatmeal flakes. Eggshells can be stored for adding to other recipes in this book and for refilling your saucer feeder.

STEP 4:
To make an easy saucer feeder, clean the meat from the coconut shell. Drill a ½-inch hole in the center of the shell. Glue the end of the dowel into the hole. For a hanging feeder, drill a hole in the end of each side of the coconut shell and place a length of twine through each hole. Tie the ends of the twine together at the top for use in hanging the feeder.

STEP 5:
Place the saucer feeder in your garden or yard and fill it with crushed eggshells and some sand for additional grit. Eggshell Salad is a great side dish in your backyard banquet!

TIP
To provide extra grit, add some crushed snail shells to the eggshell salad. Watch for wrens, martins, tanagers, warblers and juncos.

ALSO ATTRACTS: Carolina Wren; Blue, Steller's and Western Scrub Jays; Eastern Bluebird; Ovenbird; Northern Cardinal; Scarlet Tanager; Purple Martin

NOTES

Birds have beaks uniquely structured to pick up, capture and open the foods they eat. Grosbeaks have big, bulky beaks that work like a pair of strong pliers to crack open hard seeds, including cherry pits. Look to the shape and length of a bird's beak for clues to what it eats. Their dinnerware possibilities include a spoon, fork, knife, straw, strainer, net, pliers, nutcracker, saw and chopsticks!

ATTRACTS: White-breasted Nuthatch | Black-capped Chickadee | Downy Woodpecker | Evening Grosbeak

Festive Outdoor Appetizers

INGREDIENTS
Suet base
Cornmeal (optional)
Assorted seeds
Raisins and dried or
fresh cranberries

TOOLS
Assorted gelatin molds, ice cube
tray, or mini-muffin tin
Ribbon, raffia, twine, or string

DIRECTIONS

STEP 1:

Mix a full recipe of plain, pea-nutty, or fruity suet following the directions on page 9. Cornmeal may be added at a ratio of 1 part cornmeal to 2 parts suet base.

STEP 2:

Arrange raisins and cranberries in festive patterns in the bottom of individual molds. Next, press the suet firmly into the mold so there are no spaces in the mixture. A hole for hanging the appetizers can be made by placing a piece of macaroni into the mixture, one-third of the distance from the top, or insert a pipe cleaner into the suet to create a hook for hanging. Refrigerate until the mixture is hard. (Hint: A mini-muffin baking tin or ice cube tray can also be used. Place the end of a length of yarn, string, or raffia into the bottom before filling, to use for hanging, later.)

STEP 3:

To release the ornament from the mold, place the base of the mold in a shallow sink of warm water. Tip the mold and tap the bottom. String a length of bright red or natural color raffia through the middle of a circular ornament or through the macaroni hole. Hang the decorations on an outdoor tree, from a window suction-cup holder, or a feeder support.

TIP
String popcorn, pasta loops and cranberries onto button thread in 4-foot lengths. Tie several lengths together and string around a tree outdoors. Make swags from millet or sorghum stems that are in full seed to decorate your outside windows and doors.

ALSO ATTRACTS: Red-headed, Red-bellied, Hairy and Pileated Woodpeckers; Yellow-bellied Sapsucker; Gray Catbird; Northern Mockingbird; Blue and Gray Jays; Eastern Towhee; Carolina and Mountain Chickadee; Tufted Titmouse

NOTES

Wild Turkeys forage for food on the forest floor, where they find energy-rich nuts and seeds and protein-packed insects. If you live near a wooded area where Wild Turkeys live, you can invite them by providing the Gobbler Goulash in an open area with a brush pile on the edge, near trees or another edge near an open grassy area. When the goulash is left near a farm windbreak, or other edge near an open grassy area, Ring-necked Pheasants and Northern Bobwhites may come to feed. Get ready for ground-dwelling and nut-loving birds to gobble up this treat! Feeding turkeys can attract a large flock. Offering a smaller amount of food in staggered timing often works to attract fewer birds.

ATTRACTS: Wild Turkey Ring-necked Pheasant Northern Bobwhite Blue Jay

Gobbler Goulash

INGREDIENTS
4 cups of nuts: acorns,
   hickory nuts, peanuts
4 cups of cracked corn
4 cups of popped corn (hold the salt and butter)
Pasta Alfresco pieces (page 58), optional

TOOLS
Pail or large bowl

DIRECTIONS

STEP 1:

Combine the nuts, cracked and popped corn, and pasta pieces in a pail or large bowl.

STEP 2:

Before you place the goulash outside, consider making a tent-like wildlife-watching blind so that you can watch the birds by becoming a part of the habitat. Be resourceful and creative by using materials you have at home, like old sheets, blankets, or a tent.

STEP 3:

Place your blind near existing cover rather than in the open. Camouflage your blind with natural materials similar to those in or near your backyard habitat.

STEP 4:

Pour the goulash onto a raised ground feeder, or sprinkle part of the goulash directly on the ground.

STEP 5:

Be aware of the time of day that wildlife are most likely to visit. Wild Turkeys venture to feeding areas like this at dawn, sunrise and at dusk. Position yourself in your hideout and watch for the fun to begin. Record your wildlife adventure in Chef Notes (page 86) and include drawings or photographs.

ALSO ATTRACTS: Rock Pigeon; Chipping Sparrow; Mourning Dove; Wood Duck

NOTES

Celebrate the birds in your backyard with a cake. How many candles do birds have on their bird-day cake? For most birds, the first six months are the most perilous. In perching birds (Passerines), once the young have survived their first six months, they may have one, two, three, or as many as six birthdays. There are exceptional individual birds, however, like an American Robin that lived nearly 14 years!

ATTRACTS: White-breasted Nuthatch   Northern Cardinal   Downy Woodpecker   Evening Grosbeak

Happy Bird-day Cake

INGREDIENTS

1 cup oatmeal, coarsely
   ground in food processor
¼ cup cornmeal
½ teaspoon baking powder
1 tablespoon Nyjer seed
1 tablespoon sunflower chips
1 egg
½ cup milk or water, warmed
2 tablespoons melted suet
⅓ cup Raisin-berry Relish (page 62), or raisins and cranberries
Toppings: peanut butter, nuts, seeds, carrot sticks and pumpkin seeds

TOOLS

Muffin tin and liners
Food processor

DIRECTIONS

STEP 1:
   Preheat the oven to 350°F. Line a muffin tin with paper liners. Set aside.

STEP 2:
   Combine the coarsely ground oatmeal, cornmeal, baking powder, seeds and
   sunflower chips in a medium mixing bowl. Make a well in the center.

STEP 3:
   Whip the egg in a separate bowl. Add the warmed milk or water, melted suet and
   then the Raisin-berry Relish.

STEP 4:
   Pour the egg mixture into the well in the center of the oatmeal-nut mixture.
   Stir until ingredients are combined, but do not overmix. Fill muffin cups ⅔ full.

STEP 5:
   Bake for 20 minutes or until lightly browned and a toothpick inserted in the
   center comes out clean. Cool. Frost with peanut butter and decorate with seeds,
   nuts and dried mealworms. Top with a carrot candle with a pumpkin-seed flame.

TIP

This recipe can be divided into individual cake tins, baked and frozen until needed.

NOTES

New parents need all the help that they can get, especially when their chicks increase their mass by ten times in a mere ten days! To fuel this fast growth, many songbird parents feed their chicks mineral- and protein-packed insects. This can be a constant job, requiring some 15–20 trips per hour for a clutch of 4–6 chicks. Rose-breasted Grosbeaks make up to 50 food trips per hour to the nest! You can help songbird parents and the ravenous fledglings by providing a fast food café with mealworms—the Irresistible Insect Daily Special.

ATTRACTS: Brown Creeper   Eastern Bluebird   Chipping Sparrow   Black-billed Magpie

Irresistible Insects

INGREDIENTS

Mealworms, mealworms, mealworms

TOOLS

Cannonball gourd, mature and dried
Length of rawhide or twine
Small craft saw
Drill

DIRECTIONS

STEP 1:

To keep active mealworms in a feeder, it's best to use a container with sides that are at least 2 inches high. This can be the bottom of a clean coconut shell, the bottom of a gourd, or a clean recycled container.

STEP 2:

If using a gourd feeder like the one pictured here, place cornmeal in the bottom of the feeder first, or simply place the worms on the bare surface. The feeder provides a roof that will shade the contents from direct sunlight.

STEP 3:

To make a gourd feeder, first scrub the exterior of a mature, dried cannonball gourd with a copper kitchen scrubber and a strong solution of warm water and bleach. Dry.

STEP 4:

Next, cut holes in the side so that the resulting base is about 2 inches deep. A small craft saw works well for this purpose. Clean out the inside of the gourd. Drill 3 small drainage holes in the bottom. Drill 2 holes in the top for threading a piece of rawhide or twine for use in hanging the gourd. Hang the feeder at a mid-level to lower level.

TIP

If you need a source of live mealworms, you are in luck. They can be found at many pet supply stores, bait shops, bird feeding stores and online sources. Mealworms are the larval stage of the beetle *Tenebrio molitor*. The worms will stay alive for weeks in a refrigerator in a container with cornmeal for food and an apple slice for moisture. Place some holes in the top of the container, too. You might want to remind your family what is in the container. A midnight snack of mealworms could be a bit of a surprise.

ALSO ATTRACTS: Yellow-rumped Warbler; Bushtit; Ovenbird; Eastern and Western Bluebird; Carolina Wren; House Wren; Ruby-crowned and Golden-crowned Kinglet; Indigo Bunting; Mountain Chickadee

male Baltimore Oriole

NOTES

Migratory songbirds often feed on fruit in their tropical wintering habitat. On their spring migration to North American nesting areas, they rest and eat during the day. Invite these bright birds to refuel their energy in your yard by setting out grape jelly loaded with fresh grapes and oranges by May 1st. After they fill their belly with jelly, they may even stay to nest in your neighborhood.

ATTRACTS: American Robin   •   Baltimore Oriole   •   Blue Jay   •   Gray Catbird

Jelly Deli

INGREDIENTS
3 cups grape juice
5¼ cups white sugar
1 package pectin (Sure-Jell)
¾ cup water
Fresh grapes

TOOLS
String or yarn, 2 feet
Small, recycled take-out
    coffee cup with lid

DIRECTIONS

STEP 1:

Combine juice and sugar in a large bowl and mix well. Let stand 10 minutes.

STEP 2:

Add the package of pectin to the water in a heavy saucepan and stir well. Heat this mixture on medium-high heat until it comes to a boil. Boil for 1 minute, stirring constantly. Remove from heat.

STEP 3:

Pour the pectin mixture into the juice mixture and stir for about 3 minutes or until the grains of sugar are dissolved. Pour into plastic storage containers. Let the jelly set (become like a gel). This may take up to 24 hours. Freeze until needed. The jelly will keep for up to a year in the freezer.

STEP 4:

Use the point of a pencil to make a hole in each side of the coffee cup, one-third of the way down from the lip of the cup. Insert the string through the holes. Tie the ends together at the top. Place tape over the holes.

STEP 5:

Mix a dozen crushed fresh grapes with ½ cup of jelly and put in the coffee cup. Place the lid on the cup making certain that the drinking hole is open. This opening may be enlarged to make it easier for birds to get to the jelly. Avoid making sharp edges. The lid may be taped to the cup. Hang the jelly feeder from a tree branch (birds will need a perch while eating) by May 1st and watch for orioles, catbirds, robins and other birds to fill their belly with jelly!

ALSO ATTRACTS: Northern Mockingbird; Eastern Towhee;
White-breasted Nuthatch; Yellow-bellied Sapsucker; Summer Tanager

NOTES

Birds that eat fruit take cues from color, texture and taste to determine when the fruit is at its peak in energy content (sugar). Some birds can see ultraviolet (UV) light. Many ripe fruits reflect UV light, but the leaves around them do not. This directs birds to the ripe fruit and a fast lunch. Plant fruit trees in your yard for a treat both you and wildlife can enjoy.

ATTRACTS: Cedar Waxwing   Gray Jay   Summer Tanager   American Robin

Krunchy Kabobs

INGREDIENTS
Fruit: any combination of
apple, orange, cherry,
prunes, large berries
and/or fruits from
ornamental trees or shrubs, like crabapples,
and/or wild fruits like wild plums, cherries
Pasta Alfresco Pieces (page 58), Mockingbird Mini-muffins(page 52),
and/or Woodpecker Waffle Pieces (page 72)

TOOLS
Wooden kabobs or skewers
String or yarn

DIRECTIONS

STEP 1:

Hit the trail around your house and gather berries, ornamental cherries and crabapples, or use fruit that you already have on hand. Wash the fruit. If it is large, cut it into 1- to 2-inch cubes or slices. (Hint: The cut fruit must be large enough to stay together when inserted onto the kabob stick.)

STEP 2:

Arrange a combination of fruit, pasta loops, mini-muffins, and/or 2-inch waffle pieces, to make a 6-inch chain on the table or counter. Then poke each piece onto the kabob stick, leaving enough room at the ends to tie a string.

STEP 3:

Tightly tie the ends of a 16- to 20-inch length of string around each end of the kabob. Pipe cleaners can also be used. Add tape to the very ends so that the string will not slip off. The ends can also be set with glue to secure the string or pipe cleaner in place. (Hint: If you do not have kabob skewers, reuse your campfire marshmallow roasting sticks!)

STEP 4:

Hang the treats from a tree branch or feeder support and watch for birds to kkkkrunch on kabobs!

ALSO ATTRACTS: Northern Flicker; Northern Cardinal; Blue, Gray and Western Scrub Jays; Gray Catbird; Rose-breasted Grosbeak; Northern Mockingbird; Summer Tanager

NOTES

Feeling the tiny feet of a chickadee on your finger while it eats seeds from your hand is incredible! It only takes patience, practice and following a few simple guidelines. Animals have a limited amount of energy and they need to use it to survive. As a rule, we are too close to wildlife when our presence changes their behavior and requires them to expend their valuable energy unnecessarily. When we become a natural part of their habitat, by way of motion, sound and visual cues, some birds become comfortable enough to allow us very near. Invite birds to dine with you and your backyard lunch buddy!

ATTRACTS: Black-capped Chickadee   Dark-eyed Junco   Song Sparrow   Chipping Sparrow

Lunch Buddy

INGREDIENTS

1 pumpkin, melon or
  a large gourd
1 apple slice
2 grape halves (or other fruit
  to make eyes and mouth)
Tweet-tweet Trail Mix (page 66)

TOOLS

1 old pair of jeans or pants
1 old long-sleeved shirt
1 pair of old gloves
Recycled plastic shopping bags
Toothpicks
1 old hat (the best is one that
  is stiff, like a pillbox hat,
  western-style hat, top hat, etc.)
Basket

DIRECTIONS

STEP 1:
Stuff the jeans, shirt and gloves with recycled plastic bags. Make a head with the gourd or pumpkin by using fruit on toothpicks for the eyes and nose, and the apple slice for a smiling mouth.

STEP 2:
Place the hat on top of the gourd or pumpkin and put the trail mix on top.

STEP 3:
Fill the buddy's hands and a bowl or basket with the trail mix. Place this on the lunch buddy's lap. In time, birds will get used to the buddy.

STEP 4:
Sit quietly beside the lunch buddy. After the birds have eaten from their lunch buddy for some time, sit on the buddy's lap and hold the food-filled basket on your lap and the food in your hands. Sit very still and be quiet. Get ready—you will be the bird's lunch buddy too!

TIP

This is also a great opportunity to photograph, draw and journal about birds. For photography examples, visit the website (www.iwishicouldfly.com) of Alan Stankevitz, the wildlife photographer that took the recipe photos in this book.

ALSO ATTRACTS: Golden-crowned, White-throated and White-crowned Sparrows; Mourning Dove; Rock Pigeon; Eastern and Spotted Towhee, Common Redpoll; Carolina and Mountain Chickadees

NOTES

Mockingbirds can eat nearly anything. They eat insects, seeds, fruit and berries, depending on the season; they are omnivorous. During summer months they eat more insects and in the winter more fruit and berries. You can add seasonal favorites to these muffins. In winter, add cranberries, blueberries, raisins and cherries. In the summer, mix in extra protein—nuts and dried mealworms.

ATTRACTS: Northern Mockingbird — Steller's Jay — Northern Cardinal — American Robin

Mockingbird Mini-muffins

INGREDIENTS
1½ cup cornmeal
¼ cup flour
1 tablespoon baking powder
1 cup of any combination of:
  cranberries, cherries,
  blueberries, raisins,
  or nuts and dried mealworms
1 egg
⅔ cup warm milk
⅓ cup melted suet

TOOLS
Mini-muffin pan
Mini-muffin cups
Raffia, twine, or string

DIRECTIONS

STEP 1:
Preheat oven to 400°F. Place mini-muffin cups in the mini-muffin pan. In a bowl, mix together the cornmeal, flour, baking powder, and fruit, or mealworm and nuts, according to the season.

STEP 2:
Break the egg into a separate bowl and mix well. Warm the milk in a microwave. Melt the suet in a microwave. Mix the egg, milk and suet until well blended.

STEP 3:
Make a well in the middle of the cornmeal mixture. Pour the egg mixture into the center and stir all the ingredients together just until the cornmeal is moistened. It is ok if the batter is lumpy.

STEP 4:
Fill each muffin cup ⅔ full with batter. Bake for 12–15 minutes or until golden brown. Remove from the oven and cool. Remove the paper from the muffins.

STEP 5:
Make a small hook at the base of a pipe cleaner. Push the top of the pipe cleaner up through the bottom of the muffin so the long end comes through the top of the muffin. Hang the treats on plants or attach to a feeder support. Watch for mockingbirds, robins, catbirds and more to munch on your magnificent muffins.

ALSO ATTRACTS: Mourning Dove; Gray Catbird; Black-headed Grosbeak; Blue Jay

male Ruby-throated Hummingbird

NOTES

Hummingbirds feed from the nectar of up to 2,000 flowers per day to fuel their extraordinary output of energy—the most per unit of weight of any warm-blooded animal! Powered by wings that move in a unique figure-eight pattern, hummingbirds fly forward, up, down, upside down, and claim the title as the only bird with the ability to fly backward. Their tiny body is as fluid as a fish and as muscular as an Olympic gymnast as they bend toward flower heads and weave aerial paths through gardens. A nectar feeder with fresh nectar provides these tiny wonders with instant energy.

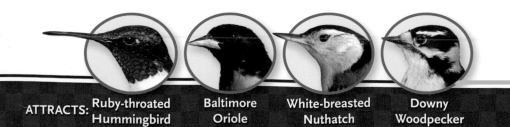

ATTRACTS: Ruby-throated Hummingbird | Baltimore Oriole | White-breasted Nuthatch | Downy Woodpecker

Nectar Punch

INGREDIENTS
4 cups water
I cup white granulated
   sugar

TOOLS
Clean nectar feeder

DIRECTIONS

STEP 1:

Measure the water and sugar into a heavy saucepan. There is no need to color the nectar. Artificial coloring agents have no nutritional value and do not enhance its attractiveness to them. Do not substitute honey or artificial sweeteners for the white sugar.

STEP 2:

Heat the mixture on medium heat until it comes to a boil. Boil for one minute, stirring well to dissolve sugar. Remove from heat.

STEP 3:

While the nectar is cooling, clean your nectar feeder and rinse it very well. (Hint: Nectar feeders need to be cleaned on a weekly basis. Cloudy nectar is a sign of bacterial growth, and the birds can become ill from it.)

STEP 4:

Place your nectar feeder in a location with partial shade to discourage bacterial growth. During peak migration weeks, the nectar punch can be made more concentrated by reducing the ratio of water to sugar to 3:1. Hummingbirds love a water mister! Add a water mister or a source of clean dripping water to attract a variety of birds to your backyard or common areas.

TIP
The "hum" of the hummingbird is a result of the air movement from some 50–70 wingbeats per second. By way of comparison, most songbirds complete just 10–25 wingbeats per second during active flight.

ALSO ATTRACTS: Eastern Towhee; White-breasted and Red-breasted Nuthatches; Brown Creeper; Yellow-bellied Sapsucker; Anna's, Black-chinned and Rufous Hummingbird

male Baltimore Oriole

NOTES

To attract fruit-loving birds to your backyard, make this simple fruit feeder, hang it outdoors and then watch for birds to munch on a free lunch. Provide year-round fruit by landscaping your yard with fruit-bearing plants: vines (Virginia creeper, wild grape, coral honeysuckle); shrubs (sumac, dogwood, nannyberry, serviceberry, elderberry); trees (cedar, juniper, wild plum, cherry).

ATTRACTS: Baltimore Oriole   Red-bellied Woodpecker   Gray Catbird   Northern Mockingbird

Oriole Oranges

INGREDIENTS
Half an orange

TOOLS
Board, approximately 6-inches
 square and 1-inch thick
Nails, two #16
Hammer

DIRECTIONS

STEP 1:
Pound one of the nails into what will be the back of the board, and drive it all the way through. The head of the nail should be flush with the back of the board.

STEP 2:
Pound the second nail into the front of the board, just far enough into the board to create a perch.

STEP 3:
Attach your fruit feeder to a vertical outdoor surface. Push an orange half onto the nail with the cut side facing out.

STEP 4 (OPTIONAL):
Once the orange half has been cleaned out by the birds, set the feeder flat and fill the orange rind cup with fresh or frozen peas and watch for parent orioles to take their chicks out for a green lunch. Other options include filling the cup with Raisin-berry Relish (page 62), or for seed-loving birds, Tweet-tweet Trail Mix (page 66).

To attract yet another group of birds, fill the orange rind with suet base, or pea-nutty or fruity suet, and place it back in the feeder. Now watch nuthatches, chickadees, woodpeckers and other birds fill up with energy!

TIP
To view from indoors, screw a "screw-eye" into the top edge of the board. Then attach a suction-cup window hanger onto the outside of a window and hang the feeder from it.

ALSO ATTRACTS: American Robin; Yellow-bellied Sapsuckers; Red-headed Woodpecker; Bullock's Oriole

NOTES

Watch pigeons long enough and you could count up to 28 different color types, or morphs! Pigeons even wear a necklace of bright iridescent purple, green and yellow feathers, called a hackle. They also have some very interesting behaviors. Count and record the different color morphs and note their behaviors to help scientists learn why pigeons can be found in so many different colors and which color morphs pigeons prefer for mates. Get to know your local ordinances about feeding pigeons and then check out the citizen science projects on page 27 for links to projects involving pigeons.

ATTRACTS: Rock Pigeon | Mourning Dove | Ring-necked Pheasant | Wild Turkey

Pasta Alfresco

INGREDIENTS
⅓ cup corn meal
¼ cup of proso millet (optional)
1 cup Masa corn flour
2 egg yolks (optional)
1 cup water

TOOLS
Rolling pin
Pizza cutter
Pasta machine (optional)

DIRECTIONS

STEP 1:
Preheat oven to 375°F. Combine the first 2 ingredients in a mixing bowl and make a well in the center.

STEP 2:
For egg noodles, add 2 egg yolks into the center and whisk with a fork, adding the water slowly. For plain pasta, omit the egg yolks and simply add the water.

STEP 3:
Gradually bring the dry ingredients into the center until a ball forms. Use your hands to work the pasta dough into 4 balls.

STEP 4:
Dust the counter top with corn flour and roll out the dough to the thickness of a nickel, or use a pasta machine. Cut and/or mold into desired pasta shapes. Twist the strips into 1-inch-long curly pasta or create your own pasta shapes. Make small donut shapes for using in Krunchy Kabobs (page 48), macaroni or shell shapes for Gobbler Goulash (page 40), and bill-size bites for Tweet-tweet Trail Mix (page 66). Brush the tops of the pasta pieces with a beaten egg and then sprinkle with proso millet seeds before baking.

STEP 5:
Bake the pasta shapes for 10–15 minutes. Cool, and prepare for some extraordinary wildlife watching!

NOTES

Gritty, grainy, smooth, hard or juicy, when a bird decides to eat one food over another, it has more to do with texture than taste. Birds generally have few taste buds and a poor sense of taste, but their tongue has a detailed system of sensors that allows them to tell food items apart. Add to the menu by landscaping with natural plants that provide migratory birds food throughout the year. In rural areas, plant rows of corn, sorghum and other grains for migratory birds. The plants will also provide winter cover for local wildlife. Also, when feeding ducks be aware that one duck can attract many others, so be sure to check your local ordinances, which sometimes prohibit feeding of waterfowl.

ATTRACTS: Mallard   American   Canada   Wood
                        Black Duck   Goose   Duck

Quacker Crackers

INGREDIENTS
½ cup cornmeal
1 cup of oatmeal
(moderately ground in
food processor)
¼ cup melted suet base
½ cup water

TOOLS
Pizza cutter
Baking sheet
Hot pad

DIRECTIONS

STEP 1:
Preheat the oven to 400°F.

STEP 2:
Combine the cornmeal, finely ground oatmeal, melted suet and water.

STEP 3:
Roll the dough with a rolling pin until thin, about the thickness of a quarter.

STEP 4:
With a pizza cutter, cut the dough into 1-inch x 1-inch squares, or be creative and make your own bird-sized cracker shapes with mini-cookie cutters. Prick the cracker tops with the tines of a fork.

STEP 5:
Bake for 10–12 minutes. Remove from the oven. Cool.

TIP
Take along a sketchbook and/or camera to record your waterside adventures. Can you determine male, female, adult and young birds from each other? Take notes on their behaviors, too.

ALSO ATTRACTS: Rock Pigeon; Mourning Dove; Eastern and
Spotted Towhees; Chipping Sparrow

male Baltimore Oriole

NOTES

In the wild, birds spend large amounts of energy foraging for food. The availability of fruit is seasonal, especially in the North. Backyard bird feeding provides birds with a wide variety of foods all year long, and scientists are still researching how much of an advantage birds receive from this type of feeding. The effects of global warming are being researched as well. Set out this fruit-filled relish and note the date, time and numbers of bird species that come to dine. Report your findings to a citizen science project (page 27) and be a part of solving the mysteries!

ATTRACTS: Northern Cardinal   Eastern Bluebird   Cedar Waxwing   Steller's Jay

Raisin-berry Relish

INGREDIENTS

½ cup orange juice
1 cup raisins or currants
1 10-ounce package (about
    3 cups) of fresh or frozen
    cranberries
1 cup brown sugar

TOOLS

Half of an orange rind, or
    another serving container

DIRECTIONS

STEP 1:

Pour the orange juice over the raisins, cranberries and sugar in a heavy sauce-pan. Stir well. Heat the mixture on medium-high until it starts to bubble. Carefully stir the hot mixture.

STEP 2:

Turn down the heat to low and put a cover on the pan. Simmer for 30 minutes or until the berries pop. Remove from the heat and cool.

STEP 3:

Be creative with your food presentation. There are many options of how to offer this treat to birds. Fill empty orange halves with the mixture (Oriole Oranges, page 56). Make surprise muffins: Fill the mini-muffin cups one-third full with Mockingbird Mini-muffin batter (page 52); next, place a teaspoon of relish on the batter, and then fill the muffin cup the remaining two-thirds full with batter. Bake as directed. For a simple presentation, place the relish in a clean, empty 6-ounce tuna can and set outside in a predator-free area.

STEP 4:

For a no-cook relish, soak the raisins and cranberries in orange juice overnight or until they are plump. Add chopped apples to the relish.

NOTES

Plant one sunflower seed in your garden in the spring and the birds will have hundreds of sunflower seeds to snack on at the end of the summer. Plant six sunflower seeds in a 4-foot-diameter circle. When they have grown to full height, tie the tops together below the blossoms. The reading room in the center is just the place to enjoy the birds while you read! While your wildlife garden grows, make this bird snack.

ATTRACTS: **Northern Cardinal**   **Blue Jay**   **Evening Grosbeak**   **Rose-breasted Grosbeak**

Sunflower Snack

INGREDIENTS

1 Woodpecker
   Waffle (page 72)
1 orange
¼ cup peanut butter
½ cup striped
   sunflower seeds
¼ cup black oil sunflower seeds

TOOLS

Biscuit cutter
8 toothpicks
12 inches of ribbon

DIRECTIONS

STEP 1:

With a biscuit cutter, cut a circle from a waffle. Poke a small hole about one-third of the way from an edge. Pull the ribbon through the hole and tie it at the ends to make a closed loop. (Hint: Placing a piece of elbow macaroni or a small section of a drinking straw in the hole first and then passing the string through it adds extra support.)

STEP 2:

Arrange the toothpicks equally around the outside edge of the waffle, pushing them in about half way. Peel an orange and set out 4 to 8 sections. Use the sections whole or cut the 4 sections in half to make eight sunflower petals. Place one section on each toothpick.

STEP 3:

Spread peanut butter on the waffle section, covering entire surface to the edges.

STEP 4:

Arrange overlapping rings of striped sunflower seeds around the outside of the center section, pressing them firmly into place. Fill in the center with black oil sunflower seeds. Hang the sunflower snack in your garden and birds will learn where snacks are found while your sunflower garden grows!

TIP

A weather-proof version can be found online at: www.birdsforkids.com.

ALSO ATTRACTS: Black-headed Grosbeak; White-breasted and Red-breasted Nuthatches; Northern Flicker; Black-billed Magpie

Blue Jay

NOTES

The food you set out in the fall may disappear from your feeder, but it may not necessarily be directly eaten by backyard birds. Some species store the nuts and seeds for eating during the coldest days of the year when their energy needs are the highest. Research indicates that during the fall, species such as chickadees can produce new brain cells to handle the additional memory they need to recover the cached food in winter. They probably do not remember where every seed is hidden, and that allows other wildlife to benefit from this store of winter food.

ATTRACTS: Eastern Towhee   Fox Sparrow   White-crowned Sparrow   Mourning Dove

Tweet-tweet Trail Mix

INGREDIENTS
1 cup cranberries
1 cup raisins
1 cup oatmeal
1 cup cornmeal
1 cup raw, unsalted peanuts
1 cup black oil sunflower seeds,
1 cup striped sunflower seeds
1 cup safflower seeds
1 cup peanut hearts

TOOLS
1-gallon bucket or large bowl

DIRECTIONS

STEP 1:
Mix all ingredients together in a bucket or container.

STEP 2:
Use this mix to fill backyard feeders (Coconut Café, page 32; Lunch Buddy, page 50) and as an extra ingredient in suet base (1 part mix to 2 parts suet base).

STEP 3:
You can make this mix in large quantities to use throughout the year. Seeds need to be kept in a sealed and rodent-proof container such as a metal garbage can with a lid or another similar container.

TIP
The question of squirrels: Squirrels like the same foods as backyard birds and can devour the supply in short order. If you enjoy watching and feeding squirrels, you can set up separate corn feeders just for them. If squirrels are not on your guest list, they can be discouraged by placing bird feeders away from trees and putting squirrel guards on standing feeders. Your local bird feeding store is a great resource to learn more about squirrels and bird feeding.

ALSO ATTRACTS: Spotted Towhee; Rock Pigeon; White-throated and Golden-crowned Sparrows; Northern Cardinal, Common Redpoll, Pine Grosbeak

male House Finch and female American Goldfinch

NOTES

American Goldfinches and raspberry-colored Purple Finches use their cone-shaped bill to break open seeds. The most popular wild seed among finches is the small, black Nyjer seed. Watch as a finch adeptly pinches a seed from the feeder with its bill, like a tiny pair of tweezers, and then maneuvers the seed with its bill and tongue to break it open at just the right spot. Have a pair of binoculars handy for a close-up view of this fascinating feeder frenzy.

ATTRACTS: Purple Finch | American Goldfinch | House Finch | White-throated Sparrow

Ultimate Finch Feeder

INGREDIENTS
Nyjer seeds

TOOLS
Stretchy nylon or sock
Length of string or twine

DIRECTIONS

STEP 1:
Find a pair of women's nylons or a pair of socks that are stretchy enough to extend the mesh. Cut the bottom end of the nylon or sock to a length of 10–12 inches.

STEP 2:
Fill the sock about half to three-quarters full with Nyjer seeds.

STEP 3:
Fold the open end over and then tie a rubber band tightly around it. Next, secure a large, heavy safety pin through the layers at the end. Tie the open end of the stocking together in a knot. Place a length of twine, string, or yarn through the middle of the knot with enough length to hang the feeder from a tree branch or feeder support.

STEP 4:
Punching a few small pencil holes in the stocking mesh may make it easier for finches to pick out the seed.

TIP
Thistle seeds that fall to the ground provide food for Mourning Doves, Dark-eyed Juncos, Song Sparrows and White-throated Sparrows.

ALSO ATTRACTS: Cassin's Finch; Lesser Goldfinch; Tufted Titmouse; Pine Siskin; Common Redpoll

NOTES

Birds that migrate long distances in the fall need extra energy for their journey. The decrease of sunlight in late summer triggers a bird's body to produce hormones (body chemicals) that stimulate them to eat more and put on extra stores of fat. This fat is what provides the energy for their long journey. You can provide foods like fresh corn that have nutrients and plenty of calories for migratory birds that are bulking up. Bring on the vittles!

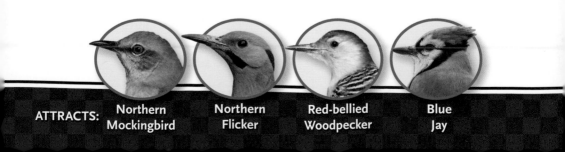

ATTRACTS: Northern Mockingbird | Northern Flicker | Red-bellied Woodpecker | Blue Jay

Veggie Vittles

INGREDIENTS
1 ear of fresh sweet corn
Fresh or frozen peas
Pumpkin or squash seeds,
    fresh or dried

TOOLS
2 feet of string or yarn
Toothpicks

DIRECTIONS

STEP 1:
Take off all husk and silk from a fresh ear of sweet corn. Leave the stem attached. Wash the corn.

STEP 2:
Make a hole through the stem of the corn large enough for a piece of string or yarn to pass through. Feed the string through the hole and tie at the ends.

STEP 3:
Poke the peas and seeds onto the toothpicks. To make this easier, the seeds can be soaked in water for up to 30 minute ahead of time.

STEP 4:
Poke the toothpicks into the ear of corn. (Hint: The toothpicks need to be pointing upward, toward the stem of the corn.)

STEP 5:
Hang the corn from a feeder support or tree branch and watch for birds to vie for vittles.

TIP
Consider purchasing the slightly more expensive blunt ended wooden cocktail picks. These could be easier on the birds should they get poked.

ALSO ATTRACTS: Yellow-bellied Sapsucker; Gray Catbird; Northern Cardinal; Rose-breasted Grosbeak

Hairy Woodpecker

NOTES

Woodpeckers and other hearty birds that live in the north all year keep up their heat-producing energy by eating winter foods high in fat and carbohydrates. Fill the square "holes" in these waffles with suet or peanut butter and then sprinkle another high-energy layer of nut meats on the top. Watch for birds to go wacky over your waffles!

ATTRACTS: Red-bellied Woodpecker | Hairy Woodpecker | Downy Woodpecker | Red-headed Woodpecker

Woodpecker Waffles

INGREDIENTS
2 eggs
1 cup milk, warmed
¼ cup melted suet
1½ cups cornmeal
2 teaspoons baking powder
¼ cup chopped walnuts
¼ cup suet or peanut butter
¼ cup safflower seeds or peanut hearts

TOOLS
Waffle iron

DIRECTIONS

STEP 1:
Preheat the waffle iron according to the manufacturer's directions. Break 2 eggs into a medium-sized bowl and whip with a wire whisk. Add the warm milk and melted suet. Mix thoroughly. (Hint: Warming the milk will keep the melted suet from cooling and turning hard.)

STEP 2:
In a large mixing bowl, stir together the cornmeal, baking powder and nuts.

STEP 3:
Make a well in the center of the dry ingredients. Pour the wet ingredients into the center. Stir until the mixture is well blended. There will be a few lumps.

STEP 4:
Spoon enough batter for 1 waffle onto the preheated waffle iron. Cook the waffle until it is well done and dark brown, but not burnt. (Hint: This recipe works best when the waffles are very stiff. This may take 2 or more pre-set heat cycles.)

STEP 5:
Fill the square spaces of the cooled waffle with suet or peanut butter and sprinkle with safflower seeds or peanut hearts, or place a large striped sunflower seed in each square hole. Generally, two waffles back-to-back will fill a typical wire mesh suet feeder.

ALSO ATTRACTS: Red-breasted and White-breasted Nuthatches; Black-billed Magpie; Tufted Titmouse; Northern Flicker; Black-capped, Carolina and Mountain Chickadees

Blue Jay

NOTES

Peanuts are a powerhouse of protein. They are also a source of vitamins B and E, and minerals such as magnesium, copper, phosphorus, potassium and zinc. Birds are the only animal on earth with feathers. Feathers are made of keratin, which is nearly all protein. Growing new feathers requires nutrients and protein. Provide peanuts to birds especially during late summer, when many molt (lose old feathers and grow new ones). Pass the peanuts, please.

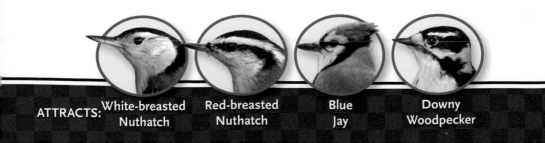

ATTRACTS: White-breasted Nuthatch   Red-breasted Nuthatch   Blue Jay   Downy Woodpecker

Xtra Pea-nutty Parfait

INGREDIENTS
1 cup suet base
¾ cup crunchy peanut butter
shelled and unshelled
    peanuts, unsalted

TOOLS
Ice cream scoop
Parfait glass or recycled dish

DIRECTIONS

STEP 1:
Warm suet in a microwave until soft, but not entirely melted. Combine suet base with ½ cup crunchy peanut butter. Mix well.

STEP 2:
Place 1 or more scoops of suet mixture in the center of a parfait dish or recycled bowl.

STEP 3:
Melt the remaining ¼ cup peanut butter in a microwave. (Hint: this will only take about three, 10-second intervals.) Drizzle the melted peanut butter over the top of the suet ball.

STEP 4:
Top with shelled and unshelled peanuts or peanut hearts. Optional toppings: crushed eggshell, a cherry (not maraschino) and squirmy mealworms.

STEP 5:
Place the pea-nutty parfait on a tree stump or other elevated stand near tree branches (but not accessible to roaming cats and squirrels). Watch for nuthatches, jays and woodpeckers as they go nutty over this scrumptious snack.

ALSO ATTRACTS: Tufted Titmouse; Carolina, Black-capped and Mountain Chickadees;
Yellow-bellied Sapsucker; Hairy, Red-headed and Red-bellied Woodpeckers

NOTES

Setting the table in your yard involves placing food at different levels of your backyard habitat. Birds that feed in trees will utilize feeders set at higher levels: nuthatches, woodpeckers, titmice, finches, chickadees and jays. Birds like cardinals that inhabit mid-level shrubs will visit mid-level feeders. Likewise, birds that naturally pick and glean foods from the ground will visit lower and ground-level feeders. Set your yard for success and enjoy the wide variety of birds that come to dine.

ATTRACTS: Rose-breasted Grosbeak | Gray Jay | Northern Flicker | Northern Mockingbird

Yum-yum Nachos

INGREDIENTS
Pasta Alfresco dough (page 58)
Raisin-berry Relish (page 62)
6-ounces of mild cheddar
cheese, cubed or
shredded
Mealworms, optional garnish

TOOLS
Rolling pin
Baking sheet
Hot pad
Cheese grater or knife
Recycled container or old plate

DIRECTIONS

STEP 1:

Preheat oven to 375°F. Prepare the pasta dough according to the directions on page 58. Roll the dough to ¼ inch thick. Cut the rolled dough into rounds with the drinking edge of a small juice glass or a 2-inch jar lid. (Hint: Dipping the cutting edge in cornmeal first may prevent the edge or lid from sticking to the dough.)

STEP 2:

Place the nacho rounds onto a greased cookie sheet. Bake for 8–10 minutes or until the tops and bottoms are browned. Remove from the oven and let cool.

STEP 3:

Cut the cheese into small (¼ inch) cubes, or grate the cheese using the largest holes in the cheese grater. Set aside.

STEP 4:

Place a spoonful of Raisin-berry Relish on top of the nacho round. Sprinkle cheese on the top. Mealworms can also be sprinkled on the top.

STEP 5:

Put the nacho rounds on a recycled plate (heavy enough to withstand wind) and place on a tree stump or another elevated stand. Yum-yum, here they come for this nutritious nacho treat.

NOTES

Providing suet, seeds and nuts to backyard birds during the winter offers the fats and carbohydrates needed to fuel their internal furnace. The smaller the bird, the greater its surface-area to volume ratio. This requires proportionally more fuel in the way of food consumption. Blue Jays need to eat about 10% of their body weight in food per day, but the much smaller chickadees need to eat about 35% of their body weight in food per day. Bring on the suet-sicles!

ATTRACTS: Black-capped Chickadee | Red-breasted Nuthatch | Tufted Titmouse | Downy Woodpecker

Zebra-striped Suet-sicles

INGREDIENTS
3 cups of suet, melted
1 cup Nyjer seed

TOOLS
Popsicle mold or small
    paper cups
Popsicle sticks or crafts sticks
String, yarn, twine, or raffia

DIRECTIONS

STEP 1:
Place the popsicle mold or paper cups on a baking sheet with wax paper under-neath. Set out a bowl of Nyjer seed seeds. Lay out the popsicle or craft sticks. Drill a hole through each stick, near the end. (Hint: Some craft sticks come with holes already made.)

STEP 2:
Melt 1 cup of suet in a glass measuring cup in the microwave.

STEP 3:
Pour 1 inch of melted suet into each cup or popsicle mold. Place in the refrig-erator for about 10 minutes, or until the suet just starts to cool. Sprinkle a layer of thistle seeds into the partially cooled suet. Push the sticks into the centers of the suet-sicles, keeping the ends with the holes on top. Place back in the refrigerator to cool for about 10 more minutes.

STEP 4:
Repeat steps 2 and 3 until the mold is full. Chill until hard. Pop the suet-sicles from the mold. If they don't release easily, place the mold in warm water for 30 seconds.

STEP 5:
Place a 12-inch length of string, yarn, twine, or raffia through the hole in the su-et-sicle stick and tie the two ends together in a slip knot. Hang the zebra-striped suet-sicles from a tree branch, feeder support, or suction-cup window hanger. Watch for woodpeckers, chickadees and other birds to zip in for a suet-sicle treat.

ALSO ATTRACTS: White-breasted Nuthatch; Hairy Woodpecker; Carolina and Mountain Chickadees

Birds You Can Attract

Each recipe page in this book includes lists of bird species that may be attracted to the recipe. All of the species listed on the recipe pages are depicted here, along with their general geographical range. Since local populations of particular species vary significantly, note that some bird species may be more prevalent than others. Whichever birds show up, these photos should help you start identifying the species attracted to your recipes. As bird species can look alike and be hard to distinguish, it's best to refer to a field guide to help you definitively identify birds.

American Black Duck
East/West

American Goldfinch
East/West

American Robin
East/West

Baltimore Oriole
East

Black-billed Magpie
West

Black-capped Chickadee
East/West

Blue Jay
East/West

Brown Creeper
North

Canada Goose
East/West

Cedar Waxwing
East

Chipping Sparrow
East/West

Dark-eyed Junco
East/West

Downy Woodpecker
East/West

Eastern Bluebird
East

Eastern Towhee
East

Birds You Can Attract

Evening Grosbeak
East/West

Fox Sparrow
East/West

Gray Catbird
East/West

Gray Jay
North

Hairy Woodpecker
East/West

House Finch
East/West

House Wren
East

Mallard
East/West

Mourning Dove
East/West

Northern Bobwhite
North/East

Northern Cardinal
East/West

Northern Flicker
East/West

Northern Mockingbird
East/West

Purple Finch
East/West

Purple Martin
East/West

Red-bellied Woodpecker
East

Red-breasted Nuthatch
East/West

Red-headed Woodpecker
East/West

Birds You Can Attract

Ring-necked Pheasant
East/West

Rock Pigeon
East/West

Rose-breasted Grosbeak
East

Ruby-throated Hummingbird
East

Song Sparrow
East/West

Steller's Jay
West

Summer Tanager
South

Tufted Titmouse
East

White-breasted Nuthatch
East/West

White-crowned Sparrow
East/West

White-throated Sparrow
East

Wild Turkey
East/West

Wood Duck
East/West

Yellow-rumped Warbler
East/West

Chef Notes

Chef Notes

About the Author

Award-winning author and science educator Adele Porter combines her passion for science and dedication to children in her new books. In fact, the students that Adele has worked with during 20 years as an educator inspired the *Wild About* series of books. Adele has also written educational materials for the Minnesota Department of Natural Resources, the U.S. Forest Service and various publications. She is a member of the National Science Teachers' Association, the American Ornithologists' Union and the Society of Children's Book Writers and Illustrators.

For Adele, one of the best parts of being an author is meeting the readers of her books at author programs and book signings and hearing their enthusiastic outdoor stories and involving readers in citizen science. She looks forward to hearing of your new wildlife adventures!

A native of Minnesota, Adele treasures the time with family and friends. She can be contacted via her author website (www.adeleporter.com), and *Birds for Kids, Where Science Takes Flight* (www.birdsforkids.com), an online resource for kids and educators that hosts a free *Wild About Birds* bookmark, an interactive bird identification key, sample lessons for using *Wild About* in the classroom, an educator-idea exchange and more!

References

Poole, A. (Editor). *The Birds of North America Online*: http://bna.birds.cornell. edu/BNA/. Cornell Laboratory of Ornithology: Ithaca, 2005.

Henderson, Carrol L.. *Wild About Birds: The DNR Bird Feeding Guide*. Minnesota's Bookstore: St. Paul, 1995.

A complete list of references can be viewed on the author's website, www.adeleporter.com

THE
KEYS
TO
TULSA

THE
KEYS
TO
TULSA
a novel by
BRIAN
FAIR
BERKEY

THE ATLANTIC MONTHLY PRESS
NEW YORK

Published simultaneously in Canada
Printed in the United States of America

Library of Congress Cataloging-in-Publication Data

Berkey, Brian Fair.
    The keys to Tulsa / Brian Fair Berkey.
    ISBN 0-87113-314-8
    I. Title.
    PS3552.E7217K4   1989   813'.54—dc19   89-30288

Design by Laura Hough

The Atlantic Monthly Press
19 Union Square West
New York, NY 10003

FIRST PRINTING

Acknowledgments

I want to thank these people publicly; they had faith in me, which is more than I can say for myself.

Here are the ones who kept me going, and how they did it:

Henry Dunow, whose friendship and support of my work existed long before he became a literary agent and sold this book; *Susan Mandler,* whose affectionate teasing finally convinced me to believe that I was a *writer,* even though I happened to be a carpenter; *Robby Barnett,* who not only taught me crucial things about the creative act but read my every draft with wild-man enthusiasm; *Ed Binns and Elizabeth Franz,* who encouraged me to keep going in every way they possibly could, including by their own example; *Gary Fisketjon,* who not only saw promise in a crude and unfinished manuscript but was willing to take a gamble on it, unlike some others I could name; and *Nancy Binns,* my wife, who put up with me all that time, under the illusion that getting this published would make me easier to live with; she loves me anyway.

Maybe the meek inherit the earth,
but I keep the mineral rights.

—attributed to

J. PAUL GETTY

Little bee suck the blossom
Big bee get the honey
Dark skin pick the cotton
White man get the money
Take me back to Tulsa
I'm too young to marry
Take me back to Tulsa
I'm too young to marry

—BOB WILLS/TOMMY DUNCAN

She looks so good
That he gets down and begs

—ELVIS COSTELLO

THURSDAY

Richter Boudreau came to a little after daybreak. Vision still smeary from the night before, he got up and went to the window to make sure her car was really gone. He looked, then dropped the blind against the eastern sun. He was naked, but the farmhouse was stifling already, the air dense with heated moisture.

Having gone without sex for months on end, there were two ways he could take it, as a freak deal or as an omen. He fell back onto the bed, the sheet silvery gray with use. He started tending toward the omen. He couldn't even remember the woman's name.

He'd met her at a bar on Sheridan. A young-looking twenty-six, she was a bank teller at a mall branch, with a humorously nervous quality to her, like she faced major decisions by making coin flips. She was tall, her body a little more corpulent than necessary. By the third drink he began to think of it as abundance.

Without being particularly articulate, she talked at some length about the hassles of bank telling. Boudreau listened, intent. He couldn't tell if she were anxious or just not too bright, but at a certain point she stopped midsentence, smiled and put her hand on his forearm.

Coming off his long dry spell, he'd forgotten what it was like to be within sniffing distance. It inspired him. He suddenly found the sweet spot of self-embellishment, the effortless groove of a musician in front of the right crowd. His rap became a thing of beauty, the horn section kicking in behind the choruses. She was clapping at all the right places.

Work? He taught out at TU. Her eyes widened. No, seriously, in the film department. Shit no, he hadn't *gone* there, he'd gone to Berkeley, theater and then film. So why'd he come back to Tulsa? Good question. He rattled his ice and made a little mouth. He'd gotten married but it didn't last long, he'd been young. She stroked his arm with her fingertips and he soloed ferociously. Also he was the movie critic for the *Tulsa Journal*—you ever see that column "Light and Dark"? Well thanks, that means a lot, it really does.

Then she set him up for the end of the tune. No, she remembered the name right: *Truman* Boudreau. He smiled as if faintly embarrassed. Yeah, I'm related, he was my grandfather. He smiled again, the black sheep of a black sheep. Coming to *gitcha*, baby.

After that Boudreau had ordered another pair of drinks, watching her from the corner of his eye. She was looking at him as though James Dean might return from the dead to play his life story.

By the time he got her home, something happened. Maybe she'd sobered up enough to develop misgivings. On the other hand, maybe it had to do with the total disarray of his farmhouse. In no way did this resemble the house of a college professor and a film critic, scion of a notorious local family. Then again, maybe it did. Maybe she'd come with a maniac to an isolated old shack of a house in Broken Arrow. She looked out the window at her car more than once.

Boudreau couldn't believe it. His timing was shot now: she wanted to hear more about the ex-wife, she wanted to get to *know* him. His life always looked better in its broad strokes than up close, and here she was asking about his feelings. He could tell this relationship wasn't going to last past daylight. This was work.

After what seemed like endless delicate bullshitting, he put some smooch music on the box and got her to share his last joint with him.

Bingo. The rest was easy, stoned smile to stoned kiss, couch to bedroom. Her dress came off and her hips began working nicely on their own. Boudreau eased his fingers under the last flimsy item of clothing, and then it happened: the lights went off, the air conditioner, the refrigerator, everything at once. Marvin Gaye stopped singing, his last few words slurring into silence. The house went dark as the bottom of a mineshaft.

Boudreau swore and got up, crab-walking in his erection-bound underwear. He felt his way down the hall, an exact image in his head of the most recent warning from the power company. The original was sitting under a pile of blue exam books on his desk, one of those things he'd been meaning to deal with. He made it into the living room and headed for the kitchen door.

The problem was that four years before, he'd stripped the wall between the kitchen and living room of its wood lath and plaster. Then Ginny had left, and after that he'd done nothing more. In the dark he tried to walk through the open stud wall, arms out front like the Mummy. They went through but he didn't, the stud clubbing him so hard it drove him to his knees.

The girl heard a loud *thunk,* followed by low moaning. Stoned and half naked in some weird guy's house, she began to see colors moving in the dark. She imagined cut power lines and hideous faces at every window. She started screaming.

On his knees in the dark, Boudreau groaned and swore, his brain still flashing. He called out that he was *okay,* the screams dropping then to a frightened whimpering.

He summoned his breath to calmness. "I said shut up, all right? I just ran into the fucking *wall.* "

This seemed reasonable enough, but in the dark the whimpers broke into sobs now, steady as a metronome. Things were getting a little hysterical here. He tried to keep his voice down. "I'm *okay,* okay?"

She kept on crying anyway. He staggered to his feet, feeling his way to the correct opening this time. An egg began to swell above his left eyebrow. He groped around for the drawer that held the candles and flashlight.

The potential for an uncomplicated sex act went downhill from there. He lit a few candles and tried to act as if nothing had happened, but she was rigid with tension. She didn't like the way he'd yelled at her. He apologized, and in a few minutes tried again with no luck. Look, she liked him but she wanted to just talk for a while, all right? Maybe it was a mistake pushing this so fast, she needed a little time. They didn't have to do it right now, maybe in the morning or something.

Boudreau stared up at the wavering candlelight on the ceiling, his patience gone. He got off the bed and started opening the double-hung windows a little harder than he needed to. The morning, he let her know, would be a problem.

She hesitated. Well okay, maybe they could just sleep on it and see each other again later in the week. He let that hang in the sweltering air until she finally took the hint.

Okay, he was a shit-head. If that's what it took to get him off the hook, fine. He was relieved. She could call him what she wanted, as long as it meant he didn't have to wake up next to her in the morning.

He heard the car leave in a spray of gravel, then got up and roamed the living room with his candle, searching for the remainder of the joint. He smoked it down to a nub and stared at the faded, horizontal lines on the kitchen studs, where the plaster and lath had once made a wall.

Three hours from start to finish: with the bank teller as a stand-in, he'd just recapitulated his entire history of misery with Ginny. So far as he could remember, it was a new record.

Valerie, thought Boudreau: she'd asked him to call her "Val." He rolled over in the heat and gave up on sleep.

Still horny in an irritable way, he scratched the itch with a few idle jerks. There was something about the quality of light coming from under the blinds. After a few seconds he closed his eyes, release at hand.

The first time he'd ever had an orgasm with a woman, he was thirteen going on fourteen. Not a woman really, just a girl, his age.

His family had been in Tulsa for a year and a half by then, but he'd gone back to True's ranch in the Osage, for a little visit to see his old "girlfriend." In fact, it turned out to be the last time he went up to the ranch, ever.

Her name was Myra and it had happened in the backseat of an old Cadillac, up on blocks in the corner of an unused tack barn. Myra's father was a hand who didn't live on the ranch but sometimes brought her and her little brother along when he came to work. Richter and Myra had really just been playmates, ranch buddies, before he moved to Tulsa; he hadn't seen her since puberty had hit them both. In the meantime, he'd acquired a new girlfriend in Tulsa who regularly let him touch her tits, but he saw no point in saying anything about that.

There had been steeply angled shafts of light, moted with tiny particles, coming down from cobwebbed windows high up on the barn walls. All the old tack and harness and rusted equipment was covered in a fine-grained fur of spider webs, heavy with dust. To touch it was to disturb it. The air smelled faintly of old hay and manure, underlaid by the odor of packed earth soaked by years of motor oil.

He didn't remember how it happened, but they somehow made it down to their underwear. The backseat of the Caddy was huge as a bed, its gray brushed velvet upholstery like another level of nakedness against his skin. It had been years since Boudreau last recalled all this. The sensation of having a teenage pecker came back to him, the throb so hard it felt like it was going to explode.

She let him take off her bra too, but not the panties. He didn't argue, stunned to have gotten so far already. Eyes open, he fastened his mouth to one of her little breasts, smooth as new snow, and watched the other small pink nipple grow tightly wrinkled and upright.

He explored underneath the panties as much as he wanted. She lay on her back while he worked his fingers in her lightly haired sex, thrilled at its slickness, its folds and heat. She breathed hard, her face flushed and eyes closed. His main sensation was thrilled disbelief: so *this* is what it's like.

She rubbed him from outside his underwear, and then, without warning, touched the bare tip of his penis just under the waistband. She loved him, this meant she loved him.

They clasped together in a crush, humping against each other in a delirious attempt to get closer. He shot forth in a warm flood and thought to himself, *This has jerking off beat by a mile.*

It still did.

Boudreau lay spent on the bed, bathed in sweat and body odor. There was an elliptical streak of dried sperm on his thigh, shiny and tight as a scar. He'd crushed the memory of Myra and the Cadillac like an eggshell; so much for lost innocence.

Vals. That's what he was into these days, *Vals.* He should've known better. He *did* know better, it was what he deserved for letting himself get so desperate. Val was not so much an omen, he decided, as a straight warning.

He wondered where Myra was now, what she looked like. For a moment he saw himself as if he'd stayed with her, as if they'd stuck together like their families had always joked, had gotten married and ranched out in the brush, had kids and horse trailers and a mortgage. Then when Ginny came to visit, he'd be Warren Beatty at the end of *Splendor in the Grass,* funky in farm clothes, surrounded by dirty-faced kids, bittersweet and extremely handsome.

It was a short-lived riff, more than a little pathetic. Who was he kidding? He'd always hated *Splendor in the Grass* anyway. What he needed was a shower.

He turned the faucet and stood there while nothing happened. He swore. No power, therefore no water. He knew the exact amount in his checking account, which was maybe enough to cover two beers and some barbecue. Nine dollars against four months' worth of utility bills, and that was just for starters.

Against his better judgment he began to consider the Big Plan again. He'd been putting it off for months, but maybe its time had finally come. What could he lose?

He waited until eight o'clock, then picked up the phone and heard the reassurance of a dial tone. At least they hadn't cut that off yet. He steeled himself.

Women weren't his problem anyway, what he needed was money.

"Mom?" he said. "It's Richter."

rla Thompson sat in the folding metal chair at the end of Boudreau's desk, one elbow planted on it, holding up the side of her head with her hand. She was slumped in the chair, legs splayed out under her dress. In spite of himself Boudreau took a quick look, the view good enough to see up to her tonsils. She nearly caught him and he looked away while she droned on.

He kept expecting her to drop the ruse of having come to discuss her final grade. Any minute now, she'd start talking about *them*. Herself and Boudreau. He stared over at the wall again.

The framed photograph hung next to the door, the very first thing he'd put on the walls back when the office was new. He went for months at a time without noticing it at all.

The picture was of his father's father, a big newsprint photo that Boudreau had cut out of the front page of the *Tulsa Tribune* when he was fourteen years old.

Truman Boudreau had been more than six and a half feet tall in cowboy boots and weighed close to 260 pounds. His flesh had sat on him in solid slabs. The photograph showed him only from the waist up, but he was a full head taller than the sheriff's deputy beside him. He'd always made other people seem small.

He was looking straight at the photographer. He held up his two huge fists, the sleeves of his cattleman's jacket fallen away to display the handcuffs. Beside him, the deputy looked up with a hick grin of admiration. A great picture, it had briefly made the national wire services. It satisfied the country's image of what a crooked Oklahoma politician should look like on his way to the state pen.

Thick black hair curled out from under his pushed-back white stock-

man's Stetson. Beneath the brim was a massive forehead underlined by
a solid block of merged eyebrows. His small eyes were set deeply under
the brows, so dark they seemed black. His complexion was dark too,
obvious even in the old newsprint: it looked east Texas swamp, French
or Indian or Spanish. He had fleshy lips and a small dark mole—a beauty
mark—above the right corner of his mouth. On a man who looked like
he did, it gave the appearance of big appetites.

He wasn't a handsome man, but he'd worn tailored western suits and
had his sideburns cut long out of his curly hair. When people said
Truman Boudreau was good-looking, what they really meant was power-
ful: whatever else you wanted to say about him, he had *style*. As a
cattleman who had established a prize breeding stock program, he believed in the dominion of superior individuals. As a politician, he
believed in the same thing. Life was politics, and politics no different
than herd management: over the years Truman came to resemble one
of his own Black Angus seed bulls.

Arla Thompson talked on, endlessly. His elbows propped on the arms
of the chair, Boudreau supported his chin with steepled fingers and
hoped this would pass for attention. He'd smoked a joint with Brinkman
at lunch, down at the paper, and the humidity had turned it into a
stunning sinus headache. He felt like shit.

At noon it had already hit ninety-seven, and now the air-conditioning
in the little concrete block building wasn't working. A smart man
would've canceled office hours and just gone over to his mother's.

He'd assumed Arla Thompson would just let things go and not show
up for the scheduled appointment. Instead, she sat there refusing to look
at him, wearing her pain deliberately as a mask. Now she was talking
about her end-of-year paper. Her *paper.*

Boudreau knew what his grandfather would've thought about Arla
Thompson. That's *cupcake material,* True would say, and lick his lips
significantly.

Arla Thompson had signed up for his noir course the second semester.
("FILM 1020: FILM NOIR. *A survey of sex, sweat, and betrayal, from
forties B pictures through* Bonnie and Clyde.") When she'd come in to
interview for the class, Boudreau decided on the spot to let her in, screw

the prerequisites. She looked Irish or Scottish, maybe Welsh, with perfect milk-pale skin framed by very fine black hair, cut short like parentheses around her face. Her eyes were gray, her eyebrows dark and full; she had a thin nose and a wide mouth with broad even teeth. She reminded him of True's ranch, of the dirt-farmer families around the ranch who seemed to have strolled right out of the British Isles until you heard them talk.

He'd pegged her from that first interview, her accent so strong you could grate cheese on it: some little town out in the brush, Choteau or Barnsdall or Pawhuska, somewhere like that, Bible class and the long bus ride to a consolidated high school, girls' basketball and Key Club, a full girdle on dates, maybe some frenching and light grinding after a year of going steady.

"So you transferred here from Tahlequah, Arla?" he'd said.

"Yessir?" A slight blush came to her cheeks no matter what he asked her.

"They have a film department up there?"

She shook her head and blushed again.

Boudreau smiled. Northeastern Oklahoma University at Tahlequah: it made TU seem like Oxford.

"What's your major?"

"Special ed?"

Boudreau cocked his head as though to hear better. *Spatial ayud?* It took him a beat to understand.

"What's that, a talking horse?"

She looked at him, confused. She was too young to get it.

"No sir?" she lilted. "These are children with learning, emotional and other severe disabilities?"

Boudreau nodded approvingly. Retards. He tried to keep from smiling too hard.

Arla Thompson blushed a furious deep pink while he watched. It was like her blood kept blooming at him. He smiled again. She was going to be in his film class, and he was going to see how that skin blushed all over, relieved of its cotton Baptist underwear.

She represented a dangerous departure from his usual taste in female

students. Even at TU there was usually some kind of thin selection from
the English department, earnest young women with politics and unshaven legs and a need to experiment with men who were bad for them.
And they came after *him*, impelled by a rotten spot, a gene, whatever
it is that brings moth to flame. In the local ecology he had a niche: tall,
dark and handsome, seminotorious, full of stories about Berkeley in the
sixties, the last rotten branch on a dead family tree.

He'd ignored the signs from that first day on. A grandfather in
handcuffs on the wall didn't have the usual effect. He'd even got a faint
whiff of disapproval, although it was nothing by comparison to when he
offered her a joint the first time. By the time he realized they played in
different leagues, with different rules of engagement, it was too late.
He'd given off the usual signals, but she just didn't get it. She kept trying
to come up after class, then once she got the hint, it turned ugly. The
whole thing had taken maybe four weeks, and then—so he thought—it
was over.

Now here she was again. She seemed to have lost weight, and she'd
been slender to begin with. She looked fragile with hurt, as though
barely able to keep talking.

"I'm sorry," said Boudreau. He'd drifted off. "What did you say,
Arla?"

"I said I guess if you don't have any other comments, then, sir?" *Inny
caw-mints?*

Boudreau looked at her and she looked carefully back, past his shoulder.

" 'Sir'?" he said.

He was amazed. She wasn't going to bring it up after all. She was in
a high flush, a glaze of sweat on her skin. He really was a bastard.

" 'Sir'?" he said again.

She met his eyes briefly, her own glittering, then grabbed the strap
of her purse.

This was perverse. The sex hadn't even been that great, but now he
had a sudden yearning to see the thin straps of the pale yellow sundress
come sliding off her shoulders. He wanted to hear the little cries one
more time, see the blush spread down over her milk-pale chest. Maybe

they could have one last go, everything understood and bittersweet. He wanted special ed.

"Listen, Arla, I feel bad about this," he began. He meant it, he really did. "Would you like to talk this over? Come over tonight and talk it over?"

She shouldered her purse and rose from the chair, brushing invisible wrinkles out of the sundress.

"Thank you sir?" She gave him a tight-lipped little smile. "For all your help?"

He smiled back at this slap in the face. *Sure, okay.* In a few years she'd be married to some assistant branch manager out in the boons, busting the seams on her jeans with those thighs, pushing an overloaded cart through the Safeway while she threatened to kill her whining kids. He needed *this?*

He expected her to slam the door, but she closed it instead with a careful, distinct click.

Then Boudreau—Boudreau who had worked for two years on a paper in an Oakland storefront with a tapped phone and nonhierarchical editors, Boudreau who had participated in endless meetings to root sexism out of the language and the workplace—then Boudreau lit a cigarette, dark faced.

"Cunt," he said.

He'd smoked the cigarette down to the butt without realizing it when the phone rang.

"Richter honey?" came the voice. "Har y'all doin'?"

Boudreau settled back in his chair and cradled the phone away from his ear. Vicky Stover turned up the volume with her exaggerated grit accent, as though you'd miss the joke without it. He played along without enthusiasm.

"Well, *Vicky* darlin'."

He heard her light a cigarette at the other end and exhale noisily.

"I'm just so glad to *hear* you?" she said. "I just been calling all *over.*"

Boudreau stayed frosty. Two weeks before he'd taken her to a screening, and on the way home she'd made some promising little signs that something might happen. Nothing definite, but still. Since then he hadn't heard word one.

"Yeah, well it's been a while," he said. "So how are you."

He had dropped his accent but she didn't seem to notice.

"Oh, coam see and coam sa?" she said. "You know, suck a wet one and you're gonna get spitty? Least that's what momma always said."

Boudreau snorted in spite of himself. Priscilla Michaels had not been called "Prissy" for nothing.

"Lord rest her soul," said Vicky Stover. "Up there with the angels and all?"

Boudreau clicked his tongue in reprimand. He changed the subject, refusing to let her joke him into a good mood. "Hey, was that Keith I saw driving down Forty-first the other day?"

"I'm sure I don't know," she said. "But yes, I've heard my big brother *is* back from his latest facility?"

"How's he doing?"

"Asking the wrong person, Richter honey," Vicky Stover said.

"You haven't talked to him."

"I don't believe I've *had* that pleasure?" She said it formally, drawling out the vowels.

Vicky and Keith were not exactly on great terms, but even so, Boudreau knew she was lying instantly. Meantime the accent was irritating the hell out of him, even though she'd switched from cracker to belle. He registered the lie without concerning himself further.

"Yeah, I'll have to call him up," said Boudreau, with no intention of doing any such thing.

"Oh, he'd *love* to hear from you, Richter, I just *know* he would?"

Boudreau heard in this a direct homage to her mother, the kind of social cheer so fake it turned brittle the moment it hit the air. He was growing tired of inferring the real Vicky, not an easy task in the best of times.

"So," he said, "so how's homelife?" He could hear the baby crying faintly in the background.

The sound in the receiver grew louder as she aimed the phone at the source. The baby threw in a good wail on cue, and then he heard Vicky's breath in his ear again.

"Oh, just fine?" It was musical with sarcasm. She dragged hard on her cigarette and her voice went husky. "But I'd love to come see y'all."

Boudreau straightened up at the sudden vision of having Vicky Stover alone in his mother's apartment.

"I mean I even got me a *sitter* tonight," she added, in wonderment at how bad things had gone, that it had come to this.

"Well," he began, just as the baby let fly with an ultimatum of noise.

"Excuse me, but I believe I'm on the *phone?*" Vicky said sweetly, away from the mouthpiece. " 'Course you *would* have to get off your butt and pick her up."

Boudreau heard a low "Fuck you" in the very near background, the first word drawn out to three bored syllables.

This changed the focus of things. Ronnie Stover sounded so close to the phone his presence had a looming quality: it was like suddenly noticing the big cat lying motionless on an overhead branch. The baby's crying petered out and Vicky stepped back in.

"So maybe we come see y'all, then?"

"Oh?" he said. *"Oh."* He tried to get some disappointment in his voice. "Listen, Vicky? Listen, I'd love to but—" He stopped and considered. "This has been a real bitch of a day, you know? I have a review to write tonight. But maybe on the weekend or something."

*"Rich*ter? I can get us hap-py?" she sing-songed.

"No, really, I can't."

"Richter," she said.

"Vicky," said Boudreau, but he'd waited a few beats too long to keep it comic. "No seriously, this piece is due tomorrow morning. Seriously."

He waited through a long silence. Vicky Stover had never once taken disappointment well.

"Sure, okay." Her voice went colorless, the accent fallen away like a dead leaf. "Sure. Some other time, then."

Involuntary with guilt, Boudreau began to offer a more detailed explanation of the demands on the working man.

"What?" she interrupted.

He began to repeat, more lamely, what he'd just said when she cut him short again.

"Ronnie says he wanted to talk to you about something." She covered the phone then, muffling a short exchange. "But not on the phone." She relayed the information in a voice as neutral as a telephone operator's.

Boudreau was nailed. He'd been avoiding Ronnie for two weeks, and now Ronnie wanted to talk to him. The shit was about to float.

"What?" Vicky said. "What? Hey, *wait* a minute." She covered the phone again.

Boudreau lit a cigarette and waited. How did he get himself into these things? Better yet, why? Just then Margo Ross, the film department secretary, walked into his office and let a memo fall from her hand onto his desk, as though she wanted to avoid touching it. She turned around and walked back out, all without saying a word.

There was a loud, indistinct noise from Vicky's end, something slammed or thrown. Boudreau cleared his throat, ready to get it over with.

"Sorry," she said. She didn't sound all that sorry.

"Listen," said Boudreau, "tell Ronnie he's just going to have to wait a little longer. I don't have it right now."

"Don't have what?"

The memo informed Boudreau that there would be no air-conditioning in the building till next Tuesday. Repairs.

"The, uh, the *money?*" He cleared his throat and tried again. "The money I owe Ronnie." He felt like a shit-heel. Money was one of the staple arguments of Vicky's marriage.

"The money you owe Ronnie," she repeated.

Boudreau readied himself with excuses and promises.

"Well, that's a switch anyway," she said then. "It's usually him owing other people. But he didn't say that's what he wanted to talk about."

Boudreau was grateful for her nasty little snort.

"If Ronnie has a fault as a small businessman"—the accent was back again: *binnisman*—"it's he don't remember these things?"

Boudreau gathered that Ronnie had left the room.

"Yeah, well," he said, "don't remind him, okay?"

When she snorted again, it occurred to Boudreau: this was her money, too.

"I mean, I'll get it to him," he added. "I will. I just don't have it now."

"Oh, I don't *care,*" Vicky said. "I'm just so sick of this shit I can't *stand* it."

Boudreau began to fry in his own guilt, speechless.

When she finally spoke again, her voice had gone small. "Oh, Richter?"

"What?"

"I *miss* you?" She sounded on the verge of tears. "And I really need to get out tonight? Even with him and all?"

Boudreau took it as a cue to hit his mark and say his lines.

"Maybe I can get my review done before you come over," he said. "You still want to?"

"I swear, you are just a *sweet*heart?" she said.

"What kind of drugs you got?" Even with Ronnie coming, Boudreau was sort of glad now. He could stand to get high. It had been a tough week.

"Oh, you know, this and that." She lowered her voice. "And listen, Richter honey? If Ronnie says anything—I know he won't but if he does—about you and me going out last Friday? You'll just go along and say we did, say we went to a show?"

Boudreau hesitated. "Yeah, okay," he said. "Sure."

"It's too complicated on the phone," she explained. "I'll tell you later."

"Whatever." He was about to hang up before he remembered. "Listen, I'm not out at the farm this week." What could it hurt, he thought. "I'm house-sitting at my mother's."

Before he knew it the dial tone was buzzing in his ear, along with the realization that he was about to throw a little party at his mother's apartment.

Boudreau gave up on the review and devoted his full attention to worrying. He couldn't remember how he'd decided that sneaking in here was such a good idea. It had only been that morning, but there was a blank spot where his reasons ought to have been. He'd just gone ahead and *done* it.

His mother and Billy had been on their way out the door to the airport when he called. He'd call again when they got back, he said, it was nothing important. Too rushed to be suspicious of an out-of-the-blue social call, his mother was merely irritable and said they'd be back late Monday. Hearing her voice made him glad he hadn't been foolish enough to trot out the Big Plan.

And then he just found himself driving straight over from the farm-house to her apartment. She owed him this much, he remembered thinking that. The apartment was huge, on the twelfth floor of a luxury tower with a spelled-out address for a name. He fingered the key she'd given him three years before, when Billy had his emergency appendectomy. Boudreau assumed it still worked.

He was in luck. As he pushed through the lobby doors, the doorman was sneaking a pull from a half-pint of cheap vodka. Boudreau gave him a big wink while the guy hurried to stash the bottle.

The doorman was a recently hired Cockney Englishman, a middle-aged little ex-actor with a lit nose. He'd somehow drifted from Brixton all the way to Tulsa, only to wear a uniform out of a bad play about the sunset of empire. Now all he had to do was act sober, and have an English accent.

Boudreau bullied him with a line about doing some work for his mother, he'd be in and out for the next few days, but he'd like to keep it secret so she'd be surprised.

This was bullshit and the doorman knew it. He weighed his prospects and glared at the unfairness of it all. This was blackmail.

Boudreau gave him another wink and strolled into the elevator, ready for a few days of luxury tower, some good central air and a big-screen TV. He figured he'd clear out Sunday evening, Monday morning at the latest, buy the doorman a pint for his trouble. Tomorrow he'd collect on his review, put the minimum down on the utility bill and get his power turned back on. No one would ever know.

The lobby intercom rang at eight. Boudreau picked it up, his anxiety spiking. The doorman's voice carried a note of betrayal.

He stood inside the door with his hand on the knob, waiting for the faint *ding!* of the elevator at the end of the hall. When it came, he opened the door and watched them come down the hallway, seeing them through the doorman's eyes. These were white trash dope fiends, come to pillage and fornicate and lose him his job. Boudreau hoped to God neither of the two neighbors on the floor would hear anything.

"*Gawd* if this air-condition don't chill my butt!" Vicky yelled.

Boudreau watched Vicky Michaels Stover sashay down the carpeted corridor. She was playing dress-up, the Girl with the Cheap Reputation: beat-up Dr. Scholl flip-flops on her pink-toenailed feet, a too small white halter top with a pack of Salems wedged in against one side of her cleavage, and a pair of faded short-short cutoffs. The outside seams had split high enough up to indicate she was at least wearing underwear, which happened to be a bright shiny red. Her blond hair was piled up stiff on her head, and she'd applied a generous amount of makeup, red lipstick as the dominant feature.

Vicky was in full grit-bimbo regalia, her very favorite. She gave it an ironic lilt by carrying herself like someone raised in a thirty-two-room house, not including servants' quarters. Although in Boudreau's opinion the whole thing had a definite fuck-me effectiveness, the irony was wearing through in places. Lately he'd been getting the feeling that maybe it was for her too.

Ronnie walked behind her, a six-pack under one arm.

"Hidy and welcome y'all," Boudreau said, extending his arm. "It might be nouveau but it's still reesh." He tried to hurry them through the door without being obvious.

Vicky heaved a mighty sigh and swept in.

"Well, it *is* tacky but it'll have to do." She planted a wet kiss on Boudreau's neck as she went by.

Boudreau could see she'd already dipped into whatever it was that was going to get them happy. She kicked off her sandals, then ran through the foyer and across the carpet of the living room to the big picture window.

"Ronnie honey?" she yelled. "Could we get us a place like this?" *Plice.* She launched herself backward to land in the deep cushions of the gray couch.

"Hey, my *man.*" Boudreau held out his hand for a slap-me-five, a drug-brother's handshake, whatever.

Ronnie Stover arranged his heart-shaped mouth into a pursed-lipped semblance of a smile, an expression that pushed up his cheeks and hinted at a secret sour taste somewhere. His eyes were unreadable behind his dark glasses.

Instead of taking Boudreau's hand, he flicked out a feint to the midsection. In the moment it took Boudreau to drop his own hands to cover, he found the other long-fingered hand laid along his cheek, cradling his jawbone. Ronnie's left gave him a stout little cuff and was gone before Boudreau knew what had happened, except that he'd just been hit in greeting by a man to whom he owed five hundred dollars.

Boudreau came up with an elaborately mimed parody of a karate move.

"That won't get it," said Ronnie. He was already past. "You got to think with your spine."

"Some people, that's all they got to think with," said Vicky from the living room.

Ronnie ignored her and walked through the foyer. He stopped to examine a painting on the wall, lit by its own little brass light.

"Hey *hey*, grunt, think with your *spine*, hey *hey*, grunt, you'll be *fine*. Yeah," Ronnie said to the painting, "real fine, till they blow your chicken-bone spine away."

"He means to say howdy and how are you?" said Vicky from her spot on the couch.

Boudreau watched Ronnie stalk around the living room like some long-boned animal of prey, his shades halfway down his sharp nose. He seemed a little strung out, but even so, the six-pack of Coors in one big hand looked light as a box of kitchen matches. He cased everything, fanning out a pile of magazines here, fingering the texture of a lamp-shade there.

For someone who made such a big point of refusing to talk about his time in Asia, Ronnie Stover's behavior had "I been to War and I'm heavy-duty" written all over it. Boudreau found it not a little preten-tious, especially since he wasn't so sure Ronnie had ever even seen combat. It was sociopathic, but in such a bush-league, secondhand sort of way, like he'd learned all his moves by watching deranged vets on made-for-TV movies.

The thing was, thought Boudreau, it fit; it was perfect. What else could Ronnie do but an update of the torn–T-shirt role? His wife might like to play cracker dress-up, but he was the real thing, a nickle-ante drug dealer from the wrong side of town who'd gotten too old to cruise burger joints. He wore straight-legged jeans with no belt, old rough-out cowboy boots and a faded denim cowboy shirt with the sleeves torn off at the shoulders. Swept back in a straw-dry DA with long sideburns, his hair was a darker blond than Vicky's, at least at the roots. Boudreau had his suspicions, reinforced by the weird orangey yellow cast at the tips.

A year or two before, Vicky had come across Ronnie's senior yearbook in a box of junk. This was when she still worshiped him, and she'd saved it to show Boudreau. The look on her face had said he wasn't going to believe it.

Ronnie had gone to a greaser school downtown, where he'd appar-ently been a basketball star, the shining light on an otherwise losing team. The sports section had shot after shot of him laying up, driving around picks, scrapping for the rebound, feathering the long jumper. He had a lanky, loose-boned build, muscles ropy and tense, a tall six four. His center of gravity looked to be right in his pelvis. He'd been the lone white starter on an otherwise all-black team.

"Ain't he purty?" Vicky had giggled, turning the pages for Boudreau.

"What, no shades?" said Boudreau. "I thought they were like a birth defect."

Boudreau had hardly recognized him. There was no trace of the sullen edge that he regarded as the quintessential Ronnie, the thing that made him seem either menacing or stupid, or more frequently both. This, of course, was preheroin and pre-Vietnam, but Boudreau didn't think either one explained things. It just seemed like a different person. RON-NIE DEAN STOVER, it said under his class picture, and then his little quote: "Going pro."

Boudreau had stared at the pictures and filled with envy, then jealousy. The black-and-whites fairly glowed with animal ease. Here was someone for whom mind-body was not a problem. Here was someone who thought with his spine as a matter of grace.

On the other hand, it was also someone who often seemed embarrassed when he had to use language. Boudreau watched Ronnie finish his tour of the living room and its objects, all without saying a word. He set his beer down on a table and walked over to stand in front of the big picture window. His wife lay on the couch just behind him. He looked out at the meadow of lights that spread away to the north twelve floors below.

"Who lives here?" he finally said, still looking.

"My mother," said Boudreau. "And Billy."

With Ronnie standing in front of her, Vicky rolled from her side onto her back in a quick thrash. It was like the couch had become a bed and there wasn't enough room. She looked up at the ceiling.

"Billy your dad?" Ronnie said.

"His dad's *dead*, Ron honey." Vicky lit a Salem and waved the match out from the wrist. "About twenty years ago? They weren't real close?"

Ronnie swiveled his head away from the window to give her a long look. She kept her gaze on the ceiling, innocent.

"That's right." He looked back out at the lights. "That's right, I knew that. I just forgot it."

"*Right.*" She drawled it out into two syllables. "You for*got* it." She blew a thin stream of smoke straight up like a geyser, then played mouth games with it, Morse code, Indian signals.

Reacting openly to things like this was not Ronnie's style. Boudreau thought maybe he stiffened a little, but otherwise he played dumb, or at least deaf.

This was great, just a great idea to have a couple of good friends over. Maybe they'd end up throwing a psychodrama in his mother's apartment, trash it and call it a night. He found himself wishing they were nodded out. At least when they shot dope they got along, or if they didn't, they couldn't tell.

Vicky laced her fingers up behind her head. There was a huge, livid bruise on the inside of her upper arm, red to purple to black, going yellow around the edges. Boudreau stared. Halfway around the arm was a matching thumbprint.

Ronnie asked something.

"What?" said Boudreau.

"Said, what they get for a place like this?" Ronnie repeated.

Boudreau didn't know. The arm seemed suddenly delicate and too pale, a child's arm, breakable. He couldn't believe she let him do that to her.

"Well, I tell you what," said Ronnie. He shook a Pall Mall up out of his pack and put it in his mouth, leaving it unlit. "Be enough to keep me high for a while." He walked away from the window, then started thumbing through another stack of magazines. The cigarette dangled from his lips like a fuse.

"What's the deal with the English guy downstairs?" Vicky said then.

"What English guy?"

"The *door*man, Richter honey."

A rush of anxiety ran through him. "What do you mean, what's the deal?" Immediately he saw a scene, an insult to other tenants, a threat. Something to report.

She rolled her eyes to the ceiling, then lowered them, assuming the patient look of someone about to explain social nuance to a moron.

"What's wrong with *colored* is what I mean." She raised herself up on one elbow. "It's just another one of these foreign fads, you *know* it is, I mean first ever'body goes and trades in their Cadillacs gets one of these Mercedes—correct me if I'm wrong, but these are German automobiles? Do you see my point, Richter honey?"

Vicky widened her eyes at the unthinking carelessness of it, then arrived at her grim conclusion.

"Then just you wait till you try and find a good Negro doorman in a few years? There just won't *be* one, that's what."

"That ain't funny," said Ronnie, without looking up. He was leafing through a stack of *Town and Countrys* and *Tulsalites*.

"Oh, uh-huh?" said Vicky.

She cast a long look at her husband, eyes narrowing. Her thin lips puckered in a tight little smile of barely veiled superiority: it was a dead ringer for the contemptuous expression her mother had used to get through the day. Boudreau assumed this was for his benefit, to further his appreciation of the layered irony involved. The problem was that he couldn't sort out the layers, crucial to an understanding of where parody stopped and something else began.

Vicky widened her eyes briefly, as though to clear her head and regain character.

"I mean, this is a precious part of our heritage, it's kind of like a folk art," she said. "Maybe the Junior League ought to get involved? They could do sort of a nigger doorman retraining academy?"

She turned on her husband. "Ronnie Dean? Maybe there's employment opportunities for some of those ex-soldier friends of yours, what do y'all think?"

Ronnie picked up the six-pack. His dark glasses were as blank as his face. "You wanna get high now?"

Vicky rolled her eyes at him.

"I told you I'm not *doing* that anymore?"

"Yeah, you told me." His cheeks went up in the pursed-lipped smile. "More for me, then." He tucked a couple of magazines under his arm. "I'm go have a beer and a bop."

Boudreau watched Ronnie disappear down the hall to his mother's bedroom, there to cook dope in a spoon and burn the building down.

"Got rid of him," Boudreau observed.

"I swear!" Vicky gave a cheerleader's sigh, her eyes fixed on the spot where Ronnie had been. With him out of the room she seemed to deflate. She stubbed out her cigarette and laid back full-length on the couch again. She put her hands back behind her head and closed her eyes.

Boudreau sat down on the couch just beyond her feet. She stretched her legs out and lightly kneaded the outside of his thigh with all ten toes. Boudreau got an immediate, gratuitous hard-on.

A tiny smile appeared on Vicky's lips.

"What's so funny?" he said. He was convinced he was giving off a hard-on vibe.

"I had dreams about you all night long," she said in a plain voice.

"Yeah?"

"Yeah," she said. "You kept *saving* me."

"Yeah? Saving you from what?"

Her smile tilted up in one corner. "Oh, you know," she said. "This and that. I think other people's dreams are boring, don't you?"

Boudreau made a sound of assent, even though he wouldn't mind hearing about these. He watched her breathe, her breasts balanced under the small white halter like delicate mounds in danger of sliding off her chest. He could smell a sweet bath oil coming off her skin. She dug her toes into his thigh, pushing him slightly. In spite of himself, Boudreau began to entertain notions again.

"So I guess things don't seem so good, huh?" He watched her face.

Her eyes remained closed. "Oh no, things are fine. Things are just great?" *Jis grite.*

"Really?" said Boudreau.

Vicky nodded, finally opening her eyes. She pushed her cheeks up until her eyes crinkled, a parody of a phony smile, and withdrew her toes from his leg.

Boudreau watched her pull the vanishing act. He took it personally that she couldn't admit it to him.

"Yeah?" he said. "So how'd you get the bruise?"

"Bruise? This old thing?" She turned her head to look at her arm, as though he'd paid her a compliment on a piece of clothing. Then she looked back at him and performed a wide-eyed shrug.

"I guess I don't know?" She smirked, a Cheshire expression that erased everything she'd said, before disappearing back into itself. "I guess maybe I bump into things a lot?"

Vicky sat up suddenly and jumped off the couch. She ran her fingers around the legs of her red panties as if adjusting a bathing suit after coming out of the pool. She went over and dug through her purse, then took out her leather stash bag, the repository of free cuts copped out of whatever passed through Ronnie's hands. Flinging herself back down on the couch, she sat cross-legged facing Boudreau and began chopping white powder on a mirror.

"Well, would you look at that," he said.

Once, when they were younger, Boudreau had handed Vicky Michaels a love note. He was home on a visit from college and she was not yet out of high school. The note was so purple he was still mortified to remember it. A *love* note: it must've been someone in an earlier incarnation who'd written love notes. It was so long ago he couldn't remember anything of what she'd said afterward, just the look of embarrassment on her face while she searched for a way to disabuse him. Even at seventeen she'd been able to shut him down with a single look.

Boudreau watched her work the powder into lines, a sensation something like physical hunger centered in his midsection.

A television went on down the hall.

"Ronnie catching up on a little tube," he said.

"What?" Vicky wasn't listening. She chopped and rearranged the lines, drawing them out again and again, finer and straighter, more parallel.

He couldn't let it be. "You know you don't have to take that," he said, low voiced.

"Take what?"

"The bruise?" he said.

She looked up at him like this was big news. "Is that right?" She said it word by word, full of fake amazement, then turned her attention back to the mirror.

Boudreau felt like he'd just put his finger in a live socket. Well, fuck *her*. If she wanted to get slapped around and then play games about it, *fine*, she could fool herself all she wanted. It wasn't exactly his problem.

Vicky cast a critical eye on the six identical white lines, then rapped the fine dust off the razor blade.

"Wouldn't daddy be happy to see me now," she said.

"Yeah," said Boudreau. He thought she meant the dope.

"You know what he told me once?"

Boudreau shook his head, still pissed at her. His expectations had devolved into waiting to get high.

"This was when he was trying to talk me out of it? He goes, 'Vicky, that boy's all dick.' I couldn't *believe* it, I mean he never even *said* that word before." She gave an astonished little laugh. "Like this was supposed to warn me off, right? He didn't know the half of it."

Boudreau wasn't sure what she meant by "the half of it."

Vicky handed him the mirror and a short section of striped soda straw.

He put his face to the mirror, then faked a sudden violent need to sneeze.

"Asshole," she said.

Boudreau grinned and did two of the lines.

"Jesus." He snorted hugely, in a better mood already. "So how come you aren't getting high with Ronnie?"

She snickered. "I don't do that shit no more. I quit."

This was news to Boudreau. She wasn't strung out, but she'd had trouble even stopping for her pregnancy. "Yeah?"

"Yeah," she said. "It's bad for you."

He started laughing.

"I'm *serious*," she said.

"Hey, I know what you mean." He watched for the crack in her deadpan. "Your body's a temple, right, it pays to worship the right drugs. This, by the way, is great dope."

He realized then that she wasn't joking. It's *bad* for you? He wondered if this had only recently occurred to her.

"Okay, now you see it, now you don't." He vacuumed up his other line and handed the mirror back to her.

"Yeah, *so,* " he said. He could chat all right. "So okay, when did you stop doing the Bad Thang?" He had a little trouble believing she'd stopped, not just like that.

"While ago." She did one of her lines and snukked a few times. "Couple three weeks, I don't know."

"How come?"

She waved the straw happily, a conductor's baton to the surge of music. "New leaf," she said. "I decided I gotta get my shit together." Vicky heard herself and laughed out loud. She snorted her other two lines in rapid succession, then blinked and stretched out her jaw in a grimace, lifting her head away from the mirror like she'd gotten socked in the face.

"I ain't going down in flames yet," she said.

They sat cross-legged on the couch, facing each other and smoking cigarettes, speed rapping. After a while they did two more hits each.

Vicky leaned on the back of the couch, one arm hung over it, and laid her head down on her arm.

"I miss Clem." She gazed out the huge window, a black screen with amazing depth, a picture tube of lights and shapes extending out into nothing.

"Yeah?" said Boudreau. "Oh, Clementine, my Clementine—"

"Yeah," she said, cutting him off. "I've been trying to get out for a week, and now I miss her." She gave a ragged laugh. "She's just starting to crawl, but she only goes backwards. Momma's girl."

"I never figured you as a mom," Boudreau said. He focused on the little roll of creamy belly that overhung the top of her cut-offs, the last physical remnant of her pregnancy. "I don't know why, I just never did."

"Yeah, me neither," she said. She closed her eyes, and made a small sound of amusement through her nose.

"What?" said Boudreau.

"Just how everything ends up," she said. "I mean, here we are, but—"

"Yeah?"

"I don't know, *all* of it," she said. "I mean it's too funny, or it's not funny at all. Who would have thought we'd end up in Tulsa? Who'd a thunk it?" She made the amused sound again, but this time it sounded involuntary. She snukked, drawing up the coke drip.

"Yeah, right." Boudreau shook his head at the enormity of the irony. *"Tulsa."*

He had returned from California with a wife, and Vicky from New York with a case of hepatitis that turned into a nervous breakdown. Then somehow they'd both stayed on, long after the wife and the hepatitis were gone. Sometimes he wasn't so sure about the nervous breakdown.

"We're like migratory animals," he joked. "It's destiny, we're just programmed to come back and start the whole thing all over again."

"Don't *say* that," said Vicky, sniffling again.

She was keeping her eyes closed, Boudreau realized, because she was trying not to cry. A strand of her hair had come loose and was hanging down in front of her face. He reached over and looped it back into place with his little finger.

Vicky started at his touch, then went still. She opened her eyes for a moment and closed them again.

"We can help each other," said Boudreau. Here he was, back again.

"Yeah?" Her mouth went tiny, the merest idea of a smile. "We gonna run away together?"

"Sure." Against all sense he found his heart thonking wildly inside his rib cage, just with the saying of it. It *was* destiny, it was. It was all destiny.

She gave him a long look, eyes glittering. "Well, so where's the bus tickets, boy?" She drew a deep breath, lifting her shoulders as though gathering a burden, then sat up abruptly and reached to her stash bag on the coffee table. "I'm getting a little wired up here."

Thick with feeling, Boudreau watched while she rolled a joint. She took out a fat wad of opium and crumbled it into tiny pieces, then sprinkled them into the pot.

"This here'll take the edge off?" she said.

Boudreau felt the thread slipping out of his grasp again. He was about to say something to pull it back when he heard a slight change in the blare of the TV down the hall.

Ronnie materialized in the doorway of the living room, his cowboy boots off but the shades still on.

"What say?" said Boudreau, immediately paranoid about how much Ronnie might've heard. "You coulda stayed in here and got all coked up."

Ronnie grunted and tossed some magazines on the nearest table, half of them sliding off onto the floor. He picked up a new batch, bored.

"Anything on?" Boudreau tried to decide if throwing magazines on the floor meant anything.

Ronnie made a dismissive motion with his mouth. "Trash." He held up one of the magazines, a *Soldier of Fortune.* "Who reads this?"

"Billy," said Boudreau.

"Who's Billy?" Ronnie paged through the magazine, carefully wetting his thumb. The heroin had made his movements a little overdeliberate, but otherwise there was no sign.

Boudreau aimed a look at Vicky to stop her from saying anything. "Billy's my half brother," he said. "He's twelve. No wait, thirteen."

Ronnie's eyebrows went up. "He read this shit?"

"Billy'd like to be a sniper when he grows up," Boudreau said.

Ronnie frowned at the magazine. "You mean like a army sniper?"

"Nah, I think Billy'll go free-lance," said Boudreau, "more like your Charles Whitman–type sniper."

Vicky started snorting and choking on the joint she was lighting.

"Snipers ain't funny," Ronnie said without looking up from the magazine. From what little information Boudreau had gleaned from Vicky, he'd served all of four months in Vietnam, just long enough to pick up the makings of his hard-drug problem, some brig time stateside and a dishonorable discharge. Now he considered himself the gentle warrior, a pacifist at heart. He flicked a fingernail at the magazine like he was getting rid of a bug.

"These assholes," he said, "they never *heard* of karma."

Vicky passed the joint to Boudreau, who hit on it and then held it out to Ronnie. Ronnie looked at it with no expression.

"What a pair a garbage-heads." Pursing his lips, he dumped all the magazines back on the table except the *Soldier of Fortune* and stood looking at Boudreau through his sunglasses.

"We got some things to talk about when you get done," he said, then walked out of the room.

Without much pleasure Boudreau finished the joint with Vicky, imagining the conversation to follow. Now he was stoned and floaty on top of his coke jitters.

He found Ronnie installed on the chintz chaise, drinking a can of beer and watching the end of a made-for-TV movie about a family who'd adopted four orphans of different races. A metal film can and Ronnie's works sat on the little table next to the chaise.

Boudreau sat down on the corner of the bed, wondering how to proceed. The fact of the matter was that Ronnie had fronted Boudreau a quarter pound of California seedless buds a month before. Bum-on-the-street broke, Boudreau had figured he could turn around reefer that cost a hundred and twenty-five an ounce wholesale for a hundred and seventy-five retail. A few phone calls and he'd be a quick two hundred bucks and some stray joints richer.

What he hadn't figured was that Ronnie would give him short weight, more like three and a half ounces instead of four. Maybe it had just dried out a little, but he had to wonder if Ronnie had deliberately taken him off. He let it go without saying anything, and then it became academic anyway. He ended up selling one for a hundred and fifty, and one at cost. The third he had to sell as light weight because he'd dipped into it after he'd already smoked the odd half. Before he knew it, he'd spent what he'd made and now he owed Ronnie five hundred dollars he didn't have.

"How's the movie?" he said. There was a little black boy, an older Latin girl, a white boy about the same age, and a tiny Asian of indeterminate gender but cute as a peanut.

Ronnie watched the TV for a moment more, then turned. He pushed his sunglasses back up on his nose while he looked at Boudreau.

"Listen, man, I know I haven't gotten that money to you but I should have it next week." This was a bald lie. "Week after that, latest."

Ronnie turned back to the TV and pursed his lips, his mouth slightly open. He licked the bottoms of his molars, the whole thing giving him a slightly wolfish look.

"Is that okay?" said Boudreau.

"Maybe you could help me with something," Ronnie said finally.

"How do you mean?" said Boudreau. "You mean like instead of the money?"

Ronnie lit a Pall Mall, still watching the TV. He exhaled and gave a shrug. "Maybe," he said. "Depends."

Boudreau screamed inside at how maddeningly vague this had already become. In spite of an intense urge to lay back on the bed and float on the opium, he made himself focus.

"So what's it depend on?" he said.

"See this film can," Ronnie asked.

Boudreau could see it.

"That's got a fucking fortune in it." Ronnie kept his eyes on the TV screen. There was some kind of conflict between the black boy and the white boy. "All's I got to do is figure out the details."

Ah, the details. Boudreau regarded the film can. It didn't look like any fortune to him, maybe an ounce or two of powdered abuse.

"What is it?" This was going mighty slow. "Is it dope?"

Ronnie gave a maybe–maybe-not smile at the TV. "Let's just say it's kind of a deal." He had himself a rare chuckle. "Kind of a deal."

"So where do I come in?" Boudreau tried to put some enthusiasm in his voice, but it wasn't easy, even for five hundred dollars. Ronnie was always alluding to big-time deals, most of which had half-lives of twenty-four hours, and it was always someone else's fault when they didn't come through. This time he had the goods in hand, but that alone didn't make the deal any more promising.

"You work for a newspaper," Ronnie answered. "I don't know, I ain't got it figured out yet, but I might need some access to the medias. Cover my butt." He tore himself away from the TV long enough to aim a significant look at Boudreau.

"Uh-*huh.*" Boudreau nodded for a long time. "And of course we're talking here about something the police might be interested in, am I right?"

Ronnie threw his head back in a soundless gesture. That was a good one. He looked back at the TV, where the black boy was in tears, trying to explain something to the mom. "Let's just say the police might already know." He said the word *poe-leece.*

Boudreau whistled to show how impressed he was. This was surreal. Whatever it was in the can, cheap diamonds or a sample of a kilo or a saint's knucklebones, Ronnie was in over his head, that much was clear. Newspapers and police my ass, thought Boudreau, here's where the paranoia comes in. Ronnie was a conspiracy theorist of broad range, from book-tower and grassy-knoll rehashes to the extraterrestrial origins of ancient cultures. Boudreau had endured his share of long, incoherently detailed explanations of the evidence at hand, and how it was being suppressed by Motherfuckers.

"Gee, I don't know," said Boudreau. Maybe it was stolen. "That's intense." This was jokey, he was getting into it.

Ronnie nodded at Boudreau's appraisal and dropped the butt of his smoke into a newly empty beer can, where it hissed out. There were three other empties neatly lined up beside the chaise.

"That's why I might need the medias."

"Meedee-*yuh,*" Boudreau corrected without thinking. "It's already plural."

"Whatever," Ronnie said.

Boudreau saw he'd pissed him off. "It's Latin," he said, stepping in deeper.

"Whatever," said Ronnie. "Like newspapers."

"Right," Boudreau said, happy to agree. "You let me know what I can do once you get it figured out."

Ronnie stared at the TV in sharp-faced profile to Boudreau, high cheeked, shades slipped partway down his hawk nose again. Stretched out on the chaise, he looked impossibly long, not just tall but long, as though his body had stretched out in the silence, from the heels of his feet out to his long-boned fingers, up to the crown of his frayed blond pompadour.

"This ain't funny, Richter," he said. "And I ain't stupid." He kept his voice flat, a statement of fact for Boudreau's information. His eyes stayed on the TV, where the white boy and the black boy were hugging each other, clearly sealing a new sibling relationship.

Boudreau watched too, a chill running through him. The mom had appeared now to join in the hug, with the dad, the Latin girl, and the Asian peanut watching in secrecy from the top of the stairs, their eyes rolling in delight.

Boudreau watched the crawl of end credits, then the commercials. He wondered what he was going to say, or if they'd both just keep watching in silence until the test pattern came on in a few hours.

"Hey, Ronnie, man, look, I didn't—" he began, winging his way into some sort of apology.

"Well, ain't this cozy?" Vicky said. "We improving our minds in here?" She came to a stop near the front of the TV, stumbling slightly. She hugged her elbows.

They all watched the local late news highlights. An enormously obese man appeared, standing in front of a pile of rubble in west Tulsa. It was apparently his former house, which had collapsed in a mysterious fashion.

"My *he's* attractive," Vicky said. "What'd he do, set on it?"

"That's real sympathetic," Ronnie said.

She regarded Ronnie as he watched the fat man from the chaise, then went over to the bed and climbed on, elaborately fluffing a pillow before arranging herself in a tight snuggle beside Boudreau.

He went rigid at the contact. She might as well have climbed on top of him and started humping. This was all he needed, to add jealousy to his catalogue of indebtedness and insult. After a minute or so he stole a glance over at Ronnie. His skin had taken on a ravaged, deep-pored look in the glow of the TV. His face looked cold as stone behind the sunglasses.

"Where *is* my cigarette?" Vicky giggled at how trashed she was. "I had one, I swear I did?"

She reached over and slid Boudreau's pack out of his shirt pocket, giving him the tiniest caress of fingertips in the process. As she lit the cigarette, he caught a glimpse of her eyes. They'd gone hollow, looking over at her husband.

FRIDAY

Boudreau woke up knowing he'd slept through the alarm. He was curled into a ball on top of the bedspread on his mother's bed, trying to stay warm. The air-conditioning was freezing; he'd slept in his clothes. He woke up a little more, then gained full consciousness with a single thought: *Shit* he was late.

He vaulted out of bed and searched the kitchen cabinets for a jar of instant coffee. He let the tap water run hot until it steamed, then made a cup. It was swill but he drank it anyway. He smoked a Kool along with it, using the saucer as his ashtray. It was running on to midmorning already, and he should've been at the paper an hour ago.

The review was of course still unwritten. He couldn't *believe* he'd overslept.

He shuffled around in his socks on the thick carpet, straightening things up in a quick once-over. If he kept the apartment picture-perfect, there wouldn't be any need for a major overhaul come Sunday. He emptied the ashtrays and rinsed a few glasses, then tried to remember how and where the various stacks of magazines had been arranged. His head felt like it was filled with mud from the night's doping.

He wandered around with a stray throw pillow, unable to decide to which couch the fucking thing belonged. He only visited there maybe twice a year, Christmas and whatever. It wasn't like his mother's decorating scheme was burnished into his memory.

He thought maybe it went on the long gray velvet couch that sat in front of the big picture window. Out the window the taller buildings of downtown Tulsa had already disappeared in the morning smog. He tucked the pillow into place behind some others, pleased with his choice until he looked down.

Boudreau groaned out loud and dropped to all fours. The curled, skeletal ash of a cigarette lay on the white carpet, a few inches away from the edge of the long coffee table in front of the couch. The cigarette had obviously rolled out of an ashtray, then smoldered all the way down to the filter. The cream-colored wool was branded halfway down to its backing, charred black. Boudreau raked at the surrounding pile, trying to comb it over.

This was making him feel less than adult. Furious, he raked at the burn harder, with no success. He tried moving the coffee table over a few inches and then out a few, so that one broad leg would cover the evidence. This left four distinct indentations in the carpet where the legs used to sit. He began rubbing in a frenzy to get the woolen pile to stand up again, and got an immediate friction burn on his knuckles. He swore and began using the edge of a thick glass ashtray instead.

Boudreau got up from his knees and stood back. The couch was centered in front of the window, but now the coffee table was no longer centered in front of the couch. The indentations in the carpet were faint but still clearly visible. He might as well leave her a map: *Here's the burn, I did it.*

The white filter had red lipstick wrapped around it, one of Vicky's Salems. He felt like throwing the ashtray through the window.

Boudreau's pulse quickened, his morning going downhill already. He began to deal out blame, all of it to Vicky Stover. He'd always measured love by the level of insecurity it aroused in him, but this was too much. When he was eighteen, he'd lined up for her along with everyone else in wheat jeans and penny loafers, hopeless and horny. Now here he was, fifteen years later, still jumping like a puppet. He'd no more "gotten over" her than he'd gotten over drugs.

This was *it*, this time; this wasn't love. What he felt was more like a grain of irritation under his skin, pearled with the passage of time, no different from the little black lump on his leg where his sister had stabbed him with a lead pencil.

We gonna run away together? He could hear the voice, rich with tease. *So where's the bus tickets, boy?*

What a joke. Boudreau could only imagine what it would be like to experience Vicky Stover on a daily basis. *Hi, honey, I'm home. Who've you been today?* Sigmund Fucking Freud couldn't deal with her. Her lurid little wife-beating scene served as fair warning. He'd had it.

He gave up worrying about the cigarette burn. What was his mother going to do, sue him? If she stopped speaking to him again, it wouldn't exactly change the quality of his life.

If he hadn't had the two of them over last night, none of this would have happened. Then again, if he hadn't snuck in here himself, it wouldn't have happened either. That, of course, depended on him not having paid his power bill.

He stopped himself. This kind of thinking was pointless, you might as well start worrying about how the planets were aligned when you were born.

Boudreau checked his watch and hurried down the long hallway to his mother's bedroom, following the gallery of family photographs along the walls, thirty years' and three husbands' worth.

Most of the pictures were of his mother and the last two husbands on various high-ticket outings, Rio and St. Moritz and Palm Springs. The second husband had died on just such a trip, collapsing on a sidewalk outside a restaurant in Tokyo. There were also a depressing number of photographs of Billy, including a recent shot of him posed in full camouflage uniform, complete with ambush makeup and what appeared to be a real .45.

Down at the very end, sequestered in the distant, rustic past, right next to the photograph of his mother's parents in front of their hardware store in Bristow, there was a large frame with four oval photos under the same matte, the whole thing bordered by a stylized lasso.

There it was, hard to believe: Mom and Dad and Richter and Betsy, orbiting each other like little planets. Boudreau was about nine, his sister then seven and a half, their parents in their midthirties. They would've still been up in Osage County, the house in Tulsa yet unbuilt by a couple of years.

Behind the studio smile, Malcolm Boudreau's face was already bloated, his eyes flat, his liver still a year and a half from blowing out. Betsy's little-featured face had ten years left to it, not quite enough to get her out of high school. Boudreau had avoided looking at these pictures the whole time he'd been there. The little boy's face, his own, gave him no clue of what it had been like to be him.

He walked by, depressed by his own kind. This was like a war memorial to life in the family, Dad and Sis lost in action. He felt like the lone survivor, Mom having transferred out to a better command.

Boudreau gave his mother's room a once-over. The bed was straightened, the TV retracted back into its cabinet, everything in place, no obvious stains or burns. They hadn't left until after one, Vicky bleary-eyed and silent, Ronnie so nodded out he could barely walk, much less talk. He'd left his beer cans stacked next to the chaise like a ritual cairn.

Boudreau made a last check in his mother's bathroom; it was a lot cleaner than he was. He sniffed a pit. It was the second day on the short-sleeved blue shirt, the third on the khaki pants, and there was no time for a shower or shave. He swabbed his teeth with some toothpaste on his finger, then ran a comb from the marble vanity through his hair, checking it for hairs before he replaced it in the same position.

He gave the mirror a cursory check, alarmed at the small dark bags under his eyes. Worse, the laugh lines to the sides of his mouth seemed to have gained pouchiness overnight. He pushed his chin forward to get rid of some of the sag, tightened his jaw. He was getting too old for this shit. No: this shit was *making* him old.

By the time he was out in the hall locking the door, Boudreau was in the throes of a familiar feeling, a train of thought that came through every morning, fueled by self-hatred and watery hope, followed by a long string of resolves. He was going to cut back on his doping, cut back on his drinking, watch his finances.

It was like a mantra that had never worked yet, but he tried it again anyway. You never could tell.

The English doorman was nowhere to be seen. Boudreau decided it was just as well, and walked through the lobby doors out into the heat. The motionless air assaulted him. He began sweating immediately, basting in it like a piece of poultry.

The sky was so bright he could hardly see, even with his sunglasses on, but there wasn't a trace of identifiable blue anywhere in it. He breathed in and felt a jab of sinus up behind his left eye. It was a Tulsa spring morning, with a light smell of refinery on the air.

He stopped and tucked his briefcase under one arm, then lit a cigarette. When he looked up, a cab was pulling in to the curb. W. K. Rowlings III climbed out of it, fat little ass first.

"Hey, Bill!" said Boudreau, too loudly. The boy jumped and turned around.

Boudreau couldn't believe his luck.

"Hey, long time!" He was almost shouting. Desperate, he extended his hand and lowered his voice. "Just thought I'd drop by on my way to work, but you guys weren't home. Where's, uh, where's your mom?"

Boudreau never knew what to call his mother between the two of them: Mom? Mother? Our mom? Cynthia? The connection wasn't something he liked to emphasize.

Billy Rowlings looked over at Boudreau, squinted at the briefcase and then at the lobby doors of the building. Finally he took his half brother's hand.

Boudreau shook the boy's chubby paw harder than he had to, hoping to imply physical threat. At least he only had the briefcase and not some more obvious piece of luggage. "So! How y'all been?"

Billy Rowlings' too large head on his boy's body gave him the look of a malevolent dwarf. He pulled his hand away, a suspicious look in his wide-set little blue eyes. He made a grunting vowel sound.

The cabdriver, a middle-aged man whose blue-black skin contrasted against an electric green sport shirt, set a suitcase down next to the boy. Boudreau watched as Billy Rowlings reached in his pocket and peeled a bill off his neatly folded wad, then paid the man with a tiny wave to indicate he should keep the change, all without looking at him.

Boudreau got the same sense of wonderment as when he'd first seen live miniature horses. Here were the gestures of a sixty-year-old oilman miraculously telescoped down to the size of a thirteen-year-old boy. How do they fucking *do* that?

The doorman on duty, another middle-aged black man, came out and fetched the suitcase, then immediately retreated back into the air-conditioning.

"When's, ah, when's your mom coming back?" Boudreau could feel his armpits getting slippery. Why wasn't she with him? He began to frantically review mental pictures of each room in the apartment. The cool dry air he'd been in for the last sixteen hours already seemed like a lost paradise.

"She gets back Sund'y," said Billy Rowlings. He kept his eyes averted. Even though he was chubby, bordering on fat, the boy's pale and freckled moon face seemed dry as powder.

"Is that right?" Boudreau smiled broadly at this information while trying to look disappointed. "Well, I guess it can wait."

Billy Rowlings gave him the briefest of looks. "What."

"Just business," explained Boudreau. "So, who's staying with you till she gets back?"

"Nobody."

"Nobody?" Boudreau kept the smile fixed on his face. She'd watched him like a goddamn convict when he was a teenager, and now this kid was getting a twelfth-floor apartment to himself for the weekend, with a wad of cash that would've funded Boudreau for the next month. "She left you here by yourself?"

"Yes, she left me here by myself," the boy said through his nose. *"Richter."*

Boudreau dropped his cigarette and crushed it under the heel of his boot, grinding it into shreds. He'd had enough. "Okay, Bill." He turned and called over his shoulder. "Tell her I stopped by if you remember. I'll talk to her sometime next week. No big deal, I'll get in touch."

The only thing Boudreau heard as he walked away was the whoosh of the lobby door closing, accepting the boy into the sanctum of cool air.

He walked across the already soft asphalt of the parking lot, unpleasantly aware of the speed of his pulse. This had been a little too close. If he were lucky, Billy Rowlings would be a slob and trash the apartment before his mother got back, erasing whatever signs of his own presence he'd neglected. It pissed him off how he'd groveled in front of the little turd; he almost walked past his car, lost in an extended fantasy of his own fingers around the fat pale neck.

Boudreau sunk into the car and cranked the key until the engine finally caught, a cloud of blue exhaust billowing out from the rear. It was a red '65 Austin Healey 3000 convertible and a mistake from the day he'd bought it, beginning with the money he'd had to borrow from his mother. When his old Toyota died, she'd grilled him like a second-mortgage officer about why he needed to spend so much. Boudreau's line was that the car was already considered a classic and could only appreciate. How could he pass up an investment like that?

That was almost two years ago, and since then whatever rare extra cash he'd mustered went immediately into keeping the thing running. Some investment: it was more like a spoiled brat with expensive tastes, never satisfied. Right now it needed new radials and shocks all around, on this car an easy fifteen hundred. The engine was burning oil and needed a major tune, but was basically sound until it lost more compression and demanded rings or valves. He preferred not to think about what would happen then.

Just lately, in addition to everything else, the Healey had showed signs of serious gear wear. Twice in the last week it had fallen out of third gear, just popped right out after sudden acceleration or deceleration. Now Boudreau had to remember to keep hand pressure on the stick when it was in third.

He drove fast as soon as he got out of the parking lot, but traffic was thicker than he expected. Stuck behind a line of cars at a red light, he sat in the little open car and baked through two full changes.

The problem was that even if the doorman kept his mouth shut and Billy muddied the trail with a weekend of slobbery, Boudreau's mother was still going to call him up. He'd called her, and Billy would say he'd stopped by. She could only assume that it had something to do with the money he owed her—like that he had it, for example, which he didn't. After two years he'd paid back exactly three hundred out of the four thousand he'd borrowed; it could be another two years easy before he came up with that much again. The Big Plan was beginning to look a little thin.

Boudreau decided to hop on the short stretch of expressway downtown. He started down the on ramp, running second gear out hard before he shifted. He never should've called, never should've sneakypeted in there. Now he was going to have to deal with it. No, not with *it:* with *her.*

He came down the ramp in third with good revs, searching the thick stream of cars for an open slot. A break in the line came abreast, the only one in sight. It was tight but the Healey could handle this kind of traffic like a rabbit in a pack of turtles. He turned the wheel and punched the pedal at the same time.

Nothing happened but noise: he heard the whine of soaring rpm's unconnected to a drive train. Then he heard a set of screaming brakes right behind him. Up close in the rearview was a pop-eyed guy in a boatlike Chevy doing sixty not quite sideways, high up on its locked tires. The sound of brakes began to multiply.

The Chevy whipped out of its skid as Boudreau clutched and got back in gear and accelerated again, while traffic flowed around him. This time he kept his hand on the stick. Pop-eyes leaned on his horn like he was trying to jam it through the wheel. The whole thing took maybe two seconds. In the mirror the guy was giving Boudreau the finger now along with the horn. He looked ready to jump through the windshield.

His top down, Boudreau felt like an oyster, fat on the half-shell. There was every possibility the asshole would start chucking bottles and tire irons at him, assuming he'd forgotten his gun. Boudreau changed lanes and wove his way through traffic until he lost him, the Healey handling like a dream.

Boudreau pulled into the parking lot downtown, covered with a thin film of sweat and road grime. He watched the sign on the Bank of Oklahoma Building change from 10:11 to 93 and then back again.

He climbed out of the Healey and discovered his legs had gone boneless. Propping himself up against the car, he lit a cigarette and sucked on it, trying to calm down.

His sister had died in a car accident, even though it took her a while to finally let go. For two and a half days he'd watched Betsy lie there in ICU, her head lopsided and tubes everywhere. She stared, eyes open but following nothing, while her body oozed blood and clear fluid. After a while the tubes couldn't keep up: her juices ran out and that was it. She'd somehow leaked away.

With the certainty of superstition, Boudreau had known for years that he would buy his in a wreck also. A last moment of total rending pain and terror, then lights out. Of the endless ways to die, his was going to be the stupidest. Tulsa was second in the world only to Los Angeles in cars per capita, so it wouldn't be hard.

He straightened up and looked around, freaking out. His mind was slipping gears also. The memory had come walloping out of a time zone, as though Betsy had returned to life only to die all over again.

Once his pulse finally slowed, Boudreau took two more deep drags of the cigarette and threw it down. A stab of anxiety knifed into him at how much the gearbox work was likely to cost. It would not be cheap, but that didn't matter. Whatever it was, he didn't have it. He kicked the car in the rocker panel, hard, then swore. Might as well add some body work to the bill.

He legged it the two blocks from the parking lot to the *Journal*, hurrying but not so much that his shirt would be soaked by the time he got there. A half block away from the building, he saw people swirling around somebody in the middle of the sidewalk like water parting around a rock in a streambed. It was a young, clean-shaven man with very long, thick reddish brown hair parted down the middle, the kind of healthy-looking hippie thought to still exist only in Vermont and Oregon.

As he drew closer, Boudreau saw he was brandishing an armful of leaflets, environmental or antinuke, which explained why people were avoiding him. It took balls to hand out stuff like that in downtown Tulsa. Boudreau copped a sample, and the guy gave him a big smile as he went past.

"Praise God!" the hippie called after him.

Boudreau stopped and looked down at the paper in his hand: it was end-of-the-world Bible shit, fire and doom and kiss it good-bye.

This was just what Boudreau needed to start the day, a little apocalypse from some religious asshole. He turned on his heel and shoved the paper back at the guy.

The hippie smiled like a rock. *"Praise* God!" he said again, his blue eyes way too clear.

Boudreau pushed through the revolving doors of the *Journal,* still furious, nearly knocking over a small woman. These people were getting out of hand. He felt like telling the guy to go praise his dick, he'd get more out of it.

Waiting at the elevator door, he checked his reflection in the little window. For a long bad moment he saw someone else looking back. The reflection had the small weak mouth of an incomplete predator, a suckling; a mouth of cirrhosis and arterial cholesterol and sour lungs; the mouth of a blind creature searching for a tit. It was, in fact, his father's mouth and not his own.

Boudreau stepped into the empty elevator and pushed the button. He waited for the doors to close as a larval anxiety uncurled in the bottom of his stomach, a fat little grub of dread that rode up with him. The end was near, indeed. This was just the kind of thing Boudreau took personally.

Stepping out of the elevator into the big newsroom of the *Tulsa Journal,* Boudreau had a failure of heart. The place seemed worse than usual, an entire industrially designed landscape of petroleum-derived, color-coordinated objects—chairs, desks, partitions, *people*—sprouting out of a monochrome carpet.

He felt like he was walking through a rat maze. Under the shadowless white lighting all the colors seemed slightly off, as though there might be a knob somewhere that could produce a better picture. The dry chill of air-conditioning carried a distinct whiff of curing plastic in it, with strange undertones that Boudreau had never been able to identify, somewhere between formaldehyde and hair spray. The only sound not swallowed by the carpet or the acoustically tiled ceiling was a continuous, deadened wash of *thuck thuck thuck,* fingers hitting computer keyboards.

Boudreau sat at his desk, dumb. After five minutes he was already staring blankly at the hateful little green television. The blinking cursor perched on the end of his sole paragraph like a dripping faucet. He slapped his pocket for his cigarettes and lit a Kool.

The *Journal* had gone computer only the year before, at which time Preston Liddey had delivered himself of a speech to commemorate the occasion of such a massive capital outlay. It was his usual booster flatulence about meeting the Information Challenges of the Future, with a Real Commitment to Excellence, to thereby better Serve the Needs of a Growing Tulsa.

There had been no surprises, contentwise. Boudreau thought Preston could've farted at the same level of meaning. But instead of delivering it in his patented Chamber of Commerce fashion, Liddey had everyone sit down at their new terminals in the grid of half-partitions. The "speech" was then displayed on their screens, scrolled one line at a time so the fast readers wouldn't jump ahead. Boudreau had stolen a look around as everyone sat in stupefied attention, peering into their new cathode-ray tubes. Preston Liddey stood in the doorway of his office and watched, arms crossed and a smile on his face: this was Meeting the Information Challenge of the Future.

Boudreau wanted to kick himself for not getting the piece done the night before. Then he could've just typed the thing into the machine, gone down to pick up the check from the comptroller, and split.

Instead he smoked and stared at the screen. Throwing back his shoulders, he took a deep breath. It was happening again. The words in his extant paragraph were beginning to lose meaning, the syntax seem random as shower singing.

The piece was supposed to run in the weekend section, due at one o'clock. He'd already missed a couple of deadlines recently, and here he was again, getting nowhere. Just to top things off, he had office hours at TU in the afternoon.

Boudreau didn't care about the review, but he needed the money. Besides the big one with his mother, he'd scattered little debts around town like litter. The paper paid him on submission, eighty-five a pop. He'd give the power company some token amount to restore his electricity, and the rest would have to get him through the weekend.

Next week three movies were opening locally; Boudreau thought he could talk Liddey into covering all three. Then in the second week of June, he had the summer film seminar for adults. Arranged through TU in conjunction with one of the museums in town, it drew mostly late-thirtyish women who loved Ingmar Bergman. He'd done it the last three summers; surely they wouldn't mind paying him up front this time. Boudreau was already counting on it.

He lit another cigarette, then stubbed it out before it was half-smoked. He'd never let things get quite so out of hand before. He got up from his desk and walked over to George Brinkman's half-cubicle.

Brinkman was uncapping his morning container of diner coffee, casting looks around the room from the corner of his eye.

"Yo, George." Boudreau slid into the molded plastic chair beside the desk.

Brinkman started, slopping out some of the coffee. He swore at it under his breath.

"Sholom," said Boudreau.

Brinkman looked at him, barely. "Fuck you," he said.

Boudreau tongued a disapproving noise and signaled for a sip of Brinkman's coffee.

George Brinkman was from urban New Jersey, a smart-mouth fresh out of journalism school and highly paranoid. He was ill-equipped on each count to handle the reality of being a swarthy little Jew at the *Tulsa Journal*. A small man with fine olive skin, Brinkman was twenty-seven, with a high forehead under thinning hair and dark circles under his eyes, both of which made him look perpetually alarmed in a hostile kind of way.

"So what brings you down today?" he said sideways, glaring at something or someone across the room.

"Everything," Boudreau cracked, but Brinkman stayed deadpan. "Brings me down," Boudreau explained. "No, but seriously folks. Just a movie review."

"Yeah? What movie?"

Brinkman snorted when Boudreau told him. Brinkman's taste in movies ran to violent urban-revenge flicks. Boudreau had once explained to him that this was basically an East Coast genre. Western audiences just didn't get the concept of real cities where people walked on the streets, and also thought that all small ethnic people were suspect, not just the bad guys. Context was all. Folks here could buy Billy Jack, just not Charles Bronson.

"Gimme that," Brinkman said, gesturing for his coffee. "You're germing it up."

Boudreau handed it back. He had blown across it repeatedly without acquiring a sip; it was too hot.

"Now the goddamn cup is falling apart." Brinkman took a single delicate sip. "It's not enough they give you pig urine, they got to boil it first, right?"

Boudreau was getting a little tired of Brinkman's unendingly critical comparisons. Oh *sure*, like Jersey diner coffee was inherently superior to Tulsa diner coffee. Brinkman had been in town now for not quite two months, and still regarded it as a missing chapter out of Flannery O'Connor. It wasn't that Boudreau disagreed, he just thought that in his total dismissiveness Brinkman was missing out on the humorous little nuances that made up local color.

Boudreau nodded, smiled. The conversation had drifted far enough, and he needed to get to the point.

"So *George*," he said, "I'm having trouble with this review, I need some inspiration." He leaned in and kept his voice low. "What say let's go for a *ride.*"

Brinkman blew across the top of his coffee, without looking up or saying anything, then let his eyes play over the room, long enough so that Boudreau began to get paranoid. He wondered, too late, if he owed Brinkman any money. He never saw Brinkman outside of the paper, and he always smoked Brinkman's dope. Maybe George was getting tired of it.

Brinkman finally looked back at him, a level gaze. "It's ten forty-five in the morning, Boudreau."

"Whatta you," said Boudreau, "my mother? You, *you* should talk."

Now that his coffee had cooled down Brinkman sipped at it loudly, the styrofoam cup close to collapsing. "The accent needs a little work." He sipped again, carefully bringing the cup to his lips, then gave a tiny, weary shrug of his eyebrows. Boudreau's heart jumped like a puppy.

"Okay okay, twist my arm," George Brinkman said. "I brought two today anyway. This heat's unbelievable, Boudreau. I got a world of *tsuris* living in this fucking place."

Boudreau drove south on the expressway, out of downtown, while Brinkman fired up the joint.

After two hits Brinkman started in. "I got to get out of here, I got to get out of this town."

"Give it time, George," said Boudreau. "The rich local traditions'll grow on you."

Brinkman snorted out his smoke. "Traditions?" His voice was thick with disbelief. "This makes L.A. seem like old-world Vienna."

Boudreau laughed and sucked on the reefer, anticipating the soothing plane from which he would gaze down upon his shambles of a morning. " 'Old-world Vienna,' " he repeated. "Now there's a name for a pricey little development. See, you could make money here, you just don't realize it."

"Some traditions," said Brinkman, "they got restaurants in New York older than this whole fucking town." He thought about it. "Forget restaurants, they got *waiters* older than this."

After another minute or two they were cruising south, stoned with their sunglasses on, the highway wind blasting hot in their faces.

Brinkman turned on the radio, punched two different stations, then snapped it back off. "Great radio, too," he said. "You get your choice between 'Stairway to Heaven' and 'Aqualung.' Maybe the Clash'll play here when they do their oldies tour. Hey, where we going, anyway?"

"I thought maybe you'd like to see one of the architectural wonders of the modern world," said Boudreau. "The Oral Roberts campus."

Brinkman moaned. "I been there."

"Yeah, but under the influence, with a personal tour guide?"

Brinkman grimaced and gestured for the dope. "Okay, whatever. My body's just along for the ride."

"Whoa, I am *ripped,*" said Boudreau. "Lighten up, George."

Brinkman took the hint and sat silently for a minute, but only a minute. "I'm sorry, man, but I can't take these prairie popes seriously."

"Oral shoots a great game of golf," Boudreau said.

Brinkman was off on his own track already. "I mean, take this guy Harmon Shaw?"

Startled, Boudreau looked over. "What about him?"

"Yesterday I got to cover a press conference about his new industrial park. Preston gives it to me like I've hit the big time. Oooh, Harmon *Shaw.*"

The subject was already making Boudreau nervous. "Next you'll be doing movie reviews."

"Funny. Anyway, I don't get this guy, you wanna hear how he leads off his press conference?" Brinkman turned in his seat to face Boudreau, letting one corner of his mouth rise slightly.

Boudreau nodded him along.

"He's talking to this porky-looking guy—I found out later he's one of his bankers—this *pig,* man, I mean actual pink skin bulging over the collar. Anyway, it's like a 'private' conversation, right, but no one else is talking much and we're all in clear earshot. He knows we're listening, is what I'm saying."

"Yeah?"

Brinkman raised a forefinger. "Joke: 'Hey, what do you get when you cross a groundhog and a nigger?' "

Boudreau waited.

" 'Six more weeks of basketball,' " said George Brinkman, snorting with laughter. "Can you *believe* it?"

Boudreau kept his eyes on the highway.

"Believe what, that Harmon Shaw tells nigger jokes? I can believe that."

Brinkman shook his head. "Naw, what got me was—okay, this was overheard and off the record, but nobody even mentioned it, man. The *World* was there, the *Trib,* two TV stations, and nobody fucking blinked. It's like he did it on purpose, you know, just to see. I mean, this guy Shaw's one of the richest pricks in Oklahoma—"

"You mean 'prominent civic figures.' "

"—and they *laughed.* This was a public event, right? I—"

Boudreau interrupted. "Here we have one of the traditions to which I was referring earlier, George. And you know what? Around here, nobody notices."

Brinkman waved his hand in dismissal. "Hey, I laughed too. I mean who cares what he thinks, everybody tells nigger jokes—"

"I don't," said Boudreau.

Brinkman ignored him and went on. "It's just this guy is a preacher, too, right? This public figure? They're supposed to know you don't say this shit out loud, that's all. It's, I don't know, it's *primitive.*" He sniffed. "Back home this'd be front page, man, next day every Raheem in Newark'd be out in the street, ready for some window shopping." Brinkman noticed the dead joint in his hand and stuck it back in the ashtray. He leaned back in his seat. "What a place."

Boudreau finished the drive to ORU in silence, wanting to argue but uncertain where to begin. Finally they arrived at the campus, and he began slaloming through the various parking lots in big loops, pointing out the giant brass praying hands, sixty feet high and modeled after Oral's own, then the Prayer Tower, which looked like the Space Needle and was covered with mirrors.

"Check it out," said Boudreau. "The radio station's in there too."

By this time Brinkman had slumped so low in his seat he could barely see over his door. Preternaturally clean-cut students were walking around. "Where do they get these twerps?"

"Just a few of the people who think you killed Jesus, George."

"Boudreau man, can we get *out* of here please?"

Boudreau chuckled. "Think of it as like a theme park."

"Yeah, I'm stoned out and this is very humorous," Brinkman said, sinking even lower in his seat. "This was a wise career move. A year or two here and I can move right up to the *Bugle-Democrat* in Horse Dick, North Dakota."

Boudreau laughed and did another loop around the parking lot. "Hey, you know my ex-wife was half-Jewish. She liked it here."

Brinkman turned and glared at him. "What, that's supposed to make me feel better?"

Boudreau laughed again. This was fun. One thing about Jews, they could be funny about their misery. This was like playing softball, he could lob these to Brinkman all day long.

"No," he said, "actually she hated it. I was just trying to make you feel better." He stopped the car and looked around, then relit the roach. "She was Quaker on the other side."

"*Quaker?*" Brinkman waved away the roach, irritated. He was thinking. "I have this, like, melancholy side of my personality?" He nodded his head slowly while he spoke, as though trying to understand himself. "Now I sign a contract to work in Jesus World. Carl Bernstein in Jesus World."

"Cheer up," Boudreau said. He started the car again. "It could be worse. I wish we had a couple of yarmics to put on so we could get out and walk around. We could talk Yiddish and shit while they try to convert us."

"Funny," said Brinkman. "That's real funny."

Boudreau kept his eyes straight ahead. It was just stoned joking, but now he'd somehow managed to offend him. "Okay, enough grins for one day," he said, then headed back out to Lewis.

"I shtupped Harmon Shaw's daughter a couple years ago," he offered after a while.

George Brinkman turned and regarded Boudreau as though he'd just arrived out of the sky, a late arrival from the old Avis ad. He lifted his eyebrows. "So how was it?"

Boudreau shrugged, a little smirk on his face. Brinkman had complained of terminal horniness ever since he'd moved to Tulsa.

"C'mon," said Brinkman. "So was it . . . religious?"

"Let's call it"—Boudreau had told the story a million times but the right word still evaded him—"*in*teresting."

Brinkman laughed and looked forward again. "Sounds like dry fucking to me." He did his Barry White imitation, all baritone hormones. " 'Well, baby, that was . . . innaresting.' " He laughed again. "That's the one they sent off to the nuthouse in Kansas—what's it, Menninger's, right?"

Boudreau turned and looked at him.

"Hey, you're looking at boy reporter on the case," Brinkman explained. "Guy from the *Trib* told me."

"Yeah, Liz Shaw," Boudreau said. "Before she was crazy," he added. Actually he wasn't all that sure. "She was in one of my classes. Things kind of got started one day under the table at the country club."

"Under the table?"

"She was, anyway," said Boudreau.

Brinkman whistled. "What a cowboy. So how did Harmon take it?"

"Ah, we arrive at my point." Boudreau held up a forefinger. "Harmon did not take it well."

Without being absolutely forthcoming about the tawdrier details of what happened with Liz Shaw, Boudreau recalled for Brinkman the subsequent visit from her father.

Harmon Shaw had shown up at the film department three days afterward, walking right in on a conference with a student.

"Son, I'd like it if you'd give us a minute or two please?"

Confused, the student looked at Boudreau and got no help, then left. Shaw shut the door behind the kid and took a position in front of Boudreau's desk. He looked at a spot somewhere over Boudreau's shoulder while he talked.

"I don't feel like a honest man ought to have to do this," he said. Shaw had the kind of harsh grit accent that made him grimace when he talked; it made speech seem like a labor. "Ever'body knows what happened down at Norman." Norman was the home of Oklahoma University, where Liz Shaw had been before he'd had her transferred to TU. Shaw paused for a long moment, then inhaled heavily. "What's done is God's will."

Boudreau's initial impulse had been to apologize, but now he opened his mouth to begin dissembling: I don't know what the hell you're talking about. Harmon Shaw lifted his chin a tiny amount, and Boudreau shut his mouth as if he had been directly threatened.

Shaw's voice rose in volume and took on a different tone. "He has instructed me to find His wisdom in my suffering, and I *have.*" His lips went white in a tight smile. "The loss of my daughter because of that buck will serve His greater purpose. I will suffer, I will *suffer* my shame so that others may see."

He turned then and looked around the office in blank regard, as if he'd come to assess the furniture and Boudreau was merely part of it. Chilled, Boudreau stared at his back. The man spoke about his daughter as if she were already dead. Worse than dead: defiled. The amazing thing was that Shaw couldn't see why she'd want to go out and bang a big spade.

Shaw settled on the picture of Truman Boudreau in handcuffs. "I *will not* be stayed in my sorrow," he said, "I *will not.* I have great *reward* in my sorrow. He has given me my flock to tend, my health, my boy Bedford, and in return I am the servant of His bidding."

Boudreau kept his mouth shut. It was hard to discuss things with people who had God on the other line.

"There are those whose eyes are not yet open, but He has also given me patience with my hardship. *Test* my faith, O Lord, and give me guidance through it."

Harmon Shaw turned then and looked directly at Boudreau, for the first and only time. His thick black hair grew a little too low on his forehead, his small brown eyes were set a little too deep under his brow. A long shiver ran through Boudreau: he got the feeling he was looking at a human from an earlier stage of development, for whom eye contact was a prelude to clubs and rocks.

"Do we understand each other," Shaw asked. He turned without waiting for the answer and walked out, leaving the door open.

"So?" George Brinkman was unimpressed. "The guy was upset you talked his crazy daughter out her pants." He snickered. "I mean, who wouldn't be?"

Boudreau shook his head. "Missing the point, George." They were back downtown now and off the expressway, waiting for a light behind a long line of cars. "He *threatened* me, man, these people are *serious.* Here's this guy worth a hundred seventy-five million, this spiritual leader in the eighth decade of the twentieth century, and to him the end of the world is his daughter sleeping with a black ball player at OU."

"Wait a minute, *wait* a minute," said Brinkman. "Wasn't it *you* he came to see about banging his daughter?"

Boudreau kept shaking his head.

"And maybe I wasn't listening close enough, but I didn't hear anything about breaking your knees or cutting your nuts off."

"He didn't have to." Boudreau searched his brain for the word *implicit* but couldn't find it. Meanwhile the Healey died sitting at the light, causing him momentary panic before he got it started again. "He made me feel like a *bug.*"

Brinkman lit the last bit of roach for a quick hit before they got back to the paper. "No offense, Boudreau, but I think you got a little guilt-and-authority problem."

Outraged, Boudreau started to argue.

Brinkman shook his head continually while he sucked on the roach. "Gimme a *break,*" he said, voice thick in withheld smoke, "you're talking *body* language?" He blew it out. "Let's hear guns and car bombs, then I'll help you sue the fucker."

Boudreau gave up: Brinkman would never understand. He reached for the roach, but Brinkman had already killed it.

"I don't know, man." Brinkman leaned back in his seat, contemplative. "This obsession with Raheems, it's not healthy. I think you people in Tulsa got a thing about big nigger dicks." He waited for Boudreau to turn, then gave him a grin.

"Know how a Jew makes his dick six inches long?"

Boudreau shook his head.

"Folds it in half," said George Brinkman.

Boudreau waited a minute or two, then strolled back into the newsroom himself. Brinkman had laid a Quaalude on him on the way in. He wasn't such a bad guy after all.

He settled into his chair and lit a Kool. This was more like it. He felt pleasingly thick, things didn't seem so pressing; he could knock off the review at will. He blew some smoke rings and ruminated on the soothing quality of menthol.

Boudreau looked around. He saw with perfect detachment, as though he were looking through a camera. The hum and thuck of the newsroom disappeared; he saw slow pans, tracking shots, the frames of great compositions. He heard some loping rockabilly piano on his mental soundtrack. It was one of the things Boudreau liked to do when he got high. Watch the movie.

He'd been working for a long time on a screenplay named *Greenwood*. He thought about it now. Greenwood was the polite name of a district in north Tulsa where most of the black population had always lived. In the old days it was also called "Little Africa." On the first of June, 1921, a nineteen-year-old black man, one Dick Rowland, had been accused of making advances to a white girl in an elevator. His arrest was reported in the evening paper. By sunset a lynch mob had gathered in front of the jail, and someone made an anonymous phone call to a crowded black theater. That was it: a day and a half later, the whole of Greenwood, twelve blocks wide and two miles long—*Niggertown*—was nothing but acres of smoking rubble. Stiff bodies swayed by rope from lampposts. Just-deputized "special police commissioners" dragged corpses around behind their Model T's while they looted what remained. No one knew for sure the exact number, but it was thought that about five hundred people had died, all but a few of them black. It was the worst race riot in American history.

This was the basis of Boudreau's screenplay. It had been years since he'd first had the idea. He had a thick stack of three-by-fives at home, notes and research, images and bits of dialogue, pieces of a story line. He just had to get back to it, get it down on paper. If there was one thing he knew, it was movies. You dealt with character and structure, and then you looked for your hook to stick in the first ten pages. Boudreau knew the value of a good hook: it was the thing that had you humming the chorus as soon as the song was off the radio. As of yet, *Greenwood* did not have a good hook. It did not, in fact, even have a beginning.

Boudreau sat up, startled at how he'd drifted off. He looked at his watch and staved off a little jolt of panic. He lit another cigarette.

The thing was, he just had to stay confident. It was no big deal. He had his problems, but so what. Things always seemed worse than they really were. The thought hit him with the force of words graven on stone: *Just stay confident.* Follow this simple rule.

A long rush went through him. He was more stoned than he'd thought. It occurred to him that confidence was exactly his problem. Now, Brinkman—Brinkman's ambition was untroubled by conscience, he was a confident guy. There were only six years between them, but he might as well have been a different generation. Still, Boudreau felt he could use a little ambition himself. Where could he get some? Ambition was bred of confidence. Just do one thing at a time, he knew that much. One thing at a time.

He turned his terminal on and was immediately distracted at the sight of Joyce Hamby walking through the newsroom. Joyce was the middle-aged Pentecostal who edited the religion section. She affected high-necked ruffled dresses with bows, giving her the look of a desiccated and oversized Victorian ten-year-old. He quickly looked away when she glanced in his direction. That was all he needed right now, to walk the minefield of a stoned conversation with Joyce. She was not without power. The religion section got more space and money than all the arts put together. Boudreau's movie reviews usually appeared alongside

"Dear Abby" and the horoscope and the kid puzzles, opposite the funny page.

Okay, time to concentrate. He was not going to let himself get blocked again. He had to find that zone of opinion that was really no opinion at all, just a gentle current that flowed right down the middle of the Tulsa mainstream, no faster and no slower.

This was unofficial mandate, but there nonetheless. Movies were supposed to be uplifting at best, harmless at least. Boudreau couldn't remember when he had given up having real opinions; he didn't worry about it. Tulsa was a sociopolitical jerkwater, an isolated pocket of oilmen, defense contractors, racists, Republicans, and religious fanatics—a place forgotten by time, like one of those tiny hamlets in the Appalachians where they still spoke Elizabethan English. Heterogeneous opinion was inappropriate; you spoke the common language or you kept your mouth shut. Living in such a place, he'd always felt, required a good sense of humor. The laughs were there if you kept your voice down.

Of course lately things had become a little intense. All year long an undifferentiated mass of unshaven Iranians had gotten prime-time air every night. It was like a countdown for the Big Game that never came. People began to spoil for it. On the TU campus two Pakistanis, an Algerian, and a dark-skinned Israeli were run down and beaten to a pulp. The rest hid. Middle Eastern enrollment in the Petroleum Engineering School dropped in rough proportion to the number of yellow ribbons flapping from the trees like prayer flags.

Then Reagan got elected in November. *Whoa:* the rest of the nation had caught up to Tulsa, not vice versa. Now it was an entire country of yellow ribbons and *We're Number One* bumper stickers and editorials lusting for heads on pikes, preferably from little dark-complexioned nations. A Tony Orlando song had become national foreign policy under the new president, a witless pantaloon whose legend had to do with impersonating a football coach.

Boudreau found himself still disturbed by his conversation with Brinkman. Something was happening lately, and it wasn't just the regression to politics as blood sport, that was easy enough to understand. He realized how nervous he'd become that people didn't seem to share his fear. He'd been wrong. It was not inappropriate to have differing opinions around here, or even funny. It was dangerous.

He reconsidered the Big Plan. The more he'd thought about it lately, the more attractive it became. He couldn't keep this shit up, that much was clear. Events were trying to tell him something. He needed to pile on some fat for the long hard winter ahead.

The trades were still full of stories about twenty-six-year-olds, fresh from nowhere, hauling down seventy-five grand for scripts that never even came close to getting produced. Seventy-five *grand:* he hadn't made that in the last four years.

Boudreau could do it, he knew he could. He just needed enough money to buy six months of time, so he could quit teaching at TU and quit writing these goddamn movie reviews. He'd go camp out somewhere with just a tent and a typewriter and his research. No booze or dope, maybe he'd quit smoking, too. He'd be a Buddha and come back with a finished screenplay. Once it sold, it would be Mexico here I come. There was no sense hanging around in times like these.

For a Big Plan it had one major hole in it, which was where the money had to come from. Boudreau realized the phone call to his mother had been providential in an unanticipated way. When she got back, he would have an actual reason for having called her. It would not be easy but it could be done. It was time to have a chat about the farmhouse.

Boudreau pressed his palms into his eyes. He was getting more sinus. Who was he kidding? This review was a loss. His mind was wandering like a stray dog, all mange and ribs, sniffing and rooting from one garbage can to the next, from his unpaid electric bill to Vicky Stover, to the cigarette burn, to the unwritten review, to his mother.

The morning had defeated him: sometimes you just had to accept these things. You had to flow. Flowing in this case meant coming up with some faintly credible excuse for Preston Liddey. Having recently missed two other deadlines was not a good place to start from, but he would come up with something.

On the other hand he wouldn't get paid: no plumbing, no lights, no air-conditioning, no bars. He'd just have to rough it. C'est la frigging vie. His decision made, he got up and went to the can.

Brinkman intercepted him on the way back to his desk. "Hey, wanna hear my idea for a screenplay?" he said.

"Not really," said Boudreau, distracted.

"There's this berserk religious kid here in T-town, he's a Baptist— what else?—and he starts getting like these messages in his teeth. It's this holy voice, it goes, Yo, *kid!* It says he should deal with the local heathens who disobey traffic laws. So the kid shaves his head into a mohawk, then goes and welds a bunch of heavy plate onto his SS 396. Then it's demolition time." Brinkman stopped and looked for approval.

"That's it?" said Boudreau.

"Yeah, that's it, that's the story," said Brinkman. "It's an *action* movie. The kid runs people down in their shitty little foreign cars. Kind of a patriotic political angle. Know what we call it? *Tulsa Driver.*"

"Very nice," said Boudreau. "Only a guy who'd worked the sardine beat would have such a delicate touch."

For the first four weeks Preston Liddey had stuck Brinkman with accident reporting to break him in. He went out day after day to look at cars flattened like tin cans, the sardines still inside.

When they arrived back at his desk, his computer monitor was on. Boudreau was sure he'd turned it off. He leaned down to switch the thing off again when he saw it, a single line in the middle of the screen.

I LEFT THE FILM CAN LAST NIGHT. YOU OWE ME. —RONNIE.

Boudreau stared at it, uncomprehending, then looked up.

Brinkman was leaning on top of the monitor, chewing gum.

"You laugh, man. I could sell it ten times easier than your thing about Greenway," he said. "Excuse me, Green*wood.*"

Boudreau gaped at him.

"You speak English, boy?" said Brinkman. He snapped his fingers to break the trance, then tapped the plastic he was leaning on. "Hey, you see the message I left?"

Boudreau breathed out. Here was the simple explanation. "You talked to Ronnie? He say anything else?"

"Said he'd break your legs if you didn't pay up."

"Funny," said Boudreau. He looked hard to make sure Brinkman was joking.

"Yeah, very nice guy to talk to," said Brinkman. He worked his gum. "Little shy but a nice phone manner. How much you owe him?"

"I owe him a favor." He was livid that Ronnie would call the paper and leave a message like that.

Brinkman did a Groucho eyebrow lift. "And what kind of a favor would that be, eh?"

Boudreau switched off the computer. The fucking *film can.* All right, maybe he'd been in a fog this morning, but he had no memory of seeing it anywhere. Billy, he had to call Billy. He picked up the phone.

Right, and what was he going to say: By the way, I happened to leave something behind after I snuck in the apartment? Save it for me, okay, but if you look I'll kill you?

"*Shit,*" said Boudreau. *Oh, it's just baking powder, Mom.* "I can't believe this."

"Film can, huh?" Brinkman lifted his eyebrows again. "Photographer friend?"

Boudreau cut him off with a look. Brinkman was getting on his nerves.

"Horned Frog was looking for you, too," Brinkman said then. He wagged his finger and shook his head sadly. "I had to tell him you were jerking off in the john."

This was Brinkman's pet name for Preston Liddey, proud alumnus of Texas Christian University. To Brinkman this was emblematic. He couldn't take seriously the idea of a football team whose players were called the Fighting Horned Frogs, or that he worked for a man who had been one.

Boudreau was suddenly very tired. "So what'd you say." He picked up the phone again.

"What'd I say?" Brinkman cocked his ear as if listening for a response. "Temme what'd I say!"

Boudreau immediately regretted his choice of words: now he was in for Brinkman's Ray Charles routine. He punched the number for Preston Liddey's office but held the button down. He waited with the receiver to his chest.

When Boudreau was in the right mood, Brinkman's stoned hostile-comic mode could be very funny, but Boudreau was nowhere close to being in the right mood. Now he'd get double takes, accents, choreographed Motown, Broadway show tunes with dirty lyrics, Carson monologues with golf swings and drum rolls. It was like being taken hostage.

"Okay, George." Brinkman was still doing Ray Charles. "Hey, *George!*" Boudreau pointed with one hand to the waiting phone receiver in the other.

Brinkman's eyes widened briefly, and then he segued into his imitation of James Brown accepting the cape and being led offstage. He shook his head in the patented palsy. *"Please! Please! Please!"* he sang.

Boudreau let up the phone button so the call could go through, to forestall Brinkman from throwing off the cape and returning to the stage.

"Preston? This is Richter. You were looking for me? . . . Yeah, I— What? . . . No, I haven't. I— Okay, sure," said Boudreau. "In a minute."

He hung up. Brinkman, working backward toward his own desk, had changed the chorus to falsetto bursts of *"Ho'ned Frog! Ho'ned Frog! Ho'ned Fuckin' Frog!"*

Boudreau stopped outside Preston Liddey's office and lit a Kool, even though the inside of his mouth already felt like wadded cloth. He knocked.

He became unpleasantly aware of his pulse as he walked into the office and shut the door behind him; he was winging it, stoned as a coot. He felt like he'd just smoked the joint.

Liddey was bent forward over his desk, reading. He didn't bother to look up. Boudreau stood there like a sharecropper called in to account for a missing crop.

Preston Liddey continued reading, his pink pate shining through the thin, fine, sandy-colored hair that was combed sideways over the top of his bald head. He wore a purplish brown three-piece suit, the jacket shed; his shirtsleeves were rolled up, according to his image of the working publisher who got in there and got inky. He had an endless supply of the three-piece suits, all made from the same material, a cloth which never quite relaxed. They always looked like he was just trying them on.

Tired of standing, Boudreau sat down in one of the big leather armchairs, then leaned over to knock the ash off his cigarette into the ashtray on the desk. Preston Liddey chose then to look up from his work. There was a weary smile on his face.

He gestured at the chair, the ashtray, with a dismissive flick. "Help yourself," he said.

Boudreau opened his mouth, then closed it. If Preston wanted to get Old Testament with him, he could handle it. Boudreau put a look of strained rue on his face: *Jeez, I guess I really flubbed up this time.*

Liddey didn't take notice. He pushed himself back from the polished desk with a lengthy and audible exhale. A man who lived by honoring the appropriate cliché, he pushed up his sleeves a little bit, in anticipation of the heavy task in front of him. His arms were the same pink as the skin on his head, covered with a nimbus of the same sandy-colored hair.

Liddey finished staring upward for inspiration, then pulled his chair back to his desk just as Boudreau realized his mouth had worked itself uncontrollably into a nervous smirk.

"Is there something funny here, Richter?"

Boudreau looked down quickly, pulling on his cigarette. "No sir." When he looked back up, Liddey's face was a slightly deeper pink than before, the muscles around his mouth tight.

"I'm going to be perfectly honest with you." Liddey thrust his chin forward to dispel any notion to the contrary. "This is not going to be easy."

Boudreau nodded, waiting. It was Preston's habit to explain what he was about to say before he said it. He had better luck that way.

"I am frankly in the dark over your attitude," Liddey said.

Boudreau leaned forward and cocked his head. "My *at*titude?" It came out sounding a little incredulous; he tried to lower the pitch of his voice. "I just thought you wanted to talk to me about that piece for the weekend section."

Preston Liddey regarded Boudreau with heavy patience. "You have the review, son?"

There it was, the first one of the lecture. *Son.* Boudreau swallowed and leaned forward again in his chair. "No sir, I don't, this week I had—"

Liddey stopped him with a raised palm. "Then I'd say we have an attitude problem, wouldn't you? You've been missing deadlines, son, and I call that attitude."

His mouth still open, Boudreau sat back as hard as if he'd been pushed.

"I'm not going to beat around the bush with you." The editor paused, squeezing his lips in consideration of his next remarks.

Boudreau had already stopped listening; he knew what was coming. It would be a kind of strange code in which certain words and phrases would recur, staples of the management workshops and seminars that Preston Liddey liked to attend. One seminar had apparently revolved around the "Five PAs," of which Boudreau could remember only two: Performance Attitude and Premium Assets. He was pretty sure he was going to hear about Performance Attitude again. Preston had come back from that particular seminar ticking off the Five PAs on his hand, clearly pleased at how neatly it worked out, one per finger.

It was just the sort of thing Liddey loved, further evidence that all things had their places. Boudreau had understood this early on, and learned to fit in himself. The problem was that lately he seemed to be inadvertently popping out of place.

Earlier that spring, he'd come into the paper one day to find the newswires going nuts. Everyone was standing around a television set, looking grave. He worked his way into the crowd. Reagan had been shot. The plucky presurgery quips were being admiringly intoned by network newscasters; there were slo-mo replays of the shots and the struggle. Boudreau stood and watched, then without thinking, straight-faced a variant of the old joke to Brinkman.

"What do you think Hinckley did with the money?"

Brinkman, the innocent new guy, looked at him.

"What money?"

"You know, that his mom gave him for the shooting lessons."

Boudreau was called into Liddey's office and made to apologize. He'd never seen Preston Liddey so worked up. Boudreau grasped that he had violated a Grave National Moment.

Boudreau was sure that was part of why he was sitting there now. Preston didn't give a rat's ass about a movie review, he was after Boudreau's *attitude*. People who didn't fit in were going to be weeded out. The Big Plan was looking better and better. He just had to sit through a little more bullshit in the meantime.

Sure enough, Liddey was saying something about excellence in goals being a direct result of commitment and . . . attitude.

Boudreau nodded intently, as though the concept required careful thought. On the back wall was a big florid oil portrait of Liddey *père*, looking over his boy's shoulder. The old man was a completely bald, narrow-faced version of the son, equally pink but harder edged. There was no trace in the thin-lipped mouth of any affinity for management seminars.

By most accounts Lewis Liddey had also been a very firm believer in the necessity of consensus. As the founder of the *Tulsa Journal* in 1917, it was important to him that people share the same thoughts. That way important things were achieved; that way Tulsa would grow into a great city.

Lewis Liddey had been a longtime crony of Boudreau's grandfather, the five-term county commissioner of Wagoner County. Then change came, and Lew Liddey changed with it. Tulsa County Republicans began to look hard at adjacent counties controlled by rural Democrats; Truman Boudreau got indicted by a state grand jury.

Staked out like live bait to see who would come feed, Truman Boudreau was charged by a grand jury with fourteen counts of vote fraud, construction kickbacks and tax evasion. Lew Liddey turned and ran like a small dog at the roar of feeding; he didn't even return phone calls. By the time the trial arrived he was already churning out editorials about how the rotten few weren't going to spoil that pure and precious thing, the Oklahoma political process. This was an important notion for good people to agree upon, even though it didn't happen to be true. Kicking back contract money and stuffing ballot boxes were jokes built into state politics; some of the more lightly rehearsed witnesses against Truman Boudreau got confused when it was suggested that these things were illegal.

A disoriented bee returning to a ghost hive, Richter Boudreau found himself pissed once again at how Lew Liddey's unconscionable treatment of his grandfather had remained undiscussed the entire time he'd worked there. Lew was on the wall; True didn't exist.

Meanwhile, Preston seemed to be wrapping up.

"—and let me rest-assure you, no matter what the situation, Richter, I don't care if it's politics or business or what have you—a newspaper even"—here he smiled with pleasure at how smoothly his own elocution had brought it all full circle—"there's two rules that make it all go round in our system. Two rules."

Preston Liddey paused to let the drama build. Boudreau leaned forward on his knees, chin on hands, a player listening to his coach. It proved instinctive.

"You can never score if everybody wants to carry the ball"—one finger went up, there to be wagged for emphasis until the second finger rose—"but if everybody is a team player, then you all score together."

Liddey leaned back in triumph. Boudreau mirrored his motion, demonstrating how fully he had absorbed the impact of the lesson. This wasn't so bad. Liddey *fils* couldn't help being an asshole, it was in his blood. Boudreau felt a lump in his pocket and remembered the Quaalude Brinkman had laid on him. The day wasn't a total loss if he'd already gotten free dope out of it. Maybe he could find somebody for some rubber-legged sex tonight.

Preston Liddey fixed him with a look. "Do you see what I'm driving at, son?"

Boudreau nodded and made a tight-lipped, I-see-it-now kind of smile. "Yessir." It was the first thing he'd said in five minutes. "I'll have that review ready for the slot on Monday. And there's a couple more for next week, too." The reefer had made his mouth so cottony the words came out thick.

The editor shrugged and waved his hand dismissively, already considering the bigger picture. "I'll be frank with you now, Richter, you know what I'd like to see us do?"

Boudreau had no idea.

Liddey laced his fingers behind his head and leaned way back, then looked up at the ceiling in a brainstorming sort of way. "I'd like to see us renew our commitment to family-oriented kind of entertainment."

Boudreau nodded and looked up at the portrait behind Preston. Lew Liddey had finally checked out with a stroke a few years back; he was still alive, but not by much. Every now and again they rolled him out for public functions. A nurse would wheel him around, his mouth hanging open a little, his head bobbing in agreement to anything at all.

"And Richter?"

Boudreau, half out of his chair, had thought it was over.

"You know, it's the little things that add up to attitude. Respect for others. You take a shave before you come in here next time, hear me, son?"

Down on the street Boudreau got caught in the noontime crush. The air pressed in on him: he felt heat radiating in every direction, bouncing up from the street, out from the buildings, down from the sky. He was

going to be late out at school, but right now this was not a major
concern. He was cutting his losses. So DuPuys would give him one of
those petulant looks; it wouldn't be the first time. He'd rather face
DuPuys than Liddey any day.

Boudreau struggled down the crowded sidewalk toward the parking
lot. He was dripping with sweat from the mere act of walking. Throat
parched, he made his way to a parasoled hotdog stand on the corner for
a soda pop.

There were a couple of businessmen and a grimy guy in a ponytail
standing around the cart, eating and drinking. The two businessmen,
pink skinned and clean shaven, clearly had an attitude about the ponytail. Boudreau gave the hippie an eye-rolling smirk of us-and-them soli-
darity while the vendor got him his pop.

Boudreau dug in his pocket for change and came up with a handful,
including the Quaalude. He decided on the spot to start the weekend
a few hours early.

He ripped the top from the orange pop and chugged a third of it,
throat aching from the cold, then laid the pill on his tongue and knocked
back more of the orange. Out of the side of his mouth, Boudreau
low-voiced a crack to the ponytail. "And remember, kids: *all* drugs are
safe with alcohol."

The guy looked back at him through blue eyes that seemed overly
clear. Too late, Boudreau recognized who he was, his hair tied back and
his leaflets gone, a morning of downtown grime on him.

"*Praise* God! Pills won't help you, brother," the guy said. "These are
end-times coming."

Boudreau blew in late to the film department, so hot and grubby his
skin hurt from the grit in its creases. He stopped at Margo Ross's desk
first. Nobody else in the department was around. She was eating a carrot
and reading Uta Hagen's *Respect for Acting*.

"Your little friend is in your office." She didn't bother to look up. "She's been here for an hour."

"Great." Boudreau knew without asking that she was referring to Arla Thompson.

He gave brief thought to sneaking back out. He wouldn't even have bothered to show up if he'd known DuPuys wasn't going to be there. Today's office hours were strictly for appearances, since grades had been posted earlier in the week. Today was *it,* the last official day of the semester.

Margo looked up from her book and regarded him with a slight tilt to her head. "Been living a little hard this last day or two?" She looked like she would have been amused if he'd come in wearing a full-body cast.

"I lead a fun life." Boudreau winked at her. "You know that." The wink felt more like a tic, his muscles already a little slack behind the Quaalude.

Margo looked at him evenly for a second more with her cat-green eyes, then expelled air through her nose in a brief expression of mirth. She looked back down to her book. "Yeah, I remember." She took a loud, cracking bite off the carrot. "Life in the low lane."

Boudreau got the mail out of his box and sat on the corner of her desk. She studiously avoided looking up. He felt a sudden pang for Margo, a rooted physical yearning. She had a tight little chunk of a body and pale, freckled skin, with short, dark red hair and those cat-green eyes. She always wore tight jeans, and either long-sleeved black turtlenecks or men's sleeveless undershirts. Hot weather was undershirt time. She had sharp little breasts, whose tips poked darkly under the thin, white-ribbed material.

His mail was all trash: a few late papers for the survey course, some junk mail, an interdepartmental memo that he'd already gotten, two flyers for film festivals he couldn't afford to attend, and one witty piece of student hate mail: "You Will Die For Flunking Me, Ass-Fuck."

He dumped everything in the trash can beside the desk and lit a cigarette. The heat seemed to radiate from the concrete block walls. Boudreau felt a little flushed. He'd gotten some shit food at the U-

Tote-M on Eleventh and eaten it on the way over. It was not at home yet.

"Nice and cool in here," he observed. They would get to the air-conditioning next week, when the building would be empty.

Margo ignored him. He'd had a brief, on-the-sly thing with her in the waning months of his marriage. But after Ginny split back to Berkeley, she began to make a few too many assumptions about his new status. The pressure was more than he could take, and he told her he just needed to be alone for a while, okay? She was all understanding until three weeks later, when she heard cries coming from his office and walked in on him having sex with an eighteen-year-old freshman from Fort Smith, Arkansas. This reshaped her opinion of him immediately.

He still felt like a jerk—he should've been honest with her and hadn't been—but she had refused to even look at him for over a year afterward. He took it as his due. Since then their relationship had developed into distinct roles, his consisting of the moral worm twisting on the hook, hers the sleek trout who couldn't believe she'd ever been tempted by such a low thing. It didn't help that she had a prime seat for watching the come-and-go of his various student affairs.

Boudreau looked down at the top of her head, at the dark thick red hair, and found himself welling up with feeling. He had been a true fool; he *needed* someone like her. She'd been so easy to be with, so comforting and hip and honest. He remembered her pubic hair being the same deep lustrous auburn, a thick cinnamon jungle. She'd been seeing some guy in the theater department for the last year or so, but he'd heard they'd split up.

He crooned a line of late-period Elvis, "Are You Lonesome Tonight." She refused to look up.

He blew a smoke ring, then another. "Maybe we could go over to your place and lay naked in the air-conditioning," he said.

Margo read the last line in a half-audible mumble, ignoring him while trying to keep her place. She turned the page with a snap.

"This has been some fucking day, Margo," he said.

"Leave me *alone*, Boudreau," she said, still reading.

Boudreau made an unconvincing chuckle and felt his spine collapse into a slump on the desk. What was *wrong* with him, where had his sexual antennae gone to? He might be horny, but getting something together with Margo was just not realistic. This was the true measure of his stink of desperation: he couldn't tell anymore.

He stubbed out his cigarette and stood up, khakis stuck in the damp crack of his ass. He had to go down and get this Arla thing over with. He picked his pants out.

"Listen, will you let me know when that summer seminar contract comes through?" He adjusted his voice to a business pitch. "I need to do a little negotiating."

Margo Ross looked up from her reading as he was turning away. "I wouldn't hold your breath."

"What?" Boudreau stopped in midstep, out of balance. "What does that mean?"

Margo regarded him as though pondering a decision about the drape of his clothes. She shrugged. "I just heard something that makes me think you shouldn't be holding your breath."

Boudreau came back and planted his face in front of hers. He leaned across her desk so that his arms propped him up like a bipod.

She leaned back from him on the other side of the desk, arching one eyebrow as she did it. "I happened to catch—inadvertently of course— part of a conversation in which Dennis told Coburn"—she illustrated the exchange with little hand flourishes—"about some details that made it sound like Coburn had the seminar." She folded her arms across her chest. "That's all. That's what I know. Now leave me alone please."

Boudreau dropped his head and let it hang between his arms. He'd done the seminar for the last three summers. This was not good. Worse, it could also easily be taken as a harbinger. DuPuys had had it in for him for a while, and now he could see the contours of more bad news to come. Boudreau felt like finding him and congratulating him. *Hey, Dennis, find some balls somewhere?*

He jerked upright from Margo's desk; it proved to be a mistake.

"Boudreau, are you all right? Hey, Boudreau? Listen, you wanna sit down?" Margo Ross was half up out of her chair. "You are *white.*"

Boudreau felt his face go cold and clammy as the blood deserted it.

He felt sick. The bottom of his stomach had momentarily dropped out, leaving the two beers and microwaved chili-beef sandwich to climb for high ground and fend for themselves. The Quaalude began to kick in for real. He held on to the edge of the desk as he felt his various limbs striking out on their own.

"Fucking *Dennis.*" Boudreau closed his eyes and willed everything back into place. He tried to stand up but immediately leaned back on the desk. "I don't feel so good," he said.

He opened his eyes as he felt some of the blood return to his head. Margo was scrutinizing him with her head cocked to one side. She worked her lower lip with her teeth in a contemplative way. Transparent to her gaze, he managed a feeble smile. He'd always been at his best with Margo when he was a little pathetic.

She arrived at her conclusion. "You'd better watch it," she said.

Boudreau nodded like it was just what he'd been thinking. She was right, absolutely right: *he'd better watch it.*

"I have not been doing so well lately, Margie." The old pet name just slipped out. He closed his eyes again for a second to clear his head, then breathed out heavily. "And I don't know why."

Margo Ross's eyes widened for a long moment, as if in surprise. Abruptly she reopened her book. "I'm sorry to hear that, Richter." She found her place. "Maybe you should get some help."

Boudreau rose from his chair to close the office door. Arla Thompson was crying now, and it was not the kind of scene he liked to have playing to the hall, even if it were only Margo Ross down at the other end. Especially if it were only Margo Ross. His legs went rubbery when he got up, a reminder of the Quaalude, and he nailed his thigh on the corner of the desk. He got the door closed and hobbled back to his chair.

The room was truly airless now, a ten-by-twelve sweatbox. Boudreau felt a trickle run down between his shoulder blades until it stopped where his shirt was stuck to the chair.

She cried without sound, her head bobbing gently. Boudreau lit a cigarette and inhaled deeply. This was going to be as predictable as one of his own fucking lectures. He should've known he wasn't going to get off so easy.

He looked away, over at the picture of his grandfather. The thing that always got him about the picture was the look on True's face. A freshly lit cigarette was stuck in one corner of his mouth, held between his teeth; the rest of his mouth widened into a big leer of a grin. Most people had taken this as good-ol'-boy bravado, but his grandson knew better: it was real. On his way to MacAlester, Truman Boudreau was still trapped by who he was, a creature of breed, unable to fathom what was about to happen to him.

In most of his memories of True, that same grin made an appearance somewhere. He remembered being ten years old and flying with him in the single-engine Cessna out to the ranch in Osage County. True sat happy as a linebacker-sized Buddha, one hand on the neck of a quart of Jack Daniel's, the bottle planted on a thigh big as a cocktail table.

When they got to the ranch, he flew low and banked hard, buzzing some of the hands out working fence. They shook their fists and gave the plane the finger.

Hey, Richterboy, wait you see my new bull. He's got a dick on him can plow ground.

Boudreau remembered looking down and blushing, delighted; he looked over at his grandfather and got the grin.

In the photograph Truman Boudreau was fifty-nine years old. Unable to accept that he was no longer the prize bull, he was about to find out how it felt to be just more meat in the pen. It was probably one of the last times he'd ever grinned like that.

Boudreau looked away, a realization settling onto his shoulders like dead weight. The yellowed piece of newsprint was almost twenty years old, and he was almost thirty-four. He slumped deeper into his chair. Nineteen sixty-one had been without question the worst year of his life, and judging by today, it seemed like twenty years had not improved a goddamn thing. This day was melting him.

Suddenly Arla Thompson sat up. Boudreau could hear the backs of her legs peeling off the metal chair. She wiped her eyes and looked at him, catching him in the nervous act of blowing a smoke ring. She stopped crying.

"I'm going home on Monday," she managed. "I guess I thought you might have something to say?"

Boudreau felt sweat collecting in his scalp. He could tell she had just passed from wounded hurt to angry hurt.

"Look," he said, "I'm sorry, but I don't know what to say. I wish I did. I didn't mean for this to happen. I'm sorry it turned out like this." He looked down, looked back up. "I'm a jerk, I don't learn."

Arla Thompson emitted a small snort, like she'd been waiting for just this kind of bullshit. The words sounded a little overpracticed even to him. She looked down, in thrall of a thought or a memory. Her face slowly twisted and flattened in the force of it, and then her chin finally gave way. She was crying again.

"I didn't *want* to come back here." Her voice rose to a hard edge. She picked at an invisible something on the corner of his desk. "But I just couldn't believe people *acted* like that." Then she looked up from the desk and shook her head in lack of comprehension. "You acted like it just, like it just, like the whole thing never happened? You wouldn't even *talk* to me? That's just not right." She fixed him with a hard look. "It was like it didn't mean *anything.*"

Boudreau's head spun, her harsh voice relentless in his ears. "What do you want, a plaque?"

Arla Thompson stopped crying in an instant. Her mouth opened, soundless. She stared at him like she'd never seen him before. "I had me an *abor*tion four weeks ago! They scraped me out!"

Boudreau turned away involuntarily. This was way more than he bargained for. The picture of his grandfather stared down at him, grinning and handcuffed. He wished he could take back the thing about the plaque, take it all back, the whole thing, but he couldn't.

"I didn't know." Then, in spite of himself, he heard the nasty little truncated phrase issuing from his own mouth. "And you're sure it's . . ."

He met her eyes for a moment but couldn't take the raw hatred of what he found.

"Well then, maybe you can just help me *pay* for it," Arla Thompson said through her teeth. "Maybe that would be enough for *you*, mister." She stared at him, waiting for the answer.

Too late, Boudreau found himself grinning at how just fucking perfect this was all working out. Now he could be a scumbag all around.

"Guess what?" he said. "I don't have it."

A sound came out of her, a kind of shriek that rose higher and higher until it choked off and devolved into hiccupped crying.

This was out of control, everything was getting out of control. Boudreau began trying to placate her, to quiet her down, suddenly aware that all his words were coming out slurred. He sounded like a wino.

She wailed. Boudreau mumbled something about how sorry he was, how he didn't mean it, how they'd figure something out. He was sorry, but this had been a terrible day for him.

Her thin cotton skirt stuck to her legs, Arla jumped up, resembling nothing so much as a big wet cat, all bones and matted fur. Her face was red, livid under a glaze of salt water and mucus. "This *day?*" she screamed. "Try this whole *year!*"

Boudreau cringed at the look of raw accusation. She hated him, she was this way because of him. But she had him *wrong,* he hadn't meant to hurt her, that had never been his intent. They'd just misunderstood each other, she had to see that.

From another world, Boudreau stood up and reached out to give her a reassuring touch, a calming pat. "Oh, come on, Arla, hey, *listen*—" he began, low voiced.

She whirled at his touch on the back of her neck and hit him, her sharp little fist catching him right on the point of the cheekbone.

Boudreau hit her back. It was only a flat-handed slap, but she bellowed with the outrage of it, a terrible wounded sound.

He couldn't believe what he'd just done. His head swam. This was like falling down the rabbit hole and coming out in a place where time ran backward from regret to regret, where he would always be too late. Now she was already at him again; when he grabbed her by the wrists, she only screamed louder.

Boudreau let go to see if that would shut her up, and jumped backward in a defensive crouch. In a Quaalude body-murk, he stumbled and fell against the desk.

Arla Thompson stood vibrating like a reed, hugging her own elbows as though trying to contract into herself. Boudreau hung on the edge of his desk, halfway to the floor, waiting helplessly for the next attack.

"You're gonna *pay.*" The words fought their way out through breath inhaled in ragged gulps. *"You're gonna pay, mister."*

In a few seconds he heard footsteps fading down the hall and that was it. She was gone.

He peeked out the open door and checked. Margo Ross was gone too. Even though the room was like an oven, he closed the door and fell into his chair. Some amount of time went by while his mind replayed endless variations of what had just happened. It was like he wasn't even there.

The phone rang; Boudreau jumped. He thought it was an alarm. He looked at the phone through the second ring, through the third. He answered it on the fourth, convinced that it would be Arla Thompson, his duty now to eat shit, to apologize for all he was worth.

"Hey, *Boo*," said the voice.

Boudreau's shoulders slumped and he started laughing. His clothes were as damp as if he'd been standing in a light rain.

"Key?" he said, unable to stop laughing. "*Key*." Boo and Key, these were names they'd used since the sixth grade.

"What's so funny?" said Vicky Michaels's brother.

"Oh, *nothing*," said Boudreau, an inflection away from hysteria. "Not a *thing*, man, just my life is turning to *shit*, that's all."

Keith started making the crude snorking noise they'd always made as teenagers. "Well, *hey* then, let's go out," he said. "I'm in *town*. Let's go out and rape some tail, jack."

Boudreau stiffened. He was no prize to women, but Keith Michaels had all the finesse of an Ozark root hog in rut. He trailed off into an unenthusiastic chuckle. Rape some tail.

"Yeah. Yeah, hey," he said, "I thought that was you driving down Peoria a couple days ago."

"Not me, Boo. I only got in yesterday."

"Whatever." Boudreau was sure it had been Tuesday, Wednesday at the latest. "At least it ain't today. What a fucking day."

"Okay, we'll celebrate," said Keith Michaels.

"I don't know if celebrate is the word for it."

"Fuck you, man, I'm *cele*brating. The pussy posse rides tonight. Against all odds, the Key is back in town." By the sound of alcohol in his voice he'd been celebrating already. "I'm buying."

Boudreau looked around his office and lit a cigarette. "Okay." He exhaled in unexpected relief. "Hey, why not?" He saw now how this day was going to end, the only way it could. They'd get drunk and have a consciousness-lowering session.

"I could use someone to talk to." Boudreau found himself laughing again, voice lowered. "I had this girl, this student of mine just in here that it turns out I got pregnant?"

Keith Michaels began snickering. "Yeah?"

"Yeah, and she was, you know, really pissed at me." Boudreau was having trouble getting his breath. "And Key, man?" he said in a near whisper. "I fucking *hit* her."

Keith Michaels burst out in laughter.

"No. No, seriously," said Boudreau, the words coming out like a straight man's punch line. "I feel bad."

Keith laughed harder.

"I feel really bad."

"Bitch *deserved* it," Keith said. "So did her hair fall out?"

Keith's laughter degenerated into a choking cough. While Boudreau waited for it to subside, he looked over at the picture of Truman Boudreau on the wall. When he was a kid, having True for a grandfather was like being sidekick to Roy Rogers.

"So where do you want to meet?" he said, voice flat.

There were only four or five cars left in the huge parking lot. The Healey sat by itself out in the middle, a little red gobbet of British steel frying on the black asphalt. Boudreau could feel radiant heat waves rolling off the car by the time he was inside of five feet. He'd stupidly left the top down, the driver's seat back. He knew without even trying that the car would be too hot to sit in, much less drive.

Boudreau fished around in the trash in back of the seats, a compost of torn magazines, student papers, fast food bags, beer bottles and empty cans of motor oil. He found a pale blue woman's sweater, wrinkled and crusted; whomever it belonged to, she didn't need it now. He draped it over the steering wheel, and leaned the driver's seat forward to cool off.

He lit a cigarette and waited. It wasn't worth the walk to shade, so he just stood and cooked. *Did her hair fall out?* This was not something he would've chosen to think about on his own.

He smoked the cigarette all the way to the filter and threw it down. When he ground it with his boot heel, it sank into the melted asphalt.

He needed to get out of here; this was like sinking into a tar pit. The distant sound of a car door slamming and an engine turning over came from the other end of the parking lot. He tested the wheel under the sweater.

Boudreau looked up as the car sound drew near. It was an old Ford Fairlane, pulling slowly up to him. He stepped away from the Healey and saw it was Arla Thompson, her mouth set in a crooked line, face still red from crying. He put his hands in his pockets, ready to lean down in an attitude of chagrin and apologize like hell.

Fifteen feet away she floored it, the tires squealing like pigs, and drove right through the spot he had just evacuated, her eyes straight ahead. She came to a neat stop at the exit, then barreled out into the side street.

Boudreau got in the car and sat, trying to still his racing pulse. A little eddy of nausea swam up behind his closed eyes, a swirl of heat and bad lunch, the Quaalude floating on top.

What a day. This felt like the last scene of *Zabriskie Point,* the only good thing in the whole fucking movie, just an endless nightmare of an explosion, a whole house and all its contents going up in spectacular slow motion, Pink Floyd screaming on the soundtrack. He opened his eyes.

Okay, so he'd had a bad day, it was nothing a few drinks wouldn't fix.

Boudreau started the car, then felt a little thrill go through him. A bad *day?* Now he was telling lies to himself as though he were someone else. The truth was right in front of him, clear as if it had just been projected on the inside of his eyelids: his life was flying apart into small pieces, and all he could do was watch.

SATURDAY

Boudreau woke up, his mind dragging its way into consciousness like some ooze-creature laboring out of the primordial slime. He looked around and ascertained he was in Vicky's old room upstairs. So far as he could tell he was somewhere between dog drunk and just hungover.

He lay motionless on the bed, body heavy as a bag of hardened cement. After a while he made himself upright, careful to observe both inertia and gravity. He hurt all over. He had to protect the thin membrane that held in the pain.

He clutched the balustrade all the way downstairs and made a straight line to the well-stocked bar off the living room. The big grandfather clock at the bottom of the stairs said ten till eight. He stood in front of the bar and debated. This, he thought, would be a bad thing to do, but he was going to do it anyway.

Margo Ross's snotty advice came back to him. *Maybe you should get some help.* Screw her, the help he needed had nothing to do with this. He mixed a gin and tonic and stood looking at it, pissed off. The drink even smelled like medicine. He recalled watching Keith Michaels the night before and poured the drink down the sink. That's what this would lead to.

He made himself a straight tonic over ice with a piece of lime, then navigated his way into the living room and lowered himself into a big wing chair. He lit a cigarette and sipped the tonic, waiting for the sloshing in his brain to subside. He sat as still as he could.

He'd met Keith at a Boston Avenue bar and had to restrain himself from doing a double take. Keith Michaels had gained forty, maybe fifty pounds since the last time he'd seen him, his features sinking back into his face as though it were quicksand.

"Key, my man." He fought to keep the rubbery Quaalude grin of disbelief off his own face. Keith had always been meaty, but now it looked like he was disappearing under his own flesh. "Long time." He figured he'd let Keith bring up the new weight.

"I got us some juleps." Keith snickered and pointed at two empty glasses on the bar, then lifted a cheek and cracked a loud fart off the bar stool. *"Whoa!"* he said, as though no one heard it. He signaled the bartender and ordered another round while Boudreau intently watched the TV above the bar.

It was the tail end of the local news, the weather. The weatherman stayed coy until the numbers hit the screen, then went cheerful with the bad news. Old and infirm better stay in the air-conditioning, folks, no letup in sight. He closed with a joke about this being the kind of weather that was only good for heat exhaustion and gunshot wounds.

"Ass hole," Keith Michaels said to the bar at large. "Turn that fucking thing *off.* "

"What a day," Boudreau said. He was still shaky from Arla's parking lot bowling, himself as the lone standing pin.

"Yeah," said Keith. "I come back to *fucking* Tulsa and I get a *fucking* heat wave." He came down hard enough on his adjectives to turn heads at the other end of the bar.

Boudreau dismissed whatever notions he'd had about trying to talk into a sympathetic ear. He'd forgotten what having a conversation with Keith was like; the correct mode was oblivion. When their juleps came, he raised his glass. "May this day be forgotten," he said.

They'd moved on from bar to bar, in the Healey. Keith had taken a cab downtown, explaining that the Beast was out of gas. The Beast was a mint-condition '68 white GTO; that he couldn't be bothered to fill it up was typical. Instead, they filled the Healey, running on vapors itself, on Keith's Exxon card. Boudreau was just as glad he was driving. The Beast had four hundred horsepower and Positraction, and Keith still drove like he was out to impress girls the day after getting his license.

By the third bar Boudreau had achieved a certain cottony dislocation.

This was helped along by Keith's relentless monologue of reminiscence, all the way back to their early adolescent years. Boudreau sat across from his barely recognizable oldest friend, feeling like he'd stumbled into a class reunion in the Twilight Zone.

Drunk, Boudreau found it funny in a sad way. Keith went on like they hadn't seen each other in years, when in fact it had only been about eight months or so. The truth was they hadn't been *friends* in years, that was the problem, ever since coming home on their first college vacations, Keith from OU and Boudreau from Berkeley. That was when Boudreau realized he'd become as interested in Vicky, still in high school, as he'd ever been in Keith. This never got talked about, but Keith clearly couldn't hack it. Since then they'd bumped into each other maybe twice a year, without having all that much to say to each other. Now Keith was acting like they were sixteen again, ready to go out and blast fire extinguishers into open windows at stoplights.

By the time they'd moved on to the fourth bar, Keith began repeating himself, picking over the old times like bones that might still hold a shred of meat. Boudreau stopped listening and began to drink with real purpose, building himself into a tower of detachment. Keith started hassling first their waitress, then any woman who came within earshot. Boudreau cringed: this was primitive, this was like winging mud clods at girls on the playground. They were asked to leave.

Not that it was anything new. Even as kids both Keith and Vicky had shown discernible rich-brat mean streaks, which Boudreau always assumed they'd inherited from Priscilla Michaels, along with blond hair and slightly upturned noses. As an adolescent, he'd frequently felt like a rube around them, afraid of what they might turn to when they got tired of bugging the maids or blowing up frogs.

But now, he realized, it was more than just a streak in Keith; it was all there was. Boudreau kept his mouth shut, watching the drinks and gas and dinner pile up on Keith's plastic. Keith could *afford* to be mean.

Boudreau hadn't gotten so drunk in at least two or three months, his bad day finally blotted out. He was aware of making it back to the Michaels' house, though he had no idea how.

Now, sipping the tonic and lime, he had a head that felt like one of the rubbers they used to fill up with water in gas station bathrooms. Moted morning light filtered in from the windows. The enormous house was quiet as a cavern, its stray noises instantly absorbed by drape and carpet and the gentle respiration of central air-conditioning. It was a place laden with sense memory; he'd spent a lot of time here as a teenager. Now Keith lived in the house by himself, had it maintained for him even when he was gone, whether for two days or six months. The numbers bewildered Boudreau: he just couldn't imagine. He figured he could live on the air-conditioning bill alone.

Boudreau thought if he were that rich, he would at least have an ironic perspective about it. But expecting irony of Keith was like hoping for higher math skills from a dog. Keith believed he deserved the money because he was a better person, and he was a better person because he had the money. How could you argue with that?

Boudreau finished the cigarette and his tonic and went outside. The air came as a warm but pleasant shock, too early yet to be truly hot. He walked down the sweep of lawn to the grove of trees that surrounded the pool, still drunk. He decided the road to rectitude had to involve pain. He would swim laps until he burned away the poison.

The pool was placid as a mirror, reflecting the trees and banks of geraniums and asters planted around it. The top of a woman's bikini draped off the end of the diving board. One of the new tiny little tape players, no larger than a thick paperback book, was lying on a table by the pool, along with three empty beer bottles and a pocket calculator.

Boudreau dove in, the shock of the water charging him with enough adrenaline to keep him from drowning immediately. He swam until his lungs screamed and his arms felt like logs, then pulled himself out and lay gasping on the edge of the pool. After a while he went to the bar in the pool house, resisting temptation again with a can of Tab.

Installed in one of the floating chairs in the pool, he still felt like shit, but at least it was virtuous shit.

It was okay, he told himself, that he let Keith treat him to a night of food and booze, that he was floating in Keith's pool. It was okay as long as he was careful to keep it straight. Several times the night before

Keith had referred to him as his best friend, as if they still had a friendship, period. This was desperate and pathetic, but it somehow made things even: at least Boudreau knew him and cared for him, in the manner of people who had known each other as children. He put up with Keith, no small task, accepted him for who he was. In the stock exchange of human feeling, that had to count for something. Boudreau sipped the Tab and floated, eyes closed. Under the heat of the sun the throb in his head spread in widening circles, until he was no longer there to notice it.

Boudreau came to drifting like a pool toy, the water perfectly still. His eyes were still closed. He'd forgotten where he was until he made a tiny movement and felt the resistance of water against his legs.

He'd been having a jittery, disconnected sex dream about Vicky Stover. No, Vicky Michaels: in the dream she was younger even though he wasn't. She just told him that she'd loved him all along. He was astonished. She laughed and told him she wasn't afraid to show it now. Then they were both naked in the swimming pool, skin against slippery skin. They were holding tight and grinding hard. In the dream he was swooning with gratification.

He slipped one hand off the armrest of the floating chair and made a little paddling motion. The chair began to slowly rotate; the sun hit his closed eyelids and filled the inside of his head with warm orange light, a spectacular display of sunlit blood vessels. He paddled more and the warm orange moved out of his head. It left behind a glow of excited rods and cones, little corpuscles trucking along, all lit up.

For a moment he still believed it, then realized it was just a dream. He tried to summon back the feeling, warm and fluid, half-there. It was too late. The sensation shriveled away from him, taking with it the belief that Vicky really told him that she loved him while squeezing his dick.

In the still air Boudreau became aware of the far-off sound of a car pulling up, the engine stopping. A door slammed, the sound clear but distant. Someone had pulled into the driveway, beyond the trees, up by the house.

Boudreau made the mistake of opening his eyes. He instantly shut them again, but the damage was already done. The light had transformed itself into a wedge of blinding headache, lodged in the exact middle of his brain.

The sun was brutal, close to straight up. There was a big pecan tree that overhung the deep end of the pool; Boudreau paddled the chair over to its shade. The skin on his face felt too tight, too warm. He swung his arm from the chair and clubbed an arc of water from the surface. The motion set off new throbbing in his head. Now he had a sunburn to go along with his hangover.

Sweat ran into Boudreau's eyes as he sat up in the chair; he had to get out of the sun. He knew he should go find who just pulled in up at the house, go find Keith then split. He'd be crazy to spend any more time with him. Then he thought of what awaited him at the farmhouse and immediately revised his threshold of tolerance. Maybe he'd hang around for a little while if he could stand it. He knew he'd feel better if he ate something.

The can of soda was still in the styrofoam armrest, a hot flat Tab, half-full. Boudreau swirled around the contents and then downed it in a gulp, forgetting about the cigarette he'd put out in it. He stepped out of the chair, spewing, and sank straight down to the bottom, soda can still in hand. Underwater, as chlorine came shooting up his nostrils, Boudreau floundered. He was in the deep end.

Boudreau walked in the delivery door at the back of the house and heard noise, then followed it through the long kitchen, through the butler's pantry and into the breakfast room.

There was Rena, in the same uniform she'd worn ever since he could remember. She was sitting at the table watching a religious show on a color portable. She was bent forward to the set even though the sound was up to speaker-rattling volume.

Boudreau moved into the periphery of her vision until she saw him. "My!" she shouted. "Oh my, Mister Ricky! Go sneaking up on me like that!"

Her eyes flashed behind her bifocals, but Boudreau knew she wasn't really mad. He leaned over and kissed her on the cheek. Her skin was cool and dry and soft with wrinkles, like close-grained old leather. She looked up at him, mollified by the kiss.

"How you been?" she yelled.

"I've been out swimming," Boudreau shouted over the television.

"Fine, fine, when my arthuritis ain't hurting me," the old lady shouted back, her smile full of gold. She said the word *hoyten*.

Boudreau nodded and smiled back.

"How that girl a yours?" she said.

It took him a moment to realize she meant Ginny. He made an expression with his eyebrows that said, Well, you know, married life . . . she's fine, thanks. If she couldn't remember, he didn't feel like reminding her.

She beamed at him again. "That's good," she hollered.

He was horrified at how small and old she had become, her shoulders gone narrow and frail, her back distinctly humped under the thin white sweater she wore against the air-conditioning. Her hands were all knuckles and her gray hair had become so thin it was mostly dark scalp.

"Is Key around?" Boudreau shouted.

The old lady looked reprovingly over the tops of her glasses. "You find Mister Keith, you tell him he should a lef' me a note you coming over for lunch."

Boudreau nodded as though they were communicating. He started his question again, but Rena had turned to catch something the TV preacher was saying. Boudreau decided to wander around until he found Keith, half hoping he wouldn't.

"In the mercy whom!" Rena shouted.

Boudreau was startled. "What?"

"Say he in the *music room.*" She kept her eyes on the set. "Corn beef samwich for lunch, you tell him."

Boudreau walked out in the long gallery that connected the kitchen to the front entry hall. He was shaken by how rickety Rena seemed. She had always seemed so indestructible, a presence he took to be far more basic to the house than any of its owners; it was Rena Almond, not Priscilla Michaels, who had really run the household. Besides taking care of Vicky and Keith since they were born, she had supervised a cook, a cleaning maid, the "man," whose name was Randolph, and a gardener. Now she was the only one left, her checks signed by a trust officer. She took care of Keith, fixed his meals, did his laundry, picked up after him.

Boudreau opened the door to the basement. There were lights on, but he got no answer when he called. He went down anyway.

Rena had unknowingly precipitated a major argument he'd had with Ginny, the first in a long sequence that he now recognized as the beginning of the end. They'd dropped by to see Keith, whom Ginny instinctively disliked, and afterward in the car she had turned and said, *"Mister* Ricky?"

Ginny had grown up in Berkeley, the only child of a sociology professor and a painter, whom she always made sure to identify as a "watercolorist." She'd made one brief trip to Tulsa with Boudreau before they moved there, a hothouse flower moved into the exhilaration of open air. It was a hoot, this exotic tribal culture that worshiped petroleum fractions and drove big gaudy cars and called each other "y'all."

Within months of moving, she was already suffering the consequences of unmediated open weather. She began to think certain people said "nigger" in front of her on purpose, as often as they could. She started picking fights, making sure to let people know she was a Jew right after they had used the word in verb form.

"I can't *believe* you let her call you 'Mister Ricky.' "

At the bottom of the basement stairs, Boudreau could hear the tinny buzz of an unamplified electric guitar coming from the billiard room. Keith Michaels was leaning back on the corner banquette down at the other end of the room, massive headphones on, eyes closed. He had a sunburst Stratocaster in his lap; except for the headphones he was naked. Cords from the 'phones and the guitar snaked over the enormous old slate-bed pool table, then across the elaborate walnut bar, where they were plugged into a solid bank of flat-black electronics, state-of-the-art and brand-new. In the jumble of components and wires a record spun silently on a turntable thin as a chromed pizza box.

Boudreau walked over and lightly tapped Keith on the shoulder. He wasn't naked after all; the guitar had hidden his jockey shorts. His doughy white flab billowed everywhere. A drink sat beside him, sweating a dark ring on the red leather cushion.

Keith opened his eyes, unsurprised. "Lemme just finish," he said, in the careful loudness of someone who can't hear himself. He closed his eyes again and kept playing.

There was a pack of Marlboros on the bar. Boudreau helped himself to one, then drew himself a Coke from the row of dispensers.

On the pool table was an overflowing ashtray, along with maybe half a rack of scattered balls, a bridge and two regular cues, one of them broken, an extremely long telephoto lens, a slew of empty beer bottles, and a velvet-lined wooden box with the lid up. Inside were a pair of matched handguns, giving off a dull oily gleam against the velvet. They were long-barreled revolvers, huge things, with ivory handles and nickeled engraving. Boudreau experimentally lifted the butt of one with his fingertips, then let it fall. It was a lot heavier than it looked. He took the ashtray and sat down on a bar stool.

Ginny hadn't begun to understand how deep the shit really ran here; you had to grow up in it for that. *Things were never that simple.* He grew up in it, but that didn't mean he was a part of it. He knew as well as anybody about the bad taste and the circus wealth and the Chamber of Commerce manifest destiny, and he *especially* knew about the racism. The mistake was in thinking you could change any of it.

Keith was in fact a perfect example; nobody was going to change

Keith. He was the third generation of a family whose money was an organism that now lived on its own, watered and tended by squads of lawyers and bankers and trustees. Its roots went back to the turn of the century, when Elton Michaels arrived from Indiana and hit oil on leases near Glenpool that he'd swindled from two Cherokee families. There was a row of old green-glass bottles full of crude oil in a display cabinet upstairs, each one labeled with the name of the well it came from. As a kid, Boudreau used to stare at them. They might as well have had genies locked inside, ready to grant houses and cars, political appointments and beautiful women.

Keith's father took over the business after an apprentice stint out roughnecking in the field. Canny where his own father had been merely ruthless, Joe Michaels proved the better businessman. Power accrued to those who could sniff out weakness while making with the glad hand. A maestro of the boardroom and the bank meeting and the legislative chamber, Elton's son parlayed his father's fortune into something much more impressive, a thickly branched, multileaved growth of pipeline contracting, oil-field equipment, agricultural chemicals.

Boudreau took in the view of Keith Michaels, the male fruit, the very culmination of this enormous and widely admired flower of American capitalism. There he sat in his underwear, an obese alcoholic who liked to wear headphones and play along with his old Rolling Stones records.

He wasn't going to change Keith, no more than he was going to make Republican oilmen gain sudden compassion for the downtrodden, teach a redneck never to say "nigger" again, bring Jews into the open arms of their Christian brethren under the smiling eyes of God. Keith was *supposed* to become a rich asshole who didn't care about anybody else. The only thing he lacked was the drive to make more, a minor tear in the genetic fabric. *People didn't change.* That was the sad fact, that was what Tulsa had thrown in Ginny's face. But she had turned her face away, first from the facts of the place, and then from Boudreau himself.

Keith hit one last tinny chord with a flourish. He took off his headphones and leaned back against the wall, guitar still in his lap, and had a sip of his drink.

"Whew," he said. "Stones, man."

"Hey, who else?" said Boudreau. "Who else?" Keith seemed perfectly sober.

"Throw me a smoke." Keith pointed at the box on the bar beside Boudreau, then looked at the shorts and T-shirt Boudreau was wearing. "You stay here last night or something?"

Boudreau stiffened. "Yeah." He threw him a cigarette. "Remember, you said stay in Vicky's room?"

Keith caught the cigarette and shrugged. "Hey, fine with me." He pointed to a plastic butane lighter on the bar. "Light," he said.

Boudreau underhanded it to him in a looping toss, restraining himself from throwing it as hard he could. It wasn't that Keith went out of his way to stomp on other people's feelings, merely that he'd never noticed they had any.

"You said you could use some company for a few days, right?" Boudreau said this with a careful smile, just something he wanted to get straight. "And I said they were doing some power-line work out at my place, remember? And then you said—"

Keith lit his cigarette, waved it in a gesture of dismissal. "Sure sure," he said. "Right. Boo and Key gone party for a few days. Thass the main thang." He was feeling funky from his work with the Stones. He got a wide-eyed look of innocence on his face. "In moderation, of course." He deadpanned the look into a smirk.

"Yeah, what moderation?" Boudreau got up from the bar stool. "Not fucked up enough, that's your motto. Jesus *Christ* did I have a head this morning."

Keith laughed and drained the last of his drink, then got up and laid the guitar down on the pool table. He picked up one of the handguns. "You see these? Colt Pythons, man, special edition. Set me back three grand." He shrugged off the price. "Presentation set."

Boudreau nodded to show he was impressed. Three grand.

"I saw that movie *Deer Hunter* while I was up in the tank?" said Keith. "Great flick." He spun the cylinder on the gun. "One bullet, six chambers."

Boudreau nodded again. The gun was making him nervous.

Keith spun the cylinder again, then whirled and dropped into a two handed cop-show crouch.

Boudreau froze.

"Check it out, Jim." Keith's eyes were narrowed, his chin down to his chest. "Think how it feels to stare up *this* anus."

"I get the idea," said Boudreau, trying to make it sound nonchalant. "Don't do that." He waited for Keith to move. "You watch too much TV."

Keith shifted to aim the gun not at Keith's head per se, but rather at the image of his head in the big mirror behind the bar, which they both faced. Boudreau looked into the barrel aimed at him in the glass, paralyzed. He blew a nervous smoke ring, which immediately blossomed from his mouth in the mirror.

Cocking the hammer first, Keith tracked the smoke ring in the mirror like someone shooting skeet, then pulled the trigger.

Boudreau jumped along with the *click!* of the firing pin.

Keith Michaels cackled, his eyes bright.

"Mother*fucker,*" said Boudreau. He'd thought he would lose his hearing at the very least. "That's not fucking funny."

Keith put the gun back down on the pool table. "Looked like the guy in the mirror was shittin' bricks." He was still laughing. "Kinda, you know, nervous?"

"Yeah, *fuck* you." Boudreau was unable to come up with a more sophisticated response. "*Fuck* you, man." There wasn't any.

"Hey, c'mon," said Keith, "It wasn't *loaded.* You know I'd never fire a loaded weapon in the house."

"Oh, well that makes me feel a lot better. Like the time you blew out the TV by accident."

"Lighten up." Keith gave Boudreau a smile that had nothing to do with fun. "That was kid shit, I had too many beers. You're looking at the new Keith, my man. The new Keith does nothing except on purpose." He turned toward the door. "Let's go see what Rena made me for lunch."

Boudreau followed Keith's fat butt up the stairs, keeping his distance. He was beginning to remember how often he'd felt the same way when they were teenagers. *The new Keith, bullshit.* This was the same one, just a new stage. People didn't change; they just went through stages, they just slowly died out. In Boudreau's opinion, Keith Michaels did not have that many stages left.

Boudreau polished off his corned beef sandwich and pushed his stool back from the island counter. His head felt marginally better. He took a dainty sip from his Seven-Up, and gave himself credit for passing up liquor yet again. He lit a cigarette.

Keith, on the other hand, mixed another drink as soon as they came upstairs. He had already finished it and started on a beer. He sat in his underwear on the opposite side of the oiled butcher block island, eating cookies. Usually Keith still dressed the same way he had as a teenager: wheat jeans and penny loafers, button-down oxford shirts. Now, with his new rolls of fat, Boudreau couldn't help thinking there was something vaguely diaperlike about Keith's attire. Maybe he was regressing all the way back.

Rena hadn't seemed to notice at all. Priscilla Michaels had died in the freak crash of a Michaels Drilling Learjet four years before, and Joe Michaels had followed her with stomach cancer less than a year later. Boudreau guessed that Rena had grown accustomed to a variety of unfettered behavior ever since. She treated Keith like a large, unruly house pet. She moved him aside or slapped his hand, all the time keeping up a monologue of commentary in her high-pitched old lady's voice.

She had set places for the two of them at the counter, each plate with a thick, neatly halved sandwich, the corned beef meltingly tender and slathered with mayonnaise and Durkee's, surrounded by a fluffy pile of potato chips and a garnish of small pickles and peppers on the side. Then she left them alone. Boudreau considered how it would feel to have someone whose job it was to fix your food for you, then clean it up afterward. You had to go potty by yourself, though.

Rena had also set out a plate heaped with still-warm chocolate chip cookies, the same cookies Boudreau had salivated over as a kid. Keith had taken two or three bites of the corned beef and eaten a few chips before going to work on the cookies.

Boudreau smoked his cigarette and watched. Keith hardly paused to chew, putting the cookies down like a cow eating hay, cookies as fodder. He ate not fast but methodically, one or two bites per cookie, a slug of beer washing down every few. Between chomps he told Boudreau about his stay in Minnesota.

After he'd finished half of the cookies on the plate, Keith got up to peer into the big, double-doored refrigerator, fingers thatching reflectively in the whorl of dark blond hair around his belly button. Finally he fished out another bottle of beer, then sat down and went back to work.

Boudreau was impressed. In the last five or six years Keith Michaels had gone off twice before to get dried out. The first time he returned to serious boozing by fits and starts over a long period of time—understandably, since his parents were still riding herd on him. By the second attempt they were gone, but it had still taken him a decent while to hit deep-end behavior again.

This time, though, he was going at it hard only a few days back. Boudreau had been with him since six the night before, and he had yet to see him without a drink. He wondered what had clicked, what step it took to abandon all pretense, to give in. Even the question made him nervous.

"So'd you meet anybody there?" Boudreau stubbed out his cigarette, bored. Keith was going on endlessly about the cold and snow, astonished that people could be so stupid as to live in such conditions.

"You mean like girls?" said Keith. *"Gurls?"* He had a long pull on his beer, and belched. "Yeah, I met this one chick from Minneapolis."

"Yeah?"

"Yeah," Keith said. He picked up a cookie and examined it. "Zane."

"Zane?"

"Yeah, Zane from Minneapolis." Keith laughed through a mouthful of cookie. "Norwegian or Danish or some fucking thing."

"And she was in the place, too?"

Keith Michaels snorted at the delicacy of Boudreau's euphemism. "Yeah, she was in the *place*. Never been in one before, though. Gonna get out and join AA and everything." He belched a laugh and reached for another cookie.

Boudreau was morbidly curious for the details. Listening to Keith talk about women was like seeing Cro-Magnon man brought to life. "So you banged this Zane?" he leered, leading Keith on.

"Repeatedly. She ate my chili, man." Keith shrugged and then inhaled the cookie he was holding. The memory didn't seem to make him that happy. "We did okay till she got on her high horse."

Boudreau watched Keith's jaw visibly tighten at the thought of Zane's high horse. He chewed as though he were grinding pebbles down to sand.

"She cute?" Boudreau knew this was somehow inappropriate, but he wanted a picture.

"Yeah, sure," Keith said, annoyed that Boudreau had bothered to ask. "Okay face. Blond. Tits to here." He sniffed. "She wasn't bad. Zane from Minneapolis."

Boudreau nodded, disappointed by the clam-up. He eyed the remainder of Keith's sandwich, then decided not to reach for it. To directly ask Keith for something was to become fair game. He wanted to keep his declared needs down.

Keith hunched over the counter then, both hands on his beer. He shook his head very slightly, his mouth disturbed. "There was something wrong with her box," he said in a low voice.

"Her what?"

"Her *box*," Keith said.

Boudreau looked at him for further meaning, confused.

"Her *vageena*," he explained, not believing he was having to do it.

"Her what?" repeated Boudreau.

"Her vageena," hissed Keith. "Her *cunt*, you asshole."

Boudreau nodded, light dawning. Keith's face was dark with anger. *Her vageena.*

"Yeah. So?" said Boudreau. "So. So what was wrong with it? I mean with her box."

Keith Michaels looked at the plate, angry. "It was too hot," he said, and turned away.

Boudreau waited for a moment, expecting more. "Too hot?" he prompted.

Keith breathed in, exhaled; he took a swig from his beer, finishing it. This did not come easily for him. He nearly whispered. "It was just like too *hot* in there, you know, I'd put my dick in and it was just *hot*. It was fucking disgusting. There was something wrong with her."

Boudreau nodded, all sympathy. "What, you mean like clap or something? Disease?"

Keith shook his head. A look came over his face, like he was trying to rid his mouth of something distasteful.

"Nah, the bitch never got laid in her life. Yeah, maybe, I dunno. There was something *wrong*, I dunno. It was too hot."

Boudreau wasn't sure what the "yeah, maybe" referred to, disease or whether the bitch ever got laid. "Well, so like did you say anything to her?" he said.

Keith tore a cookie carefully in half, then folded the two pieces into his mouth. His eyes fixed on something distant. "Not right away."

Boudreau tried to imagine what such a scene had sounded like. He waited. "So that was when she got on her high horse, huh?" he asked finally.

"What?" said Keith. By the look on his face he had already dropped the subject, banished the whole thing. "Oh. Nah, totally different thing. She started saying all this stupid shit about oil companies, some stupid book she read. So I told her, I went, Hey, baby, I happen to run some oil companies, so maybe I know a little better than you. Oil makes the world go round. I went, You use gasoline, you drive a car. She never thought of that. Stupid *bitch.*"

Boudreau winced at the level of vituperation. "So you told her you were Mister Executive?"

"Yeah, what's so funny about that?"

Boudreau's smile grew more incredulous. "Yeah, right, you run Michaels?" He could hear his own voice rising. This was too much. "C'mon, Key. You can tell that to Zane from—"

The front doorbell rang, two deep, discrete notes, the second one slightly higher.

Keith turned to the door of the kitchen that led to the middle of the house. "Rena! Hey, Rena—the *door!*"

He turned back to Boudreau. "Maybe I don't go to an office every day, but so what. I help run things. Yeah, you laugh, shit-head. Go ask Chip Carlson, he'll tell you. He calls me all the time, we talk on the phone, I get reports in the mail."

Boudreau kept his face carefully blank. Chip Carlson was the estate lawyer who managed the various family trusts. It would be like asking if three-year-olds really piloted aircraft carriers.

The doorbell rang again.

"They send me the reports even when I go to the tank. Hey, *Rena!* The fucking *doorbell!* And I read 'em too, even though I gotta deal with all this other stuff. *Reee-na?*"

Keith waited a few seconds, ear cocked, but there was no sign. The doorbell rang again, then repeatedly. Someone was leaning on it. Keith swore and got up to go answer it himself.

Boudreau watched him waddle off, still in his underwear. He was uncertain if Keith had forgotten or if he just didn't care, but it didn't matter. Keith lived in a different world.

Boudreau ate two of the remaining five cookies, then reached over and took the untouched half of Keith's corned beef sandwich. He heard muffled voices from the front of the house as he chewed.

With the exception of a forced five-month stint as an office go-fer when he flunked out of college, Keith Michaels had never shown the slightest interest in the corporation that bore his family's name. He seemed to regard it as a large bladder of wealth conveniently located for his use, an anatomical peculiarity like a yolk sac. Now, of course, he was helping run it.

Boudreau knew better, courtesy of Vicky. Keith's huge block of stock was held in trust, and Joe Michaels had left behind a set of conditions so tight it might as well have been a cage. Keith was barred from so much as breathing on anything but his trust checks.

Boudreau stuffed in the last bite of Keith's sandwich, filling himself up. Now the voices from the front of the house were growing closer, and louder. He thought he recognized the other voice.

Keith's voice rose above the muffle to confirm Boudreau's suspicion. "No *way*, Vicky! No way!"

Boudreau began to think that making it through the weekend here might be more of a chore than he was ready for.

Keith stomped back into the kitchen, mouth set in a pout, his sister following a few feet behind. Boudreau couldn't remember the last time he'd seen the two of them occupy the same room.

Vicky gave Boudreau a broad wink. "I've been looking for you, Richter Boudreau." She made it sound musical and teasing, like he'd been hiding from her, a recalcitrant kindergartner.

Keith stood by his stool as though to defend it, one arm planted on the counter. He reached for a cookie. Vicky came and stood beside him, much closer than necessary. He stiffened, refusing to look at her.

She looked across the island at Boudreau. "I swear, Richter, you can eat and look at him in his underpants?" She picked up the next to last cookie from the plate and bit it carefully in half, drawing it apart with her teeth, going for texture. "God!" She ran her tongue around her lips to catch the crumbs. "Ooh, is that *good?*" She put the rest in her mouth and did a mock swoon. "And *is* Jesus our Lord? Where's that old black gal Rena?"

His mouth still full, Keith grabbed for the last cookie. "Around." He looked straight ahead. "What do you care?"

She turned and glared at his profile, amazed. "Just thought I'd say hidy? If it's all right with y'all?"

She punctuated her question with a quick backhanded slap to her brother's gut, producing a wet sound of smacked flab. Keith brought one hand down to protect himself, giving her an opportunity to grab the cookie out of his other one. By the time he recovered, she'd gobbled the cookie in a bite and moved out of range to the end of the island.

Keith blushed a bright red, the color bleeding down his neck into his shoulders. Now he refused to look at either of them. His eyes went inward as he picked up an olive from his plate and ate it.

Vicky leaned on the island with both elbows, focusing her attention on Boudreau as if her brother were no longer there. There was the faintest trace of a smile on her face as she finished chewing and swallowing.

Boudreau looked straight back at her. In spite of the lectures he'd recently given himself, his day had just improved. "How'd you know I was here?"

"Ve heff our vays." Vicky let her eyelids drop and narrowed her gaze. "Rubber hoses?"

"Chust rubber." She arched one eyebrow. "Bleck rubber. You like rubber, eh?"

Boudreau mimed open-mouthed lust. It came easily.

Keith went to the refrigerator, took out another beer and turned his back to them, looking out the window over the sink.

Vicky grinned at Boudreau. She was in a great mood, a different person than she'd been two nights before. Her skin was clearer, her face relaxed. Her hair looked freshly washed, shiny and fluffy as corn silk. She wore a pair of tight, faded jeans and a loose, sleeveless T-shirt. The way she leaned over the counter produced a perfect sloping line down her back, a line that lifted at the curve of her buttocks and then followed her legs all the way down. "Wanna play some tennis this afternoon?" she said.

"Tennis?" said Boudreau.

She gave him a questioning look. "Little balls?" she said. "Fifteen–love, fifteen–thirty?"

"Are you serious?"

Vicky Stover rolled her eyes. "*Yes,* I'm serious, that's why I'm *here,* Richter honey."

Boudreau hesitated the merest of moments. "Sure," he said. "Sure, I'll play tennis with you." This would be the end of his freeload with Keith, but he didn't care. How Vicky could turn on and off so fast made no sense to him, but he didn't care about that, either. "Where we playing?"

Keith turned from the window with a nasty smile. "You can always play out at LaFortune." LaFortune was a city park with public courts; to Keith this was an unanswerable insult of a suggestion.

Vicky mimed her brother's expression back at him, turning it into the look of a petulant baby.

"You can't play at the club," Keith said, ignoring her. "There's no family membership anymore, just mine." He folded his arms across his chest, triumphant. He swayed a little and Boudreau suddenly saw how drunk he was.

His sister snapped her fingers in disappointment. *"Darn* it, Keithie, and here I forgot? You forget these things after a few years go by." She looked him up and then down, as though she'd just noticed his size. She measured her next words for effect, one at a time. "You might try a little exercise yourself? Kind of a lard-butt pig these days, doncha think?"

Keith's face went dark red, his eyes watering. "Eat shit, Vicky. Eat my *shit,* you slut."

Vicky averted her face slightly, letting his badly thrown rock sail right by. She turned to Boudreau, satisfied. "My, this is adult."

Boudreau hurried to fill in. They were like rats in a litter, ready to kill each other. "I'll have to go out to my place first, okay?"

"That's okay, I have to get some things here, too." Vicky turned to her brother, nothing in her tone to indicate their last exchange. "Okay if I go up and get some stuff, Keithie? I don't keep much of a tennis wardrobe at home these days."

Keith had turned to look out the window again, one hand on the sink counter. He held his beer in midair, rigid.

Vicky gave his back the finger, then kissed her fingertips and touched Boudreau's cheek.

"Come on upstairs." She gave him a stage wink. "I have something to tell you."

Keith stood motionless at the window a full minute after his sister left the kitchen. Boudreau sat equally still at the counter.

Keith turned, his whole face in a fiery blush, and addressed the

kitchen at large. "She's out to get me, man, she's out to fucking *get* me."
His eyes narrowed at something only he could see; his mouth twisted.
"We'll see who fucks who."

"Oh, come on. She's not out to get you, Key. It's just the same old
shit, right?"

"Oh yeah?" Keith turned his face to Boudreau, his anger making him
seem almost sober. "You think I don't know why she's seeing Chip
Carlson? Fucking *slut.*"

"What?" said Boudreau.

Keith's face went blank, his expression inward.

"C'mon, Key. What?"

"Shut up."

"Okay," said Boudreau. "Whatever." He waited awhile, with no
results.

"You be around tonight?" Boudreau extended the offer of company
as thinly as possible, but extended it anyway. He had to, because of his
betrayal with Vicky. That was the way Keith would see it.

Keith pouted, refusing to answer; he took a pack of cigarettes out of
a carton in the refrigerator door.

"Hey, come on, Key. Don't blame *me*, man, she's *your* sister. I'm just
here."

"Yeah," said Keith. "You're just here." He concentrated on tapping
the pack against the butt of his other hand. "Think I'll go have a drink
by the pool." He started out the delivery door.

"Keith, I'm your *friend*," Boudreau called.

"Have a nice game," Keith said, leaving the door open behind him.

Boudreau got up and closed the door; you didn't let air-conditioning
out in this kind of heat. He went to a window and watched Keith walk
down toward the pool, his body an unhealthy potato-white against the
green of the lawn. Because of the downward slope or because he was
drunk, his legs had no spring in them. His feet seemed to be hitting the
ground before they were ready to.

Boudreau went to the refrigerator and got a pack of Marlboros out
of the carton himself. What the hell, he'd had enough. He'd get a pack
of cigarettes out of the deal and that was that.

He took the curved, carpeted stairs two at a time, then went down the hall to Vicky's room. She wasn't there. He turned, confused, just as he caught a slight movement out of the corner of his eye.

Vicky stepped back from an open closet door, in profile. He was about to say something when he noticed that she was half naked, her shirt off and her jeans down to her ankles. In one hand she held a wadded-up tennis outfit. She hopped to keep her balance, then spoke over her shoulder.

" 'And who's been sleeping in *my* bed,' said the Vicky Bear."

"Whoa, sorry!" He didn't think she'd spotted him.

She turned toward him as she stepped out of the jeans, then adjusted her panties but made no other attempt to cover herself. She kept him fixed, eye to eye. Boudreau felt his face go hot. "Hey, I didn't mean to—" he finally got out.

"Sure you did," she said. "Just don't look at the stretch marks, okay?"

"Where are they?" he said. If this wasn't deliberate, he didn't know what was.

She smirked at him before pulling on the white top. Boudreau drank her in as the garment went over her head. When he and Keith were teenagers, they'd regularly watched her undress through a peephole in the hall linen closet; now she was letting him watch on purpose. He averted his eyes chivalrously as her head popped through.

Vicky stepped into the skirt and snapped the waistband into place, then spun once in front of the mirror on the closet door. She looked hard at her reflection, wincing.

"Oh Lordy, what's wrong with this picture?" Vicky smoothed the tiny skirt and sighed loudly. "They don't wear these flirty little skirts anymore, do they?" She gave a pouty cheerleader's flounce at the mirror. "I can't stand it, I just look so *old.*"

"Oh *bullshit,*" Boudreau burst out. He realized he'd been holding his breath, and now he didn't have any. "God, you look great."

"Why, *thank* you, sir." She cast her eyes down and batted them furiously. "I've always depended on the kindness of strangers?"

"Boy, are you in a good mood," he said.

"Why, 'cause I got nekkid for you?" He blushed and she laughed at him, then pointed at a little vial on the bedside table. "There's some toots there for you."

"Ah," said Boudreau.

He pulled out the little spoon and did happily as he was told; so much for getting through the day clean. This was different. He snorted and snukked while she watched. Heaven was raining manna on him, his dream in the pool beginning to look prophetic. He grinned at her.

"Yeah, I don't know, Richter, you take it when you can and don't ask questions." Vicky shook her head in mild wonderment. "This is very weird. I mean, being in this house is very weird. It's, it's—" She gestured around her. "I don't know, it's like my mother's gonna walk down the hall and find me with a *boy* in my room."

She walked back into the closet and began rummaging. "A *boy*," she said. "Now I just have to find some shoes and a racquet to complete the picture." She pulled out a stack of three racquets and began taking off the covers and examining each one.

Boudreau watched her, transfixed. He was back in love.

"But yeah," she said, "I guess I am doing better. Change is in the air." She gave him a significant look. "I'm sorry for the other night," she said, and immediately went back to scrutinizing racquet strings. She did an accent. "It's just that life is so con*fusin'* right now?"

Boudreau nodded. He understood perfectly.

"I'm even thinking about doing some acting again." She raised her eyebrows. "I don't know, I probably won't do it. Maybe Little Theatre or something."

Years before, in New York, she'd taken classes and landed some bit parts in a couple of tiny downtown productions. She came out of it with a couple of agents who wanted to sleep with her, and the case of hepatitis. The nervous breakdown came later.

"That's wonderful." Boudreau found it ineffably poignant that she still thought of acting as a possibility. He wondered where Ronnie fit into all this, then realized he didn't. "I'll come watch."

She strummed the strings of one of the racquets, shaking her head at her own folly. "Well, anyway, things *are* looking up," she said. "I really think they are."

"Getting your shit together?" he joked.

She looked at him, then remembered. "Yeah," she snorted. "Yeah, *right.* Getting my shit together."

Boudreau unscrewed the vial and had two more quick hits. He grinned at her stupidly, giddy as an ape.

"Okay, now, *shoes,*" she said. "This may take a while, you might want to go down and wait outside." She made ready to brave the depths of the closet again, then paused.

"Richter honey?" She gave him a little smile. "Thanks for being patient with me. This is *not* an easy time to be going through."

Boudreau felt his face glow.

"Go on now." She blushed and looked down, no longer able to meet his eyes. "Go on, I'll be down in a minute."

Boudreau's outlook changed the moment he stepped out the front door into the midday heat. He began sweating immediately; this was stupid, even for love. To play tennis in heat like this was like making an appointment for a heatstroke. Then he saw Ronnie Stover. The battered Mustang was fifty yards down the long brick drive, pulled onto the carpetlike lawn under the shade of a big old elm. Ronnie had parked so the car was aimed right at the front door of the house, as if it were some kind of target.

Boudreau forced himself to walk casually out to the Mustang, having somehow neglected to consider how Vicky had arrived. Just stepping out the door of the enormous house had made him feel like a conspirator. So far as he knew, Ronnie had never even set foot in the place.

The house was old for Tulsa, one of the first oil mansions, built in the twenties by Elton Michaels. It was a rambling, three-story structure of dark brick with clay-tiled hip roofs and Moorish-looking arches. It was hard to imagine how all this must have looked sixty years before—the brand new Greek Revivals, the Tudors, the Renaissance villas, with their pools and fountains and formal gardens—set plop on the raw prairie by the bumpkin millionaires who'd built them. The ground itself had still been Indian Territory only a few years before.

Now the street was lined with big trees, the huge lawns lush with the tended green of sprinkler systems and black gardeners. Everything looked as though it had been there forever. To sit in front of a house like this, knowing you missed your piece of it—that would require true Zen. In this neighborhood someone like Ronnie Stover would always be too late, by definition.

Boudreau kept forgetting that Vicky was married, and to whom. In his short walk to the car the cocaine had already resoldered a number of interesting connections in his mind, all of them paranoid.

Ronnie was lying across the two bucket seats, head hung out the window on one side, boots out the window on the other. His shades were on and he wasn't moving. The radio was playing, low. Boudreau thought maybe he was asleep, then saw a smoke ring drifting up out of his mouth.

"Vicky should be out in a minute," said Boudreau. "I think she's still trying on some tennis clothes." This was the God's honest truth, he himself had witnessed it. He leaned against the front fender, half sitting. "How you doing?"

"I don't know why she don't just wear some cutoffs." This sounded so bored it hardly qualified as a complaint.

Boudreau didn't know, either.

Ronnie took a slug from the bottle of beer he had. "Y'all're gonna die out there," he said.

Boudreau needed a moment to assign this comment its proper meaning, as a reference to the weather. "Yeah, we'll die," he said. "It's good for you."

"Never could see what people get out of tennis, anyways," Ronnie elaborated. "Ball's too small."

So far as Boudreau could see, this was an inarguable point.

"Told her she was crazy to play in this heat." Ronnie gestured with the beer bottle, a little wave of its long neck dismissing his responsibility in the matter. "She said after you beat her last week she wadn't backing out. Said she whip your ass."

"Yeah?" Boudreau nodded lengthily. He hadn't realized they'd played together so recently.

Ronnie had yet to turn his head toward Boudreau; he'd hardly moved at all. He gave the appearance of a large animal immobile in the heat, of carefully controlled reserves.

Boudreau racked his brain for a safe subject. "How's Clem?" The baby was asleep in the back, strapped into a car seat, all diaper and T-shirt and folds of sweaty pudge.

"Sleeping." Ronnie took a last drag off his cigarette, then aimed and flicked it through the car and out the window, onto the lawn. All he moved were two fingers.

"She should be out any minute," said Boudreau.

"Any hour's more like it," Ronnie said, "but that ain't why I'm waiting. You never called me back yesterday."

"Yeah?" Boudreau had forgotten all about the call to the paper. "Yeah, a bunch of things came up." Now he was caught off guard again. "I was going to call you today. But listen, you can't call me at the paper."

Ronnie rotated his head where it rested on the car door. He looked at Boudreau, his sunglasses blank.

"I mean," Boudreau backtracked, "you can't leave messages like that. There's people there I have to worry about."

Ronnie pursed his lips.

"It's just that it's not cool," said Boudreau.

Ronnie rotated his head back to the interior of the car and gazed out the passenger window; Boudreau saw him bare his teeth in the wolfish grin.

"You owe me, Richter," Ronnie said.

Boudreau breathed out. "Don't I know it." The air itself was pressing in on him, thick with heat and moisture and crud. His head was suddenly throbbing again, a hangover with a metallic coke edge.

"Listen, I can talk anytime—just not at work, okay?" He took a deep breath. "The thing is, I don't know how much there is to talk about. I'm broke. I mean I could maybe get it to—"

Ronnie held up the beer bottle to stop him, then had a swallow. He held the long neck of the bottle between two fingers as lightly as he'd held his cigarette. "Told you maybe we could work something out."

Boudreau looked away, over at the thick hedge that lined the other side of the brick drive. A candy wrapper or some other kind of trash was stuck in it, a single white blemish in its perfect green texture. He barked out a nervous little laugh. "What?" he said, "you mean like I could pay it off in baby-sitting or something?"

Ronnie turned and gave Boudreau a long look. "I told you about that deal?" His cheeks rose slightly, like he shouldn't have to say this. "I hope you got that film can safe."

Boudreau licked his dry lips. "Yeah, it's safe enough." He saw no point in describing its status any further. For all he knew Billy had found it and already snorted its entire contents.

One corner of Ronnie's mouth went up in a tiny little shrug. "Tell you what then, you come meet me tonight, we talk about this deal I got. See what happens."

"Tonight?" said Boudreau. This would mean having to come up with the film can. "Um, I'm not sure about tonight." He floundered frantically. "Yeah, maybe. I mean, I'm not sure yet what I'm doing tonight, but maybe I can."

Ronnie shifted his gaze over to the big house and found some small cause for further amusement. "Hanging out with brother Keith, are you?"

Boudreau thought maybe he'd been a little too obvious. "Yeah, we talked about it. But I can probably get out of it."

Ronnie said nothing.

"I'll try to get out of it," Boudreau repeated. Out of the corner of his eye he saw Ronnie gaze back into the car. He made himself ask. "You want me to bring the film can?"

"Keep it," said Ronnie. "Safer with you."

Enlightened, Boudreau ventured further. "What if I don't like the deal?"

"Don't sweat it, Richter." Ronnie smirked to himself again. "All you got to do is listen. Then maybe we work something out, maybe we don't. Then all you owe me is the can."

"Yeah," said Boudreau, "that and five hundred bucks."

"Yeah," Ronnie said, "that, too."

"And that's it," said Boudreau, measuring the exact boundaries of his debt. How hard could it be, coming up with five hundred dollars and the film can?

"Far as I know," Ronnie said, apparently finding more humor in Boudreau's need to rehash.

Far as I know. Boudreau had every intention of keeping it that way;

he just needed a few days of artful stalling, starting with tonight. "I'll
see if I can't ditch Keith."

This struck Ronnie as unusually funny. "Yeah, old Keith, he can't
come." Ronnie snorted out another chuckle. "I'll be at the Sixty-Six
around nine, you know that place?"

"The Sixty-Six?" Boudreau took a while. The Sixty-Six Club was the
latest incarnation of a TU jock bar called the Hurricane Lounge, a dive
in a tiny shopping center on Eleventh out past Memorial. Now it
sported blacked-out windows and a sign that said Adult Entertainment
Nitely.

"I got a connection to make," Ronnie explained. He allowed himself
another private little smile. "Might even get high myself."

"What the hell, it's Saturday night, right?" An enchanted evening
unfolded in front of Boudreau: he could hang out in a blood-bucket bar
while his good buddy Ronnie shot and sold some felony narcotics. There
would be plenty of time to chew the fat about some hairbrained drug
deal guaranteed to land everyone in jail.

"You'll meet her, too," Ronnie said then.

"Meet who?" Boudreau's mind was already made up.

"This girl, Cherry?" said Ronnie. "She dances there, chips a little."

"Cherry?" This completed the picture. Boudreau assumed he meant
she chipped dope, not men. Then again, maybe it was both. "Cherry,
huh?" Boudreau repeated.

"Y'all'll have things to talk about." Ronnie made what sounded like
a smutty chuckle low in his throat.

"I bet we will," said Boudreau. He'd never seen Ronnie in such a
humorous mood; it made him nervous.

The baby made a whimpery noise in the backseat. She was still asleep
but twitching around. Ronnie snaked himself into a sitting position, his
body making the driver's seat look small. The car's engine came to life.

Boudreau took this as a hint that he remove himself from the car and
stand away. His pants were stuck to the back of his legs.

Ronnie's left arm was braced in the window, bare to the shoulder,
muscles strung tight as cable. He was looking through the windshield
at the front door of the giant house across the lawn. After a long moment

he turned to Boudreau, shades blank of information. "Nine, nine-thirty," he said.

"See you there," Boudreau answered, with no such intention.

Ronnie put the car in gear and backed all the way out onto the street. Still rolling backward, he put it in first and laid a little patch before passing slowly in front of the mansion. It looked like he flicked a wave good-bye, until Boudreau saw the beer bottle sail across the street, hitting the manicured lawn like a chip shot clearing the trap.

Boudreau laughed out loud. It had probably taken true restraint for Ronnie to keep from just moseying up and pissing on the front door.

Boudreau drove while Vicky fiddled with the radio, catching the tail end of an auto-body commercial. The next song poured out of the radio like balm. What luck: his high came back, everything draining away except her presence. She turned it up and Boudreau drove slowly to keep the engine noise down. The Healey hugged its way down the tree-shaded residential streets like water purling over a streambed of mossy rocks.

It was the Beatles, "It's Only Love." They'd been playing a lot of Beatles since Lennon had gotten shot in the fall, but Boudreau hadn't heard the song in years.

They both started singing along as though on cue, involuntary as lab rats. He watched Vicky as they hit the chorus, his immediate recall of every word and chord sweetly unbearable. So much time had gone by, but the song was still there, and so was she. *It's only love, and that is all.* She struck a crooner's pose while she sang. *Why should I feel the way I do?*

In a trance, Boudreau waited for "Girl," the next song on the album, and got a waterbed commercial instead. Vicky started punching buttons, then snapped it off and put her hand lightly on his thigh for a moment, giving him something between a pat and a caress. He turned to look at her, but she was looking ahead, a goofy grin on her face.

Boudreau felt wise and sentimental, as though he could go back now which could be eaten in a car: Arby's and McDonald's and Kentucky Frieds and Wendy's and Big Boys and Burger Kings and Roy Rogerses and Ponderosa Steak Houses and Taco Ricos. It was all housed under fake mansard roofs, sheathed in plastic wood, plastic thatch, plastic stone; the signs were alive with electricity, signs with words misspelled, contracted, put in quotes, or just left out.

Even though it happened to be Yale, it was interchangeable with Memorial, or Harvard, or Peoria. Every town had a strip or two of this kind of development, but in Tulsa it had become all there was. Boudreau had a little epiphany, the whole thing coming into a sudden new focus. This was like a diorama of the chatter he had in his head, a physical realization of the process by which the purity of want was transmuted into the mania of need. This was *home*.

Who was he to look down on it? Created by a citizenry still convinced of its own simplicity and sturdy self-reliance, it was a vast, choking border town of distraction, the credit-card Juarez of the future. This was where you got high, got laid, got out of yourself for a few hours, the landscape of a people who bought things the way he used drugs, convinced they couldn't live without them. He could understood that.

They pulled up behind a huge line of cars at Sixty-first and sat through three light changes. Having Vicky beside him was somehow making things different, he could feel it. "I remember putting up signs with True, right on this corner," he said.

"What?" said Vicky, off in her own thoughts.

"Campaign signs." An image came back to him of driving around with True in one of his pickups, the bed piled with cardboard posters on thin lath stakes. There was a hokey picture of him in his stockman's hat, grin wide as a mile. " 'TRIED AND TRUE,' " he quoted in a big voice. " 'VOTE TRUMAN BOUDREAU FOR COUNTY COMMISSIONER.' "

"He got tried, all right," Vicky said.

"Yeah, he sure did."

The last change had brought them right up to the intersection before it went red. Occupying only one of twenty-eight lanes, they sat in the little open car and breathed exhaust, heat waves rippling a few feet above the pavement.

and give his teenage self some real advice about love. It welled up inside him; it was like being outside a spice shop, the smells too intense and yet not sufficient. He couldn't sniff deeply enough. He fought the urge to talk. What was there to say when you felt like this?

He saw her all over again: her jeans all the way down but not quite off, her breasts, tipped with the same dark pink as her lips, shimmying as she hopped for balance. He watched as she turned toward him, stepping out of the jeans, her white bikinis pulled down on one side, enough to show a glimpse of blond fluff before she pulled them back up.

"Richter, honey?" she said. "Are you there?"

Boudreau came out of it, staring at a side-street stop sign on Lewis. There was a car behind them, and it had just honked again.

He turned south on Lewis and then east when he got to Forty-first; at Harvard he went south again, then east on Fifty-first, stair-stepping his way across town, south and east, roughly following the same direction that development had taken in the last fifteen years.

The roads got wider the farther they went, but they were thick with Saturday traffic, totally clotted around the mammoth shopping centers that now seemed to occupy at least one corner of every major intersection. Light glared from the acres of cars in the giant parking lots, bounced off the buildings, off the road itself. Everything was too bright, even with sunglasses.

He hit Yale and turned south. Usually he avoided all of south Tulsa by taking the expressway out to Broken Arrow. Mile after mile the strip spread, a bristle of electric signs drab in the harsh afternoon light. The big street kept turning over with businesses that lived and died like weeds, but you had to drive it every day to actually mark the changes. It seemed like half of them were franchises, their seeds blown in from all over the country. Only the florid signs changed, gaudy big blossoms hoping for their share of the nervous bees cruising up and down, around and around.

It was a street of complicated needs: tanning salons and video parlors and performance auto-parts centers and waterbed emporiums and car stereo installation dealerships and bars with attitude adjustment hours. There were complex variations on the theme of meat fried in grease

Back then it had been farmland intersected by a pair of two-lane roads. The boy had hopped out of the truck to pound in one of the big double-staked posters on the shoulder, having just been counseled by his grandfather on the aesthetics of the situation: "I tell you what, Richter, that other fella's sign looks like shit right there, don't it? You might kind of lay it down behind them bushes where it's nicer."

Back in the truck he'd gotten a meditative little civics lesson.

"Hell, no brag, but I don't need a single sign"—it was Truman Boudreau's fourth term already—"but that ain't the point. The point is, you get out and people see you, they say, He's a good old boy, ain't he, out putting up his own posters, why he's got his handsome grandson with him. Man willing to get out and be with people, be a little friendly to the working man, give out with a job here, little favor there—I tell you what, they won't just *vote* for me—Christ, they do that anyway. They'll *remember* me."

Boudreau watched his grandfather, rapt, the steering wheel toylike under his huge paw.

"See this here?" Truman Boudreau gestured at the farmland around him with his other hand, setting up for the moral.

"Tulsa's going right here. No bullshit, son, *right* here. You get a man understands that, acts a little friendly"—he held up a forefinger big and blunt as a summer sausage, then jabbed it at his own chest—"that man's got the keys to Tulsa."

"You know what he said about south Tulsa?" said Boudreau as the light finally turned green.

"What *who* said," Vicky asked.

"Nothing," said Boudreau. "Truman."

The traffic thinned as they went further south, and Boudreau drove faster. They passed through the frontier of commerce, into more or less open countryside. There was an occasional two- or three-store cluster at the mouth of a new housing development, a Quik Trip or a U-Tote-M along with a dry cleaner or a little mom-and-pop diner, clinging to the newly bulldozed red dirt like spores for the giant shopping malls to come.

His grandfather had been half-right, anyway.

In 1925, a year after arriving in Broken Arrow from east Texas, Truman Boudreau had built the farmhouse on the edge of a gentle ridge that looked out toward Tulsa, then just beginning to burgeon in the far distance. It was a little two-story clapboard house with a gabled roof and a broad porch that wrapped around the south and west walls to keep out the sun. Its acreage stretched away from it to the north in a gradual downward sweep of rangeland, as though Tulsa itself were part of its purview.

Marrying, then burying two wives, up through the war Truman Boudreau had raised three sons in the farmhouse. After the war was over and two of the sons dead, he moved. Flush from politics and real estate deals and government beef contracts, he bought the big ranch in Osage County, thousands of acres of limestone-fed prairie, and got an apartment in Tulsa for when he had to stay in town.

After that the little farmhouse was rented to a succession of tenants, mostly hard-luck farmers who would run scrawny cattle for a few years before giving up. The last one left in '58. For a year or so, Truman's only remaining son, a lawyer named Malcolm, lived there with his wife and two children while they had a fancy new house built in Tulsa, partly financed by the sale of all but the last twenty-two acres of the farmstead. Then, in the span of the next three years, Truman Boudreau lost in rapid succession his remaining son, his ranch in Osage, his reputation, his freedom, and finally his mind. He died six years later, leaving behind a peculiar will involving the farmhouse and its land, the only thing that remained out of all he had once controlled.

Cynthia Boudreau, Malcolm's widow, then rented the house to whoever wanted it, mostly poor families who came and went suddenly, following booms and busts in oil or construction. In the late sixties three bikers lived there for a couple of years, a tenure that aged the house considerably. One of the bikers stayed on as the bass player of the rock-and-roll band that came next. The house had not been in great shape when Truman Boudreau's lone grandson, and his new wife from California, moved in next.

Boudreau killed the ignition and coasted into what used to be the front yard, a cloud of dust billowing in behind. The yard was a park-anywhere patch of dirt and dusty weeds that had never recovered from the two years of Harley parties. He stopped under a low-branched juniper for the minor shade it offered.

A scraggly Hereford mooed in the silent, overheated air, one of several belonging to the farmer down the road, a holdout who rented the remaining eighteen fenced-off acres. The cow's lowing had a pathetic sound to it, rising to a complaining note at the end.

"He feels about like I do." Vicky held out the front of her tennis dress and blew down it.

"Sure you still want to play?" Boudreau touched her forearm with his fingertips.

Vicky adjusted her sunglasses and shrugged, taking no notice of his hand. He left it there anyway. "Yeah, I think so," she said. "Might as well."

Boudreau was reluctant to get out of the car. "You're looking at my ticket out of here," he said. "The Big Plan. I know: hard to believe, but true."

She looked at him. "I don't get it."

"See, Truman left this funny will," he said, talking faster than seemed necessary. "My mother owns the place and I pay her rent." He laughed. "I mean, theoretically I pay her rent. But when I turn thirty-five, the house is *mine.*"

"Nice view," said Vicky, "if you don't mind looking at Tulsa. This land's going to be worth some money in two years."

Boudreau shook his head. "That's just it. I don't own the land, only the house. I mean, I can keep on living here as long as I want to. *If* I wanted to. That's what I meant by a weird will."

Vicky make a noise of bitter amusement. "Tell me about weird wills."

He ignored it and went on in a rush. "But see, I'm not waiting two years. I'm going to fix up the house and sell it to Cynthia and *then*"—he felt like he was offering up something—"and then I'm going to finish my screenplay."

"That's great," she said after a while. "But where will you live then?"

Boudreau shrugged. "Not here, I know that much."

"You'd leave Tulsa?"

He pressed her arm with his fingertips, important with his decision. "What's to keep me here?"

Vicky Michaels Stover said nothing and looked over at the old farmhouse. Everything about it was old and out of repair. The green asphalt shingles on the roof were curled tight as potato chips, the white paint on the clapboard was alligatored and peeling. A turned post holding up one corner of the porch roof leaned way out of plumb, the porch floor beneath it having rotted out. The old wooden screen door still leaned against the wall where Boudreau had put it after it blew off its hinges in the fall.

"That's great, Richter." She moved the arm his hand was on to slip a loose strand of hair behind her ear. "That's really great. But listen, if we're going to play, we better get going."

"Plan number four hundred ninety-two, I have 'em all the time." He looked at her. "Are you okay? You want to come in?"

She gave him a weary little smile. "I'm fine, it's just a mood. You hurry up and I'll wait for you out here."

Inside, the house was airless with heat; he'd closed the windows Wednesday morning under the laughable impression that it might rain. The living room was quiet as a vault. At first he had the eerie sensation of walking into a room where nobody had lived for a long time, as though everything in it—clothes, papers, books, dishes, ashtrays, beer bottles, cans of motor oil, his usual mess—had been left in a hurry years ago and lain untouched since. In the heat it even smelled bad. There was a faint come-and-go odor, a high thin stink whose source he couldn't identify.

Sweating, Boudreau hurried back to his bedroom and pulled the light switch in the closet. He'd forgotten about the power; no wonder it was so quiet. His flashlight sat on the night table, a reminder of his escapade with Val the Implacable. He threw open the bedroom window, disgusted.

In a rush Boudreau found what he needed, starting with an ancient swimmer's jock he knew he'd flop out of. The only tennis shorts he could find had a big grease stain, but it was up near the waistband where his shirt would cover it if he left the tail out. The strings on his racquet, an obsolete steel Wilson like the one Jimmy Connors used to play with, were in good shape, anyway; his tennis shoes were intact, if filthy. At least he had a clean T-shirt and socks.

He hadn't shaved in days, but it was too late now and there was no water anyway. He grabbed a couple changes of street clothes, without any idea where he was going to stay. He just knew he couldn't stay here, not right now. Maybe he'd spend another night with Keith, if he could stand it.

Vicky sat in the Healey in the same position he'd left her in. *Just a mood,* he told himself, *it was just a mood.* The problem was, he was catching it. "Where we playing?" he said, back out on the road.

"The club," she said and then, after he looked at her, "I'll take care of it."

After a minute he turned the radio back on and got what sounded like a staticky cat howl. Then he recognized it. Clearly it was a weather choice, but he preferred to think some cosmic deejay was up there programming the tunes for them.

He turned to Vicky with a sardonic grin while he sang along, hitting the part about *yo' daddy's rich, and yo' momma's good-lookin'.*

She reached forward and punched another station. "I *hate* Janis Joplin," she said.

The six green clay courts were empty, heat waves shimmering over their surfaces. They crossed over and went through the baseline gate behind court three. Vicky Stover reached the broad-eaved shade of the attendant's kiosk and found a big Dixie cup sweating on the courtside bench. She shook it and peered inside.

Boudreau flopped down on the bench beside her. "Okay, that's enough exercise. Got any more drugs?" He was only half kidding.

Vicky rattled the cup. "Here's some ice."

The distant sounds of splashing and children screaming and laughing drifted up from the swimming pool. Boudreau caught a faint whiff of chlorine.

Vicky looked around, then leaned over the counter into the large open window at the far end of the kiosk. She came back out with two new cans of balls and a pad of paper; she winked at Boudreau, then scrawled something on the paper and shoved it back over the counter. "So let's play," she said.

"Just for the record," said Boudreau, "exactly how many times have we been out recently? I mean, so we're both telling Ronnie the same lie?"

Vicky got a dumb look on her face. "I'm sorry." She found his eyes then avoided them. "I should've told you. Is it okay?"

"Sure, of course." It wasn't okay. He couldn't take how she kept disappearing on him. "I'd just like to get it straight."

Two little boys in bathing suits and tennis shoes materialized down on the sixth court, their racquets half as big as they were, and began slamming balls around.

"I'm sorry," she said again. "It's fucked up. I should've told you. It's

131

not that big a deal, but I can't tell you about it. Not right now. It's sort of complicated."

Boudreau nodded and lit a cigarette. "It's just," he said, "it's just that it makes it a little hard to trust you."

Vicky turned and looked down to the last court, where the two boys were already in a dispute. The larger of the kids had just yelled at the other one, who was starting to cry.

"I'm sorry." She picked up the Dixie cup of ice, thought about it, then chewed some. "I can't tell *any*body."

Boudreau couldn't let go of it. "But do you know what I mean? It just makes me think you aren't being *honest* with me." He heard his voice rise to a slight whine on "honest."

Hot faced, she looked at him. "I said I'm *sorry*, Richter, I'm not exactly thrilled to play the conniving bitch either." She took another mouthful of ice and immediately spat it out. "Don't take it personally, okay? It's got nothing to do with you." She caught the dubious look on his face and gave him a little hard-edged smile, the kind that precedes one last explanation. "It doesn't mean I don't *love* you, Richter honey, okay? *Okay?*"

Boudreau was too confused to look at her. There was no way he couldn't take this personally. "Okay."

Down on the end court the bigger boy screamed again and threw his racquet across the net. Even though it missed, the littler boy yowled and dropped his own racquet, then took off for the gate in the back fence. The first boy stood still for a few seconds, before stalking out the gate on the near side, leaving it open behind him.

Vicky stood up and began bouncing up and down on her toes. "I *really* need to work some of this off. Can we please go hit now?"

Boudreau got up, knees popping, and followed her out into the full force of the sun. The metal gate was almost too hot to touch, the heat a good twenty degrees higher on the clay itself. He felt the vestiges of his hangover reappear, lining his skull like brittle pottery.

Vicky ripped the lids off the cans of balls while he looked down at the now-empty end court. The two racquets and a dozen balls were

strewn randomly across it, as though something had vaporized whoever
had been playing there.

They'd been hitting for about ten minutes when Boudreau saw the
car, a dark maroon Mercedes, pull into the parking lot behind Vicky.
Two men in tennis clothes got out, one of them immediately waving and
yelling something to her.

When they came through the end gate, the guy who'd called out
walked directly onto Vicky's court just as Boudreau was leaning into a
forehand. He altered his swing at the last instant and barely ticked a
piece of the ball, fouling it back over the fence and nearly losing his
balance in the process. He swore under his breath and went to retrieve
the ball.

Boudreau returned to find the man had already set his equipment bag
down in the middle of the court. Big and fair skinned, he had his arm
draped over Vicky's shoulder, dwarfing her as he gestured with his other
hand and laughed. He was thick limbed but not yet fat, a jock gone to
partial seed. The other man was unloading things from his own bag at
the net.

The first man approached, his arm still over Vicky's shoulder. He
leaned down and said something to her that ended in another loud
laugh. He was about Boudreau's age, maybe a year or two older.

Boudreau took an instant dislike to everything about him: his heavy
thighs, his coordinated tennis clothes, his too hearty laugh, his blocky
head with its too blond eyebrows and lashes.

"Chip, this is Richter Boudreau? He's an old family friend?"

The man stuck out his hand from across the net. "Chip Carlson," he
said. "I guess we might have us a doubles match here, huh?"

Boudreau shook his hand while Vicky continued her introductions.
He stared at the elaborate performance, not hearing a word. Without
warning, she had become her mother's daughter again, girlish and flirta-

tious, the beautiful good sport, a future leader of charitable organizations.

An old family friend. He was amazed at how effortlessly she metered it out, as though every word and gesture weren't total bullshit. He shook hands with the other guy and watched how the two of them ate her up. Her voice was edged with tease, musical with the appreciation of being in the presence of such fine, fine gentlemen. They bought her act without a second thought: this was elegant bitch pussy, bred for their admiration, trotting around the ring like quiver-muscled breeding stock.

Satisfied with her introduction, Vicky excused herself. "I just have to go to the little girls' room?"

Boudreau nearly choked. *The little girls' room?*

Chip Carlson knelt at his equipment bag and pulled out three identical racquets, then stood up. "That's a fine girl from a fine family." He addressed this to no one in particular. "She deserves better." He tested each racquet for heft. In his beefy hand they appeared light as flyswatters. "How long you known her, Richard?"

"*Rich*ter," Boudreau enunciated. "Since we were teenagers." This was information Vicky had conveyed in her introduction, along with his correct name, but the man had turned instantly perfunctory as soon as she left the court. "Her and Keith both."

"Is that right," said Carlson. "Keith, too." He turned from Boudreau and began lashing the air with some experimental backhands.

The other man, whose name was Reynolds, continued to unload his own bag. Between the two of them they had enough to open a pro shop. Reynolds stood up and pulled on some new wrist bands. He was late thirtyish and balding, as wiry as Chip Carlson was thick, and wore eyeglasses and a floppy tennis hat.

"And what is it you do, Richter?" Reynolds said.

"I watch movies," said Boudreau, getting a raised eyebrow out of Reynolds. He'd already forgotten his first name. "I write film reviews down at the *Journal,* and I teach film out at TU." Before he could stop himself, he let on that he was finishing up a screenplay, too. What was he hoping to prove to this guy, anyway?

"Film," said Reynolds. He contemplated. "And you teach that out at TU, do you?"

"Yeah, I teach genre courses, film history, film grammar." Boudreau didn't know why he bothered; he could tell that Reynolds thought teaching movies was a notch down from basketweaving.

"Film *grammar,"* Reynolds repeated. He shook his head in smiling appreciation.

Boudreau found himself smiling back. "How about you?"

"Well, I work with Chipper here in estate law." Reynolds gestured over at his partner, who was going through some vigorous warmup stretches. "I moved here from Little Rock last year and came on board down at McCann, Barrett." Reynolds leaned against the net post, proud as an astronaut.

"Yeah?" said Boudreau. "How's business in estate law these days?"

"Oh, I guess it's always the same," he said, so self-congratulatory that Boudreau wanted to punch him. Reynolds paused. "Estate law never changes. My business is death and taxes, and that's two things there's always plenty of."

Boudreau managed a faint smile. From the way Reynolds delivered it he could tell this was a line that had gotten him some big laughs.

Reynolds grabbed a racquet and did a couple of deep knee bends. "I guess it's you and me against beauty and the beast." He laughed at his own joke, on a roll now.

"Oh?" said Boudreau. "Well, why don't you two warm each other up till Vicky gets back. I'm warm enough." He realized then he was going to have to call the man something. "I'm sorry, I didn't quite get your first name?"

"Milton?" said the estate lawyer in his Arkie accent. "Milton Reynolds?" He got a fluffy white towel out of his bag. "Call me Milt."

"Milt," repeated Boudreau. *"Milt.* Isn't that some of kind of like, fish sperm?" Unable to stop himself, he deepened his voice into a documentary narrator's. "You know, like, 'After the courtship takes place, the male largemouth sprays the egg clusters with *milt.* Reproduction is then complete.' "

The man lost his smile. He gave Boudreau a look, his head cocked, uncertain as to how much offense he should take.

"Sorry." Boudreau smiled like a jerk. "It just came to mind."

Milton Reynolds swallowed. His prominent Adam's apple shot up, then fell, as though Boudreau had just pounded the bell on a carnival strength meter. When his smile finally returned, it was even more purely condescending than it had been before.

Sitting in the shade of the still-empty attendant's booth, smoking another cigarette, he watched the two lawyers warm up. Carlson swatted the ball hard but without much control; Reynolds had corkscrew ground strokes, each shot a little aria of contortion. Boudreau anticipated his pleasure in showing these guys how bad they were.

Vicky Stover sat down next to him.

"How was the little girls' room," he asked. "Any little girls in there?"

She ignored the sarcasm and reached for his pack of Marlboros and the matches, then lit up. "Listen," she said, "Chip is going to drop me off a few blocks from home, okay, but I have to tell Ronnie you did." She flicked a quick look at him to see how it would play. "Something came up."

"Something came up?" This was getting to be a little too much. "Anything else? Did it snow today?"

She immediately leaned forward, elbows on her knees, absorbed in peeling apart the layers of the spent paper match. She took a quick drag of her cigarette. "I'm sorry. This whole scene is getting me down."

"That makes two of us."

She nodded miserably and tossed the frayed match away, keeping her eyes on it. "I said I'm sorry, okay? It's sort of complicated."

"You said that too."

"*Please*, Richter." She touched his arm. "I don't like this lying and

sneaking around, I especially don't like dragging you into it, but I—"
She trailed off. "I don't know, it's—"

"Complicated," Boudreau finished.

She snorted mirthlessly and took her hand away. "I guess it's not that complicated." She gnawed at her lower lip and exhaled her cigarette smoke, then turned her head and looked at Boudreau, blue eyes straight into his. "Do you swear you won't say anything?"

Boudreau hesitated, then held up three fingers in a scout's honor.

"How did Keith seem to you?" she said then.

"Keith?" Boudreau sat back. "You mean in general?" He lifted his shoulders. "Not good. I mean, you know, *Keith*. The same."

"Yeah," said Vicky. "Right. That's what Chip said. He's been calling me for help. I guess Keith may be in some real trouble this time." She bit off a laugh, coming out of it in an accent. "Pore little black lamb? I guess he didn't do so good at his latest facility?" She gave a tight-cheeked little smile. "Oh Lordy, *now* what're we gonna do?"

"What's the problem?"

Vicky shook the question away. "Let's just say it's nothing out of character? But so anyway, don't you just *love* it? I mean, I haven't said ten words to Chip Carlson since the day he informed me of daddy's dying wishes, which let me tell you was a *very* cordial day." She stared out at the court. "And now that daddy's trustees can't do what he couldn't do, who gets the call? Who do you think hops to it?"

Boudreau watched her. Even though she had turned to face him, he got the feeling she was talking to someone not there.

"Poor old Keithie! Well, I am just *sick* of him! I am *sick* of my fucking family!"

"Hey *hey,*" said Boudreau, holding up his palms to ward her off. "I didn't do nothing."

She took a deep breath, then bit her upper lip and leaned forward again, elbows on her knees. She supported her forehead with one hand. The cigarette dropped out of her other hand onto the ground, and her shoulders began to move slightly.

Although her back heaved gently, there was no sound. Her hair, tied

up in a ponytail that was in turn fastened with a barette to the top of
her head, left her neck exposed. Boudreau could see tiny droplets of
sweat suspended in the fine little hairs on her nape. Her neck looked
slender and vulnerable, her shoulders small and round with woe.

Boudreau felt a web of ache appear high in his chest. In spite of
himself he wanted to scoop her up in a bundle and shake her, hold her,
lick every drop of salt sweat off her body.

She finally stepped on the smoldering butt and sat up, then leaned
back in a slump against the bench, as though resting after heavy exer-
tion. She sniffed a couple of times and cleared her throat. Her eyes were
still welling over but the crying was done; she was self-contained again.

"I didn't mean to drag you into this, Richter, I swear I didn't."

"So then why'd you do it?" said Boudreau.

She looked confused by the question. "Do what?"

Boudreau could hardly wait. "Lie to Ronnie."

She stiffened slightly, fingers lacing together across her stomach. "Oh,
just he hates my family, is all, he'd *kill* me if he found out I was doing
this." Vicky stared straight ahead at the chain-link fence, clearly aware
of Boudreau watching her. "He might anyway," she added after a while.

"Excuse me?" he said.

"I believe he thinks I'm having an *affair?*" She shrugged her shoulders
in a why-not gesture. "And do you know what?" she said. "By now I
guess I just don't care what he thinks?" *Whut he thanks?* She turned
and looked right at him. "I mean, I *have* thought about it?"

Boudreau stared until she looked away, a smirk on her face. He began
nodding, conprehension arriving in successive waves. He looked at the
bruise on her arm, faded now so it looked like little smudges of dirt.
Things fell into perspective.

Boudreau put a hand on her shoulder. It was firm, moist from the
heat.

"Do you understand, Richter honey?" She put her own hand on top
of his, then removed it to stand up. "When this is over, we'll play alone
sometime, okay?"

Chip Carlson was waving them onto the court, while Milt Reynolds
toweled himself off.

"So, Vicky." He opened the baseline gate and waited. "How come you're doing it?"

She stopped halfway through. "Doing what?"

"Keith?" he said. "You know, your brother?"

"Oh, *that*. You mean what's the point?" She lifted her eyebrows in mock concern. "You mean y'all don't think I'm a concerned sister?" She thought for a moment. "Let's just say I'm tired of who I am these days?" A crooked smile appeared on her face as she continued through the gate. "And I thought it might be fun to be someone different."

"Yeah?" said Boudreau after her. "And is it?"

"Not so far," she said, and walked to the other side of the net.

It was 5–2 and 15–love; Boudreau readied himself to receive Chip Carlson's serve. It was nothing special, just an out-of-control flat wallop that could easily be blocked back. Carlson hitched up his shorts and bounced the ball a few times.

Boudreau stepped aside as the first serve boomed long, then moved up a few feet. Carlson deployed his stupid little moonball of a second serve, as though trying out a slingshot after missing with the rocket launcher. The ball floated up high on Boudreau's forehand, an invitation to him to make Chip Carlson eat the return. It was the kind of shot Boudreau could make blindfolded. He leaned into the ball and pasted it four feet past the baseline.

Boudreau swore in disbelief and walked back up to the net.

"Swing through, pard, just swing through," said Milt Reynolds behind him. "Don't have to kill it."

Boudreau grunted without turning around. If Reynolds called him "pard" one more time, he was going to recontour his throat for him. Now he was giving advice on Boudreau's strokes, this from a guy whose backhand looked like he was fending off small animals.

Carlson faulted on the next point, then served up his blooper and stomped in behind it. Reynolds fed him a nice high backhand volley,

which he put away past Boudreau, who waved his racquet, disgusted, as
it went by.

He waited for the next serve at 40–love, gingerly kneading his right
hand. He was raising blisters already.

This time Carlson got his first one in. Distracted, Boudreau became
aware of it an instant too late. He flinched and leaned away as he swung,
tipping the ball off sideways into the next court.

Chip Carlson whooped, and gave Vicky a light swat on the ass with
his racquet as he came toward the net. She kept her eyes forward, fixed
on something that apparently amused her. At the net post she said
something to him, then picked up her purse and skipped to the gate.

Carlson shook his head fondly. "She's got to powder her nose again,"
he announced, admiring her every effluvium.

Back from the can a few minutes later, she picked up her racquet and
snukked a few times, then bounced onto the court, full of chat for Chip
Carlson. He watched her, head cocked and smiling. Boudreau doubted
if Carlson knew how apt his euphemism had been.

Boudreau watched, the web of ache reappearing high in his chest.
Him? *Him?*

"Okay, pard, we got a whole new set now." Milt Reynolds turned, his
face grim with determination. "Whole new set."

"Yeah, right," said Boudreau.

A whole new set: the game was structured in discrete little increments
to keep people like Milt Reynolds going, the hope of new beginnings
dangling endlessly in front of them. If you double-faulted this point, you
could still ace the next one. If you lost this game, you could fight right
back. If you got blown away the first set, you could tie it up in the
second. And if nothing worked out—hey, you could always come back
another day.

Of course at any point the whole thing could shift as suddenly as an
avalanche. Each new point then became an opportunity to get buried
deeper under the evidence of your own failure. It was insidious, a game
that pitted you mostly against yourself and then let other people take
credit while you somehow lost.

As the whole new set progressed, he remembered once again why he only played tennis maybe once a year, ever since he'd quit the high school team in his junior year. His coach had taken him aside and delivered the standard-issue lecture about winners and quitters and the game of life. Boudreau could buy the analogy but not the conclusion. Tennis was like life, sure, insofar as most people kept playing under the false impression that things would get better if they just kept trying.

"I believe that's five–three now, friends and neighbors," Carlson called across the court in a voice buttery with satisfaction. Boudreau knew this was for his benefit; he began to hate him so much his stomach hurt.

He had just double-faulted the game point of his own serve, after already losing his serve in the second game. The racquet felt alien in his hand, no matter how he held it. He had no idea where his ground strokes were going until he saw where they went. His mind was doing him in. Even Milt Reynolds had grown silent, apparently figuring Boudreau was beyond coaching.

He cursed himself for not having folded. His hand was killing him, raw as a piece of meat, the blisters long popped. The skin on his face felt deep fried, an hour of court glare on top of his pool sunburn. He could've made any number of honest claims.

Instead, he had dumbly hung in, rejecting as untenable anything that could be construed as giving in to Chip Carlson. As the set had progressed, his mind filled between points with the same image of Vicky Stover under Carlson's meaty thighs. His tennis got worse and worse, his focus finally narrowed to the state of his own mind, a bubbling stew of self-hatred that grew richer with each missed shot. Just to embellish the spectacle, he began losing his temper. Each time he swore, he could see Chip Carlson's lips tighten. Vicky stopped looking at him entirely.

Then she lost her serve. By some fluke Boudreau hit two winners to take the game. One was lucky, a forehand that hit the tape and dribbled over. But the next was a certifiably great shot, a down-the-alley backhand ripper that caught Carlson so flat-footed he hardly saw it.

They switched courts, Boudreau and Reynolds over to the parking lot side. Milt was getting fired up again. "Five–four, pard. We can pull this thing out."

Boudreau resisted the urge to advise him on what he could pull out. The guy was still interested in winning, the farthest thing from Boudreau's mind. He wanted to hit a few more humiliating shots then lose, just enough to let them know he didn't give a shit, he'd just been fooling around.

Reynolds served and Boudreau personally lost the next two points, the second one on an extreme cross-court volley that landed four inches out. "I had the whole fucking *court!*" He couldn't believe it. The whole court was open, but no, he had to put it on the line.

Milt walked back to the baseline to serve again. Then he waited with a sour look on his face as a car pulled into a slot right behind the fence. A single figure got out of the car and hesitated to watch the point, a silhouette behind the woven green nylon that screened off the parking lot.

Reynolds, assured now that his delicately calibrated serve wouldn't be affected by the disruption, put the ball in play. When it came back to Boudreau on the baseline, he mis-hit it and lost the point, then bellowed. "Shit! *Shit!*"

Chip Carlson walked back up to the net. "I've had about enough out of you, Richard." He looked back at Vicky.

Boudreau realized the man was concerned for the purity of her ears. It was more than he could stand. "The name is *Richter,* Chipper."

Milt Reynolds hit the match-point serve to interrupt them. It went to Carlson, who played it cautiously and hit a soft, deep lob back to Reynolds. He hit a deep blooper in turn and then came up to the net, a stupid move. Carlson lobbed it over Boudreau's head to the now empty backcourt. Boudreau turned and ran as the ball receded away from him, hitting right on the baseline with a big hop. He caught up with it just as they both hit the fence.

Boudreau lost his last shred of control. It was too much, it was all way too much. He swore at a volume that made his own voice sound funny, then began to beat on the fence with his racquet. He found no satisfaction in the shock of the blows but couldn't stop. Ten feet away he caught a movement behind the scrim of green nylon.

Boudreau felt a wash of humiliation come flooding in where his rage had been. He stomped his foot, swearing now under his breath. The veiled figure moved closer, stopping on the other side of the fence, just opposite. *"Richter!"* came the voice.

He couldn't believe it. *"Mom?"* he said.

"I have *never* been so embarrassed." Cynthia Whitlow Boudreau Simpson Rowling kept her voice at a low hiss. "Are you *done?* Are you *done* now?"

Boudreau was mortified. "Yeah, I'm done."

He pressed up to the green material of the fence until he could see through it to the other side. His mother stood there in a summery floral dress with a pleated skirt. She wore white high heels and carried a white purse. Through the veil of green nylon she hardly looked any older than he did.

"So how was your trip, Mom?" he said.

Cynthia Rowling turned and began walking away down the fence line, heels clicking. "Why, thank you, Richter, I accept your gracious apology."

Boudreau followed on his side, girding himself to pay up, the price tag clear from her tone. "I'm sorry," he said. "Mom? Mom, I'm sorry, it was hardly for your benefit."

"Oh? Then I guess it must have been for yours?" She kept walking. "I hope you know those people well."

"Mom, *please.*"

She stopped. "Well, move on down to the gate so at least I can see you."

Boudreau walked to the back fence gate on the fourth court. A whole file drawer of unsettled accounts popped open, not least of which was the burned carpet and the blackmailed doorman. Ronnie's film can of dope occupied an entire cabinet of its own. He inhaled deeply, opened the gate and stepped through it.

They pantomimed a hug and a kiss like actors on a dress run-through, performed at a remove of several inches because of his sweatiness. He stood back. "Gosh you look great," he said.

Boudreau's mother straightened slightly. "Thank you." She regarded him for a moment in return, taking in his overall level of funk. "When you feel good, I think it shows, don't you?" She lifted her chin a bit, as though presenting it for scrutiny.

Boudreau hadn't seen his mother since Christmas, but that wasn't it. Her skin looked a little too tight over her cheekbones, and there was something strange about the corners of her eyes. "Well, *you* look great," Boudreau repeated, "so you must feel great."

Further mollified, she gave the skirt a little coquettish flounce. "I do. I feel pretty darn good."

She'd had another face-lift. Uncertain about the protocol of openly acknowledging a mother's cosmetic surgery, he decided to keep his mouth shut. It would be like complimenting a toupee.

"So," he said, "you're back a little early, huh?" As soon as he said it, he caught himself, too late.

"Well, I *was* supposed to get back yesterday, but then that was changed till tomorrow." She eyed him. "I guess you could say I'm early."

Boudreau struggled to keep his face neutral. In spite of his father's nominal profession, she had always been the better lawyer in the family.

"Didn't Billy tell you I bumped into him yesterday? I dropped by on the way to work, just when he was getting back from the airport. He said you weren't coming back till tomorrow."

"No," Cynthia Rowling said. "No, Billy didn't say anything. I just dashed in from the airport and then dashed out here." Her eyes narrowed. "Of course when you called Wednesday morning, I wasn't coming back till Monday."

"Yeah, I know." Boudreau gave an innocent shrug, racing to improvise. How could he have known Billy would keep his mouth shut? "I was on my way to work and I just thought I'd"—he smiled and looked down—"leave some flowers."

"Flowers?"

It sounded like shameless bullshit even to him. "Yeah, *flowers,*" he said, trying to add a note of offended pride that she would doubt him.

"Then I realized they'd be wilted by the time you got back. I should've just left them with Billy."

"Flowers?" his mother repeated. "The first phone call I've had in months, then flowers?"

He nodded and shrugged, a confused ninny in the witness stand. She'd bought the flowers, now he had to buy them back.

A tight, knowing little smile came over her face. "What is it that you want, Richter?"

He held up a palm, staving off further cross-examination. "I don't *want* anything. I'd just, I'd just like to clear the air between us."

She waited for more.

He needed a semblance of the truth. "I have some things I'd like to discuss."

His mother lifted an eyebrow and nodded, her head tilted to one side. "All right." Her tone said she'd finally gotten to the bottom of things, having suspected all along. "I happen to have a few things of my own to discuss. Let's have lunch tomorrow."

This was a lot sooner than what Boudreau had in mind. He squinted up, consulting his busy social calendar for a Sunday lunch slot. The sound of a car starting up brought him out of it.

Boudreau leaned back through the gate in the fence. The maroon Mercedes had just lurched out of reverse and pulled a U-turn at the far end of the lot. There were only two people in it, but then he saw the top of Milt Reynolds's bald head bobbing down the grassy hill beyond the courts, toward the pool and clubhouse.

He leaned back through the gate. "Sure. Yeah, sure, tomorrow's fine."

His mother cocked her head as she looked at him, as though she'd just noticed something.

"What?" He worried at what the look might mean.

"Nothing." She shrugged it away. "Just that expression on your face, it reminded me of Malcolm Boudreau." She said his father's name as though he had been a mutual but casual acquaintance. She consulted his features and shrugged again. "He was a very handsome man before he let himself go."

Boudreau searched her face for some sign of how to take this.

"Okay, then," she said. "Tomorrow at one. Why don't you come here to the grill."

"Fine." He dreaded it already.

"Good." She started to turn and then stopped. "Was that Vicky Michaels you were playing with? Or Vicky Whatever-she's-called-now?"

"Stover."

"Whatever," she said. "I thought so. And how is she?"

"Just fine," said Boudreau.

"Good, I'm glad to hear that. Okay, see you tomorrow then. And, Richter? *Please* shave."

Boudreau watched his mother make her way toward the clubhouse veranda, her heels clicking on the concrete. From behind she looked like an athletic forty-year-old.

He picked up his racquet and walked back across the green clay, the heat following him like a magnifying glass above a bug.

Leaning on the window counter of the shack, the tennis pro had finally appeared. He watched as Boudreau approached to retrieve his keys and wallet and cigarettes from the bench.

"How's it going?" said Boudreau.

The pro regarded him glum-faced and said nothing.

Boudreau tried again. "Too hot to teach?"

The guy just stared. A Scotsman from Johannesburg, he had fallen off the bottom rung of the pro tour and landed feet-first in Tulsa, opting for steady money and the occasional piece of off-court action. Boudreau had never actually met the man but had once seen him play a remarkable exhibition match three or four years before. He'd covered the court so fast and low to the ground there was something distinctly simian about it.

The pro waved a small piece of paper at him. "Who wrote this?" he said. He was short and muscular and deeply tanned, with curly blond hair and a broken nose that made him look a little thuggish.

"What?" Boudreau was taken back by the guy's tone.

Slapping the piece of paper down on the counter, the pro shoved it across with one thick finger while he stared into Boudreau's face.

Boudreau looked back at him. Perfectly cast as a club pro, he was the faintly proletarian white hunter, rough but with deferential manners, hired for muscle and sweat. Boudreau didn't really want to get any closer to him.

He stepped forward and looked down at the piece of paper. It was a club chit for two cans of balls. Where the signature was supposed to be, it said, in Vicky Stover's handwriting, "Your balls for my sweet ass."

Boudreau snickered and looked up.

The pro stared out at the empty courts, his jaw tight. "Perhaps it was whoever did all that cursing." He said the word *cursing* with a faint Scottish burr.

"Gee, there were two kids out there a little while ago," said Boudreau, pointing at the end court. There was no way he could take this seriously. "Maybe it was them."

"And are you a member?" the pro asked.

Boudreau looked at him, then smiled. He wouldn't be talking to him like this if he didn't already know the answer. "No. I am not personally a member, no."

"Then who were you playing with?"

Boudreau could feel the smile muscles tightening over his cheekbones. "Just a minute, pal," he said. "Are you saying *I* wrote that?"

"I'm asking: Who you were playing with, mister?"

Boudreau looked away and shook his head gently. *Mister.* He turned back. "I was playing in a foursome at the invitation of my good friend Chip Carlson, who you can call if you want to make a fool of yourself." Boudreau smirked at him. "Maybe if you weren't so busy hustling teenage pussy, you could have seen it for yourself."

The man's face turned ugly purple under his tan. "Get out." He said it through his teeth. "Get out of here right now."

"Sure thing, pal," said Boudreau, the jaunty smirk frozen on his face like a death mask. "Hope you find your man."

He turned and walked away, legs shaking. What was he *doing?* He was lucky the South African didn't take him apart and use the leftovers for service practice, then drag his carcass into the club to show his mother.

Someday, maybe, he was going to learn when to quit.

Boudreau fought the late-afternoon Saturday traffic back into town. There was a single long shoal of clouds to the south-west, parallel to the horizon and slightly above it. The clouds were dingy with particulates, but there was no rain in them; a colorful sunset was the most they'd produce.

No matter where he thought to turn there was already a line of cars in front of him. He waited with them, breathing exhaust fumes and taking more sun in the face, a fighter in a late-round beating.

That he was driving back to Keith's came as a surprise to him, but really, what else could he do? Of course he'd have to bad-mouth Vicky a little, which wouldn't be hard, and then Keith would let it ride after a while. He'd have a shower, and after that a drink. *Bourbon.*

No. Drink first, then shower. Okay, whatever. Drinks and shower, they ran together in his mind.

The little car felt like an industrial centrifuge, loud and hot and full of vibration. It took all the concentration he had to obey basic traffic laws and remember to keep his hand on the stick in third.

He drove on, swooning with need at the vision of amber fluid swirling in a glass.

The big trees were stretching into early-evening shadow as he raced down Keith's street and pulled into the driveway. It was empty: the white GTO was gone, along with Rena's old Chevy. Boudreau turned off the ignition, stunned. He somehow hadn't considered this as a possibility.

He was filthy and his face hurt from salt sweat and sunburn; his blister-popped hand throbbed with every beat of his heart. He got out of the car, a muscle somewhere between his hamstring and his ass alerting him to its stiffening presence.

Boudreau lit a cigarette. He could at least do a cursory check around the house. He hobbled down the driveway, around to the back.

He began a circumnavigation of the house, peering behind shrubs for an open window. In a few minutes he'd be driving all the way back out to Broken Arrow on less than a quarter tank of gas, four and a half dollars in his wallet. Then he'd arrive chez Boudreau, and there would be nothing to drink, nothing to smoke, no way to get high. In his stifling house with no water or light, fridge hot and empty, he was going to be alone with the contents of his own mind.

The big house loomed monolithically above him, silent. Boudreau decided to break a window. He picked up a rock, hefted it, then caught himself. *This was out of control.* He was acting like a skulker, someone the police would like to know about. The alarm system was probably on anyway, and besides, who knew how Keith would take it? Bullshitting him was one thing; breaking into his house was another entirely.

Boudreau decided he'd at least jump in the pool for a quick rinse. This would only add to the chlorine still on his skin from the morning swim, but at least it would delay the return home by a few minutes. He walked back to the Healey for his clothes, an image popping to the surface of his mind like a cork.

It was a view of his body—*him*—drifting facedown in the bottom of the pool.

Boudreau grew brisk. He retrieved his clothes from the car, then lit another cigarette so he could have a pleasant smoke on his walk down to the pool. Life wasn't so bad, you just had to take care to enjoy the small things.

On his way back past the house he hopped up the five steps to the delivery-entrance door, the only one he hadn't bothered to check. He prayed, then tried it on the off chance. It was open.

On the counter just inside the kitchen was a note under a beer bottle.

BOO:

THINGS ARE FUCKED UP. I'M IN OK. CITY TILL TUESDAY, I CAN'T HANDLE

IT. RENA WENT HOME FOR WEEKEND. HELP YOURSELF EVERYBODY ELSE
DOES.

KEY

At the bottom was an almost illegible "P.S.—ARE YOU REALLY MY
FRIEND."

Boudreau put his clothes on the counter beside the note, then headed
for the bar off the living room. A friend in need, now *that* was a friend
indeed.

Boudreau sat with his feet up on the giant walnut desk in Joe Michaels's study. He worked on his second drink, pleasantly lit, and
watched the local news on the huge television in the wall of bookshelves.
In a little while he'd shower up, then root through the opulent Michaels
pantry for something to eat. This was exactly the ticket: a little solitude
in which to reflect. He needed to give some thought to his life's direction, he knew he did.

Meantime he began idly ransacking Joe Michaels's desk; he had all
night to reflect. In the middle drawer he came upon a film can of
marijuana and a pack of rolling papers. Keith didn't smoke pot anymore,
but Boudreau chose not to question his good fortune. Old and dry, it
was still definitely smokable. He rolled up an item, ignoring the invitation to consider the other film can in his life. Later for that.

Halfway through the joint, Boudreau noticed that his cheeks had gone
numb. This was more like it. Now he could be there without really being
there, the exact state he'd been searching for. He let the joint go out,
then lit a cigarette and sipped at the bourbon.

He goofed on the news for a while, then a game show. Distracted as
a monkey, he began rummaging through the rest of Joe Michaels's desk.
In the last drawer he came upon one of Keith's pornographic magazines.

Boudreau spread it out on the desktop to get a better look. Boy was
he stoned. He inhaled sharply and forgot all about the TV.

Entitled *Call-Girl Cunt*, its front cover had a color photograph of a naked young blond woman on her back. She was looking up at the camera, her tongue out as far as she could get it. There was a man, too, straddling her chest. All that could be seen of him was his legs, torso and a larger than usual pecker. He was in the process of coming on the girl's face, his thin gelid loops halfway there, fixed by high-speed film.

Turgid with raunch, Boudreau unzipped his tennis shorts and began thumbing the pages, making a quick survey of the pimpled asses and stubbly-shaven pubes, shot in closeups so extreme they looked like photos of flood-lit sea creatures, bumpy and glistening. Some of the pictures were accompanied by text, apparently written by a nonnative speaker. "His huge love-meat undulated hotly inside the bitch, her pussy exploding with wild and satisfied pleasure." There was more, veering uncomfortably over the border into discipline and domination. Boudreau hurried by, staying with the pictures.

The women tried to look thrilled while clots of sperm dripped from their hair and noses and chins. Except for the occasional biker-grade tattoo, not much was shown of the men, just their wangers and all the delight they produced.

The fantasy was so transparent, and here he was with a raging hard-on. He got hung up on it. Okay, maybe it was pathetic, but horny was horny. Mind and body parted company while he theorized about it. This kind of jism worship probably had to do with how pointless the stuff had become in the face of annihilation. Why not fertilize faces? Why not pretend women liked it? It was just more late-stage culture, on a par with celebrity salutes on TV, with getting a ham-bone actor to play the president as a reassuring uncle. *Okay, bitch, the end is near. America's about to come on your face.*

He turned back to the pages that featured the woman from the cover. In one shot, on her hands and knees while the man dorked her from behind, she looked over her shoulder right at the camera. Boudreau tried to imagine what she was thinking, fucking some guy she'd probably never seen before while she stared into the lens that would preserve it. And there he was, one more in an endless row of men hunched over their magazines, jerking off.

Boudreau simply could not believe that the body here belonged to anybody real. It was like looking at pictures of dead people. Heart-knocking stoned, he stared.

The blond wasn't bad actually, fleshy but lithe, tough faced. She was penetrated here and there as casually as if the anonymous dick were some kind of weird medical instrument: tongue depressor, proctoscope and speculum rolled into one. Okay, this was just a real person in a surreal situation, that's all. He could relate to that.

There was probably a litter of empty coffee cups and overflowing ashtrays just outside the frame. Boudreau wondered what her voice sounded like, what she said while they set up the shots, what kind of clothes she wore on the way home, what kind of family she grew up in. This, he decided, would be an interesting person to know.

Here she was running her tongue along the underside of the penis. Having sex with someone like that would definitely be no-nonsense. Now she was pillowing the penis between her breasts. No fake romance, no strings, no scenes. Here, you do that. Now I'll do this. Okay, now you do that. No, *here*. Yeah. That's it.

Boudreau came a big one into the wad of Kleenex he had waiting. By the time he opened his eyes to the picture that had done the trick, his interest had wilted along with his penis; he closed the magazine immediately. It might as well have been dogs or pigs, baboons, the reproductive habits of another species. Still breathing hard, he wiped himself off and shoved the magazine back in the drawer.

He zipped up his shorts and drained the dregs of his bourbon, then focused on the task of relighting the joint. It was *hard* being a man; he was no better at it than he'd been at the age of sixteen. Stoned, he turned over this notion in his mind like a hard lump of coal, looking for some facet of it that would yield insight. From Ginny to Vicky Stover to Arla Thompson to What's-her-name, Val, he just never got any smarter, never had any better luck. The list went back, farther than he cared to review. His dick had led him around like a blind worm with a death wish. Stick it in or not, all he got was desperate. He might as well just give up.

His ex-wife had refined his flaws into just such a final charge, the summation that preceded the sentence. He was the kind of guy who *gave up*, who ran away from everything. Okay, maybe it hadn't been his finest hour. She sure as hell hadn't helped.

His marriage had collapsed like a slowly failing bridge, passion being one of the first supports to go. Maybe she could ignore the signs, but he sure couldn't: life was lonely enough already. He started stepping out whenever he could, discreetly at first, then not so much.

Somewhere in there—they were in bad shape already, though he couldn't place it exactly—Ginny's hair had fallen out. She'd had an incredible mane of hair, a blond cascade of dense corkscrew curls as wide as her shoulders; then without reason she lost it. It started with an overloaded hairbrush, but by the next day it was coming out by the fistful. A week later she was bald.

The second dermatologist diagnosed the same thing as the first: Unexplained Hair Loss. Who knows, he said, could be stress, climate change, allergy, virus, hard to say. He prescribed cortisone shots and a wig. They walked out of his office together, but from there they might as well have taken cabs to different planets.

The TV blared from across the room, the game show ending in a fanfare of cued applause and product plugs. The noise was intolerable. Boudreau wobbled over to turn it off, a wet web of stickiness blooming between him and his jockstrap, a little reminder of just how great his sex life had become since then.

Stripped of sound, the emptiness of the big house was crushing. He felt strung out, fragile in the silence. This sucked. Maybe next he should contemplate nuclear war. By the time he sat back down in the big leather chair to roll another joint he was crying.

Women were just a fucking well of loneliness, and he kept falling in.

Route 66—Eleventh Street—was lined with discount gas stations and western-clothing stores, faceless one-story commercial buildings and big used-car lots with strings of tattered plastic pennants. Once the interstate had gotten built, Eleventh had become as shabby as the rest of 66, passed by, its businesses as far out of the mainstream as the people who still traveled it. At night everything looked even more deserted, the broken curbs and littered median islands garish in the humid glow of obsolete street lights.

Boudreau passed Memorial Avenue, then missed his side street. He braked hard and whipped the wheel, pulling a U-turn to make it. Lying in the mouth of the side street was a half-flattened, rusted muffler, which he didn't see until it was too late. He cringed as he bumped over it, expecting one of his bald tires to blow.

The bar was half a block off Eleventh in a "shopping center" that consisted of a big square of cracked asphalt bordered on one side by a weed-filled lot. Along the other two sides was a collection of marginal storefronts: a children's discount shoe store, an unfranchised donut shop, a used–business-furniture place, a school-ring and athletic-trophy concern that seemed to have gone out of business, a custom van conversion shop.

In the corner of the L was the Sixty-Six Club, with a scattering of cars out in front. At night it had the whole parking lot to itself. In one of its two big paint-blackened windows was a fluorescent orange sign that said *Adult Entertainment Nitely.*

Boudreau pushed through the front door and the traffic noise from Eleventh disappeared. It was like walking into an underground cave. The world shrank down to cool air and dim light, the sound of clinking ice and low-level bullshit. Without making any eye contact, he was aware of being checked out. He stood a little taller and went straight to the bar.

The bartender sold him a "membership," then a bourbon. Taking the drink, he sat down at a table against the back wall. He made himself wait a full minute before he pulled on the drink, eyes closed. When he opened them, the whiskey was half-gone.

He was sitting in the larger of two rooms, at one of maybe twenty tiny tables. At the opposite end was a jukebox against a bare wall; next to the juke, what passed for a stage. It was a round platform, five or six feet in diameter, a single step off the floor. Next to that was a doorway "backstage" with a couple of curtains strung across it.

The bar started in the corner and ran down the length of the wall. The line of stools was already half-filled, but only four or five of the tables had occupants yet.

Across from Boudreau was a smaller room containing the exit and the johns and a pool table. He watched two pot-bellied guys in cowboy boots and leisure suits play a scratch-filled game of eight ball. Taped on one of the painted-out windows behind them was a black-light poster of the sexual positions of the zodiac. The position for Boudreau's sign looked like it would break his back.

He looked at his watch. Ronnie was never on time, but it was nine-twenty already. He'd give it till he finished this drink. Being alone at Keith's had been bad enough.

Boudreau looked up to find a small-eyed man with a greased-back DA standing over him. He wore a bar apron, and his forearms bristled with thick black hair.

"Girls ain't coming on till ten," said the man.

"Girls?" Boudreau said.

"Yeah, the *dancing* girls?" The man prompted him like a student slow to grasp a simple concept. "Not till ten."

"Oh, right." Boudreau smiled. He'd forgotten about dancers. "I don't care, I'm just waiting to meet somebody."

The barman gave him a wink devoid of humor, then folded his arms without budging, as if he expected more conversation. Finally Boudreau understood that the guy probably heard this a hundred times a night. You didn't get to just sit there with a hard-on for free.

He held up his glass. "Lemme just finish this, okay?"

"Yeah, sure," said the man. "Girls at ten." He moved on to the next table.

Boudreau sat up a little straighter and tried to look like a frat man waiting for his brothers. At least he'd showered and shaved and put on clean clothes. Out of the corner of his eye he watched the barman hassle another loner a couple of tables away.

This was a definite raincoat type, drunk already, a rangy redneck with a long, undershot jaw and no visible cheekbones at all. His glassy eyes were set in his face like marbles high on a blank wall. He wore a short-sleeved white shirt that exposed big faded tattoos on both forearms, a screaming tiger on one, a Jesus on the cross on the other.

"That big nigger gal dancing tonight?" The drunk glared at the barman. "Nigger gal ain't dancing, I ain't buying no drink."

The barman gave the guy a look like he was very impressed.

The drunk feared the worst. "She ain't dancing?"

"Tits're tits, mister," said the barman. "You want a drink or no?"

The man's cheeks went concave with woe and he nodded yes. A drink was better than nothing.

Boudreau turned away from the scene, wondering how the cracker had gotten this particular little kink in his hose.

"Ever do a nigger gal?" the man said. "You do a nigger gal, I guarantee you won't forget it."

Boudreau chanced another look and saw that the barman had already moved on. The guy was talking to *him* now.

"It's like sliding into pork fat," the man amplified.

Boudreau pretended not to have heard and looked away, busying himself with another cigarette. This was getting a little tawdry.

Standing at the bar, Boudreau tried to get the bartender's attention.

The place had become a zoo, the tables all taken and people standing two-deep behind the stools at the bar. Thick banks of cigarette smoke hung in the air. Boudreau scanned the crowd for Ronnie, trying not to look horny. He'd decided he could wait through one more drink; the place had definitely gained in sociological interest.

A good half of the crowd was couples, out on a Saturday night date to the local wiggler bar. Maybe one or two of the women were worth looking at. The clientele of the Sixty-Six Club was not a handsome bunch.

The basic patron was either skinny and gangly or lumpy and misshapen, sometimes both at the same time. Boudreau hadn't seen so much unhealthy skin since junior high. The dress code was urban redneck, the clothes cheap and ill fitting, discount-center fashions bought one payday and falling apart by the next. They had faces pinched by shit jobs or no jobs at all, bodies distorted by lack of exercise or too much of the wrong kind. Their diets were bad, and their educations would keep them from ever learning any different. They would have more kids than they could handle, and then their kids would marry each other and do it all over again.

The standard lumpen analysis held, but it was more than that. Defeat clung to them like cheap cologne. It gave Boudreau a chill: they were *pissed.* They knew that to be poor was to be ugly by definition, almost as bad as not being white. It was the motor that kept it all going, rich and pretty, poor and ugly, near the bottom but not yet on it. Boudreau felt invisible, an anthropologist at the potlatch. There was a distinctly violent vibe in the air. They were ready to party.

He finally got his drink and fought his way back through the mob, just as a couple were in the process of sitting down at his table.

" 'Scuse me, that's my table." He considered explaining how he'd been sitting there all night, then gave up. He was more drunk than he'd thought.

Short and wiry, his nose broken, the man in the couple sized up Boudreau. "I see two of us," he said. "I on'y see one of you."

"Yeah, well," said Boudreau, "I got a friend coming."

"Uh-huh." The shortie turned to his girlfriend to confirm what a lame peckerhead this dude was. "Sit down," he told her.

Boudreau was within a word or two of giving up when Ronnie appeared beside him. "This here's my friend," he said. "I guess that makes two."

"What's the deal here?" said Ronnie.

The man looked up into Ronnie's black shades. "Hey, no problem." He took his woman by the elbow and didn't look back.

Boudreau sat down, but Ronnie stood a moment longer to scope things out. He was wearing cowboy boots and jeans with no belt, a tight white T-shirt on top. His blond pompadour was carefully combed and he was clean shaven.

He pulled up a chair and sat down, pushed his shades back up on his nose.

"Hey," said Boudreau.

Ronnie looked around the club as though expecting to find someone. Drumming the table top a few times with his enormous fingers, he took a cigarette out of his pack and put it behind his ear. He ran his fingers back through his hair a few times, then patted it in place. "Just go get something," he said.

Boudreau watched him move across the room. It was easy to track him through the crowd, and not just because he towered half a head over everybody else. People parted for the big loose-boned dude in sunglasses. Women looked at him directly, the men only after he went by. They had to assume massive balls because it was the kind of information you didn't want to find out the hard way.

The light in the room dimmed slightly, and a spot came on over the tiny stage. A woman emerged from the curtained doorway and said something to the beady-eyed bartender. She fed quarters into the juke and punched her selections as fast as someone at an adding machine.

As the opening chords of "Don't Do Me Like That" came blasting out, she took a last drag off her cigarette and put it, still lit, in an ashtray on top of the jukebox; she stepped up on the little platform and started work.

The room came into immediate focus with a wave of rebel yells and whistles. The woman had teased blond hair and wore open-toed high heels, a white blouse with a placket of ruffles down the front, black panties. She seemed to be somewhere in her late twenties, though it was hard to tell. She wore so much makeup she looked like a kabuki actor.

The tops of her legs were a little thick without being fat, but she worked them hard, knees high in a standard go-go kick. She mouthed the words of the song along with Tom Petty. Periodically she threw in a single roundhouse pelvic grind, a move that drew noise from the crowd like a tent revival preacher. After each grind she undid another button of the blouse. By the end of the song she danced with the shirt completely open, revealing a jiggling belly and big bouncing bosoms in a red lace bra. Between cuts she leaned over and took a couple of quick drags from her cigarette. The next tune started and she spun around, smoke pluming from her nose.

The dancer finished her third song and left the stage. She grabbed her shirt and bra from the floor and held them to her chest, then disappeared through the curtained doorway. The spotlight went off as the noise level came back up, as though the two were controlled by the same knob.

Ronnie appeared just as suddenly back at the table, sliding onto his chair.

"So that's Cherry," said Boudreau, unimpressed. "Nice nipples anyway."

"That ain't Cherry." Ronnie raised his cheeks into an approximation of a smile. "And that ain't her nipples, either."

Boudreau looked at him. The Cherry part he could buy. "This is a joke, right?"

Ronnie had to look away from the table before glancing back. "They ain't nipples." He took the cigarette from behind his ear and stuck it between his lips.

"Then what are they, erasers?"

Ronnie lit the cigarette, taking his time. "Law says you can't show nipples," he said. "So they wear them flesh-colored band-aids. Them big round ones."

Boudreau got the picture. *Band-aids.* "Instead of like pasties."

Ronnie nodded and blew a couple of superior smoke rings. "Them big round ones," he said again.

Boudreau downed the rest of his drink. Trompe l'oeil nipples: it was more evidence of the unique quality of religious life in Tulsa. In this it was similar to the local liquor laws, which the Sixty-Six Club violated in spirit if not in letter, along with half the other bars in town. It was illegal to serve liquor by the drink, except of course in private clubs, where bartenders could mix you drinks only out of your own bottle. So the Sixty-Six Club had sold Boudreau a "membership" for four dollars. Then they sold him whiskey out of a bottle he understood to be only his, at least until the next guy came along and wanted the same brand.

He wondered whose duty it was to go around checking for nipples in topless bars, if there was big competition between the tit men in the police department. Now there was a job. It probably went to the religious types.

His mirth suddenly finished, Ronnie blew another smoke ring. "Vicky didn't come," he observed.

"Yeah?" said Boudreau, as though he'd just noticed she wasn't there. In a little bloom of paranoia he saw Ronnie playing him like a fish, waiting for the moment when he would pull him into the boat and brain him. Listen, by the way, Ron, she's been leading me on but it's not what you think.

"So how come she stayed home?" he said.

"I guess she didn't feel good," said Ronnie. One corner of his mouth went up in distaste.

"She didn't feel good?" The bruise on Vicky's arm came into view. Boudreau grew worried, first about her, then about himself.

"Not after she run the three miles home from where you dropped her," Ronnie said. "Not in this heat."

"Yeah." Boudreau relaxed a bit. At least now he knew how the story went. "Yeah, she seemed a little too wasted after the tennis to do that. I told her I didn't think she should." He shrugged at his own helplessness. "But you know Vicky."

His own ass covered, Boudreau couldn't believe how automatically he'd just covered hers. Hers and Chipper's.

"Yeah." Ronnie looked down at his drink. "Yeah, I know Vicky, all right." He rested his hands on the table around the glass, all ten fingertips lightly touching it. The glass looked tiny, encircled by his fingers like the neck of a small creature.

Ronnie raised his eyebrows, then let them fall. "I got business anyway," he said. "Just as well she didn't come."

Boudreau knew better. From the safety of his own alibi he looked down on Ronnie and felt a little pang for him. He wondered which was worse, the being a loser or the being a loser and not knowing it.

"Just as well." Ronnie said this down to his drink, voice low. "We ain't doing all that good these days."

Boudreau was astonished: for Ronnie this was a major emotional confession. He searched for some sign of a trap.

Ronnie looked up from his drink. "She say anything to you?"

"Nothing," Boudreau said. "Not a thing, man. I'd tell you."

Ronnie dropped his head under the weight of Boudreau's news, and stared at his glass.

The room lights dimmed and the spot over the stage came on again. This time a short, meaty little woman with dark hair came out through the curtains in a leopard-skin bra-and-pantie set with a short see-through baby-doll on top. Her tits were enormous. She fed the juke some quarters and kicked off her sandals to dance barefoot.

Boudreau watched for a little and then turned back to Ronnie, who didn't seem to have moved.

Ronnie ran his fingers back through his hair and straightened up a little. "It's money," he said finally. "I mean there's other shit too, but that's the big one." He considered this for a moment. "It all comes down to money." He turned to fix Boudreau with a blank look of his shades.

"Listen," said Boudreau, "I think I can borrow some money if I have to." He hadn't meant to make the offer in this context, but there it was. "I can get it to you tonight if you really need it."

Ronnie snorted at the scale of Boudreau's misunderstanding. "Five hundred bucks ain't gonna fix my problems." His heart-shaped mouth twisted into a pucker as the crowd whistled and hooted. He turned to watch the stage. "It's the way she was raised." There was a flat finality to it, like it was hardly worth saying.

"Yeah, but *Ronnie,*" Boudreau said, "she chose *you*, man. That's a fact. She kissed all that money good-bye."

Ronnie acted like he didn't hear it. Instead he watched the woman on stage, who was just now working her way out of the baby-doll. Her breasts seemed even bigger without the flimsy curtain in front of them.

Ronnie turned back to him. "Fish swim in water," he said, then knocked back the rest of his drink and got up from the table, empty glass in hand. "Dry land or no."

Fish swim in water, dry land or no: Boudreau was still sorting this out when a ragged cheer from the crowd brought his attention back to the dancing. The little dark-haired woman had just unhooked the top of the leopard-skin bikini with her back to the room. She waited for the beat, then flung the bra away and spun around at the same time, her big pillows of flesh flying out from the centrifugal force. She began bouncing her chest, hands palm up beneath her ribcage in a gesture of display. Boudreau got a hard-on in spite of the band-aids. So this was what the guys came for. Shake those cakes.

Ronnie arrived back at the table with a beer. "I tell you what, though," he said, as though Boudreau had been with him all along, "she can do what she fucking wants when I get done with this thing here. I really don't give a shit."

This thing here. Boudreau just nodded, as though the reference made sense. Ronnie turned away to watch the show, his outburst reigned in. As far as he was concerned, the issue was settled.

The dancer was finishing up her third song. She faced the audience with her legs planted shoulder-width apart, then leaned back in a limbo stance, working her big loose bosoms from side to side and pumping her crotch up and down at the crowd. Lust came rolling back at her in waves, hog calls and whistles, shouted directions for what she could do with her various body parts.

She grabbed her things and went through the curtained doorway. Ronnie fixed on the empty stage, grim as a rock.

Boudreau considered whether now was the right time to offer the money again. The sooner he ended his debtor relationship with Ronnie, the better. On the other hand he still hadn't heard anything about the legendary "deal." Having the slate wiped clean without actually coughing up borrowed money had its appeal, but he dismissed the notion as soon as it came to him. Just to be around Ronnie was to owe him.

He was contemplating how to gracefully split when a woman at the bar looked straight at him.

Boudreau smiled at her. This was no-shit meaningful eye contact: she was the best-looking woman he'd seen all night and she was checking him out. He watched while she walked away from a guy at the bar hitting on her. She made her way through the crowd, coming straight for him. Boudreau tried another smile, but she just kept coming, blank faced. By the time she was a few feet away from the table, he had turned in the other direction. He was thinking maybe she was someone he knew already but didn't want to know anymore.

She stood next to the table. "Hey, *Ron.*"

Boudreau looked up as Ronnie did. Up close, the woman's face had a distracted, not-there quality that made her look almost walleyed. She was young, with dark hair cropped so short it looked like fur. One ear was completely rimmed along its edge with silver stud earrings.

"This here's Cherry?" said Ronnie.

The woman looked down at Boudreau and gave him a smile so fleeting it seemed like a tic.

"Richter," he said, and held out his hand. "Richter Boudreau."

Cherry hesitated, then took his hand and dropped it immediately. "Hi."

Boudreau felt like he'd just touched a piece of wood.

She turned back to Ronnie as though Boudreau had disappeared. "We need to talk," she said, and gave Ronnie a freighted look.

Boudreau heard no accent in her voice. There was in fact no inflection, either, nothing there at all. The girl was like a ghost.

"He's okay," Ronnie told her. "He's the dude I told you about."

Cherry gave Boudreau another quick look, this time without benefit of the smile. He wondered what it was, exactly, that she'd been told about him. She studied him for a few moments but gave no indication of what she found, then turned back to Ronnie. Squatting down beside him, she put one hand on the table to balance herself.

Her skin had a peculiar translucence to it, so pale it seemed bloodless, like a willed absence of color. She was wearing high-heeled sandals, skin-tight designer jeans and a loose, lushly flowered Hawaiian shirt. The shirt was half-unbuttoned, Boudreau discovered. From his angle he had a perfect view of a pale, tan-tipped breast.

She kept her voice low. "I can't go back to my place."

Ronnie drew back slightly, regarding her in the light of this new information. "Where's your stuff?"

"In back." She made a single motion of her head, at the curtained doorway at the other end of the room.

"All of it?" Ronnie said.

She squinted and gave the slightest jerk of an exhale. It took Boudreau a second to understand that this was a laugh. She was squinting so hard because she was on the edge of falling apart. He stared. The woman was blank with fear, her tension reduced to a purely physiological level. She was a 'possum playing dead, a bug trying to pass for a twig.

"Yeah, *all* of it." Her voice went tremolo with sarcasm. "The big suitcase and the shopping bag too."

Ronnie pursed his lips in concentration. "It's no good at my place." He was thinking out loud. "We'll have to figure something out."

She looked at him, waiting for something more. Nothing came.

"We'll figure something out," she repeated then, a rim of moisture appearing above her lower eyelids. She shook her head in disbelief. "Oh, *man.*"

"You can stay with me," Boudreau said. "Tonight anyway. I got room."

Cherry turned and stared at him like he'd just arrived.

"I mean if you're in a jam," he added.

Ronnie looked relieved. "You still at your folks' place?" he said.

Boudreau made a vague motion with his head.

"Maybe." She kept looking at him. "Okay, but I'm not balling you, all right?"

Boudreau emitted a squeak of protest and held up his palms in a who-me gesture.

She turned to Ronnie and jerked her head backward at the room behind her.

"I can't do this tonight." Her chin rippled and quieted, just this side of crying. "I *can't,* man. I'm getting out of here."

"Hey, *listen,*" said Ronnie. "Remember? Remember what happened?"

With what seemed like a major effort, she made herself still. She looked Ronnie in the face and forced her lips together. "No, I fucking *forgot.*"

Ronnie took her arm, dwarfing it in his hand. "You be cool," he said. "We're acting like nothing's wrong, right?"

Boudreau was confused. He felt like he wasn't even sitting at the table anymore.

"Help me out, Ron," she said. "Help me *out.*"

Ronnie observed her through his sunglasses. After a long moment he let go of her arm, then smiled the pursed-lipped smile. "Okay," he said. "Let's go talk."

He got up from his chair, pulling her up by the elbow in the same motion. "We be back in a minute," he said.

Boudreau watched them to the exit. He could hear the sound of traffic out on Eleventh for a few seconds, before the door closed behind them and the raucous noise came back up.

Boudreau discreetly riffled through his wallet while the barman waited, arms folded.

He couldn't believe it: he'd already gone through the extra money. Because he was half-drunk he couldn't remember the exact number of drinks he'd had. But since he only felt half-drunk, it couldn't have been that many. He picked up his drink and gave the guy the last twenty, positive he hadn't spent that much.

He waited till he got back to the empty table, then did some more accounting. Okay, he'd had dinner and two beers at a Mexican place on Fifteenth Street. Also he'd tanked up the Healey, bought a carton of Kools and one or two magazines, a case of motor oil. Then he had a few drinks, that was it. Either someone had given him bad change or he'd miscounted to begin with, that was all there was to it.

Boudreau lit a cigarette. This sucked. He'd borrowed the money from Keith. Actually, it wasn't exactly borrowed yet, not until he told Keith, and that couldn't happen until Keith got back from Oklahoma City. In that sense, of course, it was taken.

He chose not to dwell on the distinction. Finding the money had been the only thing that got him out of the house, not to mention his suicidal mood. The ugly reality of his sex life had made him depressed, and money had lifted him back up. There was a lesson in that.

In the midst of Keith's junk strewn all over his father's desk—there were magazines, packages of photographs, a pile of mail, an open box of twelve-gauge shotgun shells, three played-out cans of Dr. Pepper and an empty bucket of Kentucky Fried Chicken—in the midst of all this Boudreau had come upon buried treasure.

There was an opened envelope, the kind with the little window on the front. It said First National Bank of Tulsa, Trust Department, and was postmarked six months earlier. He took out the check and caught his breath: it was for $22,000, unendorsed. Beside it was a neat stack of money, $540, all in twenties.

A world of possibilities opened up in front of him. Here was a short-term loan, enough to pay back Ronnie with some pocket change left over. He took sixty to be on the safe side, then put the other four-ninety in a bound volume of *The Oil and Gas Journal,* 1969. He rearranged the pile of shit over the trust check. A little charge of guilt detonated as he put the bills in his wallet, but he immediately talked himself out of it. It wasn't like he didn't plan to tell Keith, and besides, someone who forgot to deposit a check for twenty-two grand could hardly begrudge a five-hundred-dollar loan. He briefly worried that the money might be for Rena, but decided this was unlikely since she'd already gone for the weekend. He rolled another joint for the evening, then got cleaned up.

Boudreau sat at the table, working on his new drink. That was the weird thing about money, the same amount meant different things to different people. To him it was a big deal. To Keith it was just something else to leave laying around, like camera parts or guns or electronic equipment. He'd pay him back. That is, if he ever saw him again.

The thought just popped into his mind, cold but not unrealistic. The handwriting on Keith's note was shaky enough to make him wonder just how drunk he'd been when he left. The turnpike between Tulsa and Oklahoma City was ninety miles of arrow-straight road. Boudreau could see Keith Michaels flying down it in The Beast, dead drunk, then just dead. Keith used to have a girlfriend in Oklahoma City, but otherwise Boudreau could think of no reason why he'd want to go there. Then again, Keith had reached the point where he didn't need reasons in the usual sense. "Things are *fucked up,*" the note said. Keith clearly needed help. Boudreau just didn't know anyone who could give it to him. Certainly not himself.

Another dancer came on stage, chunky bodied, with hair that was a light copper color and clearly artificial. She seemed newer to the job than the other two, the smile on her face rigid with fright. She was so scared she was having trouble locating the beat in the song.

The other two dancers, tops back on, were out in the crowd now, moving from table to table, flirting and sitting on laps. They wore demure little shorty robes on top of their dancing outfits, and kept going to the bar for drinks. Boudreau realized this was part of the job description: they shilled drink money from the suckers, keeping change from the ones too drunk to notice, fending off feels and picking up the odd five or ten tucked into a bra. He was sure they must hook a little on the side.

He looked at the exit. It seemed like a long time since Ronnie and Cherry had left, and the place was beginning to get him down. He wanted them to come back in so he could clear out. Even if he didn't give Ronnie the money, at least he could tell the girl he'd changed his mind. That wouldn't be how he'd put it, of course.

She had trouble written all over her: there would be something stolen, or a crazy boyfriend, or a dope hassle. He just wished she hadn't worn the Hawaiian shirt so unbuttoned. Of course he'd invited her to come crash at his borrowed mansion. This could make a cigarette burn on the carpet look like a house-warming gift.

For a situation that his dick got him into, it showed remarkable lack of promise. *I'm not balling you, all right?* The way she'd said it had a certain weary ring to it, like the issue came up in her conversations with some regularity. Her sex life, he felt sure, was conducted strictly on a cash-and-carry basis.

Boudreau sipped at his whiskey and stubbed out his cigarette, then immediately lit another. He was out of his league, and now he had to get out of his offer. He was a jerk, but there was no reason why he should be a fool too. He began sorting through excuses.

Ronnie sat down at the table, another cigarette behind his ear and a tiny smile on his lips. He inclined his head toward the stage. "That one's kind of a dog, ain't she?" He took the cigarette from behind his ear and put in his mouth, unlit.

The copper-haired woman had just worked her way down to the bottom of a two-piece bathing suit. Her thighs were a little flabby, shoulders too narrow; her breasts were flat and sat too far apart on her chest. Also, her shaving job had left clear proof that the copper color was not her own. She closed her eyes now as she danced, to shut out the roomful of people observing her flaws.

"Where's Cherry?" Boudreau asked.

"Getting ready to dance." Ronnie drummed the table with his fingers, along with the juke.

Boudreau was amazed. "Like that?" he said.

"Naw, hell no." Ronnie was surprised at the level of Boudreau's taste. "She's better'n that."

"No no." Boudreau tried again. "I meant all upset like that."

The little smile on Ronnie's face increased until his teeth were bared. "She feels better now."

Boudreau nodded, comprehension dawning. He'd somehow assumed they wouldn't be getting high until later. "Does she hook?" he said. "I mean Cherry?"

Ronnie looked over the tops of his shades in mock reprimand. Boudreau caught a glimpse of light brown eyes that were all iris, the pupils down to pinpoints. There was nothing but surface, nothing to see down into.

Ronnie fought off the impulse to grin again. "Money ain't the issue."

Boudreau nodded some more, having no idea what this might mean.

They watched the dancer finish out her set, the fake smile dropping off her face the instant the song stopped. She ran from the stage and through the curtained doorway.

"Yeah, so I told her it was safer go ahead and dance." Ronnie said this in a reflective way, as though it completed an earlier, complex train of thought. "Just keep things looking normal."

Boudreau waited a few moments, thinking Ronnie would now make clear what he'd just said. Nothing came. "What do you mean," he asked.

"Cherry." Ronnie took the cigarette, still unlit, and put it back behind his ear. He was so fucked up he couldn't complete an action, much less a sentence.

Boudreau gave up. Maybe it was time to say he didn't really have a place for her to crash. "Listen, Ronnie?"

Ronnie tilted one cheek off his chair, like he was going to fart, then reached behind himself and fished something out of his hind pocket. He pushed it across the table, a folded-up page of newsprint, shaped to his butt. "You see this the other day?"

Boudreau recognized the column size and typeface immediately as the *Journal*'s. Drawn around a back-page police blotter item was a circle in red ink. In it was a single paragraph of generic bad news: a partially clothed body found Wednesday morning in Woodward Park. Unidentified Negro female, midtwenties, apparent cause of death, internal injuries. Sexual assault. The coroner's report was due and the police were investigating. There was a discount lumberyard ad next to it, a special on sheetrock if you bought more than ten.

Boudreau read through it twice, trying to tease out some meaning. In a town the size of Tulsa, it wasn't exactly a big piece of news. It was just the kind of assignment George Brinkman griped about getting, a nonstory, a minor entry in the big ledger of human misery. Boudreau pushed it back across the table. "Yeah?"

Ronnie left the paper where it lay and leaned over the table, struggling to keep his smile down. This was gonna make Boudreau laugh. "There was this colored girl used to work here, name Earla?" he said. "Dancer?"

Boudreau cocked his head, waiting for the punch line.

Ronnie picked up his butane lighter, finally lit his cigarette and inhaled richly. Boudreau waited.

"That's her," Ronnie said.

Boudreau watched him tap the newsprint with the corner of the lighter. It took him a moment to get it: *that's her.*

"Cherry knows who creamed her," Ronnie said. "She seen it." He leaned back in his chair and pushed his shades up on his nose.

Creamed her. Boudreau felt that he wasn't hearing correctly, and cocked his head a little.

"But nobody else did." Ronnie let the smile go now, at how good the joke was. "And that's where we'll be making us some money. That's my deal I been telling you about."

Boudreau looked at the piece of paper on the table, all the noises in the room leveling into one loud buzz. After a moment he realized it was the sound of his own blood pounding in his ears.

The rush of fear had a tonic effect, his head clearing instantly. Noise returned to the room with a hog call, the sound of a breaking glass, whoops of laughter. Boudreau thought maybe he could use another drink. "That's *black* mail," he said.

Ronnie laughed out loud. "No shit, Sherlock."

Ronnie got up to go to the can, pushing his way through the crowd like a stoned pharaoh.

Boudreau sat, immobile with fear, and watched the blond dancer try to solicit a drink from the flat-faced drunk several tables over. She sat down and admired his screaming tiger tattoo with a light caress of fingertips. The man twitched slightly at her touch. By now he was stupefied, bolt rigid with alcohol. Boudreau heard the dancer's pitch fade in midsentence as it dawned on her that nobody was home. She caught Boudreau taking it in and gave him a knowing smirk, then got up and hit the next table. The man stared at Boudreau without seeing him, as oblivious to the dancer's departure as he had been to her arrival. His lack of cheekbones made him look morose as a bloodhound.

The folded page of newspaper sat on the table in front of Boudreau like the dead girl's ashes. *That's her.* He felt a quiver of stray electricity run the length of his spine. He refolded it and turned it over, then stuck it under Ronnie's beer glass as if to weight it down. He found himself on his feet, en route to the bar.

Boudreau made his way back through the tight crowd with his glass of whiskey, cradling it from harm like the last egg of a dying species.

He had somehow come untethered from his understanding of the world, and it was not a pleasant feeling. He better start reeling himself back in, *soon;* the drink would help. The drink *had* to help.

He sat down at the empty table, Ronnie not yet back from the can. The tattooed man's table was empty now too, his vigil finally given up. The guy was going to have a long wait for the big nigger gal. Boudreau took a hard gulp of his whiskey.

This was like coming on to the first rushes of a psychedelic, a massive shift of focus. He sucked at the drink, working to integrate this new perspective. There was a reality behind the reality, something that had been there all the time, another layer of the onion that he was just now seeing.

A murdered topless dancer turned out not to be a violation of reality at all. Au contraire, it fit right in. It *was* reality: forcing early bedtime on someone was a perfectly ordinary thing. People killed each other every minute of the day, everywhere and on every scale. They killed for religion, politics, race, sex, money and sometimes sport. They killed their spouses, their parents, their children, their neighbors. They killed strangers individually and in mass, by the tribe, the cityful, by the army, the nation, by the whole gene pool. They used rocks, water, electricity, cars, plastique, rope, guns, knives, bare hands, ovens and atom bombs. Now it was refined so that two old men on opposite sides of the world could push computer buttons and rain death on everyone like a storm of shit.

The black woman's murder was no big deal, it was just what people did to each other. So why should he get upset? Boudreau saw now that it was the kind of horror with which he was perfectly familiar already. He had to accommodate this sort of thing every day.

It was just a little too close at hand: that was the only difference here, and he would take care of that soon enough. It wasn't his problem, he had no involvement whatsoever. He'd offered Cherry a place to spend the night, but this new information clearly canceled any prior obligations. *It wasn't his business.* For that matter it wasn't Ronnie's business either, except in a different sense of the word. As a way to make money, Boudreau thought it posed some difficulties.

Ronnie came back from the bathroom, hair freshly combed.

Boudreau waited till he sat down, then leaned over the table. "So who did it?"

Ronnie looked away with a little humorous shake of his head. "Think I tell you that? This ain't just gossip, Richter."

Boudreau nodded. Yeah yeah, okay. "White guy?"

Ronnie looked away again and smiled, impressed at Boudreau's uncoolness. "Let's just us say," Ronnie explained, "he can afford to pay for what he done. He can afford to pay real big." He pursed his lips, mouth slightly open. His tongue worked the bottoms of his upper molars while he let Boudreau think about it. "Now you tell me if that's a white dude."

Boudreau appreciated the logic with a nod. He wasn't going to get anything more out of him.

"You'll hear more later," Ronnie reassured him, "soon's we get some things straight. Then I'll cut you in."

Cut him in? It was time to make clear his lack of complicity in this fantasy. Maybe he'd tell Ronnie he was staying at Keith's, that Cherry would be a problem there. That wasn't bad, Ronnie'd buy that. Boudreau discovered his drink had only a tiny sip left in it. He downed it and started to get up.

"Watch this," said Ronnie.

The room lights had just dimmed again, the stage spot was back on. Another dancer pushed through the curtained doorway and stepped onto the stage, a huge cassette recorder under one arm. She put the box down on top of the juke.

It took Boudreau a while to recognize her as Cherry. Now she wore a thick pout of bright red lipstick, and her short dark hair stood out in stiff little wet-look spikes all over her head. Her metal-rimmed ear glinted in the spotlight. Pale beyond health, she wore a pair of extremely narrow black wraparound sunglasses, black high heels, and a belted, short black trench coat. On one wrist were both sides of a pair of chrome handcuffs, the chain dangling between them.

The crowd went silent, as though confused. New-wave topless had yet to hit Tulsa kicker bars.

Cherry hit the play button on the tape deck. From the way she looked, Boudreau expected to hear ear-banging noise, some kind of punker thrash that would clear the place. Instead, the music came blasting out in a tickle of memory, the slightly martial guitar line very familiar, something that had once jumped out of the radio with regularity.

Cherry spun once and faced the crowd, the collar of the trench coat up like a spy's. She began a kind of slink to the guitar line, hands in pockets, a strut that didn't go anywhere. Then she twisted and moved the trench coat open to a slit, enough so that one long, very white leg could be seen working all the way from her black spike heel up to the triangle of exposed pale buttock. Boudreau recognized the tune just as the words started: "Saturday night I was downtown / Working for the FBI."

By the third song Boudreau had moved up to the bar to be closer. The new tune was "Watching the Detectives," the tape deck turned up so loud it rattled on the opening bass notes. Still using the same angular, stylized movement, Cherry moved over to turn it down a hair.

Ten feet away, Boudreau was hypnotized. This was more than professional, this was genius tease. The girl seemed impossibly long and pale, a study in otherness. She had nothing on now but the sunglasses and handcuffs, the black heels and a black velvet G-string. Her breasts were small but round, perfectly symmetrical.

Boudreau came out of himself and looked around. The rest of the crowd watched with heads cocked, attentive but reserved. She was scary as much as sexy, a question of foreign taste carried to strangeness. They wanted grind and jiggle and oh-baby, stretch marks and hair spray and dark roots. There were traditions to uphold. She looked like a boy and she didn't use jukebox tunes. She acted like she could give a shit that they were even *there*, an exotic fish oblivious to the pressed noses and finger taps on the tank glass.

Boudreau fixed obsessively on the smooth mound under the black velvet G-string. It had perfect curved definition, its alien femaleness highlighted by the slight separation between her upper thighs. As Costello sang "She's filing her nails while they're dragging the lake," she locked into one of her angular poses. Hips cocked, she swiveled her head in Boudreau's direction, then extended the long red-nailed fingers of one hand into a claw and lightly raked it over her up-tilted crotch. She was aiming it, unmistakably.

She snapped her head back in the other direction then and just stood in one spot, insinuating her hips in a kinky little robot grind. She pouted, hollow cheeked, and whipped her face back at Boudreau, pelvis working like it was on an invisible camshaft, geared to the blips and pops of the cheesy reggae.

Boudreau watched the black triangle between her legs, a whiskey fire pooling in his own belly. *I'm not balling you, all right?* Apparently she'd changed her mind, and better yet, she was coming home with him tonight. For all he knew, Ronnie was full of shit anyway, the whole thing a joke.

One night wasn't going to hurt anybody.

A cone of dirty light hung down from the lone street lamp in the parking lot, moths as big as birds looping around in the top of it.

The Mustang sat just out of the light, on the edge of the lot, next to an empty field. From the backseat Boudreau could see the vague shapes of junk that had been dumped in the weeds; once his eyes adjusted he picked out the crumpled frame of a bicycle, a fifty-five-gallon oil drum, a flattened car door.

A few cars were still parked at the other end of the lot, in front of the Sixty-Six Club. The Healey sat off by itself, Cherry's huge suitcase protruding up from the well behind the seats.

Cherry was in the backseat opposite Boudreau, hunched into the corner. Ronnie sat sideways in the driver's bucket, one arm looped over the back of the seat to steady himself while he cooked the dope.

It was so late Boudreau had wanted to just split, but Cherry needed to get high again first. He regretted agreeing to it as soon as they got in the Mustang, sitting out in a parking lot off Eleventh Street while Ronnie spread paraphernalia and dope all over the front seat. A cop with a flashlight was all it would take. Well, *howdy*, officer, we're just making us a very small cup of coffee here.

"Dope fiends," said Boudreau. Ronnie grunted and Cherry made no response at all. Boudreau remembered his reefer, took it out and lit it. He felt like a boy with candy cigarettes, watching the big kids smoke cigars.

While Ronnie worked, Boudreau smoked pot and watched Cherry huddle in her corner of the backseat. The faint glow from the street lamp threw her face into heavily shadowed relief, her eyes closed. Between the pale translucence of her skin and her wet-spiked hair, she looked recently drowned.

Her body was the same one Boudreau had watched dance, but now it was like she'd disappeared from it, taking any promise of sex along with her. He began to kick himself all over again; he couldn't exactly withdraw the offer now. She had shrunk into a heap against the side of the car, facing him, knees bent and feet up on the seat. The tight jeans and the angle of her legs gave sharp definition to the vee of her crotch. Boudreau wondered if it were her, or just him. It had all looked so good from a distance.

Cherry handed the needle back to Ronnie and faded into her corner like a shadow, eyes closed again so she could concentrate on her rush. Boudreau watched as a thin smile appeared on her face. She was like one of those cheap, dehydrated sponge toys that starts out tiny and flat: just add heroin and watch it grow. Her smile blossomed. An invisible someone whispered good news to her, news that got better and better.

Her entire body relaxed, her features came back to life. The dope loosened her right up, dissolved away the stony anxiety. He reconsidered. Maybe it *was* just him. He couldn't tell. He'd smoked his whole joint like a cigarette, under the impression that it wasn't going to make any difference this late in the game. A minute or two or three later, it came down on his head like a load of bricks.

Liberated from any need to correspond to reality, his senses flitted around, catching the smell of hot asphalt, the distant honking of a horn, the buzz of a mosquito at extremely close range. He was slimy with sweat, but that was okay. His skin slid against the vinyl of the seat, the air so full of heat and moisture it felt like a lubricant for every mating surface. He became aware of Ronnie's breathing, of Cherry's breathing, of a car loudly downshifting several blocks away.

"Thank *God* for drugs," he said. The words hung in the thick air like invisible skywriting. They seemed funny, profound, so true.

Cherry made a sound low in her throat, pitched somewhere between assent and amusement.

The silence lengthened. Ronnie lit a cigarette and Boudreau jumped.

The match spat light in the dark, an aureole of color flaring around it. The halo lingered in his eyes long after the flame was gone. He was not just drunk; he was not just stoned. He had a need to let them know the truth of the matter. "I am *fucked up.*"

Ronnie exhaled and turned all the way around, hanging over the top of his seat. It seemed like there wasn't enough room in the car with him in it. "Whyn't we tell Richter here all about Earla," he said.

Cherry made her feelings known without using words, the kind of noise a child produces when told it's time to go to bed.

A silence followed, lengthening until Boudreau became unsure that he'd heard anything at all. *Earla?*

"Earla ain't coming back, sweetheart," Ronnie pointed out. "We got to talk about it sometime."

That's her. Boudreau's high turned the corner: this was bad news, shit he didn't need to hear. The air in the car turned stifling. Cherry expelled an odd burst of breath, like she was trying to hold back a sneeze or a giggle.

"I think you should reconsider this blackmail thing," Boudreau said. He had a whole list of reasons, but this would have to suffice for now.

"Is that right?" Ronnie had himself a chuckle. "I guess I better call them folks back, then."

Boudreau considered the implications of this. "Do what?"

Ronnie drew deeply on his smoke and exhaled with lengthy pleasure. "Said I called them again tonight," he said. "They ain't taking me serious yet, but they will. They surely will."

This was one too many things for Cherry to accept. "Oh, *man.*" Her eyes were still closed, her voice so loaded it sounded like she was falling asleep. " 'S too fucking much."

Boudreau's feeling exactly. "You called on the *phone?*"

Ronnie regarded him through his sunglasses, something in the position of his head to indicate that he was losing his good humor.

"You think I ain't seen movies too, Richter?" He flicked his butt out the far window, a tracer of sparks flying behind it. "I use pay phones, different one each time."

Boudreau was losing it. This was just the point, Ronnie had seen way too many movies.

"I told 'em we want a million even," Ronnie said.

Boudreau made an involuntary noise of disbelief, as if he were holding his breath and someone had just punched him.

Ronnie shrugged. "I could prob'bly ask more," he said, "but it ain't good business to change your offer once you made it."

Boudreau shook his head, trying to clear it, to say no, to make himself understood. "I think," he said, "I think Cherry should go to the police." The informant in question was out like a dead bulb, a dreamy little negative sound her only contribution. "I think the only—"

"The police can go fuck theirself." Ronnie pushed himself away from the back of his seat and straightened up a little, then leaned forward and pushed one finger into Boudreau's thigh. "You listen to *me* now."

Boudreau felt like he'd been prodded with a stick. He listened.

"They ain't even gotten around to finding out who she is, you know why?"

Boudreau figured it probably had something to do with lack of identification, but didn't say anything.

"Go figure it out, Richter." Ronnie snorted, a sound that said he was only explaining this once. "Rich white boy and a dead colored girl working topless, how's that look to you?"

Against all his instincts Boudreau found himself mentally defending the integrity of the Tulsa legal system. This was wrong, there was a hole in the logic of this somewhere.

"Yeah, okay," he said. "I can see your—"

"They might's well zip her up in a body bag and ship her home, that's how this deal works." Ronnie pursed his lips. "But I'm gone make him pay. I'm gone make his ears bleed."

Boudreau might've known Ronnie would work Vietnam in there somewhere. He saw no point in arguing with someone who talked about making other people's ears bleed, even as a metaphor. He hated to say it, but things were never that simple. His own life, for example.

"There ain't no justice, not for no dead colored girl." Ronnie cocked his head at the girl in the backseat. "Cherry, she don't know Tulsa, she don't even know who this dude is. But she seen him, all right. She seen his car too, real fast white car, that ring a bell?" Ronnie contemplatively worked the inside of his cheek with his tongue, then pursed his lips again. "Family like that, he ain't what you call hard to identify. Specially now he's got blood all over them white seats."

A message of alarm went out to the nerve endings in Boudreau's scalp. The missing pieces were jumping into place as though they were magnetized.

Ronnie's mouth widened into a carnivorous grin, his teeth gleaming in the dim light. "I believe you even once had a thing for his sister."

Boudreau began shaking his head. *"No,"* he said. This was more than he wanted to know. He wanted to give it back. "No. That can't be right."

"See what I mean, Richter?" Ronnie shook another cigarette out of his pack. "This here's more complicated than you thought."

Boudreau ran over the same half-flattened muffler as he pulled out onto Eleventh, the little car bucking like he'd just run over a small body. He checked in the rearview to make sure he hadn't.

He headed west, dimly amazed that he was responsible for the scenery lurching by. *Driving:* he seemed to be driving. What a peculiar thing, here he was flying along in a baroque contraption with his ass eight inches off the concrete. It was primitive, all gears and shafts and sparks and exploding gasoline; push the pedal turn the wheel. People went driving every day and never even noticed how close they were to death. It could jump up right out of the pavement. Death was *there.*

Boudreau was halfway through an intersection before he realized the light was red. A car with the green light screamed through barely missing him, horn blaring. The sound lingered in the wake of the car's jet stream, then faded and disappeared. In Boudreau's mind it intersected with the Healey, scattering body parts and the contents of Cherry's suitcase all over the street. Whoa, *close one,* he better pay attention.

The gauges on the Healey were no help, the speedometer pegged at 140, the tach permanently redlined. Even though it was two in the morning and the wide street was deserted, he thought it would be a good idea to know how fast he was going. He listened to engine noise, then got confused. Maybe it was time to shift. He was pretty sure he'd been going too fast, but now the little car seemed to be crawling.

Eyes closed, Cherry slumped motionless in the passenger bucket. She seemed propped in place, her right arm hanging out over the door, her head rolling back against the big suitcase behind the seat.

"Cherry." The word disappeared in the road noise. His tongue didn't feel right, maybe that was the problem. He tried again. "Hey, *Cherry.*"

She didn't move. Her face looked like a death mask, smiling lips in the happy repose of no more consciousness. He was driving around with a body in the car.

"*Cherry.*" This time he leaned over and yelled it. Nothing. He flipped out. "Hey, *Cherry! Cherry are you there?*"

"No, I'm in heaven." She slurred out a little snicker, eyes still closed. "Me 'n' all the other assholes."

"Just making sure," Boudreau said. *Well, fuck her.*

An air horn roared in his ear, triggering an instant dose of fight-or-flight. He yanked the Healey back into its own lane as a pickup truck on tractor-sized tires pulled even with him in the outside lane. The floor of its cab was at his eye level.

Boudreau sped up, then slowed down, then sped up again, the truck keeping exactly the same pace. Its driver, a big redneck kid with long hair and a scraggly mustache, consulted with his two friends, then turned and looked down on the little open sports car. Boudreau had the misfortune of making eye contact right as the kid leaned out the window. He pointed down at Cherry as Boudreau looked away.

"That a boy or a girl?" he yelled. Boudreau heard guffawing from inside the truck. "He gone suck my dick? Do y'all suck dicks?"

Boudreau chanced another look over to assess the seriousness of the situation, just in time to see Cherry undoing the last button on the Hawaiian shirt.

The road wind blew the shirt open like a sail, exposing her perfect little bosoms to the hot night air, so pale they seemed luminescent. He slowed down involuntarily, the big truck right along with him.

Cherry flattened a breast with one hand and peeled the flesh-colored band-aid off her nipple with the other, then did the same for the other side. She slumped back in the seat, tossing the band-aids up into the wind. She smiled beatifically, eyes closed, then gave the truck the finger.

Boudreau stomped on the accelerator and pulled a hard left for the break in the median island, making the side street but nipping the curb in the process. It sent a shudder through the dinky car, a little harbinger of how it would feel when the pickup truck caught up and drove right over them.

He stayed on the pedal down the street, a wake of exhaust noise bouncing off the tightly packed working-class houses. He whooped, awash with adrenaline. The truck didn't seem to have made the turn. Then again maybe they were doubling around. He ran stop signs and slammed into the turns, zigzagging through the neighborhood.

He made his way over to a deserted residential artery, and slowed down, moving south. *Cops,* he hadn't even thought about cops. He turned west when he got to Twenty-first, then coasted up to the light at Peoria. He'd almost taken the shortcut through Woodward Park before he remembered that was where the body had been found.

He sat at the light, shaking. On top of the murked layers of alcohol and marijuana, there was a thin layer of insight, clear as mountain air. He'd graduated from his usual low-grade worries about certain self-destructive tendencies. This was a new plateau.

The light changed and Boudreau turned south onto Peoria. It was empty as far up as he could see, a tunnel of overhanging trees and street lamps. A cruddy haze of humidity hung in the pools of light.

He'd been out of control before but never like this, never with such sickening exhilaration. Fear this big was like water, you had to let it just wash over. Underneath there would be clarity, your choice restricted to finding air again. Then you'd end up on the beach, rinsed out, clean.

Boudreau looked at Cherry, her shirt flapping open in the wind. She was boneless with dope, head lolling and body draped over her seat like a fresh-bagged trophy. Her eyes were still closed.

"You okay?" he said.

She rolled sideways in her seat, then reached over and rooted around in his crotch with one hand. After a moment's fumbling work she had him out in the night air.

Considering what he'd had to drink, it was a miracle he was even hard. He could hardly complain that he was numb too. Maybe it was appropriate, this dislocation. Getting his dick aimed down the road by a topless junkie, on the way to his childhood friend the murderer's house—this didn't happen every day.

He just hoped to Christ that Keith didn't come back early. He hoped, in fact, that Keith didn't come back at all, that somewhere on the turnpike The Beast had already rolled over and died. It would make things easier all around.

SUNDAY

I t was early, the sunlight still soft at the chintz-curtained windows of Vicky's bedroom.

Boudreau jerked awake, jumping naked from the bed and stumbling to the dormer window that overlooked the driveway. The Healey sat by itself on the brick drive. No sign of Keith.

He turned to look at the young woman. She was breathing but still out, entwined in the bedclothes.

He found his clothes and rifled through them looking for his cigarettes. No luck. He grew desperate, then remembered where he was. There were enough cigarettes in this house to open a Quik-Trip. He calmed down and pulled on his jeans. A part of him took note how his anxiety had immediately funneled itself into uncontrollable need. He tiptoed out, closing the door behind him.

It all looked different in the light of day. He went downstairs and smoked a cigarette out of a fresh pack, then took a shower in the bathroom off the kitchen. He dried himself in a narrow band of sunlight just coming in the window, latching onto the earliness of the day. He would deal with everything early and be done with it.

He made a cup of coffee in the kitchen, then decided to go out to the living room to think. This required him to pass by the main bar; he splashed two fingers of bourbon into his coffee as though it were milk and this were normal. Okay, he was working on a little abuse problem. There, he said it. But right now he had a bigger problem. These were special circumstances. He fought off the impulse to roll a joint also. He'd need his wits about him.

He settled into one of a pair of big wing chairs by a front window, then lit another cigarette and stared out. His mind kept going over the scene in the parking lot It was like one of those gruesome pieces of TV news, something a camera had caught by accident, a car plunging through a guardrail, an assassination, a child falling out a window. It played in slow motion, over and over, a piece of information that could be rolled back but never changed.

A sudden muffled sound disturbed the deep quiet of the house. Boudreau jumped, nerve shot. It sounded like something falling, a closet door closing upstairs, someone banging into something. He listened, dreading what was to come.

He drained the coffee and bourbon, to no effect. The knowledge still sat inside him like a hard little egg.

Keith had finally moved a step up from just being a rich asshole. Now he was a monster. Meanness was clearly a continuum of behavior, but Boudreau couldn't conceive what it took to jump that many notches. He still saw Keith as a teenager, wearing a Beatle wig and goofing, playing the brand-new Gibson he'd got for his fifteenth birthday. They'd been buddies.

A gardener's pickup truck laden with equipment pulled up in front of the house across the street. Two black men in bib overalls, one middle-aged and the other younger, got out of the cab and stretched. Because of the enormity of the Michaels front lawn it played as a distant panorama. They sat down on the curb and began drinking out of a thermos.

More stirring issued from upstairs, the sound of a door being closed. After a while he heard the far-off sound of plumbing, deep in the house's guts. There was the muffled boom of a flush, then the steadier sound of a shower.

If mistakes were shit, then he had plenty of shoveling. He had to get Cherry out of here, right away. He resolved to go up as soon as her shower was over. It wouldn't be nice, but right now nice was a luxury.

Boudreau lit yet another cigarette. There were some big blank spots in his memory of the night before; he still didn't understand how he'd gotten into this position. In the hard light of day, sex with Cherry didn't seem like a very good reason. He seemed to remember she'd drooped

off about the same time he had, before they even made it into the
driveway. He must have carried her upstairs.

Aside from his episode two years before with Liz Shaw, dubious sex
had never had such big warnings painted on it. He'd had plenty of time
to absorb the lesson and still hadn't learned a goddamn thing.

That one had begun when Liz Shaw turned up at TU, after Harmon
Shaw had retrieved her from Norman. He'd found out about Bubba
Duncan, the wide receiver from Mississippi known in the sports press
as Hubba Bubba.

There'd been open rumors that Harmon Shaw had tried unsuccess-
fully to get Duncan kicked off the team and out of school. This had
come as no surprise to Boudreau, who in fact thought it mild. Lynching
would've been more to Harmon Shaw's taste, but for once he'd come
up against a power that his own couldn't touch. Messing with OU
football was like spitting on the flag, and white girls with black ball
players—this was not exactly big news. Bubba Duncan was already a
two-time all-American going into his senior year, worth his weight in
bowl games and TV contracts.

By the time Boudreau came across Liz Shaw in his film history course,
she already had a distracted, hunted look about the eyes, a neurasthenic
belle on tranquilizers. She'd come on to him in the weirdest ways, but
he'd ignored all the signs. The half-finished blow job under the table at
the country club should have been the tip-off. Here was someone looking
for trouble.

As if that hadn't been enough, once he got her panties down in a more
private setting—coming face to face with a mound shaved baby clean—
she had instantly disconnected. She went chatty on him, rambling on
about this and that as though Boudreau didn't have his face buried
between her legs, tongue to salt bud, stubble to stubble.

He knew banging Liz Shaw was not quite fair, but there he was. She
kept talking and her hips kept moving, as though there were two different people here. For Boudreau, down between her legs, it was like
working while listening to the radio. After they had actually copulated,
she burst into protracted tears, reminding him a little too much of the
end of his marriage. He felt like a scumbag: no stranger to the alienated

sex act, this one had been truly fucking depressing. He did his best to forget the whole thing, and he had, at least until Harmon Shaw dropped by his office a few days later.

Boudreau got up and went for more coffee, adding three fingers this time. He lit a cigarette, then realized he already had one going.

He could redeem his bad judgment by bowing out of this, *right now;* it was that simple. You stayed away from lost causes unless you liked to lose. He worked on the coffee and bourbon, a new buzz starting up, and sank back into his chair. Her shower was taking forever, all that water streaming over her hard pale body.

The gardeners across the street got up from their seats on the curb. They took their time, stretching and yawning, then began unloading lopping shears, rakes, hedge trimmers. It was too early to make noise in a neighborhood like this, not on a Sunday. A big green Mercedes drove down the street. The gardeners busied themselves under the broad brims of their hats, waiting until the car was gone to look up again. One of the men took off his hat and mopped his brow with a red bandana, the day steamy already.

Next they laid a couple of planks off the back of the truck and rolled down a big high-wheeled mower fitted with gang cutters. After that they unloaded a small trim mower, then wheeled both pieces of equipment across the street and onto the Michaels lawn.

Boudreau had assumed they were mowing across the street. This wasn't his house, he didn't belong here. What if they came to the door? He jumped up, ready to start pulling drapes, then caught himself.

This was stupid—bad nerves, plain and simple. They weren't going to come to the door for their money; they were just more of the prepaid labor that ran Keith's life for him. Boudreau sank back into the chair, his cup suddenly empty, and watched them start the big mower. It occurred to him that Keith was a throwback, the wine-brained feudal lord who'd stumbled into a darkened hut to have his way with a peasant girl. Things had gotten a little out of hand, but it was nothing a few pieces of gold wouldn't fix. The only difference now was that most of it would go to a good law firm.

Through the window he could just make out the distant, muffled sound of the big mower, a sound that brought to mind incongruous images of summer days playing with garden hoses, of the smell of fresh-cut grass. He found it soothing in spite of himself. He had to be cool, that was all. Things would work out.

The shower noise finally stopped. Time to go upstairs and get this over with.

He went in the bedroom, then hesitated outside the bathroom door before knocking. Maybe if he said something first, she wouldn't get scared. "Cherry?"

There was no answer. He waited until he heard a slight noise and tried again.

"Yeah?" came the voice then.

"Hi," said Boudreau, trying to make things a little friendlier. There was a long pause.

"Hi."

"Hi. Hey, *listen.*" He leaned against the wall next to the door. "You want anything to eat? Some eggs or bacon or something?" He meant to say, *We have to talk,* but at the last second changed his mind. There was no sense laying it on her through a bathroom door.

The door stayed closed. "I don't do animal protein," she said.

"Oh." She didn't do animal protein. "Okay, well how about some juice or coffee or something?" He saw what he was doing, and had no power to stop it. When she didn't reply, he tried again. "You want a little wake-me-up, then?" he said.

"A what?" she said. "You mean like a drink?" There was another pause. "Yeah, okay. Sure."

"One Bloody Mary, coming up," said Boudreau. He'd gone straight from taking short order to bartending. Maybe next he'd see if she had any laundry needs he could take care of.

"Hey." She called through the door as he headed for the stairs. "Hey." She obviously didn't remember his name. "Everything's okay, right?"

"Yeah," he said. "Everything's fine."

Boudreau mixed two Bloody Marys, figuring he could use one himself. He made doubles, then dumped in extra Tabasco, under the impression it would make them healthier.

Hearing the door to the bathroom slam shut, he grabbed the drinks, nearly spilling them, and hurried to the foot of the long, curving balustrade. He was still in his jeans and no shirt, barefoot. "Down here," he called, sucking in his gut.

She appeared at the balcony, short hair toweled into a fluffy crewcut. She was lost in a man's shirt she'd found, the sleeves rolled up. Her legs seemed to go on forever before they disappeared under the shirttails at her thighs.

Cherry looked out over the stairway and the grand entry hall, eyes wide. She cracked out a laugh, not believing it. "This is for real, right?"

She began an exaggerated descent, hand arched regally over the rail. After three or four steps she leaned back and flourished the shirttails like a dress, as though she were flouncing her way down to a garden party. From his vantage point Boudreau caught an expansive view of flat pale belly instead of petticoats, a lush dark triangle beneath it. She traipsed the rest of the way down, Scarlett O'Hara gone stripper.

By the time she reached the bottom, she was grinning like a kid, her mouth full of tiny white teeth. "You *live* here?"

"Not exactly," he said. "It's a friend's place. I'm just sort of housesitting." He made himself look her in the face. "Listen, we should probably talk, okay?"

She met his eyes and saw the news immediately, her grin disappearing so fast it was like he'd hit her. "Sure." She froze on the spot, refusing to look up.

He stood speechless, drinks in hand. She was used to getting bad news on a moment's notice. "In here." Hands full, he pointed the way with his chin.

The girl walked in front of him from the entry hall into the living room, then kept going until she stood right in the middle. She did a slow pirouette, taking in the polish of wood and texture of drape, the ornately manteled fireplace, the paintings and mirrors, the vases and boxes and sculptures on all the tables, every surface bathed and shadowed in oblique morning light. The furniture was all overscaled, deep with upholstery. Wherever you looked, there was another group of chairs and couches and tables, any one of them enough to fill an ordinary room.

"How about right here?" said Boudreau in his most cordial voice. He waited beside the wing chairs by the window.

Cherry drifted over, working her bare feet in the thick pile as though it were sand on a beach. Boudreau put the drinks down on the little table between the chairs, making sure to use coasters. When he indicated her chair, she avoided his eyes and flung herself down, a teenager about to get a lecture. She huddled into a corner of the big chair, legs folded under.

"There you go." Boudreau sat down himself, feeling like he'd just maneuvered a fragile object securely into place. He made himself look away from the naked haunch and buttock that had come into view.

"Cheers," he said, taking a long pull on his Bloody Mary. "Wow." He had another big swallow, the viscous liquid burning and soothing at the same time.

Cherry picked hers up and held the glass in both hands, then drank a full third of it as though it were plain tomato juice. She made a noise of appreciation in her throat, then closed her eyes and leaned back into the chair. Her partly buttoned shirt gapped open, offering a full view of one breast.

Boudreau looked, in spite of himself. She exposed herself for a living, she could hardly be unaware of it. No harm in just looking.

Cherry opened her eyes, mouth tilting up in one corner. "These aren't bad, I could do about three of these." She looked at the glass, then tossed down the same amount again.

"Hey," Boudreau said, "I take good care of you."

She looked at him and snickered. "You mean if I get drunk, you won't kick me out?"

It was his turn to look away. "That's not really what I meant."

She snickered again. "It's been done before. Get me fucked up enough, I don't care."

Boudreau relaxed a little, the need to spell things out fading away. A few drinks would see them through, they had at least that much in common. She was no fool: there wasn't any sense beating her over the head, not when she was already way ahead of him. He worked steadily at his own drink, savoring each sip. He gave some thought to rolling a joint once all this was over.

"Sure you don't want something to eat?" he said.

Cherry shook her head, in the midst of a swallow. "Puke it up." She patted her midsection in explanation, as though it needed placating.

"You're a little strung out, aren't you?" he said in the same solicitous tone.

She turned away, offended. "I've got like this nervous stomach, okay?" She turned back and gave him a look, stunned. "I mean someone just dicked my friend to death and I'm *upset*, okay?"

Boudreau withered. "Listen, I'm sorry, I didn't mean to accuse you or anything, I just wanted to know if you were, you know, in pain. That's all I meant."

"Sure." She drained the rest of her Bloody Mary, holding the glass in two hands because it shook too much in one.

"I mean," he said, "I'm the last one to talk about drug problems." If she wasn't strung out, then he wasn't drunk. "That's my middle name, Richter Fucked-up Boudreau."

"Forget it." She gave her eyebrows a weary lift, like this was the last thing she should have to explain. "Can I have one of those cigarettes?" She waited while he lit one for her. "I'm not a junkie, okay? I just chip. Like Ronnie and what's her name."

"Vicky."

"Yeah, Vicky. I do up maybe twice a week, sometimes three." She turned to gaze out the window and exhaled a lengthy stream. "Maybe a little more lately."

"Yeah, well, you be careful." Boudreau touched her hand for emphasis. "You got enough problems right now."

Still looking out the window, she stiffened for a second before moving her hand away.

"So when did you start doping?" he said. "When you got into the life?"

She turned to him. "Into the what?"

Boudreau picked up his cigarettes, embarrassed. He'd thought it was the hip thing to say, secret hooker talk. "You know, clubs and shit. Dancing." *Men.*

She snorted. "I only started dancing three months ago, when I came to *Dullsa.* I've been getting high maybe a couple years."

"So how'd you end up here?" he said.

"I followed someone."

Her barely audible voice told the story, but he had to ask anyway. "So that's over now? You broke up?"

She moved her head slightly, staring back outside. A stricken look came over her face, as though the house were a ship, the shore steadily receding beyond the window. Her eyes widened.

"So what'd you do before you came here?" he said.

The question pulled her out of it. She shrugged, fiddled with the cuff of the shirt.

"I was in a band for a while, I don't know, I did some acting classes. Waitressed. You know." She looked at him to make sure he knew, and put out the cigarette, then immediately took another one. "In San Francisco."

"Oh yeah?" This was common turf. He lit her new cigarette. "I lived in the East Bay for eight years."

"No shit." She looked at him with new regard, like she'd just found an English-speaker in a foreign country.

They talked Bay Area, neighborhoods and street addresses, parks, stretches of coast. It all came back to him—God, he missed California. Riding his three drinks, he went into a reverie of the Haight, hippies and fucking in the park. Marches and demos. Psychedelic bands. Psychedelic *drugs.*

He went on for a while until he noticed the tilt of her head and the crooked little smile.

"It's, uh, kind of *changed* now." She rattled off a bunch of bands he'd never heard of, who apparently played at places like the Deaf Club.

"The Deaf Club?" This was making him feel old.

"Yeah, the *Deaf* Club, get it?" she said. "In the day it's this place for like, hearing-impaired people."

He found himself nodding lengthily as he looked out the window. She was laughing at him.

Outside, one of the lawn men was mowing around shrubs and flower beds and hedges. His partner was doing laps of the entire enormous lawn. He came into hearing every few minutes, then into sight, then out of hearing again.

Boudreau decided to explore an earlier topic. "You're not bad for someone who never danced before." He paused to consider the slightly hostile ring of what he'd just said. "I mean you're much better than somebody who's only danced for three months."

"Yeah, must be natural talent, right?"

Still sitting on one folded leg, she stretched out the other until it was fully extended, toe pointed. She paralleled it with an arm, then turned her head in a high-chinned parody of dancerly hauteur. Letting the leg dangle again over the chair's armrest, she blew a short burst of smoke through her nose, amused, then twisted around for the ashtray and knocked it off the table.

Boudreau found himself on his knees in front of her, picking up butts. He offered the ashtray to her, taking note of how all the twisting around had caused the front tails of her shirt to fall open.

A corner of her mouth lifted as she stubbed out her cigarette. "It ain't that hard to turn guys on," she said. "Believe me."

Within kissing distance of pink lips nestled in soft dark fluff, Boudreau believed her. He chuckled about those darn guys, his throat so tight it came out as a near whimper. In the meantime she'd twisted to look out the window again. His view lost, he wobbled to his feet, certain there would be more to follow. She was no amateur. "How old are you," he asked.

"Nineteen."

Boudreau held up his glass. "Thirty-three." He felt more like fifty. "You want another?"

After the next round was gone, Boudreau ducked out to the can, so turgid he had trouble peeing. When he came back, Cherry was standing within the big bay window, behind the chairs. She leaned against the corner as she stared out, the drape wound around one hand tight as a bandage. The two glasses sat on the table, empty.

"Hey," he said, "how about anoth—"

She released herself from the drape and turned, eyes brimming over. She made a feeble gesture with one hand, a little wave that said she couldn't talk.

"Are you okay—" he started again, but she stepped over to him and buried her face against his bare chest, her arms around him.

Boudreau stroked her head, the hair still damp and smelling of herbal shampoo. He kept things paternal and restrained himself. It was probably inappropriate to grind his throbbing crotch against her.

"Oh, *man,*" she said. "Oh, man, this *sucks.* This really sucks."

"Hey now," said Boudreau. "It's okay. There's nothing we can do about it, all right?"

She snuffled and dropped her arms to her sides. Boudreau held her, impressed by how small she was.

"I don't usually trust guys," she confessed into his chest.

Leaning back and lifting her chin with one hand, he wobbled a little on his feet, then caught his balance. He looked in her eyes and his tongue went clumsy. "No one said you had to."

Cherry closed her eyes and wrapped her arms around his neck. She laid herself into him, then made a little nuzzling kiss on his bare chest.

Boudreau closed his own eyes while a thrill raced up his spine and back down again. So far as he could tell, the bluffing was over, they'd both folded their cards at the same time. Her shirt had ridden up when she stretched, leaving his hand behind on the upper slope of her now bare ass. Boudreau gave it the slightest experimental pressure with his fingertips.

She pressed in closer and gave him another small kiss. This one was on the neck, a teethy little nibble meant to worry nerve ends; after that she squeezed him, leaving her entire body imprinted on his. Boudreau made a small swooning sound and squeezed her back, equally hard. It was *happening*.

She sniffled and let out a long sigh. "You'll take care of me, right?" Her lips moved against his chest, voice barely there.

A noise came from the back of his throat, a moan he hoped would pass for assent. This was not a smart thing to be doing, but just now he couldn't remember why.

She licked his nipple then, just as he discovered that her shirt had ridden up in front also. He went exploring, exultant; when he spoke, his voice came out thick as pudding. "I thought you said you weren't going to ball me."

She stopped, confused. "What?"

"You know, last night." He got a finger in her and she jerked a little. "What you said in the bar."

His zipper came down with a crisp ripping noise.

"Don't take it so serious," she said. "This is just friends, okay?"

Clothes off, they ended up on the floor in front of the chairs. Boudreau kissed her all over, stroked and rubbed and diddled and licked. He fingertipped her little bud to no obvious effect, until finally she sat up and pushed him onto his back, then bent to her business.

He shuddered in gratitude, his eyes closed. He'd had a thorn in him for months, and now she was pulling it. This was healing of the highest order.

On his back, the wool carpet began to get to him as he tried to savor each little lick and nip. He became itchy with distraction and concentrated harder, only to become aware of the lawn mower as it drew closer. He followed the sound mentally while she worked on him. It went down the left side of the lawn, turned the corner and came across the front of the house, toward them.

Cherry knelt over him, drawing her tongue from root to tip; if she noticed the noise, she paid it no attention. She varied the pressure and broadness of surface, giving him a wet little tongue massage. The sound got louder and louder, like it was about to come right through the window.

Boudreau opened his eyes. From his angle on the floor he caught the sweat-stained crown of a straw hat bobbing across the bottom of the window, appearing briefly again between the two chairs before it vanished.

He watched Cherry suck on his penis in pained disbelief. Okay, so maybe it was a little professional. It was still the best blow job he'd come across in years, and he was ruining it because he couldn't stop thinking about the goddamn gardeners. Now she was taking first one ball then the other into her mouth, working them around, applying gentle suction.

Boudreau closed his eyes again. He tried logic. Surely they were too low on the floor to be seen from outside. The sound of the mower receded. The guy would be telling his partner now to check out the needle-dicked white dude getting sucked off inside. The best view would probably be from the corner window.

Boudreau became locked onto the varying pitches of the two lawn mower engines. The deeper one grew more distant, following the lap pattern around the vast yard. That was a good sign. But where was the other one, the trim mower? He strained to pick out its sound, muffled through the window.

The noise began to blur in his head as Cherry took his organ into her mouth. She began doing inventive little things with teeth and tongue, meanwhile working her fingers under his spit-slickened testicles. Boudreau felt his nerves loosening up, building. His anxiety took a leap of free association.

Keith. Keith was going to walk in and they were all going to *die.*

Cherry grasped all his equipment with both hands to finish him off. She pulled his balls up around his shaft, and began jacking and sucking in concert. Boudreau informed her in a strained voice that he was about to have his orgasm. She kept going. He wondered if she heard him, and how much she'd hate him when he came in her mouth. He moaned protractedly, giving fair warning.

Eyes tightly closed, Boudreau didn't care if there were bleachers outside the windows, didn't care if Keith were armed with a meat cleaver. *Pop* went the weasel.

She began to draw a river of sensation out of him, a stream that started somewhere far up his spine, fed by a million little tributaries of helplessly firing nerves. His brain went orange.

After a while he became aware that something extremely intense was still going on. He opened his eyes and saw that she had unmouthed him and spit all the semen and saliva back onto him. She worked his reddened and beslimed genitals up and down with both hands, watching his crotch as intently as a lab technician following an experiment. In a second or two the pleasure began hopping synapses, shorting out into pain. He reached down to stop her and she let him go, wiping her hands on his thighs. She nestled into his armpit, head on his shoulder.

"Oh, *man.*" He was right back to where he had started, stomach still in knots around the dense little egg of fear. He moaned again at how fast his perspective had just changed, its sole organ of support deflated like a balloon.

She fitted herself closer against him, a whole bundle of alien wants and needs that he couldn't begin to take care of.

"Cherry's not my real name," she said into his chest.

"What?" said Boudreau.

"My real name's Eleanor," said Cherry.

The lawnmower began closing in on them again, the noise growing louder. Lying on the floor in front of the windows, lap smeared with spit and jism, Boudreau began to consider what a big mistake he'd just made. "I didn't know that," he said.

Boudreau got Eleanor Falk's life story, a lot more than he could deal with. He discovered he'd broken a basic rule: never sleep with someone whose childhood was more fucked up than your own. She had him beat by a mile.

She'd grown up all over the Southwest, an only child whose mother disappeared when she was five. The father drank and sold asphalt roofing, in that order.

When the girl was twelve, he came back for one hellish day after a five-day drunk, then left and didn't come back at all. This was in Nevada. She watched game shows and cooked for herself in the kitchenette of the little room, trying to gauge when the motel people would stop believing her about the bill so she could split before they reported her. One day the knock came, but it was a child welfare worker, not cops.

As she delivered this detail, Cherry's voice cracked, then gave way entirely. The little girl had thought she was saved.

"So he was dead?" Boudreau didn't mean to prompt so flatly, but her tale of woe was not bringing things any closer to resolution. In fact, it was making things harder.

"He was in jail watching snakes." Her voice was low with hot-faced shame, even now. "Then he had a long talk with God."

"He got religion?" Boudreau was beginning to feel pinned under her. His arm had fallen asleep and he was alive with itches, the carpet scratching him from underneath, his sodden pubic hair a bed of damp prickling. "So that stopped the drinking?"

"Yeah, he stopped drinking. But *Satan* was still around, right?" She paused. "Guess who he lived in."

Satan? In the ensuing silence Boudreau tried to shift his position a little.

Cherry took it as a signal, rolling over and withdrawing her face from his shoulder. "This is boring." She looked straight up, body stiff. "Forget it."

He tried to cue up his interest. "How do you mean, who he lived in?"

"Whorish *daughter* of a whorish *mother*," she said with the force of a hated quote.

His noise of rueful appreciation ended up sounding more like a pained grunt. He got the feeling that his incomprehension was coming to be regarded as part of the problem.

"Just because he stopped going *after* me didn't mean he stopped *beating* me, okay?"

Boudreau shifted his weight again, and she lifted her head away in response, at which point he registered the content of what she'd just said. He sat up, scalp lifting with the knowledge. She drew away from him like he'd shoved her, the side of her face red and creased from where she'd lain on him. This was the look of someone whose feelings about men were a little scary.

He looked down, searching for the right words. Listen, I'm sorry, okay, but I can't help you, I just can't. You got the wrong man here.

He looked up and disabused himself of the notion immediately. She was already fully versed about wrong men, himself included. He might as well stick with injury and forget the insult.

"Listen, Cherry?" He cleared his throat, trying to readjust the pitch of his voice. "Let's talk now."

"Yeah, sure." She kept her eyes away. "The story was over anyway, right?"

"Hey—no, go ahead, I'm sorry," said Boudreau. "I didn't realize." He touched her arm for sincerity, but it went stiff at contact. "So what happened?"

"What do you *think* happened?" She made a sneering sound at how generically these things worked out. "I got the fuck out of there, ran away to the big city."

"And you were how old?" he said.

"Fifteen." She shrugged. "Sixteen."

"Wow," he said.

"Yeah, *'wow.'*" She turned to look at him as though confirming something, then looked away, face gone neutral.

"Wow," Boudreau repeated, before he could catch himself. He was sorry he'd asked. "And now you're here."

"Yeah, now I'm here." She got to her feet, one whole leg and flank of her pale naked body textured and reddened by the carpet. "Sucking off some guy I met the night before while I wait to get killed."

"Hey—no, *wait.* You—" he began.

"Where's the kitchen?" she said, and walked out of the living room before he could answer.

Boudreau pulled on his pants and went to the bathroom again. When he came out, he found her in the kitchen, sitting on a stool at the island counter and eating yogurt, still naked.

He inhaled sharply. "Aren't you cold?"

His concern elicited a single expulsion of breath, about enough to blow out one candle.

Surging with guilt, he felt like he should show some token of affection. He went over behind her and kissed the place where her shoulder joined her neck. Now that the hard part was almost over, a perverse restirring of desire ran through him. They understood each other, they could still be friends. He reached around and hefted her bosoms. They were like firm little white peaches.

Her body went rigid, yogurt spoon in midair; she waited until he withdrew his hands, then completed her bite.

Boudreau slunk around to the other side of the island. "You sure you're okay?"

She glanced across at him, then blew out another candle. "Yeah, I'm just fine." She fixed the yogurt with a look as she readied another bite. "No worse than before, right?"

Boudreau let it drop. There was only so much shit he was willing to eat. The more attitude she came up with, the easier it was for him. He stared at her, drinking in her nakedness in long bitter swallows. It wasn't like she didn't know what she was doing.

"Listen, the thing about this house," he began, then noticed Cherry staring hard across the island counter to the sink.

He followed her gaze. On the window sill above the sink was a small framed picture that Rena liked to look at while she washed dishes. Boudreau hadn't even remembered it was there. It was of Vicky and Keith Michaels as young teenagers.

"Who's that?" Cherry pointed with her spoon. "Is that—?"

"Where?" said Boudreau.

She got up and walked over to pick it up, her mouth slightly open.

Until that moment it had somehow escaped Boudreau what he'd done, bringing the girl here. He'd succeeded in thinking about nothing but pussy, forgetting what else was involved. It was unbelievable, breathtakingly stupid, but he'd somehow done it anyway. If she had reason to hate him before, it would be nothing by comparison to this.

She turned the picture for Boudreau to see and tapped the glass. "Isn't that What's-her-name? You know, *Vicky?*"

Boudreau looked at the picture as if he weren't sure. Vicky was identifiably herself in a younger version, but Keith was not. He remembered what Keith looked like now, his features obliterated like tracks sunk in mud. In the picture he was so young, hair longer, a big grin on his face. She'd only seen him as a fat pig.

Boudreau nodded until he found his voice. "Yeah, that's Vicky. And her brother." He couldn't bring himself to say the name.

"They *live* here?"

"He does."

She shook her head. "But this is Ronnie's old lady, right?"

"Yeah."

Looking up from the picture at him, her eyes widened. "So but I don't get it, she's got this kind of—?" She finished by gesturing with the picture, waving it in a weak sweep of the kitchen, the house.

Boudreau smiled. "No. No, she and Ronnie don't have any of this shit."

"Yeah?" she said.

"It's just his. The brother's."

Her eyes narrowed. "What happened, he dick her out of it?"

"Not exactly," he said. "She didn't want it."

"She *what?*"

"Yeah, check it out." He was so relieved he found himself on the verge of laughing. It was *funny.* "It's true, I swear. It sort of came down to a choice and she, uh"—he caught himself—"and she wanted *Ronnie* instead."

Boudreau burst out laughing while Eleanor Falk stood there naked, staring at him. She waited while he wiped his eyes and caught his breath. "See, she pissed off her father by marrying Ronnie, and he disinherited her." He waved to dispel any mistaken notions. "I mean, it's a lot more complicated than that but basically"—he started to crack up again—"she went for the curtain instead of the door. She chose our man Ronnie."

Cherry looked at the picture as though trying to identify a strange odor, her cheeks raised and brow furrowed. She gave up and replaced it behind the sink, then sat back down on the stool.

"Well, ain't that fucking romantic." She picked up the yogurt again, her own smile having more to do with stupid than funny. "So where's the parents—they live here with the brother or what?"

"They're at that big country club in the sky," he said, "where the waiters are always polite." He looked at the clock on the wall, then a second later slammed the counter with his sore hand, right on the raw blisters.

"Shit!" *His mother:* he'd forgotten all about lunch. Hopping and moaning, he held the bad hand with his good one, then took an angry swipe at the air. *"Shit!"*

The girl flinched away from him, poised on her stool for flight. "Be cool, okay?" She kept her eyes on him. "I didn't do anything, man. I didn't do *any*thing."

Still pissed and hurting, it took Boudreau a while. "It's not *you.* I just gotta split right away, I got a date."

Her eyes fixed on the empty yogurt container, she appeared to be physically shrinking. "Sure."

"It's with my mother," Boudreau added.

"Whatever."

Boudreau looked at the clock. He was half-naked and smelled like pussy and alcohol; he didn't have time to deal with this.

She kept her eyes down. "Don't leave me here, okay?"

"Look, I'll be back in two hours," said Boudreau, desperate to get out. "You can lock the doors if you're scared. No one knows you're here, no one's going to come around. Keith won't be back till Tuesday."

It was out before he knew it.

"Keith?" She looked around, wild.

Boudreau locked eyes. "The brother." He watched her, but it didn't seem to register. "He won't be back till Tuesday. You'll be okay. I'll be back right away."

She'd gone motionless at the counter, some frail spotted creature hoping its protective coloration would work one more time.

"There's some aspirin with codeine in the bathroom off the study," he said, then wondered if this were such a good tip. "Just don't do too many, okay?" He realized he should just shut up. "I have to go clean up my act."

Boudreau took the front stairs two at a time. By the time he reached the landing a sharp sense memory had come to him, of being a teenager and getting chased by Keith a million times up these same stairs. He could do it with his eyes closed. He made a flying pivot-turn at the newel post, breaking the little toe of his left foot with an audible crack.

Boudreau turned onto the club road, a big dark-windowed car right on his bumper. When it honked, he looked in the rearview and gave a little wave. He pressed in the clutch pedal slowly, letting fly with a bunch of stray rpm's that died off before he made it into third, underpowered. His left foot was huge with pain.

Long and lined with trees, the drive wound its way up through the golf course. Some of the water-rationed fairways were already turning brown from the heat wave. The course was dotted with a few stalwarts out in their sporting togs, red and yellow and chartreuse. The car behind honked again, then swept out and around him to disappear over the next hill. He was twenty-five minutes late already.

The club was packed. Boudreau drove the sprawling length of the landscaped parking lot before he found an empty slot and whipped the Healey into it. He slowed down a hair too late and bumped smartly into the concrete parking block, the car's forward motion translated into rocking up and down on its played-out shocks.

He looked up to see a young teenage boy in a bathing suit jerk short, just in front of him. The kid gave Boudreau an outraged look, like he'd tried to run him over. "Where'd you learn to drive—*Sears?*" He gave the car a brief critical look then continued on, picking his way barefoot over the bark-chipped landscaping of the parking lot.

Boudreau swore under his breath, waiting for the little asshole to disappear before he opened the door. In the middle of his usual roll-and-climb, he hit his damaged toe on something, the car or the ground.

Dizzy with pain, he had to lean on the car, his toe throbbing like something out of a cartoon: whoam *whump,* whoam *whump.* He closed his eyes and tried to focus his way through it. Instead, he got an image of Keith Michaels choking Cherry to death, set to the same blood rhythm. You *bitch,* you *bitch.*

He opened his eyes in a panic. The thing to do was get in the car and drive back *right now,* blow off his mother entirely. He'd make the apology call later, after he came up with some kind of excuse.

His head swam, the air livid with heat. Fuck it. If he went back now, he'd just have to deal with the girl that much sooner. Right now he had to deal with his mother.

By the time he hobbled the length of the parking lot, his scalp prickled with sweat and he sported enormous half-moons under the arms of his light blue shirt. The too large huaraches he'd taken from Keith's closet to fit over his toe had already raised a blister across the instep of his good foot. In addition, he had a cramp in the calf of the other leg from stumping along on the heel.

A whole blond family came out of the main entrance toward him, all pastel clothes and tan skin. He vaguely recognized them, MacDermott or MacTiernan, MacAnglo-Saxon. He immediately fixed upon the col-lege-age daughter, blond and athletic in a light green sundress. He hadn't seen her for several years, and meanwhile she'd turned into a beauty. One shoulder of her sundress had fallen away, exposing the phantom strap of a bathing-suit tan line. She was drop-dead pretty, with green eyes and perfect snub-nosed features, teeth like pearls.

They made eye contact, and Boudreau gave her a jaunty little smile at how comical his limp was. Her family walked past and the girl looked away, embarrassed. If she remembered him, she sure didn't feel like acknowledging it. Boudreau saw himself on her face, some sweaty guy with a flailing-elbowed Walter Brennan gimp, grinning at her like it was funny.

Red faced and late, he took a deep breath and walked through the door of the grill, into a shock of intense air-conditioning.

Every table was full, a hot Sunday full of families at the country club. Boudreau scanned the room for his mother, trying to avoid eye contact with any of the curiously turned faces. A dark-skinned black waiter in a white serving jacket approached.

"Sah?" said the man.

"Hi," said Boudreau. "I'm just here to meet my mother?" Maybe she'd left already.

"Yes, sah?" The waiter gave him a tactful smile, waiting to find out who that might be.

Boudreau went blank. For the life of him he could not remember his mother's current married name. Maybe an earlier one would work. People were looking. He was ready to turn and run when he finally saw her, at a table in the far corner of the room. "There she is," he said.

"Yes, *sah.*"

His mother watched with alarm as he limped up to the table.

"Hi, Mom."

"What did you do to your foot?" she said, tone clear that she was not sure she really wanted to know.

Flustered, he tried to sit down too fast, then yowled halfway back out of the chair, having just rammed his broken toe into the table leg.

"*Richter!*" Cynthia Rowling leaned over the table, voice clench-jawed with suppressed volume. "What is going *on?*"

"I broke my toe right before I left the house." He looked down at his watch, dismayed at what it told him. "God, I'm *sorry* I'm so late." He rolled his eyes. "What a morning."

"Oh my *Lord.*" The way she said it left him uncertain whether this were reprimand or sympathy. She straightened up to her former posture, putting a hand to her throat in a self-calming gesture. "Well, did you at least get it looked at?"

He took this as a note of concern and relaxed a little. "No, I didn't have time." There, he'd wiped the tardiness off the slate. "All they do is tell you to tape it and stay off it anyway." He winced a brave little trouper's grin and picked up his menu. "It'll be okay."

A cafe-au-lait–skinned waiter came to take his bar order. He ordered a double mint julep, discarding his earlier strategy of seltzer only. He'd be discreet and sociable, she could buy that. He racked his brain for something easy to say.

"Can you believe this heat?"

Cynthia Rowling made a brief sound of impatience. "I tell you what," she said in her hard drawl. "After forty years I've had about as much of this as I care for." She said it as though her complaint hadn't yet traveled the proper channels.

He looked at her, waiting for the worst. She was in some kind of state, distracted or irritated. In a moment he found out.

At least it wasn't him. That morning she'd double-parked her car on Peoria to run into a store for an errand. When she came back out, another car had just finished sideswiping the Jaguar sedan, slowing down only momentarily before it drove away.

"Did you see who did it? Did you get a license?"

"No, I *didn't* get the license," Cynthia Rowling said, still mad.

Boudreau clicked his tongue in outraged sympathy. Of course she didn't get the license. Required by law to wear glasses while driving, she was too vain to wear them except in dark theaters and the privacy of her own home.

"Lot of damage?" He tried to imagine the higher realm of finance involved with body work for a Jaguar.

His mother turned on him. "That is *not* the goddamn issue!"

Never having known her to swear except at the very end of her tether, Boudreau watched nervously as she signaled the waiter back and ordered another manhattan. Usually she stretched a single drink until it was nothing but watery dregs.

By the time the drinks came, she had expanded the morning's episode to a general rant about vandalism and lawlessness. Boudreau sipped his drink, glad it wasn't him in the line of fire. Apparently it just struck her that society was falling apart. She'd found the decline of Western values in a crumpled Jaguar body panel.

After a while she steered the screed to Tulsa itself. Her notion of anarchy involved general lack of courtesy and amenity, especially having to do with automobiles. Parking. Traffic. Rudeness.

Boudreau watched his mother, shocked but cautious. Ever since he could remember, she'd had impeccable control, and now she was losing it. What's more, she had always regarded Tulsa as the end-point of social ascension, the pinnacle from which she could look fondly down on her Bristow beginnings. Now, just like him, she was saying that life in Tulsa *sucked.* Behind her mask of too tight skin, he thought he caught a glimpse of bewilderment. He felt a tiny bloom of affection for her.

She was going on now about Outsiders.

"All those big houses out south now." She waved vaguely and mentioned a new development near Eighty-first. Despite its Anglophile name, it was thirty or forty Frank Lloyd Wright imitations, great sprawling things packed together with zero lot lines, wide eaved and shake roofed. "Do you know how much people are *buying* those for?" She leaned forward over the table and quoted a shocking figure. "And you don't even know who these people are anymore."

She gazed off, contemplating exactly who these people might be. "A lot're Jews from back East, of course." She leaned back as though suddenly tired. "I mean, I guess that's where they come from."

Without her looking at Boudreau, her mouth took on a defiant set, something that accompanied her Jew commentary as naturally as "back" described "East." This was for Boudreau's benefit, but he didn't say anything. Even though it was long gone, she still regarded his marriage to a half-Jew as a symptom of his essential waywardness.

A different waiter appeared, a slender middle-aged man with a salt and pepper mustache. "Y'all ready to order now?"

Cynthia Rowling ordered a salad and a mixed grill without bothering to look at the man. Boudreau thought briefly about ordering a steak while he had the chance, then decided a big wad of animal fat would not be healthful. He opted instead for an open-faced sandwich of grilled cheese over fresh tomatoes. As the waiter wrote it down, he noticed a certain look on his mother's face; his order was a tactical error, but it was too late now. Cheese over grilled tomatoes had been Truman Boudreau's special favorite.

The waiter took the menus and thanked them.

She waited until he was a few steps away before she spoke again. "Of course it was a *colored* man," she said, coming down hard on the word to let Boudreau know she really meant *nigger.*

"What?" This made no sense to Boudreau, he could see the waiter was black.

"That hit my *car.*" There was irritation in her voice, the connection patently clear. She kept her eyes on the waiter as he moved off. "They don't care."

Boudreau got into it without thinking. "I thought you couldn't see, Mom."

His mother gave him a look. "I can still tell who's white." She pushed herself away from the table, all business. "I'm going to the little girls' room."

Boudreau watched her make her way across the room with her showy, leggy stride. He potted down the rest of his drink before she was through the door. The mustached waiter walked by and Boudreau ordered another one, trusting he'd bring it before she got back.

Boudreau first came to the club when he was about ten years old, his sister eight. His mother drove them all the way in from the ranch, just to go swimming. They had brand-new bathing suits and carried good towels instead of the old ones. He didn't get what the big deal was.

They were Truman Boudreau's guests, apparently a big deal in itself. Cynthia Boudreau had found out two nights before that her father-in-law had been a member for the last two years without saying anything. She was convinced he'd hid it from her on purpose. The young Richter lay in bed that night and listened to his father try to smooth things over: He's *not* being deliberately mean to you, Cyn, he's a *busy* man, it's just not that impor*tant* to him. During the course of his defense Malcolm Boudreau proceeded from mush-mouthed to fall-down drunk, reduced to saying the same thing over and over again in minor variations until Richter pulled the pillow over his ears.

Richter held Betsy's hand while they hot-footed it across the softened asphalt of the parking lot. She was still snurfling from her mother's attempt to brush her snarled curly hair into a pony tail. Even though their feet were getting scorched, he still had to drag her. He'd never seen so many Cadillacs and Continentals in his life, all of them new.

Finally they made it to the cooling grass of the manicured hill that led down to the pool. His mother strode along out front, sandals slapping. She wore a new white bathing suit with red piping. Richter became aware, as he watched, that other people were watching her, too. He wasn't sure he liked it.

She led them to the snack bar to show them how to order and sign for things. There were four boys—Richter's age or maybe a year or two older—lounging at one of the tables out in front. They were making fart noises and goofing around, telling nigger jokes at the expense of a young man in a white uniform, his skin so black it was almost blue. From behind his screened-in counter he worked a toothpick and occasionally shot a molasses-accented line back at them. Mostly he looked away, cultivating boredom and mild amusement, like a herdsman ignoring the antics of little white yapping dogs. He glanced through the screen, at the impatient young woman in the tight white bathing suit.

The four boys stopped talking as the counterman leaned down into the little window in the screen. Without looking at her, he lifted his eyebrows as though it required effort. "Ma'am."

Cynthia Boudreau leaned over her kids and asked, in a solicitous tone she never used at home, if either of the children would like something. Unable to talk, Betsy shook her head. Richter wanted a burger and a milk shake but was uncertain how all this got paid for. He played it safe and asked for a Dr. Pepper.

"One Dr. Pepper." The counterman wrote down the order on his pad with maybe two strokes of the pencil and then waited, eyebrows raised again. "That it?"

One of the boys at the table said something, low. The other three laughed.

"Name own atcheck," the counterman said.

"Beg pardon?" said Cynthia Boudreau.

"*Name* own atcheck."

She stared at the counterman, a smile fixed on her face. Richter hated it when she smiled like that.

"Who you a *guest* of?" he said then.

"Boudreau." The smile disappeared and she rattled off a spelling, then overenunciated the name for emphasis. *"Boudreau."*

The counterman shrugged, using nothing but his eyebrows. He pulled out the typewritten pages of the membership list and wet a broad pink-tipped finger before running it down the B's.

Richter turned around to lean against the building and look out at the pool, hoping that if he stopped watching, he would not be taken as a part of all this. Betsy tried to take his hand again but he shook it away. From the corner of his eye he could see the four boys staring like this was for their private amusement. One of them was blond and very tan and—Richter could not believe it—openly smoking a cigarette.

"That's *Truman* Boudreau," his mother said, the stiff smile back. She began to spell the name again, extremely slowly, as though the counterman was a halfwit. Richter wished he'd never asked for the fucking Dr. Pepper.

One of the boys at the table burped loudly, causing the others to burst into laughter. Richter stole a look over at the blond boy, who knew how to blow smoke rings.

The counterman found the name and said it aloud, accenting it on the first syllable. He pushed the chit through the window without saying anything else and turned to get the pop.

"Truman Boudreau happens to be county commissioner," Cynthia Boudreau said to his back, "and I'm his daughter-in-law." The man said nothing. She half-turned to Richter as she signed the chit. "Of course Truman doesn't get down here very often." Her tone indicated that she could see why. Richter nodded to show interest, even though he already knew that. He felt like he could grind his teeth into powder and it wouldn't hurt.

The blond boy stubbed out his cigarette in an ashtray, then swiveled his legs off the bench and walked toward the pool, the other three boys immediately following. Richter watched them longingly.

Cynthia Boudreau handed him his pop. "There," she said, "now they know who you are." She jerked her head back at the man standing in the window right behind her. "At least this one does."

The pool was huge, a din of screaming and splashing. He'd never gone swimming in a pool before; swimming meant the river, or one of the stock ponds at True's ranch. The water in the pool looked impossibly blue.

Cynthia Boudreau left him and Betsy by the gate, informing them they were going to have lots of fun. She was going to go get herself a grown-up drink and sit on the main veranda. Richter knew that having to baby-sit his sister ruled out lots of fun. He watched his mother walk away, feeling bad for her without knowing why.

He tried without any luck to ditch his sister, who cried loudly enough to embarrass him into coming back. He ended up squatting near her in the shallow end, over by a wall, with just his eyes and nose above water. He pretended all afternoon that he was a periscope on a sub and that no one could see him.

Although Boudreau didn't meet him for another couple of years, the blond boy smoking cigarettes by the snack bar was Keith Michaels. Keith and Vicky had practically lived at the club as teenagers, so as a coincidence, it was not a big deal. If anything, it was appropriate that Keith should be associated with one of his more sharply remembered social humiliations.

His mother was taking her time getting back. Boudreau worked on his new drink and brooded further, searching for any memories of Keith that might stand out as a first warning sign. Nothing came.

His head whirled with it. Keith had been his friend, he *knew* him. Boudreau could see now, all too easily, how Keith had arrived where he had, done what he did. It gave his act the retrospective weight of destiny, like he'd been *meant* to go take it out on some unsuspecting woman. This somehow made it worse, still harder to comprehend. You could connect the dots from A to B until you got a line, but that didn't bring people back from the dead or tell you how to feel any better.

Boudreau looked around the room at a substantial portion of Tulsa's wealth and power, porking down Sunday lunch. Probably two-thirds of these people had known Keith since the day they'd gotten his birth announcement.

Understanding had nothing to do with justice. Justice would require a locked room and someone twice as big as Keith, equipped with truncheons and dildos and a miswired libido. *He should go call the police.* The thrill of this notion faded immediately as he reconsidered the room. Going to the police would be a joke. These people would shake their heads and pity Keith, not the girl, because his was the life they understood, not hers. Some number of them had immediate forebears who'd marched Main Street in robes and hoods less than sixty years before. They would consider a black topless dancer to be asking for it by definition. In their eyes Keith's act would be an extreme form of high jinks, not so different from blowing up small animals with M-80s. Okay, so maybe the Old Testament was inappropriate; in its place would be something involving loopholes and good lawyers. Whatever justice was, Boudreau knew it wouldn't be found in the same court of law with Keith Michaels. Not around here.

Right back where he started but relieved of any personal role, Boudreau used the rest of his second drink to assuage the transition. He finished just as Cynthia Rowling finally arrived back at the table, the waiter right behind her with the food. She stood behind her chair, preening and straightening her skirt.

"I just had to go see about some business," she said to Boudreau. "I *completely* forgot about table flowers for Wednesday."

Confused, he didn't get the reference. The waiter stood patiently behind her, unable to back up. *"Ma'am?"* he said.

Cynthia Rowling became aware of the man with a slight start. Loaded tray high in the air, his position politely urged her to settle in. Boudreau watched her deliberately take her sweet time. She restraightened her skirt, then waved hello to some people three tables over and mouthed some oh-isn't-this-weather-something commentary. Finally she sat down, without a second look at the waiter.

"Ma'am," he said again, and placed her food in front of her. After he served Boudreau, he scrutinized the table to see that everything was in order. "Can I get y'all anything else?"

"No." Cynthia Rowling didn't bother to look up. "That'll be all."

Boudreau tried to catch his eye, but the man looked into neutral space and smiled professionally before leaving.

"Treated *him* like a nigger," Boudreau observed, the words out before he knew it.

Eyes bright, Cynthia Rowling sat up slightly. She looked past him, her chin lifted and a lordly little smile on her mouth. She had come back to the table in a better mood, and she was not going to let him spoil it now.

She cut off a piece of kidney and put it in her mouth. "Your food's getting cold."

Boudreau looked down at his open-face sandwich, the cheddar brown and crackled, right out of the oven. He couldn't have chosen a more foolish thing to get into with her right now.

"Just letting it settle." The words came out a little slurred and he tried again. "Letting my drink settle."

His mother stopped chewing in midbite and eyed him. After a long moment she resumed.

This was it. Somehow, against all sense, he'd gotten drunk. To his own ears he was audibly loaded. All the liquor had caught up with him, his blood chemistry achieving sudden critical mass. He didn't know why it came as such a surprise. Things were going to end badly.

He had an inspiration. "Boy," he said. "I probably shouldn't even *had* a drink." He reconsidered. Something didn't sound right. *"Have* had. A drink."

His mother stopped chewing, one eyebrow going up like a storm flag.

"I took a Darvon," he lied. "For my *toe."* The words came rolling out of his mouth like big round boulders. As long as he concentrated, they seemed to stay on the right course. "Guess I feel a little light-headed."

Cynthia Rowling had the look of someone who had been expecting much worse. "Well, be careful." She resumed chewing and motioned at his plate. "Get something on your stomach."

Boudreau nodded obediently and picked up his fork. A Darvon for his toe, that was creative. He knew his mother was preoccupied with something else or it never would have stopped there.

"Well," said Cynthia Rowling, "you're never going to guess the news *I* have." She gave him a little smile, smug with about-to-be-revealed secrecy. "Are you doing anything Wednesday afternoon?"

Boudreau shook his head, feeling it safer not to rely on words. He looked down at his plate and felt stirrings of hunger. Maybe it was a good idea to eat something.

"I have a very special someone I'd like you to meet," she said. "I'm giving a little party here."

"Party?" said Boudreau. It sounded like a new boyfriend to him. "What kind of party?"

"Well," she said coyly, "it's really more than just a party."

Boudreau focused on the complex motor task of cutting away a bite of the sandwich. An impressive cloud of fragrant steam rose from the tomato, its heat blanketed under the cheese. *God*, it smelled good. He maneuvered a bite onto his fork and looked up at his mother. "Yeah?" he said.

"Probably nobody takes it seriously anymore except me." She rolled her eyes at her own folly.

He craned the fork into his mouth.

"I got married again last week," his mother said. "To a *won*derful man."

Boudreau groaned loudly, his mouth filling with pain, not food. Tongue seared by the still broiling tomato, he spewed the whole bite back onto the table.

His mother jerked backward with a small shriek, the tight skin around the edges of her face gone waxy pale.

People at nearby tables twisted around at the noise. Cynthia Rowling stared at her son in shock, as far back in her chair as she could get.

"Oh my Lord *God,*" she whispered.

Boudreau put a hand to his mouth and groaned again. "I burn my fuckin' *thongue.*" He whimpered, tears running down his cheeks. This was less than cool.

Their waiter heard the commotion and started over before Cynthia Rowling desperately waved him away.

The nerves in Boudreau's mouth vibrated to the point of oscillation. Eyes closed, trying to escape it, he saw a strangely wounded animal, tongue swollen and useless, frantically wandering the countryside, unable to feed.

"Are you all right," said Cynthia Rowling, voice drained of affect.

Boudreau opened his eyes and nodded, his mouth throbbing. The faces at other tables began turning back again.

She looked straight through him, rigid beyond mortification.

"I'm thorry." His tongue, drunk and now burned, got bushwhacked by the *s*. He tried again. "Really *thorry.*" He put his fingers to his mouth, ready to assess the damage.

"Well, don't *play* with it."

Boudreau dropped his hand as though it were burned, too. He began picking some of the larger pieces of bread and cheese and tomato off the tablecloth, arranging them discreetly on the side of his plate.

Cynthia Rowling moved forward on her chair, picked up her knife and fork and began methodically cutting her meat without eating it, piece after little piece, as though readying the plate for a child.

Boudreau saw the mode now. Pretend it never happened. He took a tiny sip of ice water. *"Wonderful* news."

Still concentrating on cutting the meat, his mother looked up, confused. "Beg pardon?"

"So what's hith name?" he tried, his mouth hopelessly inept as an organ of communication. "Your guy?"

Cynthia Boudreau put a bite in her mouth and chewed it vigorously, then swallowed. Focus returned to her face.

"Vic," she said. "Victor Hill. I met him at Vail this spring."

Boudreau could tell she was making a conscious effort, an actress reentering character. It was time for some extra enthusiasm. "That was quick," he said, finally mastering his tongue. "Really hit it off, huh?"

His mother kept her attention on all the little bites on her plate, stabbing them one by one. "I haven't told a *soul,* it's just all happened so fast." Her brow raised for a brief qualification. "Except Billy, of course. But Vic and Billy are such great friends already, I just feel *so* lucky."

"That's great." Boudreau couldn't imagine his half brother being friends with anyone. "That's really great."

"Vic is founder and CEO," Cynthia Rowling informed him, "of Hill Leasing and Manufacturing. Of course at this point that's not all he does." She looked up from her plate, chewing a piece of kidney, and watched his face for acknowledgment.

Boudreau looked at her blankly. "Yeah?" He was finding it hard to keep up his enthusiasm. "What else does he do?"

"Victor," she said, "was just appointed to head the President's Special Commission on Future Energy Needs. He doesn't really have the time, but he's that kind of man."

This would be a bunch of oilmen, Boudreau thought, trying to figure out ways to burn more oil.

"Reagan man, huh?" Why not ask if Vic had an asshole? "I guess he must be a pretty big deal."

She looked at him, disappointed in the scope of his ignorance. "Hill Leasing just happens to be one of the biggest oil-field equipment companies in Dallas." She amended it with an admonitory whisper. "In the *world.*"

"Dallas?" Dallas was the only city Boudreau had ever been to that was like Tulsa but worse.

His mother forked a piece of sausage and gazed at it. "Of course the real money is in Houston these days."

Boudreau nodded lengthily. He cut a tiny bite of his sandwich, put it in his mouth and chewed gingerly, using the side of his tongue. "So," he said, "when do I get to meet this guy Vic?" He knew exactly what Vic would look like, how he would dress, the way he would talk. He could hardly wait.

"Wednesday," she reminded him. "Victor will be flying up so everyone can meet him."

"Great," said Boudreau, "that's just super."

"I'm *so* excited," Cynthia Rowling added.

"I'm excited *for* you," said her son.

Boudreau finished his food in the silence that followed, bite by little agonizing bite. He found himself working on an attitude. He'd burned the shit out of his tongue, and all his mother could do was get frosty because he'd embarrassed her in public. Now he was supposed to tap-dance because she was getting married a fourth time. He'd had enough of this. She was pathetic with self-deception, with her face-lifts and her husbands, the way she worshiped any jerk who came along if he had enough zeros behind his name. Meantime, she *owed* him.

"Well, listen, Mom, not to change the subject," he said, "but I have a proposition to talk about."

Cynthia Rowling sat up and arranged her knife and fork on her plate. Not so much an indication that she was finished, it was more the gesture of a banker clearing her desk for business. "All right." She averted her eyes as her face fell into straight lines.

Boudreau's train of thought came to a halt. This was the air of someone who'd been expecting to deal with an unpleasant task. She'd been waiting for him. Ronnie, Cherry, Keith: *every*one was waiting for him.

"Richter?" said Cynthia Rowling.

Boudreau lit a cigarette to buy time, exhaling an enormous cloud of smoke. "Mom, I'm in trouble," he blurted.

Cynthia Rowling's eyes widened. "Trouble?"

He saw the look of alarm on her face and panicked. "No, no, I don't mean *trouble.* I mean it's just that I've got to, I've got to change my *life,* that's all."

He'd meant to give her a line, and the truth had popped out instead. It came as a surprise to him, putting it that way. He had to change his life, and she had to help him, it was that simple. She *had* to; he would catalog for her exactly how bad things were right now. He mentally ran down the list and grew even more desperate: there was not a single detail of his existence that she could hear without melting down. For starters there were his various substance abuses, his mountain of debts, his pitiful but still renegade sex life, his increasingly tenuous employment. Occupying a special category was the fugitive topless dancer waiting for him back at Keith's empty house, a material witness to murder.

He gathered himself long enough to see her waiting for more. This was laughable, this notion he'd had of trying to explain himself. A long shiver ran through Boudreau. He was totally out of control. He was lucky not to be in jail yet.

"I don't know," he said, "I just feel like I'm in a rut, I don't feel like I'm *going* anywhere."

Staring at him, his mother nodded. He would find no argument from her on that account.

"I'd like to get ahead so I could start paying back some of the money I owe," he tried. He watched her face and wished to Christ that she weren't one of the creditors in question. This wasn't working. He held his nose and dove in. "I think I want to stop teaching."

Cynthia Rowling looked at him for a long moment before speaking. "And do what?"

"Work on *Greenwood.*"

Her eyes narrowed. "Greenwood?"

"My screenplay? Remember, the one about—"

She looked to the side, then back at him. "I remember."

"Yeah, that one." Boudreau stopped short, floundering. Bringing up race was a bad idea. "Do you know how much good screenplays are going for these days?" There, *that* was it: an investment opportunity. Business. When she didn't reply, he answered himself. "They're going for a *lot.*"

Still staring at him, his mother lifted one eyebrow. "You can't exactly count on that, can you?"

"Well, no, it's not quite finished yet," said Boudreau. "I need to buy some time."

Expressionless, she waited for him to go on. He couldn't meet her eyes anymore. "I know I'm not supposed to get the farmhouse till I'm thirty-five," he said, "but it's still mine, right?" He chanced a direct look to confirm agreement, then looked away, sorry he had. "I'd like to fix it up and sell it."

A hint of a smile appeared on her mouth. "Sell it?"

"Yeah, sell it now. Instead of waiting."

"Sell it to who?"

Trapped, Boudreau looked into his mother's eyes. "To you." The tiny smile disappeared, but he plowed on anyway. "I mean, you can't do anything with that land while I'm still on it anyway, can you?"

She arched her eyebrow again. "I believe that was your grandfather's intention, yes."

He froze. Pinned between Greenwood and Truman Boudreau, he'd just established a lost cause. "I'd do the work myself. I just need some money to get started on it, time and materials, that's all."

His mother stared down at her hands.

"It'd just be a loan until I sold it to you, and then you could deduct it from the sale price."

Cynthia Rowling looked up, but turned her face to the side.

"Well, anyway, I just thought I'd run it by you." The whole thing was beginning to sound like begging. "I really don't want to live there anyway. Not anymore."

She stared off, refusing to look at him. "You know," said Cynthia Rowling, "when Malcolm and I first got married we used to drive down here to Cain's every weekend." She followed this observation by gazing away, high color in her cheeks. *"Every weekend."*

Boudreau gaped. Cain's was an old dance hall downtown, founded in 1925 by one Madison Cain, a bowlegged little man who thought a ballroom dancing academy was just the thing to bring culture to Cowtown. It had immediately turned into a nickel-a-dance honky tonk, a rowdy but major stop on the western swing and country-music circuit.

"My *Lord*, what a place Tulsa was!" Cynthia Rowling said. "We had a little Ford roadster before the kids were born, and we'd drive for *hours* to go hear the Playboys, that's how long it took then."

Boudreau watched her trance state with mounting trepidation. She'd said "the kids" as if he hadn't been one of them, as if he weren't sitting there right now.

She was just getting warmed up. "And that was hard driving too, you'd get there all rattled up and covered with dust. One night Malcolm introduced me to Bob—I think Truman knew him or something, of course Bob Wills knew just about *every*body—and then later on, he pulled me up on the stage and dedicated a song to me. The prettiest girl in Tulsa. They played 'Time Changes Everything.' " She aimed a look at her son as if he'd just challenged her. "And that was back when KVOO used to broadcast live, fifty thousand watts. Missouri, Kansas, Texas, Arkansas—anybody listening to the radio that night heard it. God, I thought life was going to go on forever."

Cynthia Rowling raised her chin a little at the memory of it. "You just *imagine* what that was like, to a girl who'd hardly been outside of Bristow, much less Oklahoma. And *Cain's*, it was full of cowboys and roughnecks right off the rig, half the time you didn't even know if they were millionaires. People making all that *money*."

In thrall to her reverie, a crooked smile appeared on her face. "And there I was, just married to Malcolm Boudreau, this rising young attorney and one of the handsomest men in three counties. Oh, yes, *and* son of Mr. *Truman* Boudreau. So I made Malcolm promise me we'd move to Tulsa. I thought boy-howdy, I just about had it made. I'd hit the big time."

The way she said his grandfather's name gave Boudreau a bad feeling. She turned and looked at him, leaving the past behind. "Some big time. Two kids and an alcoholic skirt-chaser for a husband." She smiled again, much too hard. "I waited *years* in that ranch-hand's cottage, married to my little small-town lawyer who jumped like a rabbit when his own daddy said boo. Then one day I just woke up. I wasn't going to get used like that anymore. Malcolm had *promised* me we'd move to Tulsa, so I held him to it."

Cynthia Rowling paused, working a piece of food from between her teeth with her tongue, her lips tightly closed. "I worked like a *dog* to get that house on Thirty-eighth built. We didn't have the money, of course, but Truman was going to help me out. Oh, he helped me out all right." She fixed her son with a signal look, spelling it out for him. "And your father acting the whole time like he didn't know what was going on. Didn't even *care.*"

Cynthia Rowling leaned back from the table and folded her arms. "Of course he had some little secretary downtown to help him forget. I already had a lawyer drawing up the papers when we got word on his liver. I stayed till he went, I figured I owed him that. But I'd made up my mind about his drinking and lying. I'd *learned.* "

Boudreau's mother looked him straight in the eyes. He saw it coming, inevitable as a high-balling train. "I'm not going to let you disappoint me anymore," she said.

"No, *wait,* " Boudreau said. "I'm not Dad." The combination of words sounded outlandish, a strange defense. "I'm *not.* "

His mother looked at him as though weighing the evidence behind this assertion. "I just won't take it anymore." She shook her head. "Sneaking into my apartment like that was the last straw. I wouldn't even have known if Billy hadn't talked to the doorman."

Boudreau looked away.

"I could hardly *talk,* I was so hurt, I ended up having to call Vic about it. That poor man, him having to listen to my family problems already. That's *trespass,* I could have you arrested for a stunt like that, did you know that? And then you show up here so drunk or Lord knows what you can't even *eat* like a human being, and you have the *gall* to ask me for money." She shook her head again, case closed. "I'm having the locks changed Wednesday morning. I just won't *take* it anymore, Richter."

The muscles on Boudreau's face felt like wood, incapable of expression. "I'm sorry."

"You're sorry." His mother gave a mild sniff, hardly even angry now. "Well, I guess I'm sorry too. But sorry doesn't change things, does it?" She looked at him as though expecting him to agree with her. "Billy and I are moving to Dallas at the end of June."

Boudreau stared at her. "Dallas?"

His mother looked back, surprised. "You could hardly expect Victor to move *here,* " she said. "I mean, they've been calling it the Oil Capital all these years, but everyone knows that's a joke now. That house, by the way," she said, "isn't even worth the rent you owe me for it. I had it assessed."

"The *rent* I owe you?" Boudreau's voice broke like an adolescent's at the encompassing shock of it. He'd been assessed and found wanting. His eyes began to well up.

Now it was she who looked away. "You can go over the figures with my accountant if you want." She laced her fingers together defensively. "Or you can try to sue and find a way to pay me back, whatever you like." She thought a moment. "But my lawyer doesn't think that tenancy clause is exactly ironclad."

Boudreau examined his own hands, searching for clues as to lawyers and money. He gave up. "I guess the house is yours, okay?"

Cynthia Rowling relaxed slightly. "It's just business," she said, trying to smooth it over.

He couldn't resist, voice shaky with bitterness. "Yeah, I guess so. If you need to sell it that bad."

"It doesn't have to do with money, Richter. No amount of money is going to make me forget what I went through."

He refused to meet her eyes, his own spilling over. "So when do you want me out, end of June?"

"I'm not sure," his mother said. "I don't know what the developer's schedule is."

Boudreau felt her regard him from across the table as the news sank in. This was getting more humiliating by the second.

"It's not worth getting upset about," she told him. "You're just going to have to earn my trust back. I just think you have some growing up to do."

Boudreau snorted, his eyes drying up immediately. *Trust?* She'd made him feel like a thief ever since he could remember, prying at the locks around her affection.

"Would you still like to come to my party?" she said. "To meet Vic?"

Boudreau could tell from her tone that she felt this was a big conciliatory gesture, first stop on the road to mother-son rapprochement. He was dying to meet the guy who'd suggested she call the cops on him. "If you're sure you want me." He considered for a moment. "Can I bring a date?"

His mother hesitated in front of this concession. "Of *course,*" she said then. "Is this someone new?"

"She's a dancer," he said. "You'll like her." He got to his feet.

"I'm sure I will." Cynthia Rowling smiled up at him, clearly relieved at the prospect of his exit.

"Mom?" He found himself smiling back at her, amazed at how little had really stood between him and the decision he'd just made. A perpetual thirteen-year-old in her presence, he'd reached adulthood in the last two minutes. He'd fucking graduated. "Listen, thanks. No, I mean it. I needed this."

Boudreau gimped out the front door into the heat and glare. He made it to the Healey and sat down, careful not to bang his toe. The heat saturated his skin but came as a relief after the overchill of air-conditioning.

On the drive back to Keith's he felt a little dizzy, somehow lighter than he used to be, as though he'd shed a skin. He felt invulnerable, oblivious to hurt. He was still drunk, but with real clarity now. Decisions were like that. They clarified things.

Driving like a banshee through the Sunday traffic on Peoria, he turned on the radio and got an oldie, the Stones' "Under My Thumb." He laughed out loud, playing drums on the wheel. It was perfect. It was working out, everything was working out.

He was halfway down the long brick driveway before he noticed Keith's car parked at a sloppy angle in front of the garage, the driver's door hanging open. The Beast was home.

Boudreau jerked to a stop and stared, red flashes appearing in front of his eyes. He was hallucinating. He drove forward twenty more feet and stopped again. The car was still there, the red light still flashing in a weird, wowing rhythm. Boudreau's mind shut down. This was the death scene.

He ground the Healey into reverse, then looked in the rearview to find a Tulsa police cruiser pulled across the drive behind him. What great timing. It was still bouncing on its shocks, door open, cherry top silently rotating.

"*You!*" a voice said, shaky with confrontation. "Hands on your head! Both hands!"

He'd outrun a cop without knowing it. Boudreau thought about trying to get away as the footsteps approached, then immediately gave up. A speeding ticket was the least of his worries right now.

The voice quavered, right behind his ear. "You be *cool,* understand?"

Boudreau made a noise indicating his coolness. The cop didn't sound all that cool himself.

"Turn the ignition off and pull the key out. Do it slow."

Boudreau did it.

"Now th'ow the keys over in the grass, nice and slow. Put both hands on top of the wheel."

Boudreau gripped the wheel, glad for something to hang onto. He turned his head, as slowly as he could.

Looming above and beside him was a heavy-set black cop in sunglasses. He was bareheaded and sweating, planted in a linebacker's crouch, a three-foot nightstick in the up position.

"Why you driving like that? *Huh?* Do I know about you?"

Boudreau shook his head, speechless.

The cop stayed in his crouch, as though he might have to club the Healey into submission. Behind the sunglasses his face was pudgy and unreadable. Boudreau realized the guy was afraid of him. After a moment the cop opened his mouth to try again.

A shot went off, unbelievably loud.

The cop dropped to his knees beside the car. "Mother*fucker,*" he whispered.

The shot echoed like a cannon, rolling up from the back of the house.

Boudreau felt his sphincters unclinch slightly once he realized he wasn't dead. He looked over the door of the car. The cop's face had gone stiff as putty.

"What's going on?" he hissed. "What's going on here?"

Boudreau's throat had closed off. He stared at the cop and shook his head.

From his knees the cop grabbed the door of the car. "You don't fucking *move.*"

In a second he was on his way back from the cruiser in a bent-over combat run, both hands on a short-barreled pump shotgun. He went to his knees next to the Healey, ready to start shooting. After a few seconds he leaned over and held the oily blue length of the barrel against Boudreau's neck, levering his head back over the top of the seat until Boudreau was looking straight up at the sky. With one big hand the cop fished around in his armpits and down his belly. His lower body shuddered as the hand grabbed his crotch.

Still in a crouch, the cop lifted the gun barrel away and looked at Boudreau as though just seeing something. An ear-stretching snarl of a grin came over his face. "You just a peckerwood, right?" He leaned in closer, nearly talking into Boudreau's ear. "I'm gone find out what's going on, but you ain't moving. You too *scared*, hear me?"

Boudreau stared at him, uncomprehending.

The cop gave a sharp forearm smash to the door with the butt of the shotgun. Boudreau jumped.

"Hear me?"

His spine gone to jelly, Boudreau managed a nod. The cop gave him a last look and went forward from his knees straight into a crouching run—heavy buttocked and lumbering, the shotgun out in front—down the driveway toward the garage. It was maybe a minute and a half since the shot had been fired. He gave a last look back before rounding the corner of the house, then disappeared.

Boudreau hit his knees in the grass where he thought the keys were. Wrong spot, this had to be the wrong spot. He started scrabbling around in a wider circle on his hands and knees, raking the grass with his fingers. There was nothing, no keys at all, the lawn empty as a putting green.

Another shot rent the air, a distinct crack blossoming into a boom. An indistinguishable shout followed in the wash of echo.

Boudreau got up and ran, ignoring his bad toe. He started for the street, then reversed direction. There would be cars, more cops. On the broad plain of landscaped lawn he felt like an open target, a panicked rabbit running circles in a sunwashed meadow. He needed cover.

He started following an eight-foot-high hedge back toward the house, an impenetrable growth that divided things up with the next huge house over. It was the wrong direction to be traveling but Boudreau remembered a heavy chain-link gate, one that he and Keith had used as

teenagers for midnight skulking. It was down somewhere near the back
corner.

He reached the rear of the house and groaned. He'd remembered
wrong: the gate was another twenty or thirty feet down the hedge, out
in the open.

Boudreau peeked around the corner at a small knoll planted in low
rhododendron. Beyond it one part of the back lawn rolled down in a sort
of valley to the pool, no one in sight. He got down on his knees and
started crawling for the shadowed opening in the hedge. A few feet past
the shelter of the rhododendron, he could see the crowns of the pecan
trees around the pool, nothing else. He kept going. Halfway out there
was a garbled shout. He dropped to his belly just as the top of a head
appeared, down by the pool.

Slowly Boudreau rotated his head, nose into the grass, from one cheek
on the ground to the other. He started to belly backward when another
shout came from the pool area, a command to *stop*. Boudreau felt the
tension leave his body as he oozed flat onto the ground. He waited, eyes
closed and face dripping, for the order to get up.

The next voice was different, raised in complaint. It was Keith.

After a moment the first voice answered him. The cop was telling him
to *drop it*. Boudreau turned his head to look back.

Keith Michaels was in view from the chest up, holding one of the big
shiny Colt revolvers randomly off to the side. His doughy white chest
was bare, and he squinted in the hard light. Boudreau wondered if he
was still in his underwear. Keith shook his head, a smirk of disbelief on
his mouth.

Shifting in the grass for a better look, Boudreau saw the barrel of the
pump shotgun appear, pointed in Keith's direction. The cop followed the
barrel into view and repeated the order to drop it, followed by a longer
phrase at a lower volume. The gun fell out of Keith's hand, glinting
once before Boudreau heard it clack on the flagstones, out of sight.

The cop gestured with the barrel of the shotgun until Keith moved
backward. The cop squatted down out of sight, while Keith, disgusted,
folded his arms across his chest as though he couldn't be bothered with
this shit.

Boudreau bellied his way back toward the rhododendron. From his more elevated vantage behind the bush, Boudreau saw the cop rise from a squat. In one hand he held the pistol, its emptied cylinder hanging out like a shiny clump of guts. Now he held the shotgun in the crook of the other elbow like a duck hunter. He looked down to the side for a long moment, then looked away. After a bit he did it again, as though in spite of himself. He stared hard, then turned and said something to Keith.

After a hesitation Keith craned his head and searched the sky, exasperation giving way to a look of reluctant surrender. He drew closer to the cop, a kid caught by the teacher. He had on a pair of madras bermuda shorts, the waistband lost under his hanging belly. He fished out his wallet and handed it over, then refolded his arms while he watched the cop.

Pulling a card out of the wallet, the cop started talking. Keith broke in, agitated. He pointed at the gun, at the terraced bank of flowers over beyond the pool. He was arguing.

The cop's head went up, cocked at an angle like he couldn't believe this.

Boudreau watched, stupefied. These were random sets of animal gestures, nothing more. He got the feeling he was watching a pair of monkeys in the primate house, disputing some unknowable thing.

The cop turned a little and pointed down at the place he'd been staring at before. Boudreau raised himself up behind the rhododendron, freezing in midsquat when he saw it. Cherry's body was laid out full-length on the diving board, one arm hanging off it. The black wraparound sunglasses were still on her head.

She sat up as though hinged at the waist, a vampire in a tiny black bikini rising out of her coffin. She was all limb, the palest white with a faint red glow.

She said something to the cop; he said something back. Her shoulders went up in a shrug, and Boudreau caught a faint sound. She was laughing. She lay back down on the diving board, her hands behind her head. She was going to catch some more rays.

The cop was still glomming her up when Keith reached for the gun in his hand. The cop jerked it out of his reach and raised his voice, a threat. Keith stamped his foot and brought both fists down to his sides, as though he were pushing ski poles. He jabbed a finger at the cop, then up at the house. Boudreau caught a single phrase: *no nigger cop.*

A smile came over the cop's face. Within seconds Keith was wearing handcuffs and stumbling drunkenly up the hill, the shotgun at his kidneys helping him along. His belly jiggled as he went.

Boudreau sat down behind the bush, the base of his spine hitting the ground with a shock. Sweat dripped into his eyes. He waited until they were out of sight, then hobbled back along his side of the house. When he got to the front corner, they were already halfway down the driveway, the cop still shepherding Keith from behind. As they approached the Healey, Keith jerked his head down at it and tried to stop.

Brooking no bullshit now, the cop gave him a good sharp prod in the small of the back with the shotgun's butt. He stuffed Keith into the back of the cruiser, then stood in front of the Healey writing on a pad. Ticket under the windshield, he cast a final look around the palatial yard, then unholstered his nightstick and did in the left headlight, stepping into it like a good forehand. Satisfied, he walked back to his car.

Boudreau was back on all fours searching for his keys when a shadow fell across the grass. He started, then swore.

"*Mean* to scare you," said Cherry.

Boudreau looked around the huge empty yard, the quiet street. "I'm just looking for my keys." He avoided her eyes, the whole thing too weird for discussion.

She flopped down on the grass, a shirt on now over the bathing suit. "Missed some action," she said. "Keith got *busted.*" She gave him a big wet smile, lopsided with dope. He guessed she'd found the codeine-laced aspirin. Her head wobbled in comic dismay, like this was all a joke. "Boy's Ronnie gonna be pissed, I mean *cops* and shit?"

She began fanning through the grass with one hand, as though ruffling some animal's fur. Boudreau stared at her. She was not taking this very seriously.

"Bust him just for shooting in his *yard?*" She grimaced at the injustice of it. "He never should of talked back to that cop." She shrugged. "Asshole."

"I thought Keith did it." Boudreau burst into laughter at his own statement, a nervous laugh that stopped as soon as it started, involuntary as a fart. "But Keith didn't do it, right?"

Cherry held up Boudreau's keys, dangling them between thumb and forefinger. She looked at him through the sunglasses.

"Do what?" she said. "Shoot some flowerpots?"

Boudreau took the keys and looked down as relief flushed through him. "I thought," he said, "I thought it was, like, Keith. You know, the *guy. Keith.*" He looked at her to see if she grasped his meaning, then shook his head. "I mean, I pull in here and see his car and I think"—he gestured helplessly at the notion, a big dumb grin on his face—"oh, *shit.*"

She drew her head back to look at him, as if to gain more perspective. Her sunglasses had gone a little askew on her nose, giving her face a certain cubist effect.

Too late, he realized the implications.

"That's funny?" she said.

He found her at the kitchen counter, working the cap off the codeine bottle. The sunglasses were off, and she flicked him a look as she shook out three, then three again, and moved to the sink.

"I can explain," said Boudreau. He thought about it, but the necessary details evaded him. "It's just too complicated, take my word for it."

She swallowed the pills without expression, as if he weren't there.

"I mean it wasn't so hard to believe," he found himself saying. "Keith treats women like shit, he *hates* women."

She lifted her eyebrows and made a little "oh" mouth, not bothering to look at him. "I'll be on my toes," she said.

MONDAY

Boudreau left Cherry a note saying he had to go to work, he'd be back later. He wasn't sure if this were a lie or not, either part; he just knew he had to get out. He considered leaving his phone number at the paper, then thought about how such a call would go if he weren't there to take it. He checked again upstairs before he left. She was still out, her muscles so slack she looked like someone coming out of postop anesthesia. Keith had neither come back nor called since yesterday, but this was not Boudreau's concern. Keith was no longer his problem.

He wound up driving down to the paper after all, in lieu of having anything better to do. By the time he arrived, he had a reason. At times like these it was important to maintain control. Go to work, crank out the review he owed, be cool, act like a citizen. Maybe if he did those things, he'd have some sense of what a citizen would do next.

From his desk Boudreau took a look around the newsroom. Everybody seemed so placid and untroubled, just a herd of cattle out in the hay lot, grazing, lying around, chewing cud, flopping out cow pies. *Eat work shit die,* at least they knew what was coming. They went on about their business trusting that today was no different than yesterday and would only lead to tomorrow.

His stomach acidic with coffee, he lit another cigarette and gazed at the blur of words on his terminal. This made his usual writer's block look petty.

Boudreau had spent most of his life consciously feeling like an outsider, but now he wanted the yonder side of the fence, a membership in good standing within the greater bovine community. He didn't understand how he'd ended up out *here,* counting every breath like it might be his last.

Knowledge was exile, it kept you apart. Last night, before Cherry tuned out completely, he'd managed to pop the Big Question. As soon as she answered, he was sorry he'd asked. Her sneer was bad enough, but nothing like the answer itself. It was like that legendary psychedelic of the sixties, the one where you tripped your brains out for thirty days and then died at the end. He was still rushing just as hard today.

It gave him the sensation that he himself had not been present recently. If he'd been there he would've seen this coming. He would've known, or he could've found out. So where *had* he been? His memory of the last few days had some big ragged tears in it, an ancient text only partly restorable. *Maybe,* Boudreau thought, *maybe he was going crazy.* He wished Brinkman would hurry up and show.

A hand clapped down on his shoulder, and he spun half out of the chair.

"Early bird pulling the worm," said Preston Liddey. "That's what I like to see."

Boudreau managed a feeble smile. "Yessir," he said. *Pulling the worm?*

"I like to see my boys in early," said Liddey. "Makes me feel like I'm getting my money's worth." He winked at Boudreau to let him know it was all in good fun, then gave him a look of avuncular approval. "Kidding aside, Richter, morning's the best time for good work, that's when your good biorhythms are working for you." He looked around the newsroom. "Son of a *bitch!*"

Boudreau jumped, afraid to know.

"Pardon my French." Preston Liddey had himself a little chuckle at his own outburst. "Sometimes you get this kind of morning, know what I mean? You just know things're gonna cook all day, I mean *cook.*" He shook his head at the robust size of his good mood. "We have got us some *great* stories going today." He gave Boudreau another wink as he moved off. "You keep up the good work, son."

Boudreau watched a copyboy move around the newsroom flopping down copies of the early edition on every desk. When his phone rang, he jumped yet again. His nerves had gone so bad he thought it must be a visible condition, like his hair was on fire. He waited through another couple of rings, looking around the room. No one seemed interested in the least.

He inhaled and picked up the phone. The receptionist told him a Charles Carlson was on the line.

"Richard Boudreau?" said a secretary's voice after he punched the button.

"*Richter,*" he said, but she'd already punched her own button.

"Richard, this is Chip Carlson down at McCann, Barrett." Carlson's voice was bluff and formal, no indication in it that they'd ever even met, much less played tennis together two days before.

"Richter," said Boudreau.

Carlson hesitated just long enough to make the silent equivalent of "whatever." Boudreau could see him, fat jowled at a big desk in some carpeted suite, tasteful corporate art on the walls.

"Listen," Carlson said. "Keith Michaels is in jail."

Boudreau summoned surprise. "*No,*" he said. "Is he okay?"

"He's not hurt, if that's what you mean," said Carlson. "But I wouldn't say he's okay—else he wouldn't be in jail, now would he?"

"Oh, I don't know. I don't know that that follows."

Carlson stopped short at this. "I don't see what's to follow. Most people, they'd figure going to jail means something's *wrong,* wouldn't they?"

"I guess it depends on what you think about the police." Maybe after a few more exchanges Carlson would ask him if he'd like things better in Russia.

Carlson paused, exhaling heavily. "In case you're not aware, Keith Michaels has some mental problems."

"Really," said Boudreau. "So what's he in for?"

"Oh, reckless endangerment, illegal discharge of a firearm within city limits, threatening an officer, resisting arrest," Carlson recited. "Among other things. They picked him up yesterday after they got complaints in the neighborhood. He was shooting guns in his backyard."

Boudreau chewed this over. *Complaints in the neighborhood.* "Shooting guns in his backyard?"

"That's right. And apparently there were other people involved."

"Other people? You mean other people shooting?"

"I'm not aware of that. But I believe it was a party involving intoxication."

"Sounds like Keith." That darn Keith.

Carlson hesitated at Boudreau's tone, then pressed on. "The arresting officer said Keith was drunk out of his gourd. He was apparently quite abusive to this officer."

Boudreau whistled. "That's terrible," he said. "That sounds like mental problems to me."

Carlson breathed over the line for a few seconds. "Look, I'll come to the point. I've been baby-sitting Keith Michaels now for longer than I care to think about, and I've had about enough. I got his phone call yesterday from the station, and he had the fu—" Carlson's voice rose, "He had the *goddamn* nerve to tell me it was my fault."

"Your fault?" This was impressive, even for Keith.

"Yeah, and then, and *then* he says come down and get him out. After listening to that kind of abuse." He snorted. "I told him he could just cool his butt in jail for a while. I called up Victoria, but she won't have anything more to do with him. And frankly I don't blame her."

Victoria? Boudreau rolled his eyes at the newsroom. "Yeah, so go on."

"As an officer of the Michaels trust, I have a duty to execute." Chip Carlson took some time out from his offended tone to congratulate himself. "I made bond for him and got a court date. I know some people on the bench, maybe I can pull a few strings. I'll do my best." His voice went somber with the seriousness of it. "But it's not like Keith came to this with a clean slate. The police have seen him twice this year already."

This was news to Boudreau, but he stepped aside, unimpressed. "Let me guess—vulgar language? Moving violations?"

Carlson watched his best ball slam back past him. "I guess that's pretty funny, public drunkenness and threatening people in restaurants. For your information," he said, "Keith is looking at a stack of *shit*. You don't bargain all that down to nothing."

In Boudreau's opinion this was a double fault. "Rap sheet long as your arm, huh?"

Chip Carlson paused a long moment. "Some people, the only way they learn is to get taught a *lesson*, Richard." He said it slowly, letting the implications widen. "They just don't understand any other way."

Boudreau gave a nasty little laugh. Yeah, teach him a *lesson*. "Maybe you can work on getting him a TV."

"Beg pardon?"

"I mean for when they send him up to the Big House."

"Do you have a problem here?" Carlson said. "Do you have a problem I need to know about?"

"Yeah," said Boudreau. "My problem is I don't know why you're telling me all this. Chipper."

Chip Carlson stopped short, then snickered. "Why, 'cause you're the only friend he's got *left*, Richard." He sounded happy, like now they could get down to the business of snorting and pawing dirt. "I guess that about says it all, don't it? I guess you and Keith must be *soul brothers.*"

He snickered again, the prospect of violence bringing out the good humor in him. "Hell, I even called to see if his old colored housekeeper wouldn't go get him—but she won't even answer the phone!" Carlson laughed out loud. "See what I'm saying, Richard? Nobody'll even go down and pick him up at the fucking station!"

Boudreau listened to the lawyer breathe violently into the phone. He knew if Carlson were there in person, he'd be toe-to-toe and grinning, waiting for the first punch to get things started.

"Sure, okay," Boudreau said finally. "I'll pick him up." No problem. "And Chipper? Give my regards to Victoria. We'll play some tennis again real soon."

The line went dead on him. Boudreau recradled the phone, his mood suddenly much improved. He'd just needed a little exercise, that's all, a little conflict to get the blood flowing. It gave the world some definition, some light and shadow.

He turned off his terminal and leaned back, idly scanning the front page of his new *Daily Journal*, right where the copyboy had slung it on his desk. What a rag. In its own way it was comforting, a third-rate paper with no surprises. In a minute he'd go down to give fat Keith a ride home from the pokey.

He stood up and gave the paper a desultory flip before leaving on his errand of mercy. He could use some bang-up news about how hot it was here in Tulsa. Maybe there'd be one of their expensive four-color photos, kids playing in a sprinkler or something.

The three-column picture was below the fold, but it took him a while to understand what he was looking at. He leaned on the desk with both hands and stared. There was a caption under the picture, and a jump to the article on page three, with George Brinkman's byline. Not to knock Brinkman's journalism, but the picture told him the whole story, more than he wanted to know.

Boudreau sat on a bench opposite the desk sergeant and lit another cigarette. The cop kept looking up from his paperwork to watch him. He waited until the guy looked back down before he unfolded the newspaper once again, extracasual. You couldn't be too careful, here in the belly of the beast.

The picture showed an exploded car sitting in a parking lot, a long low piece of half-melted machinery hulked flat on all four rims. A relatively intact fragment of the front end indicated that it had previously been a new white Corvette. The middle of the car—where the two seats used to be—was blown up and out with an awful pustular quality, the source of the blast obvious even in its aftermath.

Heat had melted what remained of the fiberglass bodywork into a surreal image of car. Standing nearby was a skinny-shouldered cop holding a clipboard, a look of wonder on his face. He was like a human yardstick, his frailty giving the force of the explosion a disturbing scale.

POLICE INVESTIGATE SUSPICIOUS SOUTH TULSA BLAST

Boudreau was particularly fond of the headline editor's choice of "suspicious," like someone had blown the shit out of the car by accident.

Compulsively he turned again to page three, as if maybe this time there'd be something he'd missed before. He hadn't made it past the first paragraph when a door at the end of the hall closed with a hollow boom.

Keith Michaels walked like a zombie up to the desk, accompanied by a jailer. He still wore his madras shorts, along with a white T-shirt the jail had provided. It barely fit across the chest and shoulders and didn't even come close on the belly. His gut flab extruded between the top of the shorts and the stretched-out bottom of the T-shirt, as though he were wearing a bulging, four-inch-wide, hairy pink belt. He was unshaven and his already small eyes were swollen. He looked like Baby Huey after a three-day bender.

The desk sergeant shoved a wallet and a sheaf of paper over the counter.

"Where's my *gun*," Keith said, staring at the place where the cop pointed. "This is *bullshit.*"

"Watch your mouth," said the cop.

Boudreau got to his feet. "Key, sign the paper, man. I got to get back to work."

Keith Michaels spun around, livid. He stared at Boudreau like this was somehow his fault, then turned abruptly back to the desk. "What a fucking setup." Picking up the pen, he smiled to himself. "Okay, pal. I can play that game."

Boudreau watched the two cops exchange little smirks. He was already sorry he'd come.

Keith finished his signature with a ripping flourish halfway across the page then turned around, his face wild. He was in another world. He gestured behind him with his wallet, waving it like a talisman. "I'm gonna start by suing these pigs into the *ground,* and then I'm gonna work my way *back.*"

"You best watch who you call pig, fat boy," said the sergeant, his eyes gone flat in an instant. The other cop's smirk widened into a happy smile.

Boudreau took Keith by the arm before he could say anything else and hustled him down the hall and out the door. He steered him by the arm, Keith veering off across the heat-softened asphalt like a shopping cart with bad wheels.

The Healey's shocks bottomed out as Keith flopped down into the seat. Boudreau got in himself and put the key in the ignition. "So," he said. "You okay?"

Keith looked straight ahead through the windshield, his red face already bright with sweat.

"Hey—Key?"

"Whatever they gave you," Keith Michaels said, "it's not gonna be enough."

Ready to start the car, Boudreau craned his head to the side and stared. The moisture on Keith's cheeks was not sweat. "*What?*" he said.

Keith kept his face forward and shook his head, smiling. No way he was buying this, not for a minute. "Hey, let's do Keith. Sure, cut me in, why not?"

"Wait a minute," said Boudreau, "*wait* a minute. I don't know what the hell you're talking about."

His boyhood friend's smile curled into a snarl. "You want to play hard? Okay." He turned toward Boudreau, without actually looking at him. "You tell 'em we'll see who plays hard."

"Key?" said Boudreau. "Key, you're up*set,* man."

He shook off this notion, looking back through the windshield. "Take my advice, pal. You just better stay out of the way."

Boudreau sat for a moment. So far as he could tell, he'd just been threatened. This was hospital-grade behavior. "I'm going to take you home now," he said, turning the ignition. "You need to cool out."

"You fucking *liar,*" Keith Michaels said through his tears. He held out his hand without looking. "Just gimme a fucking cigarette, okay?"

By the time they pulled into the driveway Keith had withdrawn completely, getting out of the car without a word.

"I just need to go in and check on something," said Boudreau, standing by the car. "Okay?"

Keith shrugged on his way down to the pool, as though a cab driver had asked him for a glass of water.

The house was empty, no reply to his yell. His note to Cherry was gone. Boudreau panicked and ran upstairs. At least her stuff was still there. He sat on the bed, assigning meanings to what this might mean, then made himself get up. He had to get out of here. He had to start making some of this right.

Boudreau went down to the pool, thinking he should at least establish that Keith wasn't going to hurt anybody. No Keith. He went back up to the house and found him down in the billiards room, sitting on the banquette with his guitar and half a glass of bourbon. He was staring at the cover of *Sticky Fingers* propped next to him, his headphones on.

Boudreau went and stood in front of him, the volume audible from three feet away.

"You gonna be okay?" he said loudly.

Blank faced, Keith stared back at him. Boudreau mimed peeling away one ear of the headphones, then pointed to his own mouth. Keith Michaels closed his eyes.

"Well, fuck you," said Boudreau in a normal voice. "Tell Mick and Keith I said hi." He'd been planning to ask him to tell Cherry to stay put, if he saw her. Now that he thought about it, maybe that wasn't so important after all. He looked down at Keith. "And tell Laura I love her, okay?"

R onnie and Vicky's block was composed of small, one-family houses built in the thirties. All of them sat up on top of steeply sloped swales that ran down both sides, as though the street were a waterway, the houses set high up on its banks. Narrow little driveways, most of them no more than two concrete strips, ran up beside each house to cramped one-car garages out in back. Every house had its own set of poured concrete steps from the sidewalk up to the front door, the steps steep enough to require pipe handrails.

There were different solutions to the universal problem of "yard." Although the houses themselves sat on a level grade, the ground stayed that way only for another ten feet or so before it dove down to the street. The pitch was steep enough to make mowing nearly impossible, although that, in fact, was what the majority somehow did. A few avant-garde types had planted the front slopes in ground cover instead of grass, two houses had done a combination of ground cover and terraced flower beds, and one had simply paved the entire front slope with flat sandstone.

Ronnie and Vicky's solution was simplest, which was nothing at all. When they'd moved in two years before, the slope had been grass; now it was knee-high weeds, blasted by the heat to a yellowy brown.

The neighborhood was nothing more or less than getting-by working class, mostly a renting population in transit from job to job, marriage to marriage. There were broken toys littering the yards, and some obviously dead cars parked in the street or up in the driveways, a few of them up on blocks. Most of the houses were in need of something, paint or roofing or new concrete steps, whatever. Even so, in Boudreau's eyes the Stover household stood out like a hairy wart, its every window blank with drawn, yellow-stained shades, as good as an advertisement that the nonconformity of the occupants didn't stop with the front yard.

In the blare of sun the street was empty of life, people either gone or inside sitting next to their air conditioners. He drove down to the end of the block, then turned up a steep driveway, scraping his tailpipes on the angle between the sidewalk and the slope. He backed out onto the street, hitting the pipes again, and decided to park there behind a beat-up old schoolbus that someone had converted into a camper.

This was paranoid, but then again, this was exactly why he came. He'd had enough of thinking like this. He took his dog-eared copy of the newspaper and walked back down the block. At the top of the Stover driveway the doors to the garage were closed, the Mustang parked in front of it. In the dead heat a single forlorn insect scraped at its legs for a mate.

He knocked at the beat-up screen door, the inside door open. They were either saving on air-conditioning or the thing was broken. Through the screen he could see the TV on in the living room, the sound turned to a bare murmur.

He knocked again, then opened the door and went in. "Hello?" he said. "Hello? Hey, Ronnie? Vicky?"

An acrid reek of urine hit his nose, so strong it brought tears to his eyes. The diaper smell hung in the sweltering air; it had to be ninety-five inside, even with the shades drawn against the sun. It took him a moment to adjust to the gloom, his eyes drawn to the soap opera playing on the TV. A high-gloss woman sat hunched over in a medium shot, while an equally well-groomed man stood behind her, his hands resting on the back of her chair. He stared out a window and silently mouthed some kind of bad news. The camera came in on the woman burying her face in her hands.

Boudreau started to hello again, then caught himself. A little buzz went through the air. Something was wrong. The TV bespoke an ominous lack of presence, as though it had been hours since anybody had watched it. There was a close-up of the woman's shoulders heaving with apparent sobs, then a close-up of the man, stony faced, just as he turned from the window to look straight at the camera.

Boudreau fought the urge to run. This was just straight bad nerves, Ronnie and Vicky were sleeping or outside somewhere or in the bathroom or something. So they'd just left the TV on and gone for a drive. Yeah, a drive without the car. He'd check the house and then leave. Maybe he should just leave.

He tried the baby's bedroom first, its door closed except for a small crack. The TV still playing at his back, he pushed the door open with his foot, the creak of its hinges unbelievably loud. The room was a mess, a shadowy litter of clothes, an upended laundry basket, empty boxes of throwaway diapers. In the corner he made out the crib, just as a small cry came from it.

He went stiff with fear, then crept his way over to the crib, steeling himself for something he didn't want to see. He breathed out. The baby looked all right, fretting in the heat but still asleep on her belly, little diapered butt humped up in the air.

Leaving the door open, he backed out into the front room. He made himself check the rest of the tiny house, ending up back in front of the TV. They were gone. He kept waiting for his pulse to slow down. There were no obvious signs of struggle, although their housekeeping would camouflage anything short of smashed chairs and upended tables.

No one was home, no one but the baby. *Now what?* He couldn't just walk away from a baby. He couldn't take it along, either. His mind went blank while he watched a floor wax commercial, the action sped up to a silent-movie frenzy until the end, when the housewife on her knees silently caressed the shiny floor and mouthed the tag line. The soap opera resumed with a shot of a man, different from the first, entering a house, the front door slamming shut behind him.

Boudreau had time to criticize how poorly the soundtrack matched the shot. For such a heavy-looking door, it slammed more like a rickety screen. He remembered that the audio was still off but by then it was too late, the arm already around his neck. The newspaper fluttered up out his hand, then dropped out of sight like a wing-shot bird.

Boudreau caught a whiff of hair oil and sour breath from behind his neck, just as his own air was running out. This was like slow-dancing with an anaconda. No—go ahead, you lead. He heard himself gurgle. It was not at all the way he'd imagined death would feel.

The arm let go. "Thought you was somebody else," said Ronnie.

Bent double and gasping, Boudreau turned around. His hands went around his own throat, to make sure it was still there. He tried to speak but couldn't.

"She still asleep?" Ronnie inclined his head toward the baby's room.

Boudreau dumbly nodded his head, watching as Ronnie unrolled a fresh pack of Pall Malls out of his T-shirt sleeve and rapped them against the heel of his hand.

"Had to run down to the Git 'n' Go." He unzipped the cellophane and tapped one out. "She hears the car start, she'll wake up just like that."

Pop-eyed, Boudreau stared at him. This was apparently going to be the extent of his apology. Ronnie lit his cigarette and inhaled with exaggerated pleasure. "Man can't go without smokes when he's thinking," he said.

"You choked the *shit* out of me." Boudreau's voice came out like a cartoon character's, part helium.

Ronnie glanced over from behind the sunglasses, his head cocked. He pursed his lips and shrugged, then began looking around in the mess for an ashtray to put his burnt match in. "No car out front," he said, "then I find somebody standing in the middle of my living room. How's that look to you?"

"I parked down the block," Boudreau croaked. He stopped to massage his throat. "I thought it'd be better."

In lieu of an ashtray Ronnie laid the match carefully on the corner of a coffee table, so as not to be messy. The room was so dark Boudreau wondered how he could even see with his shades on.

"I thought you were gonna fucking *kill* me," said Boudreau, unable
to let it go. He knew it sounded wimpy.

Ronnie's pursed lips widened, then tilted up in one corner like he was
gonna let Boudreau in on a secret. "Potential lethal situation," he said,
"you don't come in saying, 'Scuse me, can I help you?" He illustrated
his point by cleavering an onion in half, one big hand into the other.
"You get the drop *first*. You don't get no second chance." The smile
still on his face, he watched Boudreau to make sure the lesson was being
absorbed. "Listen, comrade, I had people come in here with loaded guns
before. More'n once, and that was before all this shit started."

Comrade. Boudreau looked at him, speechless. *Poe-tential lethal situation*.
He was angling for an apology and Ronnie was giving him combat
tips, killer's-manual highlights. Boudreau had spent most of his adult life
regarding himself as an "outlaw," a self-image formed of political atti-
tudes, Nicholas Ray movies and certain select pieces of rock and roll.
Now he saw how Ronnie embodied something that far surpassed cul-
tural metaphor. Ronnie was an animal.

"You want some coffee," Ronnie asked, satisfied now that the problem had been dealt with. "I could dig some coffee." Without waiting
for an answer, he rolled his cigarettes back up in his shirtsleeve and
moved off to the kitchen.

Boudreau picked up his newspaper off the floor and followed behind,
still rubbing his Adam's apple like it would strengthen his resolve.

Ronnie was already rooting through the debris in the sink, moving
with unusual crispness. Without being exactly jerky, he didn't seem to
be inhabiting his body with the usual smoothness. There was something
a little off about him.

Fishing a Pyrex coffee pot out of the mess, Ronnie gave it a slop of
a rinse, then filled a kettle. Halfway to the stove he stopped and set the
kettle down, as though he'd forgotten what he was doing. He picked up
something out of the pile of cereal boxes and dirty dishes on the counter,
cleared a space on the formica table and set it down. Now Boudreau
understood. It was a mirror with four short white lines on it.

"I don't like it," said Ronnie, "but it helps me think." He licked his lips and turned back to the coffee making. "Figure I can use all the help I can get."

Ronnie never did cocaine, but Boudreau took his explanation at face value. The mirror sat in front of him like early Christmas. This was exactly what he needed to get him through the upcoming conversation.

He rolled a bill from his wallet and greedily snukked up his first line. He got a sharp bite in the nose, briefly noted how this was more heavily cut than usual, then snorted the other. His nose caught fire.

"Jesus Fucking *Christ!*" It was methedrine, not coke. Maybe he should've asked first.

Boudreau's blood accelerated through his body like one of the miniature electric slot-cars he'd raced as a kid. He held on through the rush, his paranoia instantly seizing upon his own mortal, redlining body. *What now what now what now.* What now? Oh, just a little visit to heart-attack city, followed by an out-of-control speed run for the next *x* number of hours. He couldn't believe he used to do this for fun. His nose felt like he'd just tried to run pure ammonia through it.

Boudreau turned on the faucet and leaned over the sink. He started snorting water out of his hands, trying to rinse out the burning crystals still lodged in his mucous membranes.

"Shit gets you going, don't it?" Ronnie said, then came over and did his lines in two efficient intakes of breath. "Cranked up my nose this morning, I tell you that."

Boudreau sat down at the kitchen table, his insides vibrating. *What fun.* He was impressed, truly impressed, that Ronnie'd already done this a couple hours earlier. He could hardly imagine where that put him now.

Ronnie put the kettle on the stove and sat down on the other side of the table. "Hot out."

"Yeah," said Boudreau. "Really hot." He guessed that for Ronnie this was speed rapping. He felt his own leg bouncing up and down and noticed he was drumming the tabletop with his fingers. A cigarette, that's what he needed. He lit one. *Wow* that was good, he could smoke thirty of these. Okay, now, time to be cool.

"Yeah, say, Ronnie?" he said. "Bad news, man." He turned the

newspaper over and pushed it across the table. "Check this out."
Ronnie tilted the paper up with the tips of his fingers.

"So I guess that's it, huh?" said Boudreau.

Ronnie made a face, as though he'd been given a basketball score he'd
already heard, then let the paper fall back to the table. "Yeah, I seen
that." He shrugged and leaned back in his chair.

"What do you mean, you seen it?" Boudreau was astonished. "Saw
it?"

"Yeah, I seen it at the store," said Ronnie, "but I knew already. It
was on the TV last night." Lips pursed, he licked his front teeth in a
pleased way. "Means they're starting to take me serious. I upped the
ante to one and a half."

Boudreau's heart went into overdrive. "You did *what?*"

Ronnie tilted back his chair and ran the fingers of one hand through
his hair. "Yesterday," he explained. "I called up, told 'em I was tired
of this shit. They want to fuck around, then the price goes up." The
kettle on the stove reached a boil, its shrill whistle going off like an alarm.
He reached behind himself and turned off the gas. "Usually it ain't good
business to change your offer once you made it." He lifted his eyebrows
significantly. "But this here's different. This is pressure to close the
deal."

Boudreau started laughing, a purely physical response akin to opening
a valve, something to release this new flow of chemical energy coursing
through him. Ronnie had somehow forgotten that all this was not just
illegal but dangerous, a good way to go to sleep and never wake up. He
seemed to regard it merely as a novel business opportunity, a kind of
militarized trade you could go into, like armed carpentry.

Ronnie studied him for a moment, then laughed along with him, a
sound Boudreau was not used to. They could laugh to bust a gut. Ronnie
gave the table a stylish little rap with his knuckles, a mini–drum
roll.

"It's *hap*pening." He gave the table another rap—shave and a haircut,
two bits—then brushed at the picture of the exploded car like it was an
offending fly. "Now they're taking me serious."

Wiping his tears away, Boudreau shook his head. "Yeah, but, *Ronnie.*
They just got rid of part of the *evidence,* right?"
"You mean this?" He flicked his hand again at the newspaper. "They
can blow up ever' car they got, I don't care."
Boudreau looked down at the melted Corvette, failing to see how this
could be taken as a positive sign. He smiled to show he wasn't getting
it. "Yeah, okay," he said, "but now it's just Cherry's word against *his,*
right? They aren't gonna pay for that."
Ronnie own smile faded. "It ain't a court a law, Richter, you get that?
It ever gets that far, we're dead meat anyway." He resettled his shades
on his nose with his forefinger. "But it won't. They won't let it."
Dead meat anyway. Boudreau shook his head, smiling now against his
will. This was a nightmare quiz show, first prize an exploded coronary
system. "So what'd they say? Now we're gonna blow up the car to show
good faith?"
Ronnie leaned over the table and aimed his face at Boudreau, his
patience gone. "They didn't say *nothing,* okay?" He withdrew his face
back across the table, brows flattened in anger. "They just listen and
hang up." He pointed at the car. "But this means they're taking me
serious. Next time I bump it up again."
Boudreau sat back in his chair, stunned by the illogic of it. In his
speed-shot brain he was starting to see colorful little crystalline edges
around things. If this was a war, then so far as he could see, the napalm
had already been called in. He threw up both hands.
Ronnie shoved the paper across the table at him, more than a trace
of violence in his restraint. "We got better cards than this." Ronnie
fixed him with a blank sunglass stare. "I ain't just bluffing, comrade."
Boudreau looked at him in uncomprehending panic, the wrong word
away from getting lumped in with those who refused to take him
seriously.
"Cherry took a little souvenir, remember?"
Boudreau stared at him, comprehension arriving in the form of an
all-over flush of cold, speedy sweat. *The film can.*
The screen door slammed shut.
Before Boudreau was half out of his chair, Ronnie had already made

it to the door of the living room, crouched and ready. It was like watching a cat go straight from a lap purr to a claws-out leap. Boudreau watched, paralyzed.

Ronnie straightened up, then came back to the table. He gave Boudreau a long hard look. "Vicky," he said.

"What're y'all doing, kissing in there?" she called out before coming through the door. "Both feet on the floor now."

Red faced and sweating, Vicky Stover came into the kitchen, her purse hanging from one arm and a bag of groceries in the other. She pushed a spot clear on the table with the bag and then set it down, right beside the mirror.

"Oh, *I* see. Y'all were doing something *bad*, now, weren't y'all?" She bent over and gave Boudreau a peck on the cheek. "Well, *hello*, Richter honey. So nice to see you? I walked past your car down the block, and I thought, Well, that *is* Richter's car, but I guess he forgot where we lived? 'Course that wouldn't surprise me since I can't even remember the last time he came to visit. Oh, is that *coffee* y'all're making?"

She turned on the kettle again, then bustled around the table and stood behind Ronnie. She put both her hands down to massage his chest in wifely affection. "And how's my Ronnie Dean, is ever' little thing okay around here?"

Boudreau watched her. She was so wired she was practically singing. Ronnie stared down at the table, his lips moving silently as he played with a book of matches, shifting it corner to corner between his fingers. From behind Ronnie's back Vicky looked across at Boudreau, a smirk of complicity on her face.

"I just had so much *fun* playing tennis the other day?" she said.

"Yeah," he said, trying to control his face. "It was great. I had a lot of fun, too." He had to look down, shifty eyed as a thief. When he looked back up, he found Ronnie staring at him, face blank behind the sunglasses. He went rigid.

Vicky's fingers abruptly stopped working Ronnie's chest. She searched out Boudreau's eyes for another moment, then looked away at the sink mounded high with dishes. "I guess I've hardly recovered from the other day, but I *would* like to play again real soon?"

"Yeah, maybe." Boudreau lifted his eyebrows noncommittally, avoiding the danger of looking at her. "This heat's a little intense, though." He couldn't believe she was doing this to him, it was like talking pig latin and hoping Ronnie hadn't figured it out yet.

Her lips went thin with self-knowledge, then tipped up in one corner. She looked down into her husband's hair, as if she'd just noticed something. "Ronnie honey, I swear you're going a little thin on top here?"

He grunted as she ruffled his pompadour, mussing it up as her final gesture of affection. She moved aside and began digging in the top of the grocery bag, coming up with a pack of Pall Malls.

"Here's your nasty unfiltered—" she began to Ronnie, then saw the pack rolled up in his sleeve. She straightened up. "God*dammit*, did you wake Clem up just to go get a pack of cigarettes? Did you? You couldn't fucking *wait?*"

"She's asleep," said Ronnie to the matchbook cover between his fingers. He looked at it hard. "Richter baby-sat while I ran out." He looked up just long enough to cast a short look somewhere in her direction.

She whirled on Boudreau, who trotted out his noncommittal look again.

"I didn't know how long before you got back," Ronnie said.

Vicky watched him work the matchbook, then stalked out of the kitchen.

Ronnie sat like a stone; neither of them said a word for a solid minute. Boudreau emitted a nervous little speed chuckle. The mighty blackmailer had no tips for this kind of combat.

"Poor little child, she's still asleep," Vicky reported back. Her outburst had abated, but she looked frazzled in its aftermath, eyes pinched, no longer there. "Now be an honest friend, Richter honey, will this house pass the white glove test?" She looked around her and sighed heavily. "I guess I ought to clean while I'm buzzing around like this. 'Course our darn air-condition's broke, and Ronnie never took care of it the way he said he would? I mean, God *knows* he's got a lot on his mind." She smiled down at him after this potshot, then smirked at

Boudreau. "I like to clean house bare naked anyway, did you know that?"

The kettle interrupted her aria as it returned to a rattling whistle. She turned it off and stood dramatically with one hand on her cocked hip.

"God, I just *hate* speed, I don't know why I do it?" She chuckled at her own helplessness. "But then, it *does* help me get my shopping done?"

Boudreau watched as a frayed look suddenly widened her eyes.

"Oh, *shit!*" She rushed over to the table and pulled a half-gallon box of cheap ice cream out of the grocery bag, thin liquid streaming out of its soggy bottom.

"Shit!" she screamed, soaring past her threshold. "Shit, shit, *shit!*" Vicky jerked the sodden carton away from her, the motion just enough to make the box collapse entirely. She flung it spewing into the sink, where it hit the mound of dishes and slid off the counter onto the floor.

Holding her dripping hands away from her, she looked down in disbelief at the trail of molten ice cream down her front, across the floor and up the cabinet. She closed her eyes and whimpered.

"They should've put it in one of them ice cream bags," Ronnie observed, getting up from the table. "I got some things to see to," he said over his shoulder.

Dumb as a post, Boudreau was still sitting at the table when he heard the front door creak open, then slam shut. He'd assumed Ronnie was just getting out of the kitchen.

"Be right back," Boudreau said, making it out the front door just in time to watch Ronnie back the Mustang at high speed down the driveway, exhaust pipes crunching when they hit the street. Boudreau waved frantically. The tires squealed a little on the hot pavement as Ronnie let out the clutch and disappeared down the block.

"*Bastard,*" Vicky said, her voice shaking. She was right behind Boudreau, on the other side of the screen door.

He turned around. The sudden sprint had caused sweat to pour off him, his whole speeding body a radiator about to blow. "I just wanted to ask him something before he left," he said. "Listen, I'd help you clean up, but I've got to get back to work."

"Come in and stay for a while," she said. "Have some coffee or something? *Please?*"

Her tone made him risk a look through the door. Although she was standing in the shadowed interior, he could see her shoulders bobbing slightly.

"I can't, really. I'm supposed to be there right now."

She moved into the light, just behind the screen. Her features were pinched and blotchy, her front covered with ice cream. *"Please,"* she said. "I can't stay here alone. I need to talk to you."

Boudreau stood rooted. Not this time.

She started in with the accent, half crying. "Richter honey, I can't take this," she said. *Tike.* "I just can't take it no more."

"I got Keith out of jail this morning," he said. "After your friend Chipper called up." He paused. "We're gonna play us some tennis again real soon."

She hugged her elbows across her sticky shirt and looked down, shaking her head. "It's *not* what you think."

"I'd like to know what I think," he said. "Why don't you tell me."

She sniffled while catching her breath, a jagged sound that metamorphosed into a self-mocking snort. "I can explain everything."

"I bet you can," said Boudreau.

She opened the door and stepped out in front of him. "That's over, believe me." Inside, the baby gave a single wake-up cry that immediately turned into steady screaming. She didn't seem to hear it. "Believe me, I just got embarrassed at what you'd think."

He looked at her, then away. "I'm still waiting to hear what I think."

"Richter!" She tried to move in front of his line of vision. "Will you *look* at me? Will you let me *explain?*"

Boudreau avoided her eyes. "I think I hear Clem," he said. The baby was wailing now, short ragged-breath screams that ran across his amphetamined nerves like a rake over a sidewalk.

Vicky breathed out, her shoulders slumping. She looked down at the front of her shirt.

"Well, isn't this appealing." She pulled it away from her chest with two fingers, then let go with a derisive little laugh. "I always wear ice cream on hot days."

"Listen, Vicky, it's not that—"

She shook her head, cutting him off. "It's okay, I won't keep you anymore." She put her ear to the screen. "Here I *am*, Clemmy honey." She turned back to face him, eyes bright. "I mean, I'd go to bed with you right now if I thought I could get away with it."

Boudreau stared. "What?"

She stepped inside the door, out of reach. "You better go," she said, "because I'm gonna do some falling apart now." She looked through the screen, a sudden shudder coming over her. "The pieces are *not* gonna be attractive."

His mind working like a chemically driven yo-yo, Boudreau drove back to the paper. *I'd go to bed with you right now if I thought I could get away with it.*

The go-to-bed part he got, it was the get-away-with-it he didn't understand. On second thought, he was unsure of the first part too. It was instant hard-on material, but what did it *mean?* What was he supposed to do about it? Wait for a sign? *I can explain.*

Maybe he'd call her later.

Boudreau caught himself, a rush of speed-fueled paranoia surging through him. In retrospect it seemed that Ronnie had choked him a lot longer than he'd needed to. He kept forgetting who she was married to, the way bruises had a way of appearing on her arm. He was already burning the candle at both ends, and now he was considering going at the middle with a blowtorch.

There were big issues at hand here, life and death, possibly his own. The bare facts loomed up at him, as if for the first time: an unidentified body, a junkie of a witness who didn't seem to care one way or the other, a partner in blackmail who took it as progress when they hung up on the other end of the phone. That didn't even take into account the identity of the blackmailee, which bumped all the rest a quantum level higher. This was just not real, this was *lunacy*, even without plotting how to bang the violence-prone partner's wife. These people were crazy, but he wasn't. He had no part in it. If you listened to bullshit for too long, you could believe anything; this was the way mass hysteria got started. This was the way Republicans got into office.

Boudreau parked and tucked his copy of today's edition under his arm, then limped his way toward the *Journal* building. Who was he kidding? The newspaper stuck to his moist flesh like a homunculus, infusing his bloodstream with a toxic certitude. If he wasn't neck-deep in shit, then America was standing tall again.

He took the elevator up and went straight to the can, guts churning, reading material in hand.

Harmon Shaw had become a millionaire businessman first, and only then a fundamentalist preacher, instead of the other way around. This was a good twist in itself, but for writers of business-section profiles on his spectacular rise to empire, the details of Shaw's colorful persona were a dream come true. Among these were the interrupted high school education, the wardrobe of discount house clothes, the antiunion campaigns augmented in his own companies by high wages and personally taught "optional" Bible classes, the establishment of a heavily funded survivalist school known by wags as the Armageddon Outward Bound, the offhanded public statements on minority IQ and school prayer and sex education. To top things off, he had a peculiar mania for grass and lawn-keeping, acquiring seed-research and agrichemical companies as a kind of personal hobby.

Depending on the politics of the particular business section, his revealed character was then summed up in a range that ran from "eccentric" to "controversial" to "bizarre." But whatever the conclusion, some mention of his wife and daughter was always a staple of these articles.

In something of a Shaw family tradition, the wife, like the daughter, had done some hard time at the Menninger Clinic. A thin, fretful woman, as colorless as her husband was vivid, she'd eventually had her medicine cabinet for breakfast one day. The daughter had yet to swim back from deep water.

Set next to the accounts of Harmon Shaw's ruthless will, next to the breathtaking figures of his fortune, the fates of Henrietta and Liz were usually offered as a humbling lesson in the way things got balanced out. He was really just a cornball family man at heart, but his family kept checking out on him: his was therefore a life "touched by tragedy." A deeply private man in front of the media, he was thought to cling all the more tightly to the twenty-six-year-old heir apparent, the son cut whole from the father's cloth. Now someone had tried to hurt his boy Bedford.

Like everybody else in Tulsa, Boudreau had seen it all a dozen times before, Brinkman having raided the files for a shameless cut-and-paste job. The skimpy details of the bombing itself comprised only a minor part of the article. Bedford Shaw had been inside the restaurant when the explosion went off, the fortunate timing of the thing leaving Boudreau less than surprised. After questioning by the police, the badly shaken Bedford had gone into seclusion at His Fiery Grace, the fortress-like ranch that his daddy maintained in the Ozarks as a business and religious retreat. Preliminary evidence suggested someone with professional demolition experience, but so far, no one had a darn clue. There was a single quote from Harmon Shaw that whoever did this was clearly trying to get to him through his boy, and it would only be a matter of time before these "vermin" were brought to justice. He would personally assist the police in whatever way he knew how.

Boudreau got off the pot sweating and shivering at the same time, head full of white noise. Bedford Shaw, he happened to know, had been named after Nathan Bedford Forrest, the Confederate general whose footnote in history consisted of founding the Ku Klux Klan.

Spying Brinkman at his desk, Boudreau made like he was just gimping over to say howdy. "Yo, George."

"Yeah," said Brinkman, idly leafing through a *Newsweek.*

Boudreau slid heavily into the chair beside the desk. "Have a nice weekend?"

"A nice weekend." Brinkman looked up at him, pissed. "Yeah, I had a nice weekend. I did some champion sweating and then at night I went to bars and slobbered down on blond goddesses." Off and running, he reenacted the scene for Boudreau. "Hi, babe, my name's Shlomo, can I hit on you? Am I *what?*" He did a take. "*Joosh?* What, just 'cause I have have a nose instead of a button? Hey, wanna see my horns?"

Boudreau chuckled, trying to sit still.

"Where do these fucking women *come* from, Boudreau, the white-bread factory?" Brinkman cast a hooded look around the newsroom, like it might be just such a place. "I swear to God, it's like they came to life out of an old *Playboy*. I'm thinking, Jesus, I ever see any pussy in this town, it won't have any hair on it. It'll be airbrushed."

It was an unfortunate image for Boudreau: a certain shaven crotch came to mind. His carefully casual approach disappeared on him.

"Hey, you got yourself a big byline today. Nice piece." He tapped his paper, hoping to indicate how it had just caught his eye.

Brinkman gave him a look. Boudreau was interrupting his riff. He frowned down at the paper. "Boudreau, you know they give 'em away free here, you don't got to take it out of the trash. Now some bum won't have sheets tonight, you ever think about that?"

Boudreau regarded the newspaper, ink-smeared and ripped, limp as tissue from the humidity and his own sweat. It sat on the desk like evidence. "No seriously, nice work." He didn't get why Brinkman was being so cavalier. "Some deal, huh."

"Yeah, that car sucked a big one, didn't it?" Brinkman had a little snicker at the expense of the melted 'Vette, then shrugged. "Great picture anyway."

"*Great* picture," Boudreau agreed. "Great piece, too."

"Great piece, bullshit."

"What do you mean? I liked it."

Brinkman gave him an irritated look. "I mean the piece was shit and you know it. Horned Frog cut nearly every word I wrote except my name," said Brinkman. "Asshole."

"He cut it?" Boudreau couldn't believe his luck. This meant there was more.

"Boudreau, can you hear me okay? Here, look at my mouth while I talk." Brinkman glared at him. "He went at it with a *chain saw*, okay?"

"Why?"

" 'Cause it had some color to it, you know, I got the facts but I added some color." Brinkman grimaced. "A little random violence and sweat out in the shit-kicker heartland. Rich prairie preacher froths at the mouth 'cause somebody's after his goldarn *boy*. It was funny, man. Subtle but funny. I mean, I got there first and I wrote a great piece, anywhere else they'd be lining up to kiss my ass today." Brinkman caught himself and shook his head. "But *new*ooo. I don't know why I fucking bother."

"You got there first?"

Brinkman looked at him for a long moment. "When the call came in, they had it as just a car wreck. The new sardine guy wasn't here, so I picked it up."

Boudreau leaned back with a smirk, like he couldn't wait for the lurid details. "Yeah?"

"Right out of Fellini," said Brinkman. "Fellini goes to Tulsa. I pull up to this huge parking lot at this barbecue joint on Seventy-first. There's two fire engines and an ambulance and about nineteen squad cars coming in behind me, and this stinking pile of burned rubber and metal out in the middle of it all. That thing fucking *went*. Meantime, there's this geek parade pouring out of the barbecue place, still dribbling sauce down their chin, and they are *wild*. Something like that, you want to see some body count. The cops're pushing 'em back."

Boudreau interrupted with a weak chuckle. "So where was Bedford Shaw during all this?"

"Camped out in the old man's stretch." Brinkman clucked and shook his head in sympathy. "*Very* emotionally distraught."

Boudreau straightened up a little. "Harmon was there?" He couldn't believe how patent this was. "Got there kind of fast, didn't he?"

Brinkman shrugged. "I don't know, he was on his way there to meet the kid for dinner or something. Anyway, he's there, okay? But then he sets up shop with the cops and reporters and gets right into it, I mean he's almost giving *speeches.* " Brinkman shook his head at his lost opportunity. "See what I'm saying about great copy?"

Boudreau lifted his eyebrows, yeah-maybe.

"I don't know, Boudreau, I'm getting to kind of like this guy. Someone blows the shit out of his kid's car, and it's like he's *happy.* See now, we don't have that back home, that kind of joy in the face of adversity. I gave the guy your regards."

"You did what?" He bought the line like an exploding cigar.

Brinkman eyed Boudreau. "Sure," he said. "Hey, *Harmon,* remember your old friend Richter Boudreau—you know, the one who bomped your weak-minded daughter? He says hi."

"Fuck you." Boudreau lit a cigarette, covering his shaky hands by waving out the match.

Brinkman leaned back in mock alarm. He lifted his eyebrows, ready to match wits, when his phone rang.

While Brinkman answered the call, Boudreau realized he'd been leaning so far forward it looked like he was ready to run from his chair. This was not cool. He leaned back again and rearranged his features, just hanging out.

Brinkman kept trying to get off the line, only to be interrupted for another bout of listening. He held the phone away from his ear and made yapping faces at Boudreau, then switched to moronic nodding at the earpiece.

Boudreau summoned up a little smile. His cigarette had burned down to the filter so he lit another. He was jumping out of his skin.

Brinkman shivered in disgust and dropped the receiver back in its cradle with two fingers. "*Ass*hole."

"Yeah?" said Boudreau, without the slightest idea where his mind had just been.

"No, not *you,* " said Brinkman. "Horned Frog. Now he wants me to go cover a press conference Shaw's giving tomorrow. You know, since I'm already on the story. Well, fuck him."

"What kind of press conference?"

Brinkman jerked his head back at the speed of the question. He examined Boudreau through his half-lidded eyes, a knowing smile on his face. "Correct me if I'm wrong," he said, holding up a hand as disclaimer, "but you seem a tad *energetic* today?"

Boudreau smiled slyly, then drummed his fingers on the desk at exaggerated speed. "Here's a hint," he said. "It's like caffeine but better."

Brinkman snorted, shaking his head. "Why not just trade in your brain cells for motor oil and get it over with?" He peeled his finger like a carrot and made shame-shame noises. "Very unhip. Very sixties."

Boudreau ignored him. "So what do you think old Harmon's gonna have to say."

" 'Old Harmon'?" Brinkman leaned back in his chair, eyeing Boudreau. "My guess is old Harmon'll do some major ranting. He seems to think he's got a lot of enemies."

Boudreau gave him a cagey look. "So maybe he does."

"Oh, c'mon, Boudreau, the guy is totally off the wall, he's out there talking about 'terrorist elements at large today.' " Brinkman rolled his eyes. "Gimme a fucking break."

"I wouldn't be so sure, George."

Brinkman put up a hand to cut short any such foolish bullshit. "Okay, granted, somebody blew up junior's ride. But ten to one it's like he was banging somebody's wife or something. You know, some vet who remembered how to use blasting caps. This smells weird to me. Harmon's just using it as an excuse to beat his drum. This is private laundry, man."

Boudreau tried to look thoughtful. "I think it's more than that," he said. "A lot more."

Brinkman studied him for a moment. "Okay, what do you know? You know something?"

"I didn't say I *knew* anything." Boudreau shrugged elaborately. "I just think you have a social obligation to follow this up. The guy's a major racist, *major* anti-Semite. You can change things with a story like this."

"*Change* things," Brinkman repeated, nodding to himself. "This is where we get stories about Berkeley in the good old days, right? What's it Cleaver's up to now—designer codpieces?"

Boudreau's face twitched. "Go ahead, laugh, I just think maybe you should take Harmon at his word." He saw his opening now. "I think maybe there's a big story here, and I'm not just talking about a color piece. I think you should find out what you can, then find out what the *Voice* or *Rolling Stone* might have to say. I think this is major."

Brinkman listened without looking up. "You *think*," he said. "You think too fucking much." He shook his head, irritated. "Color is all there *is*, Boudreau, the dude's a car*toon*, he looks under his mattress at night for communists and Jew bankers. You can't take people down just for thinking bad thoughts. That's not news."

"You left out abortion-mongers and homos."

"My point exactly," said Brinkman. "That's one lumpy bed. I mean, who takes this shit seriously?"

"Most of the electorate? You know, the mandate?"

"Yeah, okay." Brinkman grimaced, then licked his finger and chalked one up for Boudreau. "But that's just politics, nobody cares about that. Just because it's in Harmon Shaw's mind doesn't mean it's real."

"It's real." Saying this, Boudreau realized he'd lost all sense about what exactly the word meant. "You treat people like enemies, maybe some of them become enemies." He paused. "I know people who might want to do this kind of thing."

Brinkman regarded his own hands, then slowly looked back up. "Stop dicking around, Boudreau, this is pissing me off. What are you saying?"

Boudreau looked around the newsroom, taking his time before he met Brinkman's gaze again. "Just that you'll be sorry if you don't follow this up." He gave it as much portentous significance as he could. "All I can say is it would behoove you to go to that press conference. Then we'll talk."

Brinkman whooped out a contemptuous little laugh. "You're a fucking *crack*pot, Boudreau." His smile disappeared and he stared at him, eyes bright. "I hope."

Boudreau stood up, aware that something had just shifted but unconvinced he could joke his way out of it now. "Yeah, okay." He looked around the room with narrow-eyed care. "It's these *drugs* they keep giving me. Take this down: they ever dig up Marilyn Monroe, some heads're gonna roll over this one."

"Go somewhere else, will you?" said Brinkman, waving him away with both hands. "I got work to do."

Aquiver with the stupidity of what he'd just done, Boudreau tucked the newspaper under his arm and walked to the elevator. He was either rushing to beat the band or having a heart attack. Turning around as the doors closed, he found George Brinkman scrutinizing him from across the newsroom, phone in hand.

Getting no answer upstairs, Boudreau checked down in the billiards room and found Keith passed out, innocent as an overfed barnyard hog. The guitar was on the floor, strings down, and a lap blanket was pulled over him. His mouth was hanging open and his breath came and went in a gentle snore.

Boudreau was wandering the living room, wondering what to do next, when he heard a radio come on, somewhere upstairs. The song was the girl's cover of "Alison."

He froze, taking a while to realize it was Cherry singing, not a radio. She had a beautiful clear voice, but she sang it like Costello, not Ronstadt. When she got to the chorus, it sounded like crystal with chipped edges.

Aaaal-lison, I know this world is killing you.
Ohhh, Aal-lison: my aim is true.

He shivered. A cappella, she made the song sound like a spiritual for the Coming Age, remorseful and disbelieving, not a trace of faith or redemption to be found. This was like overhearing someone cry. He waited till the singing stopped to start up the stairs, stepping heavily so she'd hear him coming.

He knocked, then looked around the door. She sat cross-legged in a mound of covers on the bed, a litter of magazines, ashtrays and empty dishes surrounding her like a nest. A bottle of vodka, one-third down, sat on the bedside table.

"Listen, you can't just disappear like that again." He sat down on the edge of the bed. "Not without telling me."

She gave him the smile that seemed more like a tic and looked away, face blank. His own smile withered.

"Hey," he said. "Are you okay?" She looked strung out, pale skin stretched tight as parchment.

"Yeah, sure." She leaned back against the headboard, hands laced across her stomach, and flicked her eyes around Vicky Michaels's frilly, all-white teenager's room. "The little princess back in her cage."

This was starting out badly. Boudreau tried to take it back. "I didn't mean it to sound like that," he said. "Something might've happened and I wouldn't have *known*, okay? I worried about you, that's all."

Cherry turned on him. "Oh yeah, like really *concerned.*" Her eyes burned for a moment before she gave a tiny facial shrug and looked away again. "I went out for a little while, is that all right? I mean now that I don't have to worry about Keith."

Boudreau drew in a deep breath. "Look," he began. "I was confused." He found himself focusing on her skinny tank top, the breasts perfectly displayed. "I made a mistake. People make mistakes, then they say they're sorry."

"Yeah," she said, "then they say they're sorry."

Boudreau watched the sarcastic smirk come and go, fast as a blip on an empty radar screen. He had a flash of recognition: underneath everything else she was a teenager, convinced the world was bullshit but still afraid of it anyway. He stood up.

"We need to start this over again," he said, and walked out of the room.

"Honey?" he yelled. "I'm ho-ome." He poked his head around the door. "Okay, now *you* say, My hero!"

Eyes pinched, she picked at the edge of the bedspread over her crossed legs.

Boudreau crossed again to the bed and sat down. Start over again, now there was a notion. Exactly how far did you have to backtrack? He picked up the bottle of vodka. "Ronnie and I did some speed," he explained, and hit the bottle for a hard swallow. "I'm a little wired up."

She gave a small snort at the humor of this. "Jeez, I thought it must've been *downs.*"

Boudreau looked at her, chagrined at his own transparency. He had another big chug, then put his hand on her knee, protruding up through the covers. "I heard you singing," he said. "You have a great voice." She stared at his hand, immobile.

"Seriously, you have a really beautiful voice." Boudreau found himself working for sincerity. "You could sing professionally."

Her mouth twitched, as though someone had just pinched her. "Thanks."

Boudreau drank again, closing his eyes. For a moment he imagined her on a stage, fronting a band. It wasn't so farfetched. He began to feel the alcohol coursing through him, unfurling into the methedrine like a tributary stream in a cold deep current.

"Maybe wherever we end up after all this," he said, "we could record some demos."

Cherry made a noise, then reached for the vodka.

In a few minutes the bottle was another third down and Boudreau had worked his way onto the middle of the bed, sitting cross-legged facing her. So far, it felt like a pajama party between people who didn't know each other all that well. She wasn't making things any easier.

"So did you talk to Keith any?"

"A little," she said. "Before he passed out."

"Must've been quick."

"What do you mean?"

"I mean he passes out a lot."

She shrugged, like this was beside the point. "So maybe he's upset."

Boudreau took the bottle and had a slug. "Yeah, it's a tough life. Sometimes the *trust* check is late, the *maid* doesn't show up when she's supposed to—I tell you, it's fucking *stress*ful."

Cherry listened without reacting. She got out a cigarette, studying it. "I like him," she said. "I feel sorry for him."

Boudreau stiffened a little, surprised that this should bother him.

"Yeah, well, you haven't done twenty years as his friend," he said. "He thinks the world owes him something, and when he doesn't get it, he thinks it's after him." The moment he finished saying this he realized it could also function as a perfect description of his own outlook. "I'm just a little tired of sticking my neck out for him."

She gave him a quick look of appraisal. For someone who couldn't look him in the face more than a second at a time, she made him feel like his lies came translated, subtitled on his forehead.

She fiddled with the covers, holding a fold in one hand, smoothing it out into a long ridge with the other. "His sister, you know, What's-her-name—"

"Vicky."

"Yeah, *Vicky* is trying to get rid of him. Put him away."

He cut her off. "I already got that rap on the way home from jail." He laughed nastily. "I think Keith's pickled his brain. I think there's some real damage. You don't know Vicky, or you'd see how stupid that is. Vicky couldn't be bothered."

She made a little mouth of feigned surprise. "You got a thing for her, right?"

Boudreau went still. "Not anymore. I used to." He looked at her. "Who told you that?"

She avoided his look, concentrating on rolling the ash off her cigarette in the ashtray.

"Did Ronnie tell you that?"

Still sculpting the ash, she lifted her eyebrows without actually looking up. He grabbed her by the elbow. "I'm *asking:* did Ronnie say something to you?"

She pulled her arm away like he'd tried to hurt her or something.

"Cherry?" She'd suddenly gone inward, a tiny private smile on her mouth. He tried to bring his voice down, to erase the elbow business. "Cherry, listen: this is real important, okay? What did Ronnie say?"

She put out the cigarette, then folded her arms across her chest. *"Ronnie* didn't say nothing." The smile went up in one corner. "Keith's guy says you and her got a little something going."

Boudreau sat back. "Keith's guy?"

"Some guy he hired. Some PI in Oklahoma City."

"PI?"

"You know, private investigator?" she said, enunciating it a little too clearly.

Boudreau found himself nodding his head. They'd been watched.

"Yeah, apparently," Cherry continued, "apparently little Vicky gets around. This PI was watching her while Keith was in detox up north, and guess what? She's been putting in overtime with some other guy, too."

Boudreau looked at her, his face gone slack. Some other guy. It seemed to him she was enjoying this more than was necessary. "So what?" he said finally. "That's her business, right?"

Her shoulders lifted a hair, like maybe it was. "It's just the PI seems to think maybe she wants her room back."

Boudreau went still for a long moment, then reached for the bottle. "I can't believe that."

She looked to the side, as though it didn't make any difference to her. "Believe what you want. That's what the guy said."

"You mean that's what Keith said. There's a difference."

"Whatever." A grimace flickered and went out. "I don't know these people like you. I just feel sorry for him."

Boudreau sat on it for a moment. "So why do you suppose Keith told you all this shit?"

"How do I know?" She held out her hand for the bottle. "Maybe he just needed a friend."

He smoked a cigarette, his mind swirling with dark thoughts as they traded swigs in silence for a couple of minutes. In spite of everything, he seemed to be trying to crowd closer to her on the bed.

"Hey, this is fun," he said. "I'm drunk."

She stared down at the litter on the bed, the bottle in her hand like a prop. She was like a sheer rock wall, without a crack or a finger hold.

He followed her eyes and picked up a small photograph from the trash. It had the matte finish and broad white borders of an old junior-high picture, one of many handed out and then forgotten. A young black woman, hair processed into a lacquered upsweep, stared out of it. She was pretty but nothing special. Boudreau searched for anything unusual behind the school-picture smile, some secret rebellion in the eyes, something in the flare of nose or fullness of lip.

Cherry watched him, lifting the picture out of his hands before he could read the message in lavender ink on the back.

"I didn't know she was from Tulsa," Boudreau said. Along with the school year, the picture was captioned with the name of a junior high in Greenwood. "Were you tight?"

"She split and went to LA in the ninth grade," she said. "Kind of like me. She lived in Watts and then in Oakland."

"So how'd she end up back here?"

Cherry looked at the picture for a moment longer, then tossed it back onto the bed. "I don't know, she had this thing about wanting to talk to her father. Make up or something." The way she said "father" made it clear how she felt about such an enterprise. "So she gets back here and tries calling him, he *hangs up* on her." She looked up, her eyes in slits. "She flipped out about it; started doping way too much. Me and her were dancing. I said, Don't let it get to you, man, it's not worth it. It's not worth it."

"Yeah?" said Boudreau after a while.

Cherry's thin lips went crooked. "So finally she gets up her nerve, this is like two months later, and she goes out to where he works at, he's a janitor at some college, and he fucking *died* the day before."

"Whoa," said Boudreau.

"Heart attack," she said. "If she hadn't come here, she never would've—" She trailed off, staring. "She was getting set to go back out to the Coast."

"Jesus *Christ.*" Boudreau was shaking his head. "That is truly fucking pathetic. That's the most pathetic story I ever heard."

She cast a long look at Boudreau, eyes glittering, then looked away.

"Yeah, what a great story." She smirked over at Vicky Michaels's shelf of stuffed animals. "But it happens, right? Happens every day."

Boudreau swore at it, half laughing. "So what do you do," he said, "stop believing in God?" He laughed again. "Maybe you *start*, I don't know."

Cherry lifted the bottle of vodka as though in a toast. "Not me, man." She slugged the bottle hard, eyes watering. "Not me."

Boudreau reached for the bottle. "So listen," he said. "What's in the film can?"

Cherry sat back against the headboard of the bed and examined the ceiling. Something came over her face, not quite a smile. She shook her head. "That's private." She thought a while and shook her head again. "I gotta pee."

"Oh, that's *private*," Boudreau repeated out loud, while she swung her legs out of the nest of covers and stood up beside the bed.

She was naked from the waist down, with a tattoo of a little blue butterfly on her left buttock that he'd somehow missed before. He caught a glimpse of belly, how it flattened before it sloped back into the dense curls between her legs. She went up once on the balls of her feet, stretching, then went to the bathroom.

Boudreau considered what this meant. She was telling him something, offering it like a dare. What he did about it was his business; that was the message.

He lay back on the bed, the alcohol settling into a distinct stratum above the speed, the chemicals layered in him like something you'd get served in a pony glass. He felt jittery, but it was weighted down with the booze, so he couldn't really tell where the various feelings were coming from. He was *fucked up*, he knew that much. What a story, Earla the dancer. He swigged from the bottle, the moisture burning his speed-cracked lips. Little chemical tendrils curled their way up his urinary tract, a nervous flutter somewhere between an incipient hard-on and a distant need to pee.

The toilet flushed and she came back in, stopping at the side of the bed. He looked up at her, and she gave him the vanishing smirk. If this wasn't some kind of hostile little invitation, then he'd lost his instincts altogether. "You don't trust me, do you?" he said, voice thick.

She laughed without amusement, sounding a little drunk herself. "You mean like I have a choice?"

He reached out and put a hand on her naked flank, cool and smooth as polished stone. She looked down but didn't move. "Maybe we should take our minds off things," he said.

She looked at him, not getting it. "Do what?"

Boudreau lowered his voice. "I mean, let's make love, okay?"

"Make love," Cherry repeated. She gave a quick look around the room for witnesses to this, like he'd just suggested badminton, or skydiving. She shrugged. "Yeah, okay."

Boudreau watched as she grabbed the bottom of the tank top with both hands and pulled it over her head. She told him to get up and then flung the covers aside, scattering the bed trash onto the floor. She lay back on the bare sheet, naked, hands behind her head, while he got his own clothes off.

In a world where nothing worked out the way it was supposed to, Boudreau couldn't believe his luck. Maybe it wasn't all that friendly, but at least it was straightforward. She liked him this much anyway. Maybe "like" wasn't the right word.

After some basic kissing and fondling, he went upside down on her, working to find something that would get her going. In the meantime he found himself at the mercy of one of her blow jobs. After a while he decided it was time to get to the point. He pulled away from her, got himself right side up again, and knelt between her legs. He wanted *in* there. She made a small negative-sounding noise.

"Huh-*uh,*" said Cherry as he tried to nudge himself in.

What the hell, he could be chivalrous. He backed off, returning to kissing and stroking, then tried again a minute later. She went stiff as a log on him.

"What's wrong?" he said.

"I don't want to *do* that, all right?"

Boudreau rolled over and lay on his back. He stared at the ceiling, exhaling mightily. "I don't get it," he said. "What's the difference." They'd been lapping away at each other's genitals, and now all he wanted to do was put his inside hers. What was the big deal?

"Yeah, but that's just, you know, that's just fooling around." She sounded pissed that he could miss the distinction.

Boudreau kept his eyes on the ceiling, unable to believe how this was turning out.

"It's just the way I *feel,* okay?" she said. "I just don't want to do that."

"Right," he said, taking pleasure in the defensiveness in her voice. Maybe he'd brought it on himself, but he failed to understand how this didn't qualify as prime cock-teasing.

"Here," she said.

She sucked and sucked, but it seemed to take him forever. Boudreau didn't understand how something he would've bargained his arm for half an hour earlier could feel so pleasureless now. He was hard enough, but the speed made him feel irritated, febrile. When he finally came, it felt like he was passing BBs.

Wordless, she disappeared back into the bathroom. Boudreau sat up and pulled on his pants immediately, listening to her rinse out her mouth.

When she came back out, he tried to give her a kiss to bring the routine to an end. She turned and took it on the cheek, then got on the bed, blank. She was still naked, but now she looked like exactly what she was, a scared skinny teenager he'd just pounded further into the ground. He offered her the bottle and she shook her head, barely. He took a long pull and set it back on the bedside table.

"Did you hear about the car," he said.

"What car?" Now she wouldn't look at him at all.

He listened to himself add the last straw. "Bedford Shaw's Corvette, it was in the paper today. They blew it up in a parking lot." He watched, numb, as though monitoring an inhumane experiment. "You know, like someone else did it."

She moved so slightly he hardly saw it, less a shrug than a minute twitch of nerve response.

"Yeah, and so meantime," he said, "Ronnie's calling them up and asking *more.*" He laughed helplessly, his fingers turning up the dial. "A million and half, can you fucking believe that?"

Cherry stared like she hadn't heard a word, like she was counting the toes down at the end of her stretched-out legs. She snuffled heavily, then again.

"We," she began, "we had this *thing,* you know, we were gonna get a place up on the Oregon coast, some farm or something. Get some goats and stuff." She tried to laugh, her voice catching. "Just a dykey little goat farm."

The twilight coming through the bedroom window dimmed into nothing, a curtain lowering around him. This night was going to be endless. He cradled the bottle to his chest like a baby as she broke down, a single keening whimper that rose and rose until it burst on a note of release.

"Oh, Earla *baby.*" Her crying sounded like out of control shivering. "Nobody gives a shit about you now." She tried to catch her sobs. "Nobody but me."

TUESDAY

The TV was still on—that was the voices—but the ringing, it took him a while to understand the ringing. He picked up the phone without knowing who he was.

"Hello, Michaels residence," Boudreau said, unaccountably somewhere back in his teenage years.

There was a hesitation. "Boudreau?" said a woman's voice.

"Ginny?" He didn't know why he thought it was his ex-wife, but at least he was getting closer to the present.

"Not quite," said the voice.

It came back to him: he'd found some Valium and sat in the study watching TV until at some point his mind had mercifully checked out. Now it was morning and he was still miserably Boudreau. Now Margo Ross was in his ear, openly hostile.

"What time is it, Margo?" he said.

"Ten-thirty by my watch. Sorry to wake you up." Her voice gave no hint of any such sorrow.

"How did you get this number," he asked.

"I tried your house first, but the phone's disconnected." This was news, but he wasn't surprised. "Then I called the paper and some guy there told me to try here. I was about to give up." She made it sound like this would have been equally acceptable. "You need to put in an appearance here, okay?"

Boudreau hesitated. "Listen, I'm kind of tied up today. I'm taking care of a friend."

"Whatever," said Margo Ross. "If you want to save anything from your office, you better get down here."

The information took a while to sink in. "What's going on?"

"That's what everyone's dying to find out," she said, and hung up.

He sat immobile in the chair behind Joe Michaels's desk, staring at the TV. Every joint in his body felt like it had been sandpapered. A local newsbreak announced the sixth day of hundred-degree weather. There were some big storm formations circling around a five-state area, but the weatherman wasn't making any promises about when they'd clear the heat.

The phone rang again. He looked at it, then finally picked it up, keeping his voice low. "Hello."

"Yeah," said Cherry at the same time.

They both paused, listening to the staticky clicking of the line between them.

"Hello," said Boudreau again.

"That you, Richter?" said Ronnie.

"Yeah. I've got it, Cherry."

"How's it going over there?" Ronnie said. "Ever'thing okay?"

"Good," said Boudreau, "We're cool. I *got* it, Cherry."

"Listen, Ron?" said Cherry. "I need to get high, okay? Can you get me high?"

Ronnie thought about this for a moment. "Yeah, I could do that." His lighter clicked and he exhaled a moment later. "I got to swing by anyways."

Boudreau stood up, phone in hand.

"You still there, comrade?" said Ronnie.

"I'm here."

"You got that film can?"

Boudreau waited a little too long. "In my hot little hand," he said.

"*Wait* a minute," Cherry burst in. Everybody listened. "That's not what you told *me*, Ron." Her voice rose a notch. "You didn't tell me he had it."

Ronnie waited till she was finished, ignoring her. "I'll pick it up when I swing by, then."

Boudreau's brain felt like a fist. "I mean, I have it meta*phor*ically."

"You have it *what?*" said Ronnie after a pause.

"I mean I *have* it, just not here." Boudreau tried to keep his voice straight. "I just meant it's safe."

Cherry broke in, right on cue. Boudreau considered running upstairs and gagging her.

"This is bullshit, Ron, it doesn't *belong* to him!" From her end of the line came the sound of something breaking, something falling off a table. "You fucking *lied* to me!"

"You hush up," said Ronnie, "I didn't lie to nobody. You got the can a film, comrade?"

Boudreau took a breath. Ronnie's term of endearment had gained an edge he didn't care for. "Yeah," he said, "it's out at the farmhouse. But there's a bunch of shit I got to take care of first. When do you need it?"

"Tonight," Ronnie said. "Tomorrow morning."

"Okay, good. I'll have it to you in the morning."

Cherry talked through her teeth, speaking to Ronnie as if Boudreau weren't listening. "He's doing us, Ron! He's just gonna split with it, you can't see that?"

Ronnie lost patience with his troops. "I told you to shut your face," he said. "You're just strung out, he ain't going nowhere." He paused, the phone equivalent of the teacher leaning down to the other kid. "Are you, now, comrade?"

Boudreau made himself laugh. "Not hardly."

Cherry was half crying. "*Listen* to him, Ron!"

"You want to get high, you can just leave off, okay?" he said. "You want me to come by? You want to stay strung out?"

She shut up.

"I'll call you in the morning," said Boudreau.

"What?" said Ronnie, then connected it. "Yeah, all right." He thought for a moment. "I don't need this kind of shit right now." He hung up.

Boudreau found himself on the phone with Cherry. "Maybe he'll bring *Vicky* with him," she said.

Boudreau considered whether to threaten or placate. He could hear

her breathing. "Listen," he said, "it'd be a mistake if you came downstairs for a while. You have a nice day, now."

He went to the kitchen and made a cup of coffee, his heart doing
a funny skip beat. His bones felt hollow, too rickety to support his
weight. He checked out the service-door window for Keith's car. It was
gone. He took two more Valium and sat drinking the coffee, waiting
for the tranks to kick in and erase the hangover, the methedrine de-
pression, the bad news. He had the day, one day. By the end of it he'd
have a decision. He walked out into the heat, the air bearing on him
like water.

The main lot at TU was empty except for three or four cars, parked
randomly as dead steers left behind on a trail drive. He felt waves of heat
rising off the asphalt before he even got out of the Healey. By the time
he pushed through the doors of the film building, his eyes were stinging
with salt.

Inside the air was stifling, an overheated fake forest of floor wax and
sweeping compound and urinal cakes, the piney smell of education itself.
He walked down the echoing hallway to the stairwell, and it came to
him: this felt like getting thrown out of high school, the same sinking
sensation he'd had when he was sixteen. This was a *mistake*, he lived
in a world that ran by accident. Parents and principals, employers and
politicians—they were all *assholes*, people whose power over him might
as well have been accumulated by lottery.

Margo Ross watched him walk up to her desk without a hint of
greeting.

"Hot enough for you," he asked.

She picked up a blue departmental envelope and held it out like a
turd.

Boudreau took it and turned it around in his hands. There wasn't any
point in opening it. "So what's his problem? Just out of curiosity."

Margo Ross kept her eyes on him. "I'd call it your problem, not his."

"Oh? And what's that?"

"Your problem?" said Margo Ross. "I couldn't speculate on that. Not in the general sense."

"Okay, then." She was playing him and Boudreau didn't like it. "Let's get specific."

"Specific?" She looked down at her desk as if she'd left the answer under a pile of paper, then looked him straight in the face again. "Let's see, we could start with the phone call your little friend made to DuPuys Friday night."

"My who?"

"Oh, *you* know," said Margo Ross, "the one that you—what's the phrase—*knocked up* this semester? That you slapped around a little on Friday afternoon?"

An involuntary smile came to Boudreau's mouth. "That's not the way it happened."

"Really?"

She kept staring, until finally it occurred to him that this was more than the usual barbed banter. It was a stare of fascinated revulsion, the kind you might use to check out Charlie Manson: maybe if you looked hard enough you could see why he did it.

"Then, of course, there was the phone call from the police department."

A metallic taste came into Boudreau's mouth. "The what?"

"The p*olice?*" she enunciated. "Yesterday. I had the pleasure of answering that one."

Boudreau digested this for a while. "And?"

"What you'd expect." Her smile bared her teeth.

"Margo, I've had *enough*, okay?" He moved to the edge of the desk. "You tell me and tell me now."

"Or what?" She raised her voice and leaned away from him. "You'll knock me around a little?"

Boudreau caught himself and straightened up. "Look, I'm sorry. I'm sorry." He controlled himself, the effort bringing him close to tears. "I've got a lot on my mind. Please."

Without leaning forward again, she eyed him for a long moment. "I assume it was to figure out whether there was anything worth filing charges about. He asked a bunch of questions about your—about your relationships with female students, if there was any history of trouble I knew about. If I knew any names. That kind of thing."

Boudreau closed his eyes. "And what'd you say?"

"I told him not that I knew of."

He breathed out and opened his eyes. "Thanks."

"Don't thank *me*, Boudreau." Her eyes widened. "I'd nail you to the fucking wall if I got the chance. If the cop hadn't been such a prick, I probably would have."

Boudreau stiffened. "You're sure it was a cop?"

Her eyebrows lifted. "Yeah, he showed me his ID over the phone."

Boudreau gave up. He turned to walk away, then did a little spin of miserable indecision in front of her desk. "I could fight this, but I'm not going to." He pitched the blue envelope back on her desk. "I don't need to read this shit. Tell Dennis it's been a pleasure." He started down the hall before he stopped and turned around again.

"Listen, I don't really have the time to clean everything out now, I'm just going to take a few things. I'll leave a note for Reuben, maybe he could just leave the books in boxes or something."

"I guess you didn't read that memo," said Margo Ross.

"What?" Boudreau shook his head to clear it.

"Reuben's dead," she said. "Two weeks ago? Two and half? He was having an argument with personnel and his heart went. The memorial was last Monday."

"No." He searched her face for some further clue about why the world was losing its edges. "*No,* I mean I saw—"

Margo Ross interrupted him. "I think whatever you want you better take with you today." She got up from her desk and slung her purse over her shoulder. "And you know what? I don't even want to be in the same building while you're doing it."

She walked past him down the hall and opened the door to the stairwell before she turned around. "It's your business how you fuck up your own life, Richter. I stopped caring about that a long time ago." She expelled a little breath of wonder, shaking her head at the thought that she ever had. "But it's different when you hurt other people in the process. I don't think you understand that."

$\mathbf{B}$oudreau went into his office and stood blankly, searching his mind for the last time he'd seen Reuben Armstrong. Maybe it'd been longer than he thought. He summoned up his last image of the wiry little old man, bald head shiny as polished walnut, mouth fixed in a permanent downturn from bad dentures and a lifetime of cleaning up after white people. He'd been pushing his cart loaded with cleaning supplies down the hall, muttering to himself. Boudreau tried to avoid him as usual, breezing by with a quick "Hey, Reuben," but Reuben had stepped in front of him and launched into a hostile tirade, something having to do with a pension dispute on the eve of his retirement.

Boudreau was obliged to stand and listen, to be a dumb witness. Four years before, he'd felt exactly the same way, somehow implicated in the old man's anger.

"You tell *me!*" said Reuben Armstrong. "You tell *me* why they got to fuck a old man out of his money!"

After a while Boudreau had just excused himself and walked away, leaving the janitor to rant to himself. What the hell was *he* supposed to do about it?

This was his last fond memory of Reuben Armstrong, a mixture of guilt and irritation. He didn't know why it should bother him now, since guilt and irritation had been the sum total of his relationship all along.

He went to his desk and emptied the drawers, piling the result on the top. He looked around him at the trash of six years of work life, the books, papers, magazines, posters, the picture of his handcuffed grandfather on the back of the door. He was going to need boxes.

He stopped himself.

Why, exactly, was he bothering to pack up this shit? For his next teaching job? He felt a tightening in his chest.

Tulsa University: the two words were never meant to go together.

There was the joke, but he'd taken it seriously. It was a school with a better basketball team than English department, and not by accident.

You a fool. the sound of it rang in his head, fresh as if it had been spoken the day before.

He spun and slammed the door as hard as he could. The framed picture of Truman Boudreau flew off its nail, hitting the floor in a spray of shattering glass. Boudreau swore through his Valium haze, then squatted down to pick it up. He rocked on the broken toe, then pitched forward off balance, catching himself palm-first in the broken glass. Pain flared in his hand like a rose blooming at high speed.

He rose to his knees and bellowed. The congestion high in his chest instantly clarified. This was *home,* Boudreau had known this place since he was a boy. This was where he would *destroy.*

Still on his knees, Boudreau took a full backhand at a stack of books on his desk. He caught a mug half-full of ancient coffee in the bargain; it broke when it hit the wall, spraying him in the face. He grabbed the framed photograph and slammed it back against the floor, then again. He blew hard. The last half hour came spewing out, then a day's worth, the day before no better, this awful week's worth, a year's, whatever. He'd been *born* this way, a thin shell around a yolk of rage.

He got to his feet, kicked the desk, kicked the chair next to it, kicked the bookcase. He wanted to attain dervish status, connect solidly, speak in tongues, go for the fence. He took a wild kick at the biggest remaining piece of the coffee mug, missed and lost his balance. Catching himself on the edge of the desk, he barked his wrist and reached critical mass.

Boudreau turned and threw his whole shoulder into a punch at the back of the door. *Wrong hand.* A bolt of pain shot up his arm and lit him like neon, illuminating every sorry aspect of his current delusions.

He hopped around, curled into a question mark, holding the hand between his knees and whimpering between his teeth.

He held his hand up close for examination. The pain was clear as ice water: HAND HAND HAND. There was a shard of glass embedded deep in the thumb of his palm, where he'd driven it in with the punch. Meat was involved. He pulled it like an arrowhead, blood following the glass.

He collapsed into his chair, sweat dripping off his nose, blood off his paw. His fury had titrated down into its essence of simple self-loathing. It was only a tantrum after all, not a higher state of consciousness. He caught his breath in ragged gulps. Okay, so they were assholes. What did that make him?

Drained, he fiddled simplemindedly with the corner of a file folder marked "Greenwood Interviews."

Inside there was a single page with "Reuben Armstrong" at the top of it, otherwise blank except for the words "Mt. Zion Baptist Church." It was the sole note he had taken from the three-hour interview.

You a fool.

On that particular Saturday four years ago, out of his janitor's uniform and dressed in an ill-fitting white shirt and buttoned gray sweater, Reuben Armstrong had looked across at him like someone brought in to see the warden.

Boudreau had run off at the mouth like a clown, trying to explain why he wanted to interview him. He'd already done some fair amount of research about the Greenwood riot. He knew all about it.

While Reuben Armstrong stared at him through rheumy yellowed eyes, Boudreau talked about early Tulsa, how the Chamber of Commerce crushed every attempt at unionizing, how the local press characterized any talk of racial equality as Bolshevism. The *Tulsa Tribune* had blamed the whole riot on the "bad element of niggertown," and the police wrote it off to the IWW fomenting "so-called equality." By the next year, 1922, the Ku Klux Klan held parades down Main Street in broad daylight, nearly two thousand strong in full robes and hoods, and the year after that, Klan terrorism had gotten bad enough that the governor declared martial law and sent in the National Guard. Soon thereafter, Tulsa businessmen were able to get the governor impeached by the state legislature. Warming to the bigger picture, Boudreau threw in the Civil War draft riots and the textile massacres in Lowell. Power had always had its way. The old man kept staring at him after he was done. Then Boudreau asked him what he could remember.

It was not a question of hearing anything different or particularly more complete. After all, Reuben Armstrong had lived through the

Greenwood riot as a five-year-old. The facts were not in dispute, but what Boudreau heard changed his mental image permanently. He felt like a fencepost stuck in the path of a prairie tornado. He could still hear the old man's words grinding in his ears, even now. Hiding behind a wrecked truck, the little boy had watched his mother and two sisters, pinned with fifty others behind shrubs on Standpipe Hill, die in a roar of machine gun fire that thundered on for three hours. He found his way to the Mount Zion Baptist Church, where the last holdouts in Greenwood had barricaded themselves, until it too was set on fire and the war was over. He was herded into the fairgrounds with a thousand others, where an aunt found him two days later.

Boudreau had somehow expected him to be cleansed by what he'd been though, as though there were some kind of special survivor's perspective that made people wiser, but this was not the case. Race war did not turn people into saints. Over the course of fifty-five years, Reuben Armstrong had pickled in his own hatred, and Boudreau got to hear about it. Women, especially his no-good wife and his whorish daughter, automobile companies, unions, preachers, the university, Indians, politicians, Texans, farmers: it was a world of motherfuckers. White people only stood out as the ugliest examples.

Boudreau could hardly blame him, but after a while he couldn't listen to it anymore. He was repulsed by the way Reuben Armstrong talked about the ones who died, like they'd been too stupid to get away. He finally interrupted the old man at what seemed like a point of marginal agreement.

He could still hear himself saying it: "That's why I want to write about this. So it won't happen again."

"Do what?" Reuben Armstrong said.

Boudreau repeated himself: "So it won't happen again."

Reuben Armstrong made a wet, gravelly sound, over and over. It was apparently his version of a laugh. "You a *fool,*" he said, then got up from his chair.

The old man stood there, waiting. It took Boudreau a while to understand: he was expecting a little something for his time.

Boudreau tried to explain. "When I get some money, I'll make sure you get paid. My screenplay's still in the development stages."

"Yo' what?" said Reuben.

"Screenplay?" Boudreau had explained all this before. "You know, for a movie?"

"Movie?" Armstrong got a look on his face like he couldn't believe what he'd just eaten. "*Movie?*" he said again, and then he walked out.

Boudreau found himself staring down at the piece of paper with "Mount Zion Baptist Church" on it. He'd bled on it. Something was nagging at him, something he'd forgotten, the edge of a dream he couldn't quite remember. He shook it off and closed the folder, put it with the stack of dialogue note cards. That and the picture of True, that was all he'd take. When all this was done and he was resettled somewhere, then he'd—

Yeah, right. Like the current political climate was going to produce a sudden clamor for movies about home-grown race war. The current climate, my ass: it wasn't so different now than when Reuben Armstrong was five years old and terrified. Now a right-wing racist could wear a business suit instead of a hood, call himself a CEO while his kid went out and dicked some pathetic black girl to death. No one gave a shit, any more than they cared about a bitter old janitor croaking of a heart attack while he argued about his pension.

Boudreau's own heart began racing. *He's a janitor at some college,* she'd said. *He fucking* died *the day before.*

He sat up straight at the realization, adrenalin spiking through him at the sinister coincidence, the sheer synchronicity of it. Earla was Reuben's *daughter.*

He was going crazy. It was too weird, too neat to be real, a fiction of ironies that he alone was in a position to read. It felt like a *déjà vu* but worse, a sense that his life was being bent to grotesque purpose by unseen forces.

You a fool, indeed.

Someone was sending him a message. You a *coward.*

Cherry was ensconced in one of the big wing chairs, on a righteous nod. She watched him come in without saying anything. "Partner in crime came by," she slurred. "Gives his regards."

Boudreau looked down at her. "Where's Keith?"

She gave him a big high-cheeked smile. "Out."

Boudreau turned and went to the bar. He made himself a double gin and tonic, then came back in and stood in front of her chair.

"I was just out at TU," he said. "What was Earla's last name?"

She looked up. "Armstrong," she said after a while.

Boudreau smiled down at her, then looked up at the ceiling. He took a massive gulp of the drink. "Check this out, I just found out I knew him. I *knew* the man."

She didn't know what he was talking about.

He shook his head in disbelief, still smiling. "Her *father*, I knew him for years. Reuben Armstrong."

She regarded him through eyes dark and liquid as black coffee. "Yeah," she said. "So."

Boudreau was taken aback. He'd had a whole speech planned, and now it was suddenly beside the point. "I interviewed him, he was in a race riot here when he was a little boy." He kept his eyes on her for some sign of shock or surprise.

She looked out the window as though waiting for somebody. "Far out, man," she drawled.

Boudreau ignored her tone. "I mean, isn't that just a little coincidental, that I knew both of them?"

Without turning from the window, she shook her head. "You didn't know Earla," she said. "Didn't know her at *all.*"

Boudreau sagged into the other chair. She was missing the point, but there was obviously no sense in pursuing it. She was in junkie's time mode, future blank, past erased: fate was a straight line to oblivion, not the snaky thing he knew it to be.

"Well," he said lamely, "it means something to me." He had another slug of the gin and tonic.

Outside a horn honked, then again. Boudreau looked out. It was Keith in The Beast, waiting in the driveway.

"Whups, there's my ride." Cherry singsonged it like she was late for her schoolbus. She made it unsteadily to her feet and started for the front door.

Boudreau followed right behind. "Where're you going?"

She shrugged elaborately. "Wants me to come along be a *witness;* " she said. "See some lawyer."

"What?"

"I make a *good* witness," she said, still walking. "Keith's my *friend.* "

Boudreau grabbed her by the upper arm and she went limp, more stoned than civilly disobedient.

"Listen," he said. "Just out of curiosity, I need to know what's in that film can."

She looked into his chest, then smiled as it dawned on her. "You pig," she said. *"Pig. "*

Boudreau gave a nasty little snort as she tried to pull away.

"What'd, you *sell* it?"

"Oh, I have it." He was squeezing her arm, hard. "I just wanted to hear it from you."

She jerked loose, stumbling a little at the release. "Go take a look, then. *Pig. "*

Boudreau watched her drive off with Keith, then found his way back to the chair. Pig? He was just out of control, he wasn't a pig. On the other hand, maybe it was too late to make that kind of distinction. He picked up his drink and looked at it, swirling the ice. He could pot down ten of them and it wouldn't make any difference.

He got up and locked the front door. The house was cool and quiet, silent as an empty museum after hours.

Not a museum, he thought, a *tomb*. It lacked only cobwebs and dusty sarcophagi to function as the lone inscrutable artifact of a dead ruler. The Michaels family still lived on in its corporate way, scattered around on deckle-edged paper, shuttled between microchips, but aside from the weak-willed son and the exiled daughter, there was no trace left except the house.

The house: he'd been enthralled by this place ever since he was a kid, and now he felt like trashing it, pulling down the drapes, setting fire to the Persian rugs, pissing on the furniture. He'd spent most of his life around people who lived in houses like this one without ever lifting a finger, acting like they'd deserved them since before they were born.

The house, of course, was widely regarded as a monument to the family, but the lives of the people whose work made it possible—the roughnecks on the Michaels rigs, the truck drivers, the pipeline construction men, the refinery workers, even the masons and carpenters who actually built the thing—these were as invisible and forgotten as the poor fuckers who hauled rock for the pyramids, the peasant drones who kept Versailles spic and span for the Sun King.

He'd been about to walk away from his five hundred grand, certifying his own chump status. He didn't deserve the money, either, but that was precisely the point. Recent elections had reaffirmed the way things were: it was food chain, pure and simple. You were supposed to scrabble and claw for what you could get, creep up like a hyena under fear of death and rip off any piece still light enough to carry away. You had to *believe* in it; you had to dream of becoming the lion himself, gorging and snoozing and leaving the rest to rot.

He'd gotten hung up on the connection between Reuben and Earla, but what, really, was so ironic about that? It was what every family came to, a fantastic snarling of fates, a messy web relevant only to itself. So Reuben got shot at as a kid, so his daughter Earla died with all the dignity of a slaughterhouse sheep. Reuben Armstrong's line had been knotted and cut by white men beginning with the day his ancestor was snared like an animal a full ocean away. Where was the irony in that? Cherry was right, it wasn't a big deal. Irony wasn't just cheap, it was a distraction, no different than the drink in his hand. It was another kind of religion, a way of making you think that you could see everything for something other than what it was. His own family offered proof enough of that.

During Boudreau's entire childhood the phrase "going to Vinita" had been code for losing your mind. Vinita was the site of a state mental hospital, which was where he'd last seen his grandfather alive. Home from California on vacation, Boudreau had gone for a visit, figuring at least it was better than prison. He smoked a joint on the drive up.

It had been years since he'd seen him, but he hadn't expected this. True walked across the room hanging on the arm of a ward orderly, his flesh melted away. The beefy giant had become a fragile crane of a man, a tower of skin-stretched bones with an oversized skull on top. His luxuriant black curls remained oddly ungrayed and stuck out from his head like an ill-fitting wig. From the sides of his face, waxy folds of skin hung in dewlaps.

The old man kept confusing him with his dead father, the son for the grandson. Boudreau corrected him after the third "Malcolm." True blinked several times, then gave him a reassessing look, all in slow motion; he was carrying a load of tranks heavy as bricks. Cagey, he changed the subject and began a discourse about livestock breeding.

Boudreau listened with half an ear to the talk of sires and dams and their get. If it didn't get any worse than this, he could handle it. It was almost like being back at the ranch. So what if True had ended up living in the past, it was indisputably a better place. He could hardly blame him.

His grandfather rambled on for a while about "seed," then stopped as though reconsidering.

He sized up Boudreau through the narrowed eyes of the practiced stockman. " 'Course *bad* seed can run true as *good* seed," he said, "till the Lord culls it out." He grinned, the same face-splitting expression that used to punctuate his bawdy punchlines, but now it was skull-like, his teeth long and discolored. "He culls for *fornicators* and in*tox*icators and dee-*cei*vers."

Boudreau stared, stomach dropping away like he was taking a free-fall in an elevator. True had been a cheerfully cynical blasphemer all his life, and now he'd come to this. The joke was Boudreau's alone to appreciate.

Truman Boudreau leaned across the worn formica table. "He culled *me* out, Malcolm," he whispered, the surprise still on him. He turned, giving a sly look behind himself at the orderly, then turned back around and lunged across the table.

The orderly, a squat Indian who couldn't have held the old Truman Boudreau for an instant, folded him in his arms from behind, the old man squawking like a spindly-limbed swamp bird.

"Lord made you bad seed, Malcolm, sure as a one-nut bull!" True's eyes burned with it, the eyes of a prophet with no return ticket from the wilderness. "You can sow bad seed in your whores and harlots," he roared, *"but it will not flourish!"*

Boudreau slugged down the rest of his gin and tonic. In the years that had passed since then, he'd defended himself from its truth with irony. He stood up. Not anymore.

Okay, he was a venal son of a bitch, the bad seed of bad seed. He was who he was. He needed to get that film can and find out what was in it. The keys to his mother's apartment were still in the pocket of the pants he'd left out at the farmhouse, the day he and Vicky played tennis. He wasn't sure how he'd do it, but he'd figure a way.

He'd always dreamed of the day when his guilt would wash away, and now that day had come. All that was left at the bottom of the pan was straight greed, shining and pure, good as enlightened self-interest.

Boudreau pulled into his dust bowl of a front yard and got out. Not a breath of air stirred on the ridge, the silence like an extension of the heat. In the distance to the north a toxic-looking yellow-gray pall hung over Tulsa like the aftermath of a bomb strike.

A sudden gear-grinding whar *whar*, whar *whar* broke the silence. He recognized the sound of a big engine laboring to turn over. There was a cough and the air cracked with an explosion of ether, a mammoth diesel roaring to life. It sounded like a panzer division was ready to crest the hill.

Boudreau ran to the edge of the ridge behind the house. A big yellow bulldozer was tracking down off a trailer, a good half mile away down at the bottom of the ridge. The noise carried up the shallow slope in waves as the operator put more throttle to it.

Boudreau lit a cigarette and watched the dozer skin back the top layer of prairie, leaving a broad incision of bare red earth behind it. It seemed to be cutting in a road.

He found himself standing next to the overgrown garden plot that Ginny had put in that first summer.

The deteriorated remnants of his earlier life were still all over the place, distinct as slug trails in morning dew. There were unfinished projects everywhere, the marriage done before they were. The second summer, Ginny had wanted Boudreau to build a deck off the north side of the house, to enjoy the view. They argued about it. He saw no reason to watch the process that was inexorably turning Broken Arrow into a colorfully named suburb. By the end of August he'd dug the postholes and that was as far as he ever got. She left in October, bald as a baby.

For the life of him he still couldn't understand how it could've happened any differently.

Boudreau squatted next to the garden plot and looked at the deck site, a rectangular grid of twelve holes with weather-slumped mounds of dirt beside each one. The whole weed-grown thing suggested an ancient, mathematically advanced colony of giant burrowing ants.

He watched the dozer for a while, then looked past it at the "view" Ginny had loved so much. Five years before, Tulsa could only be seen on a rare clear day. Today was by no means such a day, but it didn't make any difference. Smog no longer hid the evidence. Tulsa had crept across the rolling prairie like a slowly spreading stain on a tablecloth, the edges of the stain red with newly routed Oklahoma dirt. The dozer began pushing the topsoil into a big pile.

The New Year's Eve after Ginny left, he threw a party to prove his independence, only to wake up hungover and alone the next morning. The heat had gone off in the night and the pipes were frozen. Someone had thrown up in the sink and that was frozen too. The sum total of nourishment in the house was a popcorn bowl with a few unpopped kernels stuck in congealed butter, and two inches left in a bottle of Jack Daniel's. He'd gone outside to pee, standing in this exact same place, and he'd thought, *Wow, it's kind of exhilarating to hit dead rock bottom.* The steers grazing behind the house had lowed miserably in the cold. He ended up firing bottle rockets at them while he killed the bourbon, then went back inside and threw up himself.

Boudreau let his cigarette fall down into one of the old postholes and stood up. Somehow he'd had to go through all that to arrive here. He hadn't known then exactly how bad it had to get. Now he did.

The front door was open by a few inches, in itself not a big deal. The door sagged enough on its hinges that the latch didn't catch unless you slammed it just right. He found it open all the time.

He walked in and the stench hit him before anything else. He gagged until his eyes watered. When they cleared and adjusted to the gloom, his heart began slamming around inside him like a bird trying to batter its way out of a cage. He grabbed the Louisville slugger he kept behind the door and looked around in nose-flared fear, inhaling the distinct smell of deteriorated flesh. Something had *died* in here.

He stood rigid for thirty solid seconds, telling himself, This is only a dream, I'll wake up from it now.

Bat in hand, he forced himself to move, creeping across the debris of the silent living room, sucking shallow breaths in the stifling overheated reek. There were drifts of torn books and emptied drawers, broken furniture.

Somebody had taken the place apart, trashed it with simpleminded thoroughness. They had thrown in some Mansonesque touches, the walls spray-painted with FUCK YOU and DIE YOU PIG, his longest kitchen knife left embedded in the back of the sofa after it had been used to disembowel all the cushions.

He followed the smell to the kitchen, bracing himself. The refrigerator had been pushed over onto its side. A low buzzing hum came from behind it. He looked over and the stink jumped up into his nose like a bacterial assault wave. There were two buttock-sized clumps liquefying on the floor, alive with shiny green flies. His gorge rose and he went faint. He was looking at body parts.

The flies shifted and he caught sight then of one corner of a square of waxed paper. The clumps were a couple stacks of cheap cube steaks he'd bought the week before his power went out. They *had been* cheap cube steaks: now they were a collective life form, a science-fair project.

Holding his nose, Boudreau backed his way out of the kitchen. His panic blossomed. Lately he'd been having these repeated episodes where he thought he was going to die in a minute or two. Now he'd just been reasonably convinced there was a dismembered body in his house. Somehow he hadn't been taking these signals seriously; this wasn't just paranoia. He was going to die.

He caught himself. He was doing it again, talking himself into things. Arla Thompson, this had to be Arla's doing. Okay, she'd gotten hers now, this was just the most extreme form of breaking up he'd experienced so far. He could live with that.

On the way back to the bedroom he swung the bat into the wall, hard enough to bring plaster off.

He pushed open the bedroom door and a new smell hit him. At the head of his slashed mattress, a white circle with a dark center shone dimly in the gloom. He edged closer. It was a dinner plate, and someone had left a straightforward message on it. The fly-covered turds lay coiled on the plate like a nightmare dessert.

He fell to his knees and got right to work. The floor was a tangled mess of ripped and strewn clothes, smashed drawers. Suddenly he was uncertain which pants he'd been wearing—*khakis,* he was pretty sure they'd been khakis. He started rooting through the pile.

Boudreau went through every pair of pants on the floor with no luck, then went through the pile again. He found khakis but they weren't the right ones. He went through it a third time, searching every pocket of every pair of pants. He lost track of where he'd looked and where he hadn't, then started over, this time doing the shirts as well. Twice more and he gave up. The keys were gone. He'd lost them, and that was that.

On his knees, it occurred to him. The house looked searched, not just destroyed. Search and destroy. Dread rippled through him like a gust of hot wind. How could they know about it? They couldn't, could they?

He hit his feet. What the fuck did it *matter?*

Through the distant background noise of the bulldozer, he heard a car door slam shut. The hair on his arms stood up straight as bristles. This was it, then. He'd always had trouble with deadlines.

He made it into position behind the front door, just as a pair of boots clumped up onto the porch. He felt his feet grip the floor like an ape's as he raised the bat. The door wasn't even closed all the way, much less locked.

Nothing happened, then finally the door creaked forward a little further, pushed by a hand or a foot. A swatch of sunlight lit the floor, a motionless shadow within it. He went up on tiptoe to bring the bat down. The shadow shortened into an elongated crouch. Arms out, it advanced into the room, followed by a matte-gray automatic.

He went for it but hit wood instead, the door slamming into him with the weight of a full shoulder behind it.

Boudreau found himself senseless on the floor, without breath, a knee on his chest and the cold metal snout of the gun jammed into the soft hollow under his jaw. His brain went sparkly waiting for the instant of impact.

"You want to get killed, comrade?"

Boudreau opened his eyes.

Ronnie looked down at him through his sunglasses, his lips pursed over to one side. He worked his cheek with his teeth, as if waiting for the answer.

Boudreau moved his head slightly and made a noise in his throat, the gun still pushed up against it.

"You want to get killed," Ronnie said, "that's ⸚ ʳood way to do it."

He looked around the room, then pulleᴄ ⸺ⁱᵉ gun from its niche in Boudreau's flesh and stood up. The automatic looked like it was part of his hand, the barrel an exceptionally deadly finger.

Boudreau got to his feet and his legs collapsed. He leaned against the wall to hold himself up.

"Looks like you had a visitor," said Ronnie. "What's that smell?"

Boudreau's muscles were firing in random quivers. This was the second time in as many days that Ronnie Dean Stover had taken him right up to the edge and made him look over. Boudreau massaged the spot under his jaw. Both times it seemed like there had been an actual decision to make first.

Ronnie turned around, smiling. "You lucky I didn't take you out." He said it as though he were discussing road directions, a wrong turn that ended up being right after all. "First I look in, see all this shit." He indicated the ruined living room with a nod. "Then I see some asshole behind the door with a club." He looked at Boudreau, his lips pouted together, then shook his head at the stunning lack of combat sense.

Boudreau stared at him, voice still out of commission.

Ronnie held up the automatic, out from his palm with his fingertips around the edges, as though Boudreau had just asked for some handgun advice.

"Nine millimeter," he said. "Eighteen to a clip if it don't jam." He pulled out the waist of his jeans with one hand and slid the gun under with the other, then hitched his pants up. He looked around at the room again. "You know who done this?"

"Yeah," croaked Boudreau. "Some girl at school."

Ronnie had himself a thin smile at this. "Well, hell, I guess that's true love."

Boudreau coughed out an attempt at a laugh.

Ronnie leaned around for a look into the kitchen, wrinkling his nose against the stink. "She must've been pretty mad, push over that fridge." He turned back around, the little smile twitching on his face. "You must've been poking it around some, Richter."

"Not really." Ronnie seemed to be taking this pretty lightly. Boudreau mentally measured Arla Thompson against the refrigerator, then reconsidered Ronnie's last comment in a whole new light. In a panic, he eyed the bat on the floor. He had one thing left in his favor, *one thing.* Of course he didn't *really* have it, but Ronnie didn't know that. He massaged his throat, buying time. "Listen, I need to get out of this smell."

They went outside onto the porch, Ronnie waiting for Boudreau to go first.

"I tried to call you back," Boudreau said, "after I got out of the house."

Ronnie regarded him, head tilted. "Is that right? Good thing I come out here, then."

Yeah, good thing, thought Boudreau. "Cherry's getting too weird, I don't trust her." He considered. "That's why I said on the phone it was out here." Out of his mouth it had the squishy blurt of excuse to it, obvious as a whoopee cushion. "I mean, I didn't want her knowing where it was."

Ronnie squatted on his boot heels, using the house to lean against. He shook a Pall Mall out of his pack and looked at it. "I don't take ever'thing Cherry says serious." He lit the cigarette and exhaled, looking out at the dirt road that dead-ended just past the yard. "So where is it?"

Boudreau sagged against the house, down into a squat of his own.

Ronnie's question had come right on the beat. "Right where it's been all along, at my mother's."

Ronnie picked a fleck of tobacco from his lip and examined it before he flicked it away. "You aren't doing me now, are you, Richter?"

Boudreau looked out at the dirt road himself, rigid, then chanced a look back at Ronnie. Now everything was out front.

"You think I'm *stupid?*" He held up his hand, scout's honor at the very thought. "I'm going over there ten o'clock tomorrow morning, I'll be back at Keith's by eleven."

Ronnie rose from his crouch in a single fluid motion, then ran his fingers through his hair. Boudreau found himself staring at the knees of Ronnie's jeans, frayed white into horizontal threads. Ronnie reached down, offering him a hand up. The hand swallowed his own and brought him to his feet with the ease of something hydraulic.

"Okay," said Ronnie. "You do that." He stared at Boudreau through his sunglasses, his pursed lips slowly blossoming into a bare-toothed grin. "You *do* that, comrade."

Boudreau smiled back and breathed out slightly, his heart jumping with what he'd just accomplished.

"See, that's our hole card," Ronnie explained, "and we got to be ready to show it. I put on some pressure this morning, I told 'em they better start taking me serious or our man at the *Journal* sees the hole card before they do."

"The *Journal?*" Boudreau squealed, hysterical. "Oh, *man!* I fucking *work* there, they'll be looking for any—"

Smiling again, Ronnie reached out and grabbed him by the chin, thumb hooked under the hollow and fingers on top. Boudreau felt like there was a vise on his face. "You think this is just a little blackmail gig?"

Boudreau squeezed out a "No" between his teeth, terrified. Ronnie looked at him for a moment longer, then let go. Boudreau moved back against the wall.

"There's some shit I ain't told you yet," Ronnie said, "but we'll talk about that later."

Boudreau looked away from the smile, then made himself turn back. "Like what?"

Ronnie allowed himself a little laugh, the smile gone by the end of it. "It's kind of a personal thing, Richter." He reconsidered, then shrugged to minimize it, like it might be jock rot, or maybe hemorrhoids. "I'll tell you soon's you give me them pictures."

Boudreau looked into the dark glasses.

Sure, just as soon as he gave him the *pitchers.* Somehow it had never occurred to him that the film can might actually have film in it. This was a good joke, and he felt sure he'd laugh about it later. Right now he was scared out of his mind, but this was clearly what Ronnie wanted to see.

"Okay, I'll wait," Boudreau said. "But I'm dying to find out."

Ronnie adjusted the automatic in the waist of his jeans, then stepped off the porch. "You will," he said, unable to suppress a tiny smile at the felicity of his double meaning. If human relations were chess, Ronnie was still playing double-jump checkers. "I guess meantime you got some cleaning up to do."

Boudreau went straight over to Brinkman's desk. "George, we need to talk. George?"

Brinkman was reading the front page, smiling broadly. "You see this?" He shook the paper to straighten it and pushed it across to Boudreau. "Read this. One of the Horned Frog's finer efforts."

It was an editorial, banner headlined TERRORISM IN TULSA. Aside from election-day endorsements, the last time Preston Liddey had run a front page editorial was during the Mayaguez incident. That one had been headlined GOD BLESS THE MAYAGUEZ. Boudreau scanned the thing in no time, made easier by the high cliché quotient. The gist was that, even though some people thought Harmon Shaw to be a politically controversial figure, some did not. Regardless, his was an important economic voice in the community, valuable for its distinctive addition to the social discourse, whether or not you agreed with him. To bomb somebody you disagreed with was a direct curtailment of freedom of expression, a treasured American right. Maybe they did that sort of thing in the Middle East, but there was no call for it here, especially not in Tulsa. The police department was pursuing some promising leads, and the *Tulsa Daily Journal* called for widespread support of both the department and of Harmon Shaw in bringing the bomber to the justice he so richly deserved.

"I think we ought to run a Spot-Carlos-the-Jackal sweepstakes," Brinkman said while Boudreau finished. "Maybe get McDonald's to cosponsor. Ten percent circulation increase, I guarantee it."

Boudreau pushed the paper back across the desk.

"Hey, why so glum, chum?" said Brinkman. "You lose your sense of humor?"

Boudreau managed a sickly smile.

"Ah, a *mood.*" Brinkman nodded in judicious understanding. "Well, my fran', I have these cousin of mine from South America? He sends me recently a herbal cure for these kind of mood? Perhaps you would like some of these cure? To share with me, eh?"

Boudreau thought about it. He didn't see how it could help. On the other hand, he didn't see how it could hurt.

"My fran'?"

"Sure," said Boudreau.

They went down the hall to a large office-supply closet that Brinkman had the key to. Brinkman kept up his irritating Spanish riff through the whole joint.

"Listen," said Boudreau. "I need to get out of here."

"What, you don't like the decor?" Brinkman looked around. "It's kind of, I don't know, Early Office Supply. You have your twenty-pound bond, your boxes of Ticonderoga number two, very yellow, very colorful, your—"

"George, I need to get *out* of here."

"A little paranoid today, aren't we?" Brinkman peered at him squinty-eyed, waving a hand as though to clear vast clouds of smoke. "Okay."

Boudreau revised his estimate about how it couldn't hurt. He was instantly a lot more stoned than he'd planned to be. Faces turned as he reentered the newsroom. Getting around common obstacles required

careful calculation. After a long journey he arrived at his safe seat beside
Brinkman's desk, convinced that a colored trail wafted behind him,
marked Intense Marijuana Odor.

Brinkman was already seated, red eyed and grinning. "So don't you
want to hear about what happened at the press conference?"

Boudreau stared. "Press conference?"

Brinkman smacked his own head. "Oh, you mean *press* conference."
He regarded Boudreau, eyebrows lifted. "The pot ain't *that* good."

Boudreau connected, like he'd just been plugged in. "You went to the
press conference?"

"*Yeah*, I went," said Brinkman, indignant. "Very enlightening experience, I might add." He looked carefully around the room, then leaned
toward Boudreau. "Listen to this, you won't fucking believe it."

Boudreau leaned forward, heart wild.

"I learned—quote—that there are *dark forces* at work in America
today. *Yeah*. Dark forces in America."

Boudreau sagged. "You asshole."

"What," said Brinkman, leaning back, "it's good enough for Liddey,
but it ain't good enough for you? I thought you had this conspiracy all
worked out."

Boudreau gestured vaguely down at the editorial, shaking his head like
he didn't understand.

"You mean where's the aforementioned promising leads?" Brinkman's mouth went down in the corners. "Like did he say it was the
Trilateral Commission or the Clamshell Alliance or something? Well,
they're hot on the trail but they aren't telling, Boudreau, they aren't
telling. Dark forces, my man."

Boudreau looked at him. He didn't know why he'd expected anything
at this point.

Brinkman smirked back at him, then sat up suddenly. "Oh no, *wait.*"
He held up his hand and wiggled it in excitement. "Dark—*dark* forces."
He looked at Boudreau, eyes widening. "Could that be *Negroes?*"

Boudreau fell back in his chair, exhausted. He stared.

Brinkman smiled, enjoying every second. He held up a forefinger,
then opened the drawer of his desk. "Here, look at what I took." He

pushed a large black and white glossy over to Boudreau. "They should've run this under the editorial."

The picture caught Harmon Shaw with his mouth open, waving one arm in pop-eyed midphrase. The camera had frozen the wave in what could be taken for a weird straight-arm salute, except it looked like he was giving the finger at the same time.

"Rat-cheer's yur dangerous demagogue with lots of enemies," said Brinkman. "Check out his fucking body guards, in the shades and white shirts." He pointed. "Mutt and Jeff here."

Of the two men in short-sleeved white shirts, one faced the camera directly, a barrel-chested little fireplug of a man. His partner was looking away in partial profile, a rope-lean mountain cracker, flat faced, arms folded across his chest. He looked vaguely familiar behind the air force shades, someone Boudreau had seen driving Liz Shaw to school or something.

Brinkman was chortling. "My favorite's the tall one with the tattoos, he looks like he eats live squirrels for breakfast and washes it down with gasoline. *Very* high quality security force."

The words went through Boudreau like a miracle fever, appearing on his skin a few seconds later as cold sweat.

"What kind of tattoos?" he said. "I mean, what were they of."

"Tattoos?" Brinkman sniffed. "I don't know, 'Born To Be Dumb,' whatever." He made a mouth. "Jews don't get tattooed. Except in special circumstances."

Boudreau kept looking at the picture, like it was an amusing image worth the extended regard. He couldn't tell. His mind was playing tricks on him.

"Boudreau?"

He looked up to find George Brinkman searching his face. Brinkman leaned over, homing in on whatever he'd just found. "C'mon, Boudreau," he said. "I smell fish."

Boudreau looked back at the picture. "Can I keep this? I mean, this is pretty funny."

Brinkman's mouth widened into a smile, his bloodshot eyes burning in.

Boudreau met them, locked in. "Is there any way you can find out about those tattoos?"

"Yeah, sure." George Brinkman lifted his eyebrows a hair without shifting his gaze. "I got more pictures I haven't printed." He grinned outright as he pounced. "C'mon, man, you know something. *Give.*"

Boudreau looked away and lit a cigarette. By the time he exhaled, the decision was made. Brinkman was already scanning the newsroom behind him, eyes narrowed with conspiracy. He held up a palm to keep it low, as if Boudreau didn't know any better.

"George," he whispered, voice wavering. "George, if you fucking breathe a *word* of this—" Someone tapped him on the shoulder and his nerves shot him half out of his chair.

Preston Liddey's secretary jumped back, both hands to her chest. "*Excuse* me!"

Wild eyed, Boudreau stared up at her.

"I didn't mean—" she began, then dropped it. "Mr. Liddey wants to see you in his office."

"We're *busy*, Lida," Brinkman said. He kept his eyes on Boudreau. "Tell him just a minute."

She grimaced and shook her head. "He said right away."

Boudreau got up like a zombie, the picture in hand.

Brinkman caught his eyes again and held them. "I'll be here," he said.

Preston Liddey was looking out the window of his office when Boudreau came in. He gestured at a chair, his face grim.

"I don't know how to say this." He paused for extra gravity, then found a way. "I'm going to have to let you go."

Boudreau stared at him for a long moment, his head cocked. *Let you go?* Go where? What did this mean? When the words finally clicked into place they seemed laughable. "Yeah?"

Liddey's face turned a darker red. "I have to tell you this disappoints me deeply."

"Okay," said Boudreau. He waited to be told, his powers of comprehension growing more literal by the second.

"I don't know why I expected you to be any different now. You've flaunted the rules of convention right along."

"Flouted," said Boudreau.

Liddey looked at him, confused, already following his next thought. "You missed your deadline on Friday and I gave you one more break, against my better judgment. Then you missed it again yesterday. This is a pattern. All I can think is, you must psychologically want to be punished. That's all I can come up with, so that's what I'm going to do."

Boudreau thought about it. "I've been real busy," he said.

Preston Liddey deflated, his shoulders sagging for a moment before his anger brought him around. He pointed at Boudreau, arm straight out for drama. "You're looking for *trouble*, son. I'm not a headshrinker, but that's a mental problem. That's all I can think, you're looking for *trouble.*"

All things considered, Boudreau couldn't argue. It seemed true enough. "Yeah, I guess so." He stared openmouthed at the picture of Lew Liddey on the wall.

Stunned, the younger Liddey's eyes widened. "Are you on narcotics?"

Boudreau continued to stare.

The publisher held his palms out as though pushing something away. "I wash my hands of you. I wash my hands." He put his newly washed hands on his hips. "I won't put up with it. I've got people coming around here asking questions about you and your friends. I can't have that."

Boudreau straightened up in his chair. "You what?"

Liddey looked at him, grateful for the first sign of interest. "That's right, some detective came in here this morning asking questions. I don't know what you've been up to, but I can't have that kind of thing. No way." He looked at Boudreau for affirmation that he couldn't have that kind of thing.

Boudreau found himself on the edge of his chair. "Did you get a name? Did you see ID?"

Preston Liddey was taken aback. As far as he was concerned, a detective was a detective. He looked at Boudreau sideways. "I don't see how that concerns you."

"You don't *what?*" Boudreau felt like his face was thawing. "It doesn't *concern* me?" His voice rose. "What the fuck did you *tell* him?"

Liddey went and stood behind his desk. "This has gone about far enough."

"They threatened you, right? They threatened you and you caved in." Boudreau stood too. "You chicken-shit."

Liddey's mouth worked soundlessly, like a fish wondering where the water went. "I don't know what you're talking about but you can start walking right now, mister. *Right* now! Nobody talks to *me* like that! Not a Boudreau."

Richter Boudreau gaped at him. Liddey had used his name like it was a synonym for generic criminal. History was repeating itself. "You chicken-shit *ass*hole."

Preston Liddey's face went slack with disbelief. He picked up the phone and punched a button. *"You leave my building,"* he said, mouth tight, "you leave my building, or I'll have your person removed."

"I guess chicken-shit just runs in the family, huh?" Boudreau pointed up at the portrait of Lew Liddey for evidence.

"Lida! Lida, will you *please* get building security up here for me, please?" He pointed the hand piece at Boudreau like a cross at an advancing vampire. Spit had accumulated at the corners of his mouth.

"Family, *bull*shit, mister! I bent over *back*wards for you! The only reason I even *hired* you was because of your mother!"

Boudreau moved toward the desk, his eyes fixed on the widening conspiracy. "Preston," he said, *"did you fuck my mom?"*

"Lida!" Preston Liddey shouted into the phone. *"Lida!"*

Boudreau was rooting through the drawers of his desk for anything incriminating when he heard the elevator arrive with a lingering *bong*.

He became aware of a slight hum to the newsroom. Someone was behind him.

"Mr. Boudreau?"

The voice said it country fashion, accent on the first syllable.

"That's me," said Boudreau, and turned around.

It was the green-uniformed man who sat behind the security desk in the lobby. Boudreau had never seen him out of his chair. He was forty-ish and overweight, his face pink with fried food, a pensioned cop with high blood pressure. He had a head that seemed to go straight down into his shoulders, with tiny ears that were flat to his scalp. It gave him the aspect of an extremely large woodchuck.

Boudreau smiled in recognition, involuntarily.

The man looked back at him through watery blue eyes, face devoid of expression. He was a good five inches shorter than Boudreau, but now that he was standing up, he didn't look short, just low to the ground.

Boudreau kept smiling at him. "Hi," he said.

"Come with me to the elevator, please sir?"

Okay, so it was going to be like that. "Let me just check these drawers first, is that all right?"

"I said *right* now, friend." The guard hooked his thumbs over his belt, which carried an elaborately tooled holster with a walnut-handled .38 in it.

Boudreau straightened up, a little crackle to the air. They were rounding him up like a stray. He was having his person removed.

"Sure thing." Boudreau grabbed his briefcase, suddenly sure he should recheck it for the picture. That would be a mistake.

The guard stayed on his heels to the elevator, two steps behind. The hum in the newsroom had dropped to nothing while people watched. Boudreau saw Brinkman standing up at his desk, mouth open and arms dropped to his sides.

Boudreau raised his fist in a power salute, then dropped it, his arm too weak to hold it up.

Someone laughed, a single burst of nervous laughter that went off like the report of a gun.

Brinkman made eye contact and pointed to himself, then mimed holding a phone.

When the elevator doors opened, the guard walked forward, herding Boudreau in. He got to the back wall, then turned around while the guard punched the button.

"Elevator escort, too, huh?" The muscles on his face hurt from the fixed grin.

"Out the front doors." The guard explained it to the wall, professionally bored. "That's what the man said."

"You do just what the man says, right?" Boudreau couldn't stop himself. "The man says, Fart, you say, How loud, right?"

Without gaining any expression, the guard reached down and unsnapped the holster strap across the butt of the .38. He worked the gun with the heel of his hand until it creaked loosely in the leather. "I'll crack your hat, smart boy. Do that on my own." He still talked to the wall. "Free a charge."

Boudreau froze against the wall and shut up. He held his briefcase against his chest until it struck him that, body-language-wise, this was a vaguely purselike gesture.

He came out of the elevator fast, relieved to see a lobby full of people. He crossed it like a broken-field runner. The guard stayed right behind him with a rolling fat-hammed lope, as if maybe he was planning on some free-lance parking lot action. Boudreau hit the revolving door at a full run, a last-second shove in the lower back putting him into orbit.

The door launched him out into downtown Tulsa, the heat slamming into him like a hostile alien atmosphere. He tripped forward, bumped a business suit and got shoved off balance. Briefcase flying, he hit the sidewalk hands and knees first before rolling to a stop on his back. Feet in the air like a bug, he looked up at the rush-hour flow of horrified faces stepping around him. In a second they would start trampling him, stoning him. He couldn't breathe.

Someone squatted beside him and grabbed his elbow. He panicked and tried to jerk it away, but the grasp stayed firm. It pulled him upright. He found himself sitting, hard butt on hot concrete.

"You all right, brother?" said a voice.

Boudreau couldn't focus through his tears. He nodded, breathless.

"What's wrong?" the voice said.

Boudreau blinked hard, looking down at his raw palms. His head wobbled.

"In your heart," the voice answered for him, "you *know* what's wrong, don't you?"

Boudreau looked up into the too clear blue eyes, boring into him. The guy was a pod person, and he was going to turn him into plant life.

The Christer took the look for affirmation, an eerie smile blooming in slow motion. "You talk about it in your heart all the time," he said, "but you keep doin' it anyway, don't you?" The smile stayed fixed, immobile, as though the words were issuing from further down. "That's just the way of mankind. Bible says man born of woman is born to *sin.*"

Boudreau stared at him, hypnotized.

"And the wages of sin is *death.*" The pod's smile widened without seeming to involve his facial muscles. "You need the Son of God on your side, friend."

Boudreau got his feet under himself. If he listened a second longer, he was going to start photosynthesizing. He grabbed his briefcase and stood up.

Inside the building the guard was watching from the chair behind his desk.

When the Christer touched him lightly on the chest, Boudreau shrunk back as if burned.

"Can I just get one of them cigarettes off you, brother?" the man said.

Boudreau parked way down at the end of the block, then hiked back to the huge empty house, staying well back on the broad landscaped lawns. He locked the door behind him and hit the bar.

The light outside the living room windows had already gone from gray to purple by the end of the second drink, and he didn't even have a detectable buzz. He didn't understand. Where was the safe booze cocoon, the reassuring perspective of the fort under the card table, draped with blankets? His next move was obvious, so why couldn't he make it? What did he need now?

He smoked another cigarette while the minutes limped by. He was a sack of bubbling guts and nerves. The human body, what an amazing thing. He couldn't remember the exact details, but he knew that in the last few days he'd ingested every substance known to chemistry and it hadn't made any difference, none whatsoever. He'd gone right on with his business and it hadn't changed a *thing.*

He needed another drink, that's what, then he'd split. It became the only thing in his mind. *He needed another drink.* He turned the notion around, he held it up and looked at it. One more road-pop, how could that hurt. He'd just proved it wouldn't make any difference. He got up and went to the bar.

You *jerk:* this was just how he kept stepping out of the room for major decisions; this was exactly how the water had reached such a hard boil. He knew it, had known it all along, had known it for years, and here he was about to do it again.

Drinkless, he went back to his chair and looked out the window. The street had almost disappeared in the darkness. At least the house was safe, dark as a castle. Well, pretty safe. For a while, anyway.

He might as well just pull the fucking covers over his head and hope the boogeyman would go away. *What the hell was he doing here?* The smart thing was to get some clothes out of Keith's closet, take the rest of the money from the book in Joe Michaels's study, then walk out and drive away.

Okay, it was a plan. He went straight to the bar and poured himself a lowball glass full of bourbon, then took his seat again. He took a long pull, then another, fire burning through him. That was better. Fifteen more minutes. He riffed for a while on where he'd go. Maybe he'd hit Padre Island first, he used to go there as a teenager, he could be there by midday tomorrow. Then he'd slip over the border and make his way across to Baja. He knew Baja, he'd improvise from there. That is, if the Healey held up. He worried, sipping at the whiskey. He'd just have to deal with it. He lit a cigarette, match flaring in the dark, then cursed himself. Anyone could see that from outside.

He had to *go.* He had to go *now,* and that meant he had to make it down the street to where he'd parked the goddamn Healey.

He socked down the last of the whiskey and went down to the basement. It was stone dark. He thought hard about whether there were any windows down here, then made himself turn on a light.

The gun cabinet was in the den off the billiards room, its walls covered with stuffed fur and fin, the dead fruit of Joe Michaels's expeditions to Alaska and Nova Scotia and Africa.

The glass doors of the big cabinet were locked, an arsenal of heavy metal gleaming dully inside. Boudreau considered how best to break the glass then tried one of the lower drawers. Inside it were boxes of ammunition and a chromed .38 caliber revolver.

The hard weight of the thing terrified him. He was in a new league now. He hefted it, broke the chamber open. It was loaded, six little brass circles with white metal pimples in their middles. He picked up a box of .38 shells, then caught himself.

What noirish little movie did he have in mind, the one where the drunk guy is frantically reloading behind the corner of a building while bullets ricochet nearby? If six shots weren't sufficient, then he might as well use one right now and leave the other five for somebody else.

He calmed himself down. Okay, the gun was enough, he had to defend himself. He stuffed it down the front of his jeans like Ronnie had, then pulled it right back out. It was too heavy for that, he'd rather carry it than have it fall down and shoot his dick off.

With the lights off he mounted the stairs, gun in hand. Some small part of his mind stood off to the side and watched, bug-eyed. Who *was* this guy, armed and drunk and seeing things in the dark? He was going to hurt himself before anybody else had the chance. He was making this shit up, no one was coming after him here. He should just crash and leave at dawn. Maybe he'd think about it over one more drink.

From the gallery-hall end of the kitchen he heard the noise of someone fiddling with the door down at the other end. He went rigid, unwilling to believe his ears. The gun got slippery as a fish in his hand, the cross-hatching disappearing in sweat. He strained to pick something out of the dark, something more than the colorful retinal arrays detonating in his own skull. *Just a branch against a window or something.*

Right after he decided he'd been hearing things, he did: the distinct suck of weatherstrip and click of latch as the door pushed open.

He aimed the gun in the general direction, waiting for some kind of outline to appear in the pantry doorway. It did, and went still. It knew he was there. Time stopped. He knew he should pull the trigger, but waited for the next moment, the one that would tell him he had no choice.

The outline moved.

"Don't move," he said.

The lights went on.

The two of them stood frozen at opposite ends of the kitchen, actors in a poorly blocked play.

"Jesus *God!*" Vicky Stover's hand was still on the wall switch, stuck there. She breathed out like a deflating balloon, a squeak at the end of it. "Are we being a little hostile here?"

Boudreau kept the gun on her.

"Richter honey, I *had* to come over here." She kept her body motionless, as though she'd lose her balance if she moved. "Things between me and Ronnie have gotten bad," she said. *"Real* bad."

"Yeah?" He didn't like the way she kept her eyes on him, like she'd somehow expected this.

"I need to *talk* to you."

He thought about it. "Sure, go ahead."

Hand still on the light switch, she cringed back against the wall, turning her shoulder. She made a low, whining cry. "Could you not point that at me?"

Boudreau turned the outstretched gun slightly and regarded it. He looked at her, then back at it, as if he'd just understood the connection. He got rid of the gun on the counter like it was a living thing. He started laughing, his breath coming in insufficient gulps, hiccups gone hysterical.

"God, I'm sorry." He repeated it again, and again, and again, the words and breath taking on a life of their own, a cleansing yogic regime for regretful assholes. He went limp.

"*There*, honey," she said. "There, now." She had his head on her shoulder. "I know you hate me." Her voice quavered. "Well, guess what, I hate me, too."

He shook his head on her shoulder, denying it hotly. "I don't *hate* you, how could I hate you? You're *Vicky.*"

She ran her fingers through his hair, then grabbed it hard at the back of his head and pulled back. Her eyes burned. "Well, would you kiss me, then?"

After the first brush of lips she whimpered in the back of her throat and opened her mouth wide. It was like falling into warm clear ocean water, an invertebrate weightlessness that made Boudreau want to swim deeper and deeper, forget he'd ever had a spine or been a land creature.

She made the urgent little noise again, then caught the fat of his lower lip between her teeth and worked it, ran her tongue around on the surface of his teeth for a quick loop-de-loop.

She pulled away and put her head on his chest, breathing hard. "Oh, this is just so bad?" she said. "This is bad and I *knew* it would happen?"

She pushed him away by the shoulders and exhaled heavily, then fixed him with a glittery smile. "I come in and this boy points a *hand*gun at

me, Lord only knows, then here I am wanting to go to *bed* with him?"
She ran her hands down her sides and hitched her body inside her
clothes. "And the worst thing is, I think I like it?"

She'd disappeared inside the accent, but Boudreau didn't care. All he
heard was the part about going to bed.

He reached for her again, but she grabbed his hand and pulled him
along behind her, out of the kitchen. "Come on, boy."

Dragging him behind her, she started flipping on lights without
looking, a childhood's worth of wall-switch sense memory.

Boudreau stopped dead. He'd forgotten. He flipped the last one right
back off, then turned to get the others.

She switched it back on and faced him. "This is Keith, isn't it?" she
said. "Did he threaten you, Richter honey? Is that what all this is
about?"

Boudreau looked down, then shrugged. Her husband or her brother,
what difference did it make?

Tight lipped, Vicky smiled at the confirmation of her guess. Through
his haze he noticed for the first time the overbrightness of her eyes. She
was wired. "We don't need to worry about him." She stopped as though
remembering something. "Not right now, anyways."

Boudreau looked at her, head cocked in confusion, and her eyes darted
away.

"I happen to know he's with Chip right now," she said. "Carlson."

Boudreau dropped her hand. "Oh, you mean *that* Chip."

She glanced down, then back up. "They're having a meeting with a
judge friend of his. I didn't want to say anything."

"What else did you not want to say?" He couldn't look at her.

"Richter! Don't you do me like this!" She put a palm on his cheek
and moved it until they were face to face. "It is *not* what you think!"

"I'm waiting," said Boudreau.

Her eyes were an impossible blue, intense and icy at the same time.
"I think it's time you and me had us a heart-to-heart?" *Thank.* She
caught up his hand and gave it a kiss. "But first I have a little something?"

Boudreau watched her get out ice, rum, and daiquiri mix. She ran it through the blender, then pulled a small medical-looking bottle out of her jeans pocket and dumped it into the froth. After pulsing it one more quick turn through the blender, she poured it into two glasses, big as drugstore milkshakes.

He took his and looked at it. "What is this?"

She licked icy froth from her own glass. "Frozen daiquiri, you silly."

"I mean in the bottle." He reached for it, but she jerked it away, giggling, then pocketed it.

"Just some spice." She gave him a smirky little grin, then raised her eyebrows in an oh-if-you-must-know. "Banana flavor Demerol."

Boudreau regarded his glass.

"They give it to those real sick little children? You know those poor things with cancer or something, make it feel better while they're waitin' to die?"

Boudreau looked back up at her.

"Poor little angels." She slurped a gulp down and make a face. "It *does* taste a little chemical, but I guess that's kind of the point, ain't it?" She stared at him. "Richter honey?"

Vicky, mouth set, surveyed her bedroom from the doorway. Her eye fell on the trash next to the bed, on Cherry's big suitcase against the wall, lid open. She went over to the bed and picked up a pair of bikini panties between thumb and forefinger. "Have you been dressing up without telling me?"

"It's this friend of Keith's," Boudreau lied. "Some topless dancer he met."

She snickered and flung the panties over at the suitcase. "Oh, a topless dancer, is that right? I bet that's a real healthy relationship."

"She's actually not so bad," said Boudreau. "I mean, she's fucked up but who isn't?"

"Yeah, right," said Vicky Stover. "Who isn't?" She put her drink down on the night table, then picked up everything not belonging to her and dumped it into a heap on top of the suitcase. Plopping down on the bed, she had a long drink from her glass. She closed her eyes and smiled. "I'm gonna have this house back, Mr. Boudreau."

Boudreau took a mighty drink himself before he said anything. "You mean you and Chip, ain't that the deal?"

The smile fell off her face and she opened her eyes. "I wish you'd just let go of that."

"Don't *lie* to me, Vicky. I know all about it."

She stared at him, eyes going wider until her face seemed to split open and fall apart. He watched her cry. She looked up at him and started shaking her head, furious through her tears. "Are you just gonna watch me?" She patted the bed next to her. "Please?"

He put his drink on the night table, took hers and put it there too. When he sat, she pulled him over, arms around his neck. She sobbed into his nape, shaking her head back and forth.

"I've been lying to myself so long I can't *tell* anymore." She gulped, trying to catch her breath. "I just can't *tell*, Richter!"

She dissolved again, struggling like a child too tired to go to sleep. He restrained her, massaging her back until finally she went quiet against him. The sharper edges around things were beginning to go soft. After a while she inhaled deeply and snuggled into him.

"But I'm not lying now." She said it in a tiny voice against his neck, then pulled her head back. "This isn't lying, is it?" Her cheeks were wet, eyes febrile and distant.

He fastened onto her mouth, and within a second he was lost, a water creature again as she lured his tongue in and captured it. A wave of euphoric lust washed over him. She was a trip to the tropics, salt and rum and banana, all the ganja he could smoke.

She pulled out of the kiss with a sudden intake of air, leaving him beached like a whale. "Oh, *Lordy.*" Vicky exhaled with a huge sigh and pushed him away, then gave a whole-body stretch, arms above her head. She rose to one elbow and looked him over, eyes bright, then handed him his drink. She drank so heavily from her own she had to send her little pink tongue out to collect the froth from around her upper lip. She closed her eyes. "God *help* me if this ain't wrong?"

Boudreau understood she'd just disappeared on him, leaving a weary but not-so-dumb cracker bimbo to sit down at the bar and explain things in her absence.

Without opening her eyes she took a daintier sip, then arranged herself against him, lying on her side with her head nestled in his shoulder. He'd never felt so fine with nerves, a melting energy in his flesh wherever she was in contact with it.

"Lemme just tell you a little story first, get all this old business settled up?"

Binnis. He took a massive gulp of his own drink and put his other hand lightly on her shoulder. He was starting to float, his ancient dream of flying brought to life. He didn't care if she explained it in an Irish brogue.

Vicky sighed again and closed her eyes in concentration. "There's this sweet young couple which ever'body goes is all wrong for each other?" she began. "She's this spoiled little rich thing, and the boy, he's just trash but handsome as Elvis Presley?

"Well, but then it don't take long, they get to *fightin'* all the time? She's thinkin' maybe she made a mistake? They're just gettin' by, gettin' high, like that song goes, arguin' about ever' little thing? If it ain't money, it's sex, and if it ain't sex, it's dishes, and why don't he get a regular job?"

Boudreau began to move his hand on her shoulder, massaging the front of it with his fingers, his palm in the hollow below.

"So this gal, she gets herself pregnant? Like maybe a child will fix things up?

"*Right,* so now they got shit dipes and no money and no sleep on top of ever'thing else? And she's got this little girl-baby to worry about? Her future and all?"

She paused for breath, eyes still closed. Boudreau watched her face from a few inches away, transfixed. It was hard to remember she was talking about herself. He varied the pressure of his palm so he could feel the slight pull of her breast below it. She smiled, dreamy. She wanted hm, she was going to *let* him. He grew huge with the fact of it.

"So that's when she starts gettin' these phone calls from this lawyer fella about her brother. How he's a drunk and a no-good, like all this is news to her?" She snorted. "But this lawyer, he starts putting these *ideas* in her head. You know, how it ain't right the brother got all the family money and she didn't git a nickel? And how he—this *law*yer—how he's gonna fix things up for her?"

She lowered her voice to a conspiratorial, I-can't-believe-it tone.

"He gets to sweet-talkin' her how she deserves better? And how the way the brother's been actin', she can get what's rightfully hers, without hurtin' the brother? You know, he'll get taken care of like one of them cats you read about, gets left a million dollars and all the cat food they can eat?"

She opened her eyes just long enough to have another swallow of her drink.

"Well, this gal, she starts to feelin' her whole *life* has just been *one big mistake.* She can see it now, how folks was right about her marriage, how she's been lyin' to herself right along? Why, she knew it the day she got married! Down there in the basement of that little Baptist church, there's her husband's poor little family actin' like it was a funeral? 'Course her own family didn't even *come.*" Her brow furrowed and she shrugged. "It's just as well, I mean, there's his poor daddy over in the corner smokin' cigarettes the whole time, he's this retired *postal* carrier? He's wearin' white socks to his own boy's weddin'?"

Boudreau insinuated his hand under the collar of her shirt, then placed it back where it had been.

" 'Course you know what happens then?" She grimaced at the way of all flesh, then answered herself darkly. "She starts goin' to *bed* with the lawyer fella, she starts thinkin' how he'll save her from all her mistakes?"

His hand on her shoulder flinched and she grabbed it, tight as a claw. It came as a shock, a reminder that all this was intended for him. She raised her voice.

"But then she goes, Am I *crazy?* Here she's already cheatin' on her husband, but now she's thinkin' about this other boy all the time? This other boy, he's always been her best friend, he always sticks right with her?"

She smiled.

"Why she remembers when this boy and her brother used to peep while she was gettin' undressed, right through the hole in the linen closet? And it's really *him* she's been wantin' right along, but she's been lyin' to ever'body so much she just can't tell no more? It's just too confusin'?"

Vicky's features pinched together in soulful concentration, eyes still closed. Boudreau watched as her cheeks squeezed up in contempt.

"What it takes is this *lawyer*, he finds out she likes to party a little, and he gets Re*pub*lican with her and calls her a dope addict and all? Tries to lay down the law on her?" She caught her breath. "Well, that's when she *wakes up.* She can leave her husband anyway and still get what she wants. She can get it on her *own.*"

Vicky opened her eyes and stared into Boudreau's. He looked back at her, confused.

"And she just hopes this other boy, he'll forgive her? He won't think she's cheap?"

She moved what was left of her drink to the night table, then closed her eyes again and took the hand under her shirt with both of her own. She moved it down onto her breast and pressed it against her in a slow circular movement. She let the hand go and slid down in the bed, arms above her head.

Boudreau felt her nipple spring up under his palm. She made a low moan, and he moved his hand under the loose shirt, then pulled it up and bent to her. The nipple was sweet as a hard little cherry between his lips.

" 'Course that's just what she is," Vicky exulted in a thick voice above him. "Just a cheap little tramp."

Boudreau watched her ride on top of him, watched her bouncing tits and the distant look of concentration on her face. She ground against him roughly, leaning over to rake her nails down his chest. He bucked back into her, his movement somehow coming out in slow motion. He wasn't even sure who she was now, but he didn't care. He couldn't believe he was finally *in* there.

She reached behind her, arching her back, and grabbed his nuts. He came in a shuddering spasm but she kept going. This was no time to quit. To stop now was to risk dismemberment.

She began an escalating set of moans, finally going rigid on the last one, straightening up like someone had just hit her with a board. She collapsed on top of him, breathing hard, then not at all.

He waited a minute. "You okay?"

She started making funny noises, face buried in his chest.

"Hey, Vicky?" He couldn't tell if she were laughing or crying.

When she spoke, the accent was still there, but she wasn't. "Oh, honey? My life is just such a mess?" She nibbled at his chest, then bit him, hard enough to hurt.

My laff is a may-us. Boudreau suddenly felt sleepy, his head a lead weight. This was a mistake. Somewhere between the Demerol and booze, he understood that Vicky Michaels Stover had just gone through the thin ice, and now he was in the cold water with her. If she just wouldn't *talk.* He cupped his hands on her ass and tried to steer things back to the past, where all this would've made him think he'd died and gone to heaven.

"That hole in the linen closet?" he managed to get out. The thing was probably still there, just off the lower corner of the bureau. "I can't believe you knew that."

"Uh-huh." She moved her head in a nuzzle against his chest.

He tensed a little, sure she was going to bite him again. "How'd you know?"

She made a little shrug against him. "Keith did it all the time."

"You didn't tell on him?"

She shook her head, going coy on him.

"How come?" She didn't answer and he tried again. "How come you didn't tell?" He gave her a little shake. He wanted to hear this. She struggled away from him.

"Don't act like you didn't know." Her voice was barely audible. "You know what he did."

Boudreau's mind circled around it, a dog analyzing a pile of garbage before nosing in. "Wait a minute," he said, "what do you mean? What do you mean, I knew what he did? Did what?"

He squeezed her, then shook her again, harder.

She flopped him out in a single motion, leaving a trail of warm drool behind, and rolled over to the edge of the bed. She shook her head, over and over again.

Boudreau sat up, dizziness rushing in on him. The air felt like it was filled with jello. "You can't do that, you can't just tell me something like that and n⌐ᵗ—"

She stood. "Let's just not talk about it please?" She said it as if they'd just had a spat over who was supposed to take out the trash. She gulped down the last inch of melted dregs from her glass, then set it back down on the edge of the night table. It fell off.

"Vicky?"

She picked up her panties and turned to face him, naked. "Just let it *be*, okay?"

He grabbed her elbow.

"You let *go* of me."

Boudreau held on and considered. "What'd he do?" he slurred. "What'd Keith do?"

Her whole body was blotchy, face bright red. "*Well, who do you think he blamed it on?*" She was practically shouting, her eyes burning with a glassy unfocused glare. "*His precious little boy?*"

She pulled hard but only managed to stumble into his lap. He restrained her around the shoulders until she finally went still.

"Oh, Richter honey, it just makes me want to die? I swear I just can't take this no more?" *Tike this.* She cuddled into him, wiggling her bottom into his lap. "But you know what I did?"

Boudreau was afraid to find out. In the same little voice she informed him.

"Me and Clem checked into this nice little motel room today, it's got that paper strip over the toilet and all?" She said it *mo-tel.* "I think I've run away from home?"

Run away from home. It took Boudreau a moment to remember home meant Ronnie, not her parents. *Ronnie.*

"So I was thinkin', maybe tomorrow mornin' let's you and me just go somewhere? You be a daddy to my little Clem? I mean till this whole thing blows over for a while?"

Boudreau stared at the downy white-blond hair on the back of her neck. This was a little more than he'd bargained for.

She took his hesitation poorly and began struggling to get out of his arms. "You don't want to do it, do you?" She was crying again. "You just *hate* me now, don't you?"

Boudreau took note with whatever was left of his better judgment that he'd somehow grown another hard-on. He was still trying to factor this into his answer when the door of the bedroom flew open behind him.

Vicky Stover shrieked and leapt off his lap. "He's got a gun! My *Lord,* he's got a gun!"

They were like naked fish in a barrel. Boudreau wanted to turn around, but his muscles refused to answer. In front of him Vicky moved in a rigid crouch backward toward the wall, panties still balled up in one hand.

"Don't you *dare!*" She sounded like someone trying to ward off a rabid dog with stern vocal commands. "Don't you *dare!*"

"Hey, this looks like a *party.* "

Boudreau turned around.

Keith Michaels filled the doorway, so drunk he had to lean against the jamb with one shoulder. His shirttail was half out, and his hair spiked up at odd angles. A 35-mm camera hung by a strap around his neck, giving him the look of a tourist who'd concentrated on bars. This was offset by the remaining half of the Colt Python presentation set he carried in one hand. He waved the gun vaguely in their direction, as if he were conducting.

"*Key,* " said Boudreau. "Key, this is *not funny.* "

" 'Key this is not funny,' " Keith Michaels mimicked, lowering the gun to scratch his leg with the barrel. It reached all the way to his frigging kneecap. "No way, man. This is *very* funny, this is *cute.* "

"Put . . . the . . . gun . . . *down,* " said Boudreau, adopting the stern dog-command tone.

"Shut up," said Keith.

"Don't be an asshole, Key."

Keith Michaels leveled the gun at Boudreau's crotch. "You shut up."

Both hands over his genitals, Boudreau moved backward on the bed a few inches. His hearing was starting to blank on and off.

Keith smiled at the results. "Call *me* an asshole, you *asshole.* "

Keeping her eyes on her brother, Vicky stepped into her underpants. She stumbled forward and froze, panties around one ankle. Keith caught the motion and spun, gun at arm's length, as far out as he could get it.

She started begging. "Keithie, *please.* Please don't."

"This's how it feels," he said. "How's it feel, Vicky?" Keith's eyes were watering over now. "You like it?"

She stared at him, mouth open.

"*Yeah,* " he said. "Yeah, now it's *your* turn, slut. You like it?" She shook her head but this was not good enough. He cocked the hammer back, the click loud as a bomb. "*You like it?*"

"No," she got out. "*No.* "

Keith Michaels jerked the barrel of the gun to his own temple, hammer still cocked. "Watch this." His face twisted until it was unrecognizable. "This's what you want, right?"

Vicky and Boudreau made eye contact. Keith caught it, the final evidence of conspiracy.

"Do it," Vicky hissed. *"Do it."*

"You fucking slut," he said, squeezing his eyes shut.

Boudreau leaned away instinctively as Keith pulled the trigger. Vicky screamed.

"Jesus Fucking *Christ,*" Boudreau swore.

Keith Michaels's eyes bugged open at what he'd just done, his mouth working as if he'd just taken a sock in the jaw. He started laughing.

Vicky Stover pulled up her underpants with a snap. She was breathing hard and her eyes glinted. "I thought you were going to do us all a favor, you fat pig. You coward."

Keith's features fell to the middle of his face, mouth in a tight sphincter of rage. "Yeah?" He broke open the cylinder to show the single bullet. "See that?" He closed it and spun it, then aimed it at his sister. "How's your luck?"

She made a motion toward her clothes, keeping her eyes on the gun. "Why don't you just go jerk off somewhere." Her voice cracked and she stopped, giving the lie to her bluff.

Keith Michaels fumbled the camera into one hand while aiming the gun in the other. "One more picture." He cackled, eyebrows pinching together. "Then maybe I'll jerk off."

Boudreau, on the bed, guessed that maybe the peephole was still there. "Key," he said, "that's blackmail."

"You shut the fuck up." He turned slightly, ready to shoot or photograph. "What do you think *she's* doing?"

"Keithie." Vicky moved toward him cautiously. "Keithie, you give me that camera."

"Think you're so smart," he said, "we'll see who likes these pictures."

"You *give me* that camera."

Keith cocked the hammer back, aimed it at her feet, and fired. She shrieked and jumped, the hammer clicking.

He kept the gun on her, his mouth wide with excitement. "Try again? No? You wanna try again?" He waved her toward the bed with the revolver. "Sit down."

She sat on the bed, so rigid she was trembling.

"Now grab his cock."

Lips set in a line, she shook her head no.

He thumbed the hammer back again, aiming more or less at the both of them. "C'mon," he said. *"Grab* it. I just need this one more."

"Do it," Boudreau croaked.

Vicky Stover reached out and wrapped her hand around his limp little weenie, holding her eyes on her brother.

"Say 'cheese.' " He snapped the picture, then let the camera fall to its strap. "Okay, that's a good one." His brows lowered, he backed to the door with the gun still trained on them. "You come out the front door before I'm gone, you're *dead.* You're dead meat."

By the time his lumbering footsteps hit the bottom of the stairs, Vicky had already begun gathering her clothes.

Boudreau grabbed at her as the front door slammed shut. He was hysterical. "Didn't you *hear* him?"

She looked at him, but her eyes were focused somewhere in the middle distance. "He's a sick boy," she said. "You can't take someone like that seriously."

Outside, The Beast's engine came to life at full throttle. Its tires squealed in reverse, braked, squealed again out in the street.

Drunk, Demeroled, petrified, Boudreau sat inanimate on the edge of the bed. Vicky bent over and gave him a peck on the lips.

She straightened up, instructing him like a teacher. "You stay put, sweetheart," she said. "I'll call, you hear? I'll call by midnight."

She stopped at the door and looked back at him. She was still in her underpants, clothes in her hands like an athlete on the way to the locker room. "Don't you worry, Richter honey. I know where he's going."

After a few minutes Boudreau got his clothes on and made it downstairs. In the kitchen he stumbled onto Cherry, sitting dull as a stump at the counter, eyes half-lidded.

"Where'd Keith go?" he said.

She made a dismissive little noise without looking at him. "Howdy, pardner," she said.

Boudreau's head felt like it had a clamp on it. Just staying conscious was hard enough, he didn't need any more junkie shit now. "I asked you, Where did Keith go?"

She made a taffy-faced grimace. "Out," she said. "Went *out*, okay?"

Boudreau worked to bring her into focus. She'd been thin before, but now she looked just plain strung out, *burned*, down to skin and bone and connective tissue, no need for the burden of flesh. She had so many loose screws the only question was which part would fall off first. He stepped up right in front of her. "Where'd he go? Ronnie's?"

Cherry made it to her feet and swayed backward to avoid contact with him. Her face looked feral, features honed to deathly sharpness. *"Hassle me,"* she slurred.

"He's got something of mine," said Boudreau. "I just want it back, okay?"

"What?" she said. "Like a *film* can?" She smirked, then tried to ambulate past him. "Mean like he took some *pictures?"*

He grabbed her by the shoulders. "What'd you say?" He gave her a single shake, setting her head bobbing like a rearwindow car toy. "What'd he tell you?"

She broke free and lurched her way around the island. He watched her get as far as the doorway to the gallery, then went after her.

"I don't want to hurt you." From above he watched himself stand in front of her, as if he were screening one of those overhead Hitchcock shots down into the cell as the door clangs shut.

She offered her face up to him like a speed bag. "Fuck you."

From inside his cocoon Boudreau watched his hand go out.

Her head snapped back into position, a line of drool trailing sideways out of the corner of her mouth. She tried a smile, one cheek jumping and twitching above it. "Big *man,"* she said. "Hit me again?"

Boudreau was getting ready to do just that before he suddenly reentered himself, horrified. This had gotten out of hand. For a moment there, he'd wanted to kill her, just flat *kill* her. There had to be another way.

In a jerky-gaited stumble she made it down the gallery to an elaborately upholstered fainting couch, collapsing onto it like a badly made windup doll.

She was sick, she was just working him into this. Boudreau couldn't believe what he'd just done. "Jesus *Christ,* I didn't mean to do that."

Her eyes widened from their half-liddedness, then narrowed again. "Did it by *ac*cident? *Fuck* you, man."

When he groped for her hand, she jerked it away. "Just tell me, okay?" He was begging. "Just tell me where Keith went."

She regarded him for a moment, head weaving. " 'S a matter, you never did pictures before?" She looked at him like he'd just confessed to having grown up without eating a hamburger. " 'S no big deal, I did pictures before. Good money, man. Pay extra for anal, but I never did anal." She shook her head. "No way."

Boudreau tried to assess the creature in front of him, if she was doing him again. He felt woozy.

"Don't believe me?" *Belee me?* She squinted at him through her own haze, then licked her lips. "Wanna hear about some pictures?"

He was about to ask, one more time, then give up.

"Wanna hear about *private* pictures?" It sounded like a taunt.

He looked at her.

"We did a thing, okay?" she said. "Me 'n' Earla." She snukked up some postnasal drip, then paused like a drunk on a barstool, enchanted with the telling of her own story. "Dude comes on to her after the show, white dude." Cherry kept her gaze on him, smirking at the very species. "Go out with me, baby?" She tucked in her chin and widened her eyes. "*Sure,* sugar." She thought a moment. "This's Earla." She shrugged. "*Money.*"

Boudreau started shaking his head. "I don't want to hear this."

"So Earla comes *home,*" said Cherry, "an' she's all upset, right? Dude's weird shit, takes her some motel. Wants her suck him off while he curses her. Call her *nigger* and shit.

"He *hurt* you, Earla baby? No no, baby, it's *okay.* He didn't hurt me. Paid her two hunnert dollars. 'S a rich little fuck, got a lotta money. So dude comes back two nights later, wants her go out again. Okay, 's backstage. I go, Fuck him. I go, *Fuck* him, Earla, I got a camera. Less do a *thing*, okay, Earla?"

Boudreau leaned away.

"So I go, Leave the blind open at the motel, Earla. 'M outside with my *Nikon.*" Cherry restrained herself from crying, face distorted with rage. Boudreau could hardly understand her.

"So dude's calling her *nigger*, comes right away. All over. 'S really pissed, *yell*ing her. Big *nigger* dick, that what you want baby? Show *you* big nigger dick." She glared at Boudreau. " 'S got a *club*, man! Big fucking *club* an' he's *stick*ing her an' she's yelling an' he's *hit*ting her. Hitting her an' hitting her an' *hit*ting her."

Boudreau winced and turned, trying to get the voice out of his ears.

Her tears came in a sudden but steady flow, like a summer shower. "An' I couldn't *move*, I couldn't move, an' then"—her voice choked, tiny with the wonder of it—"and then it was *over.*"

Boudreau got the picture.

WEDNESDAY

Boudreau came back to life from the dreamless shroud of Demerol, skull packed with fine mud, neck muscles like iron from his posture in the chair. On the table next to him were a telephone and the .38.

He'd taken up his post in the breakfast room, next to a window on the driveway. First he'd told himself midnight, then one. Okay, two o'clock was the limit of acceptability, and he was a fool for even believing that. Then he thought about how she'd looked bouncing up and down on him.

So what was it now, three-thirty, four? *Whatever.* If he'd needed proof, he had it now.

He parted the drapes and had to squint, the colors of daylight already bleached out by harsh sun. He got up and ran.

Boudreau rooted through Keith's voluminous closet and discovered a whole section of clothes that by their look went back to his short try at college. The tags were still on half of them. They weren't the hippest clothes in the world, but at least they'd fit. Back then, he and Keith were the same size. He found a small carryall and began throwing things into it, furious.

What was *wrong* with him? This was no longer self-destructive, in the pure sense of the phrase. At least suicide meant by your own hand, but now someone else was going to do it for him. He just didn't know who yet.

He couldn't understand how he'd arrived at a point where other people would want to kill him. What had he done? What did he have in common with *any* of them, except inhabiting the same place? But maybe that was just it: *to coexist was to be at risk.* Everybody liked to think they lived their own lives, but this was bullshit and he knew it, the myth of the individual woven right into the social contract. The truth was that other people were *dangerous*. Other people were all the time leaving the lug nuts loosened, or thinking about something else while they administered the incorrect dose; they turned left from the right lane, they misread the label, they sprayed the wrong hillside, they voted for the fool because he seemed friendly on TV; sure as shit, some faceless guy was going to hit the wrong switch at the fuel-rod console, or wake up in a panic in front of the radar screen.

What could you do, except run?

He found one last pair of wide-wale corduroy bell-bottoms and stuffed them in, then put the revolver on top and left the bag unzipped.

Boudreau made a quick stop in Vicky's room. Cherry was still dressed, limbs splayed out over the bed as if she'd been dropped from several stories up. Her mouth was slack and hung open, her breathing shallow but steady. In sleep she looked innocent, at peace. Maybe she was off feeding goats on the coast of Oregon, with Earla. If she were lucky, she'd stay there.

He went down to Joe Michaels's study and took the rest of the money from the book, then hit the kitchen. He was at the counter trying to get the zipper over eight packs of cigarettes when the door to the service entrance opened.

He jumped. "You *scared* me," he said, "I thought you were *Keith*. I brought a bag from my house and he fucking rifled it."

Ronnie looked at him through his shades, then closed the door behind him. He walked across the room and went to the refrigerator, opened it and looked inside. "You mean you got something he don't?" Ronnie said into the refrigerator. He pulled out a beer.

Boudreau tried to assess the inflection. *Those pictures were taken at gunpoint, man, your wife didn't really grab my nuts and fire me like a roman candle last night.* "Keith makes things up," he got out.

"Is that right?" Ronnie pushed the icebox door shut with one hip, then leaned against it to regard Boudreau. The automatic was tucked in the waist of his jeans, casual as a fashion accessory. He held the beer between thumb and forefinger, fingering the bottle repeatedly as though practicing scales. "So where is brother Keith?"

Boudreau shrugged. "I haven't seen him since I got him out of jail." He tried another shrug that felt absurdly out of register, his every gesture radiating inept calculation. "Listen, man, I've been trying to call you."

Ronnie Dean Stover shifted position from one hip to the other, fingering the bottle now with both hands like a tenor sax. He was either speeding again or about to blow his stack, maybe both. He stared at Boudreau without saying anything, shades unreadable as a monster bug's compound eyes.

Boudreau flinched as Ronnie abruptly took his first swig on the beer. "I kept getting no answer, I don't know, maybe the phone wasn't—"

Ronnie belched loudly, a grim smile appearing in the aftermath. "Vicky split," he said.

"She what?" Boudreau had to lean on one arm on the counter. He should ask questions. "The baby, too?"

Ronnie lifted his eyebrows above the sunglasses, then lowered them, then tilted his head to get a different angle on Boudreau. "I thought maybe you knew."

"How would *I* know?" Boudreau went rigid at the sound of panic in his own voice. "Did she leave a note or anything?"

Ronnie shook his head, barely. "Didn't have to. She come home with a big bruise on her arm while ago." He held the beer by the neck and drained half of it. "She's been fucking around. I seen it coming."

Boudreau's face collapsed into a shit-eating grin that he tried to get rid of but couldn't. The phrase *fucking around* had never seemed so descriptive. "Listen, you don't think—"

"I don't think *nothing,*" said Ronnie. "I got other things to deal with first." He pursed his lips. "One thing you learn in the bush, you deal with what's in your face." The pursed lips moved into a brief smile for Boudreau's benefit. "I can wait my time."

A little short of breath, Boudreau closed his eyes and inhaled deeply.

"You got the film can?" said Ronnie, right on schedule.

Boudreau exhaled and opened his eyes. It would be important to look him in the face. "That's why," he began, "that's why I kept trying to *call* you." He tried to bring his voice down from the cracking point. "There's a problem."

Without a single visible motion, Ronnie's body came into remarkable focus. He levered himself away from the refrigerator with his elbow, then came and leaned on the edge of the counter next to Boudreau, beer in the other hand. "What problem?"

Boudreau collapsed onto a stool. "I don't have the pictures here."

Ronnie's lips tightened into something like a smile. "Then I guess you better go *get* the pictures."

Boudreau shook his head, grinning like a demented man. He cleared his throat, like the idiot smile was some kind of bronchial problem. "The thing is," he began, "I'm not sure how easy they're gonna be to get to."

Ronnie stood straight up, then put his beer down on the counter.

"I mean, I know where the can *is*, it's still in a safe place," said Boudreau, not having seen the fucking thing since the night Ronnie left it behind.

"So where's it at?" said Ronnie.

"My mother's," Boudreau said, "I haven't *touched* it. Except to hide it, I mean. But see, she came back last night before I had a chance to get it out of there." He looked into Ronnie's sunglasses and saw a globed distortion of his own face staring back, a big-nosed dork burrowing deeper in his own shit. "But that's not the only problem."

Ronnie pursed his lips, then widened them, several times in a row, so that it seemed like an involuntary flexing of jaws, a warm-up exercise. "You're dicking around with me, comrade."

Boudreau put up both his hands in an instinctive move, palms out, an unarmed man. "I swear I'm not, I swear it! Listen to me!" Maybe this was where he should kneel. He swallowed, trying to get the words out. "There's this reporter I know—that guy who did the car story?"

Boudreau blurted out the details about the tattooed man, Harmon Shaw's bodyguard. He didn't really believe it anymore, but the more he talked it up, the worse it seemed. "I mean, if that's the guy, he was sitting right *there*, he was two tables away!" Boudreau stopped short. "I think maybe they know who we *are.*" Having said it, he found it eminently believable. He was hysterical.

Ronnie picked up his beer and had a healthy swallow. He thought about it, then shrugged using only his mouth. "Maybe they do," he said. "I ain't surprised."

Boudreau's mouth came open and he rose up from his stool. His tour of duty had just ended, he was going to walk out through those gates.

"Where you going, college boy?"

Ronnie reached out and sat him back down, his tailbone hitting the stool with a shock. He stood so close Boudreau could smell him, a skanky armpit odor of amphetamines and male hormones.

"You *listen* to me," Ronnie said. "You figure they did her like that 'cause she was a nigger, right?"

Boudreau nodded, speechless. He was here to learn his lessons. He was a *college boy.*

"What else you know about Harmon Shaw?"

Boudreau thought. "Nothing," he said. "I fucked his daughter once." He realized this was swampy ground as soon as he said it.

Ronnie's cheeks tightened. "Yeah, you told me that story before. I guess that makes you a stud hoss." Ronnie snorted once and the joke was over. "So I guess you never heard what he's doing up there in the Ozarks? You never heard that?"

Boudreau was unwilling to hazard a guess.

"Harmon thinks he's going to *war.* He's got himself a little army a assholes, got a hit list of politicians and whatnot." He pushed his shades up on his nose then watched Boudreau's face. "You know that colored judge in Arkansas got shot last month?" He pursed his lips and smiled. "That wadn't no ex-con with a hard-on like the papers said."

Boudreau was already shaking his head. *A hit list, a dead judge.* He smiled against his will. "You're telling me What's-her-name . . . you're saying *Earla* was on this list?"

Ronnie looked at him, disappointed. "That's just some pussy Junior got himself in trouble with, that girl don't mean shit. But you best believe it's coming, it's coming *soon,* comrade. People better get their ass ready."

Boudreau made himself look right at him, just to get this straight.
"You mean like a race war?"

Ronnie had a swallow of beer, then smirked. "You get the gold star,
college boy."

Boudreau had to look down. *No.* No, this was just a little tarnished;
he'd heard all this before in a different version, but the revolution never
came. It was what people like Ronnie told themselves to have something
to believe in. Not Boudreau. As much as he'd believed it back then—
wished for it, even—the hard rain never fell. It never would, the American way had to do with living in a steady drizzle. Back then it petered
out with hokey acronyms and names from pop songs, some randomly
murdered cops and a couple of robbed banks, a house that got perforated
to the ground while he watched on live TV, sick to his stomach.

A race war, what bullshit. He looked up, smiling again in spite of
himself.

"I have a little trouble with that, man," he said. "I guess I have a hard
time believing that."

Ronnie looked down at the counter as if reassessing things in this new
light. He looked up and hit Boudreau, an open-palmed warning cuff to
the side of the head.

Boudreau cringed away, the inside of his skull ringing like a gong.

Ronnie brought his own face closer, teeth bared in a vicious smile.
With his shades and his skin-stretched cheekbones his face looked
ancient as a battle mask, violence molded into it. "I don't care *what* you
believe, college boy. I seen just a little too much of it to be that stupid."
His lips relaxed slightly, then went up in one corner. "You wouldn't
know about that, now would you?"

Boudreau nodded, with no idea what he was talking about.

Ronnie snukked hard, trying to clear his amphetamined sinuses. "I
was 1-A right out of fucking high school, Here's your helmet and don't

forget your ass. Don't forget your ass 'cause I *own* it. You know what that's like?"

Boudreau shook his head, childlike.

Ronnie brought his lips together in a tight o, then thought a moment. "I had this friend a mine over there? Odell Raines, colored dude. We'd get high together and talk hoops, he played hoops. Stand-up dude, man, he didn't give a shit about colored clicks and white clicks." Ronnie cleared his throat. "This Georgia lieutenant, he didn't like it, he come down on him for being tight with whitey—you know, hassle him, give him shit duty all the time. Odell'd just laugh at him, piss him off more. So this peach lieutenant, he made him go out on point through a unmarked mine field." Ronnie waited a beat, still working on his phlegm. "That fucker knew what he was doing, ever'body knew he done it on purpose. It wadn't no secret but nobody done *nothing*. So I made a deal in my head with Odell."

He cocked his head and smiled at the memory of it. "I waited my time, I didn't say nothing to that little faggot. I waited a whole *month.*" Ronnie cleared his throat once more, and this time got results. He worked it around in his cheek, then turned and hocked a big wad onto the kitchen floor. "I seen my chance and I took that sorry redneck out."

Boudreau stared at the splat of snot on the spotless kitchen tiles, the exact worth of one sorry redneck lieutenant. His voice cracked. "You mean you fragged him?" The word seemed bizarre, too specific.

"Yeah, I *fragged* him," Ronnie sneered. "It felt real good. That shock you, comrade?"

Boudreau had to shake his head. In truth it didn't.

"I ain't playing around," said Ronnie. "These guys ain't no different, they're trying to take me for some asshole. They want a war, they want to go skin for skin, they *got* it." He pursed his lips, happy at the thought. "They see a print, they'll come buy those pictures," he said. "They're gone come thinking they got some little asshole blackmailer, and that's when I get in close and *jam.*"

Boudreau nodded. The circle was drawn, Vietnam to Harmon Shaw, Odell Raines to Earla Armstrong and somehow he'd ended up inside it all. Ronnie was *pissed.* He'd been pissed once, too, but never like this. This was different. This was *random,* this had to do with rogue genes and childhood slights, shell-damaged synapses, the kind of private ledger that added up unseen for years or even decades, until it spewed out on some downtown street, in some suburban shopping mall. The snarled little strand of human history known as R. D. Stover had finally come whipping loose from the weave.

"All right," said Ronnie. "Let's go get them pictures, then."

Boudreau was afraid of this. He shook his head, unable to summon words.

Ronnie inhaled slowly, his chest expanding to a point of stillness.

"You don't under*stand,"* said Boudreau. He was crying. Ronnie was going to kill him, for one reason or another.

Ronnie exhaled and Boudreau kept going. "I mean, I think she had the *locks* changed. My mother. It's not like we can just go over and wait till she goes *out."*

Ronnie sagged against the counter, a little smile appearing at this latest ploy. He took off his sunglasses and rubbed the bridge of his nose, then looked into Boudreau's face, twelve inches away.

If Boudreau had ever seen Ronnie's eyes up close before, he didn't remember it. They were an orangey brown, too big and too far apart, the eyes of a nocturnal predator. There was an animal flatness to them, no indication of anything behind but cortical reflex and hard-bred instinct.

Ronnie pulled the automatic out of his waist, the one that held eighteen in a clip, and put it down on the counter between them.

"You're not taking me serious, Richter."

"Mom?" said Boudreau.

"Richter?" There was a note of surprise in Cynthia Rowling's voice.

"Yeah, hi," he said. "Listen, I've been thinking, you know all that stuff we talked about the other day?"

"Yes?" She sounded impatient.

"Well, I was just thinking, you know, that maybe we—" He looked over at Ronnie, then foundered.

"*Yes?*"

"I mean, I thought, you know, I thought maybe we could talk about it some more. If you have some time."

"*Today?*" she said.

Boudreau ignored the disbelief in her voice and jumped on the suggestion. His voice quaked. "Well, I thought if you had a min—"

His mother cut him off, speaking with exaggerated care. "Let's just put it all be*hind* us, Richter, shall we?"

"Well, yeah, okay, but I—"

Her voice went hard. "I have been on the *phone* since eight o'clock taking care of last-minute details, this has been *very* hard on Billy, I worried myself *sick* about Vic flying here safely with all these weather warnings—"

"What?" he interrupted.

"Well, of course I told him we'd just postpone the whole thing, I didn't want him flying in a *storm* alert, for God's sake, but he knew how disappointed I'd be. He said his pilot flew a jet in Vietnam, I just thank *God* he made it in one—"

"I didn't know there was a storm alert," he said, as if this explained everything.

"I don't know how you could miss it, it's all over the news," his mother said, running out of steam. "Tornadoes. In the four-state area, through tomorrow."

Boudreau thought about it and risked a look at Ronnie. This was as good as it was going to get. "Listen, I'm sorry, Mom. You're right, there's no need to talk about it anymore. I'll see you at the club, okay?"

Cynthia Rowling paused at the sudden lack of resistance, then caught her balance. "Well, all right, then. And are you still bringing your dancer friend?"

"If it's still okay," said Boudreau.

"I can't *wait* to meet her," said his mother.

Boudreau went over to the bed and started shaking Cherry by the shoulder. Ronnie leaned in the doorway behind him, exactly where Keith had stood. Boudreau became convinced that Vicky's odor from the night before still permeated the room, just as his eyes fell on the motel key she'd left behind on the night table.

Cherry's face swam up to consciousness as he shook her. When she saw him looming above her, she jerked away reflexively. He palmed the key as he straightened up.

"It's okay, it's *okay,*" said Boudreau, voice full of panic at what he'd just done. He'd drawn attention to the key, he should've just left it where it was.

Cherry sat part way up in the bed. Eyes wild, she looked from Ronnie to Boudreau and then back to Ronnie. She scrabbled backward toward the headboard.

"Wake up, girl," said Ronnie. "Big day today."

She looked back at Boudreau.

"Do you have anything you can wear to a wedding reception," he said.

Uncomprehending, she stared at him, then closed her eyes. A long shiver went through her. "I feel like shit," she whimpered. "Be a buddy, Ron. Be a buddy, okay?"

Boudreau pulled to a stop under the portico in front of the main entrance, Ronnie right behind him in the Mustang. A regal view of Tulsa lay to the north, down below the sprawling golf course. When people emerged from the club, it was the first thing they saw, increasing their sense of well-being.

A jacketed valet opened Cherry's door for her. She rolled out of the Healey, stood up and nearly fell over as the attendant tried to help. Swaying like a palm tree, she shook him off, then carefully adjusted her look-of-the-future sunglasses. The attendant watched, raising his eyebrows to no one in particular. He slammed the door and came around to Boudreau's side.

Boudreau put on the parking brake and got out, already soaked with sweat under the madras sport jacket he'd taken from Keith's closet. The air closed in on him. It was sullen with humidity, so charged it was hard to breathe.

"The brakes might need a couple of pumps," he warned the guy as he got in.

Ronnie opened his own door and stood half out of the car, one knee on the seat. To his horror, Boudreau saw the butt of the automatic peeking out of his jeans.

Another attendant approached the Mustang, hubcapless and measled all over with splotches of black primer. "Help you, sir?"

Ronnie ignored him. With his bleached pompadour and shades and sleeveless T-shirt, he looked like he'd gotten lost on the way to a different event, maybe the holdup of a convenience store.

"How long you figure it'll take?" he called across the apron of the portico.

Boudreau stood on the curb, trying to prop Cherry upright without being too obvious. This little scene was overripe already. Two other couples had paused to stare halfway through the door, along with the doorman holding it open. A third parking attendant leaning against a post was grinning around his toothpick.

"I don't know," Boudreau said, "hard to say." He gave Ronnie a big social smile. "You know how these things are."

"You bullshit me again, that's it," said Ronnie. "I'm giving you a half hour."

A Lincoln and a Mercedes were idling now in back of the Mustang, their exhaust fumes hanging under the portico in the laden air.

"We'll just have to see how it goes," said Boudreau, the smile molded to his face.

Ronnie looked across at him without moving.

The driver of the Lincoln beeped his horn, then took both hands off the wheel and gestured in dismay through the darkened windshield.

The parking attendant leaned over the top of the Mustang. "Sir?"

"You get off a my car," Ronnie said, then turned back to Boudreau. "You better not be jerking me off, Richter." He gave the attendant a long look, slid down into his seat and closed the door in a single motion. He drove through the portico looking straight ahead.

Boudreau nodded pleasantly for the benefit of the remaining audience and pushed through the doors, his stomach turning over when he steered Cherry into the main ballroom. There were not that many people yet, some clumps scattered here and there, and it seemed as if every one of them had just turned around to look. From the corner of his eye he saw his mother, her hand on the arm of a beefy red-faced man. She was performing a tinkly-laughed introduction to one of the clumps.

He turned around and found a white-jacketed waiter in front of him, offering a tray of champagne. Boudreau took one.

The waiter managed to get Cherry's attention. "Ma'am?"

Coming into focus, she gave the man a sloppy grin and took one, spilling half of it in the subsequent exchange of the little napkin. "Whoa!" she said. "Whoa, *sorry.*"

The waiter smiled politely, assuring her it was all right in a soft accent.

"No," she said. "No, man, *I'll* get it." She held up the tiny napkin significantly. Boudreau realized she was about to get down and start mopping up. He gave the man a lighthearted conspiratorial smile and maneuvered her away by the elbow.

He bent close to her and talked through his fixed smile. "We gotta do better than that, okay?"

She opened her mouth, the teeth wet and tiny. "Fuck you, man," she warned. *"Has*sle me."

Boudreau straightened up and gave a quick look around. He took one sip of his champagne, then chugged the rest. They were *bad news;* they stood out like thumbs smashed with a hammer. Blending in here was not going to be easy.

He'd found one of Vicky's old prom dresses in the closet, a light green satin strapless sheath. A solid decade out of fashion, it fit except for the bodice, which was a little loose around Cherry's smaller chest. He was caught in the same time warp, wearing some honky chalk-striped bell-bottoms from back when Keith was skinny. They set off the madras jacket nicely.

He looked at Cherry, her earful of metal and her spiked punker hair and her inch-wide wraparound shades. She looked like she'd just climbed off the back of a chopper.

"You should take these off," Boudreau said, and reached for the sunglasses.

Cherry wrenched away from him, spilling more champagne. *"Has*sle me." His date hitched up the top of her dress with her free hand. "Fucking *pig.*"

Boudreau took another quick look around. At least the place was filling up. He saw a waiter and waved his empty.

"Mom, you wouldn't have any aspirin in your purse, would you?" This was the best he'd been able to come up with.

His mother turned around.

"*Rich*ter," she trilled. "I have someone very special for you to meet." The man stood planted in front of Boudreau like a tree, a prim little smile in the middle of his big red face. His wife moved between them like a referee.

"Victor, this is my other son. Richter."

The guy averted his eyes slightly, a National Guardsman trained to look just past the stoned hippie putting a flower in his rifle barrel. He forced the tight smile back to his lips and stuck out his hand. "Vic Hill," he said.

Boudreau gave him a crazy taunt of a grin as the man tried to crush his hand. He couldn't help himself. "Hi, I'm the other son," he said. "You've heard all about me. Congratulations."

Vic Hill's smile went wider and tighter. "Your mother is a wonderful woman," he recited in his clench-jawed Texas accent. "I couldn't be a happier man."

Your mother is a candy-ass, and I'd kick the shit out of you if I got a chance.

"I bet," said Boudreau, "I bet you're a hell of a happy guy."

"And who is *this?*" Cynthia Hill put on her brightest voice as she moved in to break up the clinch.

Cherry had drifted a few feet from her moorings, goofing open-mouthed on the shindig. Boudreau retrieved her, an arm around her shoulders to hold her upright.

"Mom, Vic, this is my friend Eleanor." He turned her to face them.

Cherry took her sweet time returning to earth, then hitched up the bodice of the dress and gave a short wiggle, settling her tits in more comfortably. She held out a hand, dangling it limp from the wrist.

"Cherry," she said. Her brow furrowed above the strip of new-wave dark plastic as the time-lagged introduction caught up with her. She grinned. "I mean *El*eanor. Meetcha."

Vic and Cynthia Hill regarded Boudreau's new girl, his-and-hers smiles of polite alarm on their faces.

"Well!" said Cynthia Hill after a few seconds. "Well, Richter tells me you're a . . . a *dan*cer."

Cherry found this funny. "Yeah, ri-hight. A dancer."

Victor Hill took his wife's empty champagne glass and jumped ship. "I'll just go see I can't freshen this up, honey."

Cynthia Hill turned in panic to watch him. Boudreau let go of Cherry and stepped closer.

"So, Mom," he said, "do you have any aspirin in your purse?"

She turned back around and gave him a quizzically fixed smile, as though she'd just been introduced but had already forgotten his name.

"I've got a headache," he explained.

She stared at him, still trying to remember who he was. "I don't have my purse, it's in the check room." Her eyes looked suddenly fearful and exhausted, peering from behind the surgically tightened skin as if through a mask. "Go ask Howard, he'll find you something." She indicated a tall thin black man in a waiter's jacket. "I'm sure there's some aspirin here somewhere." The frozen smile remained in place as she turned away, desperate to escape. "I just have to go say hello to Ellie and Leon."

Boudreau hung out in the grand foyer near the check room, trying to make conversation with his half brother.

"So, Billy," he said, "how do you like your new dad?"

Billy Rowling shrugged his fat shoulders and snagged a glass of champagne from a tray going by. Boudreau took one too, his fourth, and checked his watch. They'd been here nearly forty-five minutes now.

The kid hadn't budged from the foyer for a solid twenty, taking it upon himself to function as inspector-general of all coming and going. Ronnie was somewhere outside, prowling the perimeter. Cherry sat in an open-mouthed nod, slumped on a deep leather couch across the foyer. Boudreau was losing his mind.

"Hey, Billy, how about getting me one of those plates of food?"

"Git it yourself," said Billy Rowling, keeping his eyes on the doorman and one of the parking attendants talking outside in the heat.

Boudreau smiled brightly. "I bet you can't drink that down like this," he said, and drained his glass.

The boy looked up him with his piggish little eyes and drank his own down without blinking. He wiped his mouth with his sleeve, leaving behind a so-what smirk.

"Waiter?" called Boudreau. "We get some more champagne over here, please?"

After the fourth glass Billy's eyes were watering, but he still hadn't moved a foot from his station in front of the check room. He was taking this personally. Boudreau was drunk, a hyper champagne buzz. He began to consider going for broke and asking the attendant for his mother's purse anyway.

Cherry appeared in front of him, sunglasses crooked and the aureole of one of her nipples peeking above the fallen top of her dress. *"Pee,"* she explained.

"You met Cherry?" Boudreau asked Billy. "My brother Billy."

Blinking and weaving, the boy stared at her tits. "Half brother," he got out.

"Meetcha," said Cherry without looking at him. *"Pee,* man."

Boudreau saw his opportunity. He put his arm around Cherry, then carefully pulled up the top of her dress with his other hand, making sure to brush her breast while Billy watched.

"Billy, Cherry needs some help finding the ladies' room, okay?" He pulled the two of them together and molded Billy's fat little arm around her waist. "Go on now."

Boudreau leaned casually against the wall as he waited for them to stumble out of sight. Inside the ballroom the orchestra struck up its first tune. This would do it. Hi, I'm the new bride's son, she wanted me to get her purse for her. *Hey, thanks a lot.*

He turned and caught the eye of the check-room attendant, a young black woman with a processed ponytail. She got up from her stool and came to the counter. "Help you, sir?"

"Hey, how's it going?" he began. "Listen, do you have—"

"Well, Richter Bou*dreau,* what the hell're you doing out *here?"*

Boudreau turned, his heart clenched. A late-arriving middle-aged couple had just pushed through the glass front doors, the man advancing toward him, glad hand out.

"Why aren't y'all in where all the *fun* is?" said the man.

"Well," said Boudreau, "actually I was just leaving. Work."

The man turned to his wife. "Marie, you remember Richter, don't you? Richter Boudreau, Cynthia's first boy?"

The woman squinted at Boudreau, smiling uncertainly.

Elton and Marie Bonner had lived in the house across the street on Thirty-eighth. When Boudreau was thirteen, he'd put a too well hit hardball through their front picture window one afternoon. Sure that no one was home, he went across the street and peered in, just as Mrs. Bonner emerged from a back hallway stark naked and wild-eyed. He saw a naked man who was not Mr. Bonner slam the door behind her before she was halfway across the room.

Elton Bonner folded his arms and rocked on his heels, ready to set up shop and have some conversation. "So," he said, "staying out of trouble?"

"Trying to," Boudreau said thickly. "Trying to."

"Haven't been breaking any *win*dows lately?" He gave Boudreau a big wink to let him know it was all in fun.

Marie Bonner's face blanched as the encrusted memory broke loose. Boudreau gave a weak smile and looked past them.

"*Shit,* I gotta go," he said. " 'Scuse me "

Ronnie Stover stood right outside the doors, nose all but pressed against the glass as the doorman tried to tell him something.

Boudreau opened the door a crack and felt a blast of wet heat on his face. Behind Ronnie's shoulder the sky over Tulsa had taken on an ugly yellow tinge, livid with dark thunderheads around the edges.

"It's okay, I'll take care of it," Boudreau said to the doorman. He waited until the man moved away a few feet, then turned to Ronnie. "You can't just stand here," he whispered. "I've almost got it but this is *not cool.* "

Ronnie's mouth went up in one corner and he shook his head, as if he'd been expecting just this kind of bullshit. He took out a cigarette to help him think about it.

Boudreau turned and checked over his shoulder. His mother stood in midstep at the far end of the foyer, brows together and mouth in a straight line. He smiled at her and held up his hand. *I got it, Mom.* He turned back to Ronnie, dizzy with panic. "Okay?" he said. *"Okay?"*

Ronnie lit up without taking his eyes off Boudreau. "I'm giving you one hour to meet me back at brother Keith's. One hour." He exhaled two thin plumes from his nose and adjusted his sunglasses. "I got nothing to lose, Richter, you understand me on that?"

Boudreau nodded and looked over his shoulder again. His mother was fifteen feet away. "I gotta go," he said through the open door. "I gotta *go.*"

He started to close the door, but Ronnie stopped it solid with one huge hand. "I'll hunt you down, comrade." Ronnie looked at him for a long moment, then took his hand away, satisfied.

Boudreau had just enough time to turn around and get two steps forward. "Having a good time, Mom?"

His mother eyed him. "Who was that?"

"I don't know, some guy who works on the golf course or something." He shrugged, looking over his shoulder to check that Ronnie was really gone. "Someone parked a car that blocked him or something. I told him the attendants would take care of it."

Her mouth tightened as she considered whether to believe him.

Blood rushed to his brain. He shrugged again, denying any further knowledge. A plan came to him.

"I was looking for Billy," he tried. "I think the excitement's kind of gotten to him."

His mother's head cocked over at an angle, eyes narrowing. "Excitement?"

"I don't know, little too much champagne maybe." His whole last phrase came out in a slur. He watched her face. "Just a *kid,* Mom, don't be too hard on him."

She spun around and he followed along behind.

"I'll take him home if you want." She didn't reply and he upped the offer to three birds for the price of one stone. "We're thinking of going now anyway."

In the ballroom the dance floor was full as the orchestra cranked up its honk version of "Twist and Shout." Boudreau spotted Billy on the fringe of the dance floor next to a buffet table, dancing up a storm with Cherry. Boudreau's heart leapt like a spring fawn: the kid was visibly, gloriously drunk, his eyes at half-mast and his mouth hanging open, his nasty little body spastic with alcohol.

Before they could get to him, he boogied backward and tripped on his own feet. He fell against the buffet table and went down, catching the table cloth and pulling a platter of tomato aspic down on top of himself.

Cynthia Hill stopped short. "Oh my *Lord.*"

Boudreau grabbed Billy under the arms, trying to avoid the dripping aspic. He was dead weight. He got him to his feet and held him upright, prize evidence.

"*Billy!*" the boy's mother said. "William Rowling, you *listen* to me!"

Boudreau looked down on the inert kid with a big brother's gaze, all fond understanding. "Hey, it's *okay*, Billy, it's okay. Happens to everybody. Be okay."

Billy's head oscillated on his shoulders as he tried to understand.

Boudreau raised his eyebrows at his mother and gave a little smile. "Why don't you just let me take him home for you, okay?"

The new Mrs. Hill inhaled and looked around, frantic to distraction. A few people directly around them had become aware of the little scene over the noise of the band.

"You don't need to worry about this *now*, Mom." He lowered his voice reverently. "Not on a day like today."

She inhaled again, then threw her shoulders back to bear the extra burden. "Oh, all *right.* All right. He's got his keys."

Boudreau kept a straight face as he heard the magic word. He was going to get out of this alive.

He started to move away with Billy in tow as his mother watched, stricken. He gave her a consoling smile to nail the deal down, then realized she was no longer looking at them.

Cherry had continued dancing by herself, blank faced behind the shades, oblivious to the loss of her partner. Rooted to the floor, she was moving to her own slow-motion funk beat, an empty champagne glass in one hand and a cigarette drooping long ash in the other. The top of her dress had sagged to a halt around the waist, her little brown-nippled breasts out in the world, surprising as a newborn's just-opened eyes. The man dancing next to her did a spin, then wrenched to a halt in midbop, then went down.

Cynthia Hill stared openmouthed for a moment longer, before something jolted her out of the spell and she craned her head up wildly, a chicken panicked at the whereabouts of the rest of the flock. She looked right through Boudreau, then took off. Boudreau followed her line of sight and saw Victor Hill across the crowded floor. He got a body under each arm and made his retreat.

Boudreau pulled into the far end of the parking lot. Rolling out of the Healey, he stood up too fast and felt sick. Cherry was slumped in the front seat, Billy stowed in the luggage area behind her.

He hauled Billy out by the armpits, propped him up against the car and started searching him for the keys. A pat-down yielded nothing. He tried to get a hand in one of the kid's tight trouser pockets. From the depths of his stupor Billy realized something was going on and struggled feebly to stand up. His eyes came open.

"Where's the *keys*, Billy?" said Boudreau, leaning close.

Billy's head wobbled a little and his eyes closed again.

Boudreau shoved him back against the car, harder than he needed to. "Have it your way," he said. "Little fucking twerp."

The boy's pants were so tight around the thighs he couldn't get a hand in the pockets. He unbuckled the belt and unzipped him, then realized what he was doing and took a quick look around. Now they could add molesting a drunk thirteen-year-old boy to his rap sheet.

He found a piece of metal in one moist pocket and pulled out a single key on an NRA key ring. *Bingo.*

Boudreau humped the kid across the parking lot, a distinct rivulet of sweat dripping off his nose. This was hard work. He stopped under the awning and saw their reflection in the glass doors. The aspic had melted all over Billy's front and looked disturbingly like blood; his pants were half off because the zipper had jammed on his shirttail partway up. Boudreau himself was purple faced and crazy. The two of them together were like some terrible parody of buddies in combat.

The doorman on duty moved toward the doors, then stopped when he got a load of them. Boudreau groaned out loud. It was the Cockney.

He only opened the door partway, but Boudreau lugged Billy on through. "Little too much fun," he explained.

The doorman stepped in front of him. "You near got my arse fired last time."

Boudreau held up Billy's key.

"See this?" he said. "You gimme the phone and we'll just put in a call to my mother at her wedding reception, okay?"

"Don't you threaten me," said the doorman. His face had already gone slack in a panic of indecision.

Billy moaned and Boudreau tried to hold him away without letting go, then looked at the Cockney. "You want him to puke down here or upstairs?"

The doorman made up his mind. "I'll be coming up with you, then."

Boudreau closed his eyes, breathing out heavily, then opened them again. The guy was like a border guard who hadn't understood a word he said. He didn't budge. "Great," said Boudreau. "Fine with me."

Inside the apartment entry Boudreau felt like dropping Billy and running. He was already running out of time and now he'd run out of ideas. It was happening too fast, or not fast enough. The doorman stood arms folded, his eyes watchful as a prison guard's.

A phone rang deep in the apartment. Both men stiffened like burglars, wondering whether to answer it. It rang a second time, and Billy moaned again, this time with urgency.

"Shit!" said Boudreau. "There's my mother calling to see if I got him here okay."

Boudreau shoved Billy at the doorman and ran. He was halfway down the hallway to his mother's bedroom when he heard the sound of heaving.

He went straight to the chaise and hit his knees. The film can was gone. Gone, *gone.*

Still on his knees, he went on autopilot, numbly answering the phone anyway. "Yeah."

"You," said George Brinkman, "are an elusive man."

Boudreau sagged, his air gone. "How'd you get this number?"

"It's your mother's, right?" said Brinkman. "I got it from your other place of employment. Excuse me, your other *former* place of employment."

Boudreau rose and sat down heavily on the chaise. Down the hall came the sound of Billy puking and a sharp "Fookin' *Ada!*" from the doorman. He closed his eyes and leaned forward elbows on knees, a man with terminal constipation. "What do you want, George?"

"What do I *want?*" said Brinkman, incredulous. "Boudreau, man, pardon me for saying this, but you're in some amount of trouble. Correct me if I'm wrong."

"Listen, George, this isn't a good time for me right now, can I call you back?"

"And I don't mean your erratic employment," Brinkman pushed. "I mean like *H* as in Harmon, *S* as in Shaw, *D* as in Deep Shit."

Boudreau opened his eyes and looked down. His shoe had pushed back the chintz valance around the bottom of the chaise, exposing the best Easter egg he'd ever found.

"Where are you, the paper?" He shook it and heard a reassuring rattle, then pocketed it. "I'll call you right back."

Brinkman put his mouth closer to the phone. "Listen, Boudreau. I don't know just what it is you've been up to, but you're gonna tell me about it or I'm going to the cops, okay?"

Boudreau listened to a crackle of static on the line. "George, that's blackmail," he said, and hung up.

Billy sat propped against the wall in the living room, legs spraddled out like a baby at the beach, lap full of barf. The doorman was bent in a crouch over him, holding the bottom of his uniform jacket away from himself.

"My mom said to be sure and say thanks for the help," said Boudreau. He hoofed it for the door as the phone began ringing, again and again.

The Healey popped out of third as Boudreau accelerated to catch the light, but he caught it in time and slammed through the intersection without hitting anyone.

"Whoa," said Cherry, eyes opening only briefly.

He hung a right off Peoria onto Keith's street, fifteen minutes late. He slowed down, realizing that his delivery of the film was also when his Vicky note with Ronnie would come due. Okay, he'd just drop off Cherry with the goods and keep on going. In a matter of minutes he'd be Mexico-bound.

He drove past Keith's house without slowing down. The Mustang wasn't there, but Keith's GTO was. At the end of the block he ran the stop sign and turned. He panicked. Without the money he'd ripped off from Keith, he'd get exactly as far as a half tank of gas would carry him. He didn't have a dime.

The second time around, the Mustang still wasn't there. Boudreau stopped at the mouth of the drive. Ronnie had obviously waited and then split. *I'll hunt you down, comrade.* He was probably after Boudreau at his mother's right now.

Okay, Boudreau told himself. He'd leave the motor running, go inside and grab the bag, it couldn't take more than thirty seconds. All he had to do was hold his nose and dive, and after that he'd be in clear water. He checked both ends of the block.

Boudreau pulled in, drove to the end of the driveway and turned the Healey around, aiming it back out at the street. He set the parking brake and left the engine running.

He opened Cherry's door and took her arm. "End of the line," he said.

She opened her eyes long enough to make a weak try at pulling away, then closed them again.

He squeezed until she yelped, then leaned down into her face. "I'm not fucking around now," he said. *"I am not fucking around."*

She came to a clumsy halt in front of the service door. "You going somewhere?" she asked, then saw the film can in his hand. "Gimme that. *Gimme* that."

"Not yet," he said, pushing her through the door.

She stumbled through the kitchen, yelling. "Keeee-th!" she called out. *"Keeee-th!"*

The bag was missing from its position on the counter. Ronnie had taken it, or maybe Keith. He'd give himself a two-minute search, no more. One minute.

"Keeee-th!" he heard Cherry yelling as she went through the living room. She sounded like a lost child looking for its mother. "Keeee-th!"

He'd just made it through the door to Joe Michaels's study when he heard a new sound from Cherry, a kind of *"ackk"* like you'd make bumping into something. He stopped and listened.

The noise came again, this time with a strangled quality to it.

Keith, thought Boudreau, then thought again.

Ronnie.

He bolted out of the study at a full run, then caught sight of Cherry out of the corner of his eye, standing in the front hall off the living room.

She stood, arms at her sides and shoulders hunched way up, eyes popping out of her junkie stupor as if too much pressure had built up inside her head. She started screaming.

Boudreau clapped his hand over her mouth and looked down.

Keith Michaels had had it. He lay on the floor on his side, limbs splayed out in a kind of twisted running position, the afterimage of a cartoon character who'd just run through a wall. From five feet away Boudreau could still smell the reek of alcohol. There was a small powder-burned hole in his temple, right at the hairline. His jaw hung open, slackly out of register with the rest of his face. Under what was left of the other side of his head was a pool of blood, so velvety dark and viscous that it sat on top of the carpet like fake vomit. The Colt Python lay near his hand.

Boudreau couldn't breathe. He'd never seen a dead person up close in his life, and this was a terrible place to start. He couldn't stop looking at the ruined body, its lifeless gut sagged to the floor, its eyes bulged out as though staring at the camera right beside it, strap still pathetically around its neck. There was a flecked expressionist spray of white and gray and red on the drapes a few feet away.

This was not Keith. *Oh yes it was.*

Boudreau understood he was going to throw up if he looked a second longer.

Cherry whimpered violently from behind his hand and tried to move her head. He let her go.

He couldn't believe it. Then again, what was there to believe. Keith had done it, he'd finally come around to the wrong chamber, the right chamber, whatever. There was nothing to do about it now.

He made himself creep closer without looking at the body, then bend over.

The camera was empty.

The gun, however, was not. It was loaded for bear and not for chance, all six chambers full and not a one of them fired.

Keith had had some help.

Boudreau clicked the cylinder back in, then realized what he'd done. He held the thing in one tail of the madras jacket and wiped at it frantically with the other, shaking so hard he was sure it was going to go off again.

Someone bad was out there, and he didn't want to know who it was.

Boudreau stood in a phone booth at the Quick Trip on Thirty-sixth and Harvard and dialed the motel number on the plastic key ring. It was a hundred and ten degrees in the booth, even with the door open.

"Good afternoon, Skyline Tulsa," said the perky voice. "May I he'p yew?"

Boudreau gave her the room number and waited while the phone rang, over and over again.

Finally the operator came back on the line. "The party doesn't seem to answer, sir? Would you like to leave a message?"

"Um, yeah," he said. "Yeah, no, listen, that's not necessary, but could I just make sure who's registered at that number?"

The operator went official on him. "I'm sorry, sir," she said. "I can't give out that information."

"Okay. Listen, operator, this is sort of an emergency, okay?" Without thinking, he continued. "This is her brother calling and I really need to locate her. *Please?*"

She paused. *Here the brother's brains are all over the floor and this scumbag's using his name.*

"Just a minute, please?"

Boudreau breathed out, trying to calm down. He looked out at the car. Cherry sat upright as a mannequin, a wax-museum Frankenstein's bride out on a prom date.

"I have a Victoria S. Richter through tomorrow," said the operator. "You're sure there's no message?"

Boudreau said he was no place he could be reached, then assured her he'd keep trying.

The motel was out south at the intersection of two major streets, a shrimp-cocktail conventioneer's palace surrounded by traffic and median strips and chain-link fence. Boudreau found his way into one of the enormous parking lots and circled it twice before parking.

Cherry's head was propped motionless on the back of her seat. He couldn't tell if her eyes were open behind the sunglasses.

"Come on," he said, opening her door. "We're going in."

Her head moved backward as if it were on a balky pulley system. She pointed up.

Boudreau looked. The heat had remained unabated, but he hadn't noticed the sun. It was gone. The sky squatted on top of the city like a huge dark griddle, pressing down almost as far as he could see in any direction. At the distant horizon the thinnest layer of dirty yellow seemed to squeeze out from under the edges, more like pus than air. She pointed again, to the south, and he caught a silent forking of heat lightning.

The room was on the second floor balcony, overlooking the parking lot. Cherry stood behind him.

"Who's this?" she got out. "Whosis *this?*"

Looking around first, he put his ear to the door, thought about it, then knocked. He listened again, then tried the key.

The anonymous erotic atmosphere of the motel room had a faint current of something familiar running through it, a presence. He realized it was the distinct floral smell of Vicky Stover's body.

"Vicky?"

Besides the smell there was nothing except a baby's rattle ring of multicolored plastic keys lying on the floor, next to one of the unmade double beds. He sniffed again and the ammonia tang of used diapers hit his nose. In the bathroom the trash can was crammed with disposables. He came back out, hung the Do Not Disturb sign over the knob and locked up.

Cherry was slumped sideways inside the door, barely standing. Her hands were spread out against the wall, as if it might move or fall on top of her. "We do now?" she said.

Boudreau looked at her, then collapsed on one of the beds. There was a painful lump in his pocket. He took out the film can and shut it in the drawer of the bedside table. He didn't want it on him anymore.

"We *do* now?" she said again.

He stared up at the ceiling. "Wait," he said.

He heard a rustle and looked over. The green party dress lay in a circle at her feet like a shucked chrysalis. She stood looking at him, head cocked, nothing on but the sunglasses and a pair of red bikini underwear. She stumbled over to the other bed and fell onto it.

"*Wait?*" The word came whining out in two syllables. "*Wait?*"

It wasn't like Boudreau had arranged for Ronnie to go over the wall and take Keith with him. He lay on the bed, trying to clear the image of Keith out of his head. He could see it now all too clearly, the gun gets waved, threats follow insults, the last thread finally snaps. The drunk picks a fight on the sidewalk with the overwound Golden Gloves finalist.

Hey, man, wanna see who's fucking your wife?

Okay, maybe he'd had a minor role in it, but no way this was his fault, no *way*. It was *fate,* the famous Accident Waiting to Happen. He could no more have stopped them than he could have derailed two highballing trains.

Boudreau got up and went to the window, peeked out between the drapes into the darkness. He was sure it couldn't be that late, it was just the sky, the approaching storm. How long had he been lying there— three hours, four? It didn't make any difference, the facts wouldn't change, he could spend forever and never get any closer than "fate."

He'd take back all of it, if only he could. He'd give Ronnie a basketball scholarship to a Big Ten school; he'd tell Priscilla Michaels not to treat her little boy like a defective version of the empire builder she was married to; he'd take away the junk and the booze so both of them could think straight. He'd give them productive lives and meaningful employment, erase the war in Vietnam and change the inheritance laws. He'd do anything if he could. *Anything.*

Boudreau stumbled his way back to the bed, his head splitting, a hot flush spreading to the surface of his face. His chest tightened. He found himself facedown, crying soundlessly into the pillow. Okay, he was *sorry.* Did that make things any better?

Boudreau caught a small but distinct whiff of Vicky Stover's essence, trapped in the pillow. He sniffed at it and it disappeared. Victoria S. *Richter,* that was worth something, wasn't it? If he waited, she'd be back, he knew she would. A little squirt of illicit hope escaped from his heart.

She'd said she loved him and then fucked him silly. Granted, it was a little frenzied. But Jesus Christ, who wouldn't be weird? He wondered if she'd ever told her husband about the stuff with Keith. Then he wondered if that stuff was even true, and what it meant if it was, and then what it meant if it wasn't.

Whatever. Crazy was his stock-in-trade, everyone had their quirks. When she got back, they could deal with this, they could deal with it together. A thought clicked: she was probably a few hearings and back-room meetings away from being a rich woman.

Life goes on, he thought.

Rooting in the pillow like a pig, he snorted for another tiny bloom to feed the sudden fantasy of taking up residence chez Michaels with Vicky. Of course they'd have to get the living room steam-cleaned first.

Ronnie. Of course they'd have to arrange things with Ronnie, custody rights and so on, no guns during visitation.

Boudreau spun over and opened his eyes, his head beating like a drum. He needed a bottle, a couple of joints, a half gram of toot, whatever. *Anything,* so long as it would mash his wits into paste and he could come up with a different set of results.

He sat up and the room closed in on him. He didn't even have enough in his wallet to hit the motel bar.

"I have a cigarette?" said Cherry.

She was up on one elbow, the sunglasses finally off. Her eyes looked small and colorless, dark pouches underneath.

Boudreau had four left in the pack. She drew back with a nervous cringe while he lit one for her, as if touching him might contaminate her. He was getting just a little tired of this.

"Have a nice rest?" He lit one himself, hands shaking.

She gave him her snotty little tic of a smile, then sat up in the bed, hugging her knees to her chest. "Looks like maybe Keith wasn't the only one she did."

"What?" The door to the adjacent room slammed and he went still, listening. Only then did it penetrate. "What exactly," he said, "was that supposed to mean?"

She took another drag on her cigarette and looked away. "You figure it out," she said. "Loverboy."

Boudreau's mouth hung open. This was transparent as the cheap underwear she had on, hostile junkie intellect at its best. "I don't know what you're talking about."

Cherry's eyes went wide in disbelief. "What do you take me for, an *ass*hole? You think I can't see what's going on?"

A muscle on Boudreau's cheek started jumping, in time with the throbbing in his temple. "Try again," he said. "Try again, *Eleanor*. Ronnie did it, maybe if you weren't so strung out you'd see that."

She looked at him, her head tilted. "What, 'cause of *you?*" Her mouth started to go up in one corner. "C'mon, man, Ronnie knew she was balling anything that *walked.*" She looked at him again and the smile widened. "You really believe that?"

Boudreau felt his face go hot, then willed a smile onto it. "Shut up."

She shook her head. "You really fucking be—" She stopped and laughed out loud, crazy with it. "I mean, figure it *out:* she sets it up so Keith is supposed to go sign this *thing* today with her *boy*friend— What's-his-name, *Chick*—but Keith's got some *pic*tures, right, he's no—"

"I said shut up."

"Yeah, and meantime you're still waiting for Santa Claus, you're like out on a *ride* but you can't—"

Boudreau moved closer to the bed. "I said *shut the fuck up.*"

When she started to open her mouth again, he jerked his arm back in a warning. She flinched. He did it again and got another flinch, as if they were in some brutal puppet show, the strings invisible.

She flattened herself back against the wall, eyes locked on his. "Go ahead." She bared her little teeth. "Go ahead, it'll make you feel better."

Over in the next room the TV blared on suddenly, so loud he jumped. He could hear it clearly, the start of the local news. He started to worry about how much their voices had carried, then thought again. He got up and ran to their own TV.

The sound and picture flared into the room. It was the number-one story.

All hair and teeth, a reporter stood on-camera in front of a long shot of the house. He was just finishing something breathless about this tangled tragedy in one of Tulsa's most prominent families. His eyes went earnest as he turned with the camera to the scene behind.

The house looked huge, imperial. It was here, the reporter said, mentioning the thirty-two rooms, that the violence had erupted.

The camera panned to the driveway, filled with a circus of official vehicles and flashing lights. Boudreau held his breath as the picture cut to the living room.

Here was the chalked outline on the carpet, a dark stain gruesomely enlarging the head. A black-and-white photograph filled the screen, a picture Boudreau was used to seeing on the wall of the gallery off the kitchen. He heard himself make a little noise in the back of his throat. It was Keith before he was fat, Keith blond and handsome and arrogant. *Keith when he still had all of his brains.* The voice described the dead man as the ne'er-do-well scion with a history of alcoholism and emotional problems, including recent run-ins with the police.

Then came a picture of a young sharp-faced man, crew-cut and unsmiling, a service picture in full uniform. It was Ronnie Dean Stover, without sunglasses or the pompadour. It took Boudreau a moment to understand. *They'd caught him.* Boudreau saw how it would play already, the brother-in-law from the other side of the tracks, recently estranged from the sister, bitter and distraught, unemployed, the dishonorably discharged vet with a suspected drug problem.

They'd *caught* him.

Boudreau turned from the TV to catch Cherry's eye. She was aware of it but kept her gaze on the screen. Her face fell, and then she pointed.

The screen filled with a shot of the service entrance to the kitchen. There was blood everywhere and another chalked outline on the floor. The other dead man, also armed, had been found here shot in the head also, an apparent suicide. In his possession, said the reporter, was a roll of film that may or may not have been related to the violence. As yet, the police weren't saying.

Suicide? Boudreau watched, stupefied, while the scene changed to an interview with a phlegmatic Tulsa cop standing by the line of squad cars out in the driveway. Both deceased had been armed, and there was a history of bad blood between the two. The police were looking for a man and a woman known to have been staying at the house for further questioning, but until then they were calling it a murder and subsequent suicide by a disturbed individual. They'd have to wait for ballistics results and the coroner's report, but in his opinion you got these kind of things under the influence of drugs and alcohol.

The picture cut to the front of the downtown police station. The family, the reporter let his viewers know, was in deep shock.

Boudreau's stomach clenched. Charles Carlson, described as a long-time family friend and lawyer, stood on the station steps, apparently reading a statement. The reporter's voice-over included some more information about what an important family it was, the Michaels Companies currently holding down number 214 on the Fortune 500. Boudreau caught a glimpse of George Brinkman in the melee of reporters and popping flashbulbs. He felt like he'd died; he was watching people he knew carry on without him.

The audio cut in for the last part of Chip Carlson's statement. The Michaels family was stunned and deeply grieved by the senseless violence that had occurred between these two obviously troubled young men. The family would do everything to assist the police in their investigation, but right now there was nothing to contradict the initial findings.

Carlson turned away and the camera caught a few seconds of the doubly grieving woman described as the sister and widow: the Michaels family, such as it was. Vicky Michaels Stover, continued the reporter, had been going over family business at Carlson's office when the awful news arrived.

She wore a light green skirt and a white sleeveless Peter Pan blouse, arms tan and smooth. She looked born for the role, rich and beautiful and stricken-faced. Her hair was tied back in an athletic ponytail, as though she'd just come in off the golf course. She shushed the baby she was holding, cooing to it. Carlson fended off further questions and said something into her ear, then gathered her under his arm and hustled her into the police station.

A tremor went through Boudreau. The collection of information he'd taken for stable ground shifted under his feet, then settled, an earthquake of bad news.

He fought his own face while the reporter delivered his on-camera wrap-up back in front of the Michaels house, about family tragedy striking even in a home like this one. In an afternoon of violence whose motives and details would apparently remain a mystery, the only certainty was the tragic outcome.

"So what do you think?" said Cherry from the other bed. "She still coming back?"

Boudreau looked at her, then jerked open the drawer of the bedside table. The film can bounced like a pinball and came to rest against the Gideon Bible, good and evil laid out for him like a shell game. It occurred to him that this was his last remaining problem; this and nothing else.

In his hand it radiated evil like a lump of plutonium. Somewhere on it was an unspeakable image, but it was never going to see the light of day. A weight lifted from him. Just because Bedford Shaw had ripped another branch off Reuben Armstrong's hapless family tree didn't mean he could do anything about it. It wasn't exactly unique in the annals.

"All yours now, right?" said Cherry.

Boudreau started like he'd been caught doing something. "You stupid *bitch,*" he said. "Here, you *want* it?" He underhanded the film can at her, hard enough to bounce it off the wall.

She retrieved it off the bed, keeping her eyes on him.

Boudreau picked up the phone. He dialed and listened to it ring, watching the TV to avoid looking at Cherry. The news had moved on to the second-biggest story of the hour, a weatherman looking professionally worried in front of a satellite map. The picture changed to a town right on the Missouri border, debris scattered like broken matchsticks.

Brinkman picked up on the fifth ring.

"George. It's me."

"*Who?*" Brinkman waited a beat and laughed. "I thought maybe you'd call back." He rattled ice in a glass next to the receiver. "You're in the bag, Boudreau, you're my Pulitzer on the hoof. Tulsa Throat has come to Georgie."

"George, *lis*ten, I need something," said Boudreau, "I need a piece of information." He swallowed. "It's kind of personal."

"Hey, that's what I'm *here* for." Brinkman was all unctuous cheer. "That's what friends are for, right?"

"Listen," said Boudreau, "you know that murder thing that happened today? I saw you covering it on the news, but were you at the house? I mean, did you talk to any of the cops?"

"Yeah, I talked to 'em." Brinkman guarded his tone, uncertain where this was leading. "So?"

Boudreau looked at Cherry over on the other bed. She was playing with the film with exaggerated nonchalance, as if she wasn't listening.

"You know that film they found on the guy in the kitchen? On Ronnie? Have they looked at it?"

Brinkman's interest perked up. "You *knew* that guy?"

"Um, yeah, I knew him. Not very well. But I mean, are they *say*ing anything about it, about what's on the film?"

Brinkman let Boudreau's question flutter in the breeze. "I have to say that's kind of a weird question."

"Look, I need to *know*, okay? This means a lot to me. Do you know if they've developed it?"

"Take take take," said Brinkman, "whatever happened to give, Boudreau, the pleasure of giving? First you're plotzing about the tattoos on some *goon*, now you want to know about this film they found in the house with two *dead* guys." Brinkman made the sucking mouth sound of a trader considering a shrewd offer, then came up with his Chinese detective. "Ve-lly inta-lesting."

"George," Boudreau said, "George, I'm *asking* you: do they fucking know what's on it?"

Brinkman listened, then did his side-of-the-mouth tough guy routine. "What's in it for me, pal?"

Boudreau breathed in and played his last card. "The biggest story you'll ever get."

"Ooooh!" yelped Brinkman, "the mystery *widens.*" He hesitated, and then when he spoke again, his voice was normal. "Hey, what the hell. Okay, *yeah.* Yeah, they know what's on it."

Boudreau waited. *"George,"* he said.

Brinkman let it hang there, then laughed. "Not a goddamn thing, that's what's on it. The whole roll was ex*posed,* your friend pulled it out of the cartridge before he nailed himself. Or maybe the other guy pulled it out before *he* bought it." He paused. "Truth to tell, Boudreau, you're not the only one wondering about the mystery film. We're all betting it was some juicy shit. It's gotta be blackmail, right?" Brinkman laughed again. "C'mon, Boudreau, what was *on* it? You knew this guy, was he like sucking off horses or something?"

Boudreau pressed the button down and closed his eyes. Another little landslide occurred inside him, a kaleidoscope of sharp hard facts tumbling downward, their facets packing against one another to produce an incontrovertible surface, one that could not be rearranged. He was a fool. He might be home free, but he was a dick-for-brains *fool.*

"What?" said Cherry. When he didn't answer, she looked down at the film can in her hand, her lip curled in a ripe sneer.

He stood up and held out his hand, the situation self-evident. "Give me that. We're getting rid of it."

She closed her hand around it and shook her head. "You think it makes any difference to me she likes his peenie better?"

Boudreau turned slightly and looked down, as if searching for something on the floor. She was fucking with his head.

After a moment he turned back. *"Here."* He grabbed the phone off the nightstand. "Here, *feel free*, you want to call Harmon and set things up?" He jerked it out at her, hard enough to make her flinch back against the wall. "There's two people dead, you want to go for more?"

She stared at him so hard her eyes pinched together, shaking her head like she'd always known it would come to this. "No, *three.*" Her voice was going. "*Three*, you—"

Boudreau slammed the phone down and turned back. He would explain this patiently, once and for all. "Hey, *look*, you and your girlfriend wanted to pick up some extra change and it turned out real bad. I'm sorry, okay? But don't lay it on me, cause *I can't fix it.*" He moved up to the edge of the bed and held out his hand.

She crabbed down the wall to the corner, cheeks up and her eyes narrowed to slits. "You prick," she said. "You hard-on *prick.*"

His hand was shaking. "Now *give* it to me."

Cherry's knuckles went white around the film can. She closed her eyes for strength, then shook her head.

Boudreau leaned over and hit her hard across the face, a roundhouse open-palmed smack. "I said *give it to me.*" The words sounded like they were bubbling up from a hole in the ground.

She hunched herself into the corner. All her features jammed into the center of her face, one whole side of which glowed red. "What a man."

Boudreau was having trouble breathing. Dimly, he understood something was about to veer off. He leaned over one more time and held out his hand. "This is *over, cunt,*" he explained through his teeth.

Cherry tried to smirk, mouth crooked, then spat in his face.

She rolled off the bed as he lunged, making it halfway across the room before he got a hand on her. She twisted away again, slippery skinned, and Boudreau fell, catching the back of her red panties as he hit the carpet. The underwear tore and rolled down into a flimsy rope around her thighs, just enough to bring her down.

Half on top of her, he pinned her wrists to the floor.

Cherry's eyes locked into his while she struggled. She gave one last thrash and went limp, breathing hard. "Hit me some more?" He could feel the fear and hatred radiating up into him like heat. "Gonna hit me some more, then *ball* me?"

Boudreau felt his face distort at how wrong she had him. Not if you paid me, he thought, but all that came out of his mouth was an ugly snort. This was the worst relationship he'd ever had, bar none. He squeezed her wrists until she squealed and the can rolled out of her palm. When he went for it, she brought up a knee and caught him in the stretch, hard bone to soft nuts.

Boudreau jackknifed into a dead heap on top of her. The pain kept inflating, filling him up to the bursting point. She clawed at his face, frantic to get out from under.

He beat her methodically, the rhythm of blows to her face convincing him that pain for pain was a satisfying exchange, that he'd never have to endure this again. She went limp and it got easier. There were urgent noises, apparently coming from his own throat. It was only when he heard a strange sucking sound that he saw his own hands around her neck, her eyes rolled up white.

Electric with fear, Boudreau jerked himself away as if breaking free of something. This was back-alley shit, this put him in league with razor artists and shallow-grave specialists, people who had extra chromosomes. *He'd killed her.*

After a long moment she drew breath in a raspy sucking gulp. She made a little moan, then breathed again and rolled over on her side.

Boudreau's heart came down out of his throat. If they'd just talked more, they could've worked things out. She was strung out and upset; she'd pushed him and he lost it. She was going to be okay, the main thing was she'd be okay.

He touched her and a tiny cry leaked out. She drew her knees up to her chest, awaiting the worst.

Boudreau groaned. He was one of *them;* one thing had led to another and he stood revealed as one of *them.* The veneer got ripped back and all that was left was the raw *me:* my life, not yours; your death, not mine. For something to believe in, it wasn't much.

He grabbed the film can and stood up, his knees buckling immediately. Okay, he'd deal with it down here on the floor. He pulled off the top and got out the cartridge, then took one of his shoes and beat on the metal until it crumpled.

Boudreau ripped the black celluloid out into the light like so much flat plastic intestine. He crawled over to the phone book and looked up the number, then dialed it.

A male voice was in his ear before the first ring had finished. "Yeah?" came the voice.

It was not Harmon Shaw. Boudreau breathed out, trying to regain whatever confidence he'd had a few seconds before.

"This here's a friend," he said. "Y'all tell Harmon he can re-lax, we won't bother him no more." He listened through a long silence. "You tell him the evidence is *gone* now."

"Hold on just a minute please," the voice said.

Boudreau considered hanging up as another, deeper voice came on the line. It still wasn't Harmon Shaw's, but it seemed rich with authority. "How can I help you?" it said in a grit accent. *He'p.*

Boudreau repeated it word for word, this time hopelessly corn-pone, like a desperate actor trying a different reading.

"Is that right?" The man seemed amused. "Have you and me talked before, friend?"

"You just *tell* Harmon, okay?" Boudreau panicked. Now he'd just used his own voice. "Tell him the evidence is *gone.*"

"We been waiting to hear from you." The man's tone took on an intimate, cajoling tone. "You wouldn't be the one blew up Bedford's car, now would you?"

Boudreau pushed the button down. He let it back up after a few seconds and listened to the dial tone, as if for confirmation that the connection was really broken.

He put the phone back in its cradle and waited for the sense of closure. It was *over*, it was over and done with. So why did he feel worse instead of better? The man's voice still felt present, like it had somehow lodged in his mind. That call had been a big mistake. A prickly sensation blossomed all over his skin.

So what had he expected the guy to say? Oh, you mean *that*, that dead nigger gal? Well, *hell*, why didn't you *say* so?

You ever do a nigger gal?

The man's voice came unlodged. Boudreau heard it all over again, heard it pretending to be lip-smacking drunk, heard it as clearly as if the flat-faced man with the tattoos had just whispered it into the phone. *It's like sliding into pork fat.*

In the bar he'd taken it as just another piece of ambient racism, no big deal. For a mind otherwise paved flat, it seemed more curious than anything, a hardy little sexual weed that had somehow come up through the cracks in the bigotry.

Boudreau understood it now as the talk of a butcher, not just a killer. Ronnie was *right*. This was the sound of someone who *liked* it, a believer: a butcher, a baker, a lamp-shade maker. A homegrown Nazi. This was a man who had sat and watched him and Ronnie and Cherry, who'd followed and listened and watched, who knew car licenses and addresses and phone numbers.

It felt like insects were crawling all over his skin. Maybe he was hallucinating, maybe this was what happened when you got DTs, things fell apart and you kept putting them back together wrong. A man looking for a roll of film.

He stopped himself. This was crazy. It was just a voice on the phone. There was no need to be like this.

"George," he said.

Brinkman sighed heavily. "Look, don't even think about hanging up on me again. This is giving me blue balls."

Boudreau blurted it out. "You know that picture with the guy on it? I need to know about that guy. The tattooed guy."

"What a surprise," said Brinkman. "I happen to have the picture of your tattooed man sitting right in front of me. First you tell me where you are."

Boudreau got a hallucinatory echo over the wire, a distant click as though this were coming to him secondhand. "I can't do that."

Brinkman sighed again. "Why's that?"

"I don't think this phone is good." Boudreau lowered his voice, illogically. "I mean, I think it might be *tapped.*"

"Tapped?" Brinkman made a sound of exasperation. "Boudreau, what movie is it you're starring in? Come on, man, this is getting tedious. Address first, then picture."

"Don't Jew me, George, I *can't.*"

There was a long pause. " 'Don't *Jew* me, George'? Did I really hear that?"

"I'm sorry. Listen, I'm sorry, okay, I'm *sorry.*" He tried to get his breath. "I can't."

"Okay," Brinkman said after a moment. "Okay, picture first to show good faith." He cleared his throat. "This is hard to make out, but let's see, it says F, then U, F-U, all right, I got it, on one arm it says 'FUCK.' Now the other one says, what's it say? —okay, here it is. 'FUCK YOU,' I guess the whole thing says 'FUCK YOU.' Must be some kind of biker deal."

Boudreau couldn't get out anything more than a cracked whisper. "Please," he said. *"Please."*

"So tell me where you are," said Brinkman.

Boudreau drew in a breath and held it. On the exhale he told him. What difference did it make?

"Okay, *good,*" said Brinkman, writing it down. "Good. There's sort of a snarling panther on the left forearm," he said, "and your boy Jesus Himself on the right arm, you know that goyische thing where they nail him to the fence? That ring a bell?"

Boudreau moaned audibly over the phone, his guts turning to water.

"Boudreau," said Brinkman, "you there?"

"Yeah, I'm here." Boudreau made a quakey attempt at a laugh. "I'm dead meat, but I'm here." His throat felt thick and he tried to clear it. "I need protection, I got people after me. They're gonna *kill* me."

Brinkman considered this during a long pause. "Okay, calm down, just tell me what's going on."

Boudreau worked on his breath. "You won't believe this. It was Harmon Shaw who blew up the car."

"Harmon Shaw blew up the car," said Brinkman after a moment. "You're right."

"No, *no.* See, his son *killed* someone, there was blood all over the fucking *car,* it was a *coverup.*" Boudreau could hear his credibility coming apart like wet tissue. "George, he killed a *black* girl." He lowered his voice. "He's got this fucking *army* in the Ozarks—not Bedford, I mean *Harmon,* Harmon does—it's a white supremacist thing, they shot that black judge in Arkansas. I'm not positive about that, but there's three people dead here. Here in *Tulsa.* Two that I definitely know about, that guy with the film, he's one of them." He stopped, suddenly uncertain who might have shot Keith, Ronnie or the butcher with the tattoos. What difference did it make? "I think there's three, I'm not sure." He added an afterthought. "I think it's possible some of the police department might already know."

George Brinkman didn't say anything for what seemed like several minutes. "Let's see, a white supremacist thing." There was the sound of a chair creaking back. "A dead black judge, but no, wait, you can't be sure of that. Okay. Anyway, two people definitely dead, the guy with the film and somebody else, that must be the black chick. Maybe *three,* but you don't know." Brinkman paused, then went portentous. "And the police are in on it." He leaned into the phone. "You know what you did, Boudreau? You died and went back to the *sixties.*" Brinkman was getting a charge out of his own irritation. "What's it *like* back there? They got marijuana growing on trees, lotta conspiracies and shit?"

Boudreau found himself looking down at the unraveled celluloid on the floor. "I had evidence," said Boudreau. "I can testify to evidence."

"You *had* evidence?" Brinkman snorted. "What'd it do, die in the jungle with Che? This is refried beans, man, it *stinks.* What the fuck do you take me for?" Brinkman caught his breath. "You need a fucking hospital."

Boudreau stared at the hair on his own knuckles, the last real thing in the world. "I have proof about the black girl."

"What, you mean a *fact?* Isn't it kind of lonely?"

Boudreau looked over at the woman he'd just tried to strangle. "I have," he said, "an eyewitness to Bedford Shaw's murder of a topless dancer named Earla Armstrong. She's right here."

Brinkman thought about it, then exhaled loudly. "All right," he said. "This better check out, pal. I'll be there in a few minutes."

Boudreau caught him before he hung up. "Hey, George?" he said. "George, could you bring a joint with you?"

George Brinkman waited for a while before answering, like this was just what he'd been afraid of. "Whatever gets you through the night," he said.

Cherry had made it to a semireclining position against the side of the bed. One eye was starting to swell and there was blood from her nose and a split lip. Her neck was ringed by a livid red band.

"Are you okay?"

She looked up at him the way you'd look at a tree or a cow or a telephone pole.

He turned away and made it painfully over to Vicky's green dress. Cherry was still naked except for the torn underwear halfway down her thighs.

"You better put this on." He held out the dress without being able to look directly at her. "My friend from the paper's coming to talk to us. To you."

She shook her head, speech gone.

"You don't have a choice," he said. "*We* don't have a choice."

She stared blankly.

Boudreau hobbled to the end of the room, the dress still in his hand. He felt a sudden painful churning in the bottom of his abdomen, as though his nuts had just recruited his bowels in a ruthless regional offensive.

He leaned on the top of the TV to hold himself up. "It wasn't Vicky." They'd both been wrong, maybe this would patch things up. "It was *them.*"

He made his way over to stand in front of her. "They'll *kill* us," he tried to explain. "They'll kill us unless we go public."

She looked right through him.

"Here, put it on." He held out the dress, and she cringed away in slow motion.

He bent over to put it next to her and felt his guts cramp so hard it felt like they were exploding. He grunted and dropped the dress, then tried to straighten up.

Boudreau's face flushed hard, a dizzying wave of nausea breaking over him. He felt deathly. Something had burst inside him. This was going to be his fitting end, some kind of abdominal rupture, a spew of the poisoned shit he carried around inside himself. Tight legged and doubled over, he stumbled to the bathroom.

After a few minutes he flushed the toilet and stood up, the foulness of his own odor enveloping him. He'd thought he was dying, and it was only diarrhea. Other people were dying all around and he'd panicked about a case of the trots. He looked in the mirror, his face mime-white.

He came out of the bathroom and she was gone, the dress with her.

From the balcony walkway he scanned the huge arc-lit parking lot. He couldn't make out anyone in the shadowless gleaming light, an eerie pale salmon glow that seemed to emanate from the rows of cars themselves, as though they were spaceships, newly arrived from some other world.

She was out in the middle of seven lanes with a green light, a shadowy figure on the median strip, hand on the post of a traffic sign. He started yelling her name, again and again, the words floating up like lost balloons over the traffic noise.

She sleep-walked off the curb and made it to the middle south-bound lane before crossing the path of a car with one headlight. She disappeared from view and the car kept going as though nothing had happened.

For a long second he thought she'd somehow made it, until the one-eyed car slid sideways to a stop in the middle of the huge intersection. The stream of traffic noise was cut by a squall of brakes, cars

jamming to halt in all four directions, as distinctly as if someone had just
bent a kink in a garden hose.

There was a long harmonic burst of horns, thinning into a few stray
honks and then nothing. A woman's scream fountained up in the sudden
blank of silence, a rocket in the dark sky.

Boudreau walked purposefully down to the Healey as a pandemonium
of people began pouring out of the lounge down at the other end of the
hotel, yelling and running out to the street. *He might as well have pushed
her.*

He backed the Healey out of the slot, jammed it in first. At the other
end of the parking lot a car pulled in and stopped, its headlights on him.
For some reason he knew who it was immediately and whipped the car
around in a tight U. He looked in the mirror and felt a rush of confirmation as the double headlights accelerated after him.

The parking lot surrounded the motel like a racetrack, and he cor-
nered crazily around it, already in second gear by the time he hit the
straightaway toward the side-street exit.

A solid triple line of stopped cars blocked the exit, people already
standing next to their open doors, craning to see what was going on in
the intersection. The lanes on the other side, beyond the median strip,
were empty as a runway. He looked in the rearview at the advancing
headlights and wrenched the wheel, scraping over a curb divider into the
adjacent parking lot of the little mall of stores next door. He drove the
length of it, looking out at the road as more and more cars came to a
halt, bottlenecking like sand in an hourglass. A single car thought better
of the wait and turned into the convenience store at the end of the lot.
He saw the gap and punched the accelerator, hitting the median strip
hard enough to make the little car buck like a wild thing as it went over.

He did it. He headed east, driving legally in case of cops, the road
wind in his face hot as exhaust from a furnace. The street behind him
was empty.

He wasn't sure how much gas was in the tank, but when it ran out, he'd walk, and when he couldn't walk, he'd crawl. The thought of getting killed would keep him going, plenty of motivation for the time being. That was really all it was anyway, right? Just *motion*, just a swirl of random particles colliding in chaos, brief specks of heat and light the only record of the exchange. He pulled up to a safe distance behind the only other car on the road and tooled along in its wake.

The road had narrowed to two lanes by the time he noticed the headlights in his mirror, maybe a half mile behind. It stayed there and he relaxed. It was just another car.

The next time he looked it was screaming up on him, doing eighty to his fifty. He saw the headlights coalesce into double lamps and realized he'd been entirely too theoretical about death. Brief specks of light, bullshit. It would *hurt.*

The other car came up way too fast and hit its brakes, just as he downshifted into third and pulled out from behind the one he'd been following. He punched the pedal, the Healey streaking around it in a silky leap of acceleration.

Boudreau watched in the rearview, ecstatic, as the double headlights snaked all over the road in an out-of-control skid. The Healey could do 140 in overdrive. He could outrun these guys all day long.

When he returned his eyes to the road, the stop sign was in his face. He punched the pedal again and the car popped out of gear, all momentum and no acceleration. He wrenched the wheel hard left to avoid the northbound pickup truck and missed it clean by a matter of inches.

Whoa *shit,* what a close one! The whoop of triumph was still in his throat as the little car became airborne. He must have hit a curb or something.

It was the damnedest feeling, this upsidedown rolling, this tumbling freedom from gravity—it was like no other ride he'd ever taken.

Hurtling through the air into the dark maw of his own future, Boudreau experienced an elongated moment of clarity, just like they always said. It was a comforting thing, it placed him in the larger community. He had spent his life believing he wasn't one of them, that he was somehow different or better, but he wasn't really, he was just like everybody else, just another hairless primate too smart to know any better. This was a good thing to learn. He saw the utility pole coming up but had no fear of it.

The moment stretched on, swelling him with a remorse unbelievably sweet for all the moments gone before it, the endless sentence with the punctuation now in sight. He'd done so many bad things out of fear and confusion, he had lied and cowered and screwed up, *hurt* people. He'd treated men like competition or outright threats, women like targets; he'd treated himself like an asshole he didn't want to be around. This didn't change what he'd done, of course, but it put things in perspective. He was not a bad person, but his life had somehow hardened around him imperceptibly, layer after layer, as though he'd gotten trapped in a body not his own. He saw it so clearly: now that he could slip right out of it, he saw that it had never been truly *him*.

This, he understood, was grace, the opportunity to regard his life as a complete thing, in place in the world. It filled him with sadness as the phone pole approached. Boudreau felt people would behave better if they knew it came to this. He knew he would have.

THURSDAY

G eorge Brinkman rolled up to the bullet-pocked stop sign and hesitated a moment before continuing on. This was no-shit boondocks out here. According to his directions he didn't have that much farther to go; he figured if it started looking really bad, he could always turn around.

It was eight o'clock in the morning, but the sky looked like a warm-up for the end of creation. It was low lying and dark, *vengeful,* shafted through in a couple places by a dirty light that let him see how thick the roiling mass was. He was sweating like a field hand, the windows rolled up against the wind. It was so intense the car kept lurching away from him, these periodic little sneak attacks as though an unseen demented hitchhiker was trying to grab the wheel away.

Brinkman's shoulders felt like iron. He'd been listening to weather broadcasts since before dawn, and now off to the east he could see fuzzy dark things hanging down to the ground like tentacles. He hoped to God they were just thunderclouds or whatever.

He kept driving, craning under the windshield to see if there were any sudden changes up there. At least in Jersey the shit in the sky was man-made. This was different.

Brinkman didn't regard himself as a superstitious guy, but he was a believer in vibes and these sucked. This was the kind of landscape that would make you feel like a bug even on a clear day. He'd gone past the outer fringes of development and now it was just rolling brown *nothing,* your occasional stunted tree and a lot of fence. He watched the road and thought of Boudreau, how he was always mouthing off about developers raping the farmland around Tulsa. In Brinkman's humble opinion there was nothing here worth fucking.

Tulsa. *Tulsa.* People around here were different and it wasn't just that they all had blond hair and bad taste. How could you want to live in a place like this? You couldn't, that's how, but these people were *believers,* they lived in air-conditioning and convinced themselves the heat wasn't real.

A clear indication of this was the widespread local belief in the end of the world. Brinkman took no issue with the basic notion; every time he heard a civil defense test on the radio he cringed and thought, *Here we go.* That was natural, anybody who could add megatons had to know it was coming. But *these* people, they acted like it would be some kind of *festival* and they had the only advance tickets. *Rapture,* they were always going on about rapture and the select few. What a laugh. So far as he could tell, they thought it would be sort of like Christmas and the Super Bowl wrapped together, with a lot of special effects and then *God,* a superfriendly talk-show host who would know them all personally.

Believers made Brinkman nervous.

Boudreau, primo example. Maybe once Boudreau had been a smart guy, but he'd taken all this shit way too seriously. You took these people too serious it was like a fucking *virus,* you ended up on wild-goose chases through your own mind. This weird fixation with Raheems, the obsession about Greenwood, for instance—now there was a key to Boudreau. He'd latched on to this clown Shaw like a sucking wound who'd just found true love. Brinkman suspected that maybe Boudreau had a little tar brush somewhere back in the family. More likely it was an old girlfriend or something, that was probably it. Whatever else he could say about him, Boudreau got laid more than any one white boy deserved, he had to give him that. Maybe it was just talk, but women were such suckers for that burned-out, I'm-so-weary-with-the-world schtick.

But what really burned Brinkman's ass was that meantime, Boudreau-the-less-racist-than-thou played fast and loose along anti-Semitic lines, with his little assumptions and his cute little Yiddishisms. This was liberal Tulsa in spades, pardon the expression. Boudreau could worry all he wanted about oppression of the colored, but that didn't give him license to think he knew what it was like to be a Jew. No way.

Brinkman had no quarrel with black people; he appreciated them for the best power forwards and funk musicians the human race had to offer, no small achievement in his view. He would trade the whole of opera or tennis for either one.

But that didn't mean he'd go out of his way to have one for a friend, or even that he felt all that comfortable around them. Call it racist if you want; in his view it was more like in*stinc*tual, more like *tribal*. He himself had a finely tuned sense of tribe, a couple thousand years' worth, and so far as he could see, the Soul Brothers weren't exactly lining up to get intramural with the Chosen People, either.

And that was cool, no reason it should be any different. They understood each other, blacks and Jews; it was only when they got jammed into each other's faces that it became kike and nigger.

Brinkman had met a *schwartze* Jew one time, a pious Ethiopian, and he'd just stood and stared like an asshole, unable to connect the one with the other. Sammy Davis was one thing, but this was totally disorienting, like seeing a beautiful woman and finding out it was a guy in drag.

An invisible gust, a vicious little dybbuk of wind, came along and wrenched the car over into the opposite lane. It was a good thing no one else was fool enough to be driving out here. Brinkman slowed down until his pulse stopped racing, then relit the joint he'd rolled last night for Boudreau. This whole thing was getting to be a joke anyway.

"Hey, Boudreau," he said over his shoulder. "You sure you don't want any of this reefer?"

A small moan issued from the backseat, pathetic enough to make him pull over and look.

Boudreau was out cold, somewhere in another world. The doctor in the ER said it wasn't that bad, a minor concussion and a hairline crack in his skull. After he'd x-rayed him and stitched him up, the doc gave him a needle full of dreamland, and Brinkman had had to shoulder him out to the backseat, no mean feat after a sleepless night hanging out in a hospital waiting room.

A hairline crack, now there was a chuckle, what did that mean if you were crackbrained already? Against every grain of his better judgment, Brinkman had trucked his ass over to the motel, swearing at himself the whole time, not believing for a minute that anything would come of it.

Still, he'd gotten royally pissed when he saw Boudreau trying to pull another fast one. When he caught up, he was personally going to beat the shit out of him.

The stupid little sports car was wrapped around the bottom of the pole like a horseshoe, one wheel still spinning. Whatever saint it was that looked after assholes had given Boudreau a circus catapult ride for final measure. Brinkman found him on the ground thirty or forty yards away, convinced he was dead, then amazed that he wasn't. The bastard wasn't even unconscious.

He drove to the hospital while Boudreau sat beside him, his face streaming blood, rapping away like he hadn't just been shot out of a cannon in his snazzy chalk-striped bell-bottoms. It was the worst kind of deep-end speed babble, Harmon Shaw and blackmail and a roll of film, race war, dead people, the beautiful light you saw right before you died, the works. He was *excited.* Oh yeah, and something about how he'd just murdered some girl, that was a brand new one. Brinkman kicked himself for not having the recorder going to capture this for posterity.

Still out in the backseat, Boudreau mumbled something, then moaned again. "Mom?" he said.

Mom? Brinkman snorted to keep from losing his smoke. This guy was truly a refugee from another planet, slack jawed and swollen faced, with big black Frankenstein-stitches following the shaved path up over the top of his head, like someone had gone nuts with a miniature lawn mower and then planted dead shrubs down the middle of it.

Mom. Brinkman laughed out loud and put the car back in gear. Even a mother would have trouble believing someone like this.

So why, exactly, was he paying a visit to Harmon Shaw during a storm right out of the Bible? He could ask himself that. He'd come this far, that's what it boiled down to. Call it reporter's curiosity, he figured at the least all this would be good color for the long piece he planned to send around. Crackpot right-wing millionaire in the land of the yahoo, threats and accusations all around, it had possibilities on both coasts, where people could see the humor in it. Now *there* was a ticket for the ride out; it had major metropolitan daily written all over it. Feature writer. Boudreau had certainly earned an appearance in it somewhere, Brinkman just didn't know where yet. He calmed down a little, considering the possibilities. He had to start thinking about the hook, the through line, the thing that would tie it together.

It came to him: this was what happened when people had no sense of history. They just made it up as they went along. People out here *had* no sense of tribe, history made them uncomfortable, like they might have to pay some dues on how they got there, who they were. They were *lost.*

They were a lost people.

With that thought, Brinkman pulled up in front of Harmon Shaw's. Even without a mailbox or sign it was unmistakable. There was a gravel drive, a good quarter mile long and straight as a bowling alley, leading to a huge one-story modern structure that squatted at the end of it. An eight-foot-high chain-link fence began at the road and went nearly as far as he could see in both directions. Brinkman got a nervous charge out of it. This was the house of a comically paranoid dude, homey as a concrete bunker.

The gates in the chain-link had been left open. What the hell? he figured, and drove through. At least when the tornado hit, he'd have a bomb shelter to wait it out in.

Brinkman got out of the car, the hot wind nearly whipping the door off its hinges before he got it closed. Boudreau was comatose in the backseat, down for the count.

He rang the front doorbell and waited. Nothing happened and he rang it again, only then noticing a pair of video security cameras aimed at him from above the door. He mugged at them, getting himself in the mood.

"Yo!" he said. "Yo, anybody home?"

The door opened noiselessly, courtesy of the flunky bodyguard who'd given Boudreau such a case of the shits.

"Yeah, hi," said Brinkman. "George Brinkman, from the *Tulsa Journal?*"

The man looked at him without saying anything. Brinkman's antennae went up and he smiled. What a cracker. He watched the single thought form behind the guy's flat eyes as surely as if JEW in red neon had just appeared on his forehead, flashing on and off.

"I don't have an appointment or anything," he said, "but I was hoping Mr. Shaw might have a few minutes for me."

The man raised his eyebrows, confirming that he had hearing, anyway.

Brinkman began to reconsider. This guy's bags weren't unpacked yet from his last road tour with the Visigoths. Maybe he'd missed out on all the big changes in civilization, like language.

"I realize it's early," Brinkman said, "I can come back some other time if it's inconvenient." Next year, maybe.

The bodyguard indicated entry with one arm, then stepped aside.

Brinkman walked into a big, echoey hall, terrazzo floored and blank walled. The door closed behind him with the heavy sound of a vault being sealed.

"You heard any more weather?" said Brinkman, turning around. His case of bad vibes had returned, with a vengeance. "What's happening with this tornado thing?"

The man smiled. "I ain't heard a thing," he said, and flattened Brinkman against the wall.

Brinkman had never been frisked before, so he had no sense of how you usually felt, but this was violation, he'd just been violated. It felt like the motherfucker was *processing* him.

The bodyguard took his recorder and picked up a big militarylooking walkie-talkie from a table.

"Hey, this is *bullshit.*" Brinkman heard his outrage struggle to stand up under the sheer weight of fear. There was something seriously wrong about this. "Look, I can understand how you're concerned about security, but you could've *asked,* man, I'm gonna have to file a—"

"Mister Shaw?" the man said into the walkie-talkie. "Mister Shaw?"

Brinkman heard a squawk of incomprehensible static.

"No, he's alone." There was another squawk and the man smiled. "Yessir."

He examined the recorder, popped out the tape and then handed it back to Brinkman. "Let's go."

On the way out in the golf cart, Brinkman had the momentary insane thought that Harmon Shaw had installed acres of Astro Turf as his major landscaping effort. He'd never seen such an expanse of perfectly flat featureless green, something that looked like it had been rolled down and stitched together rather than grown. Then he began to notice regularly placed sprinkler heads and caught an occasional whiff of cut grass laced with a vaguely wet chemical smell. Okay, so it was grass. It might be real, but that didn't make it right.

They rode long enough that Brinkman began to wonder. Maybe this was some kind of primitive Christian ritual, maybe the guy was going to stake him down in the middle of all that green and leave him for the tornado. Gusts of wind rocked the golf cart with violent shudders, all the more surreal because they seemed to come out of nowhere. If it were water, at least you'd be able to see waves.

Brinkman was beginning to panic when he caught sight of something in the distance, a moving point sandwiched between the plane of unnaturally bright green below and the hulking dark mass above.

Harmon Shaw was out mowing the lawn. He was on a riding machine, not just any mower but a fairway-designed monster pulling six big gang cutters. The bodyguard stopped the golf cart thirty yards away and indicated that this was it.

Brinkman walked toward the mower, the flunky trailing behind. Harmon Shaw stopped his contraption and got off.

"Mr. Shaw?" said Brinkman, holding out his hand. "George Brinkman, I've been covering—"

"I know who you are." Harmon Shaw kept his eyes roving over the expanse of green. His mouth moved briefly in an expression of satisfaction or amusement that in no way affected the top half of his face. "I keep track of what the Jew-run media has to say about me."

Brinkman's jaw dropped before his hand did. Shaw had said it without venom, as if he were talking about a minor irritation like mosquitoes or chiggers.

"The Jew-run media?" The man was either joking or seriously out of whack with reality. Brinkman had trouble keeping the smile off his face, then made the mistake of looking over at the flunky. No one thought it was funny here, himself now included.

"Go ahead," said Harmon Shaw. "Ask your questions."

Brinkman considered. Maybe Shaw was a scary loon of an anti-Semite, but that didn't exactly make him unusual, much less a murderer. *Fuck it,* he thought, you have to play these things by ear.

"I've been following the investigation," he yelled into the wind, "of the incident involving your son's car. There's a name that keeps coming up." He smiled like he was sorry to have to ask this next question. "Are you familiar with an Earla Armstrong?"

Shaw lifted his solid bar of an eyebrow without looking at Brinkman, genuinely curious. "Earla *Arm*strong?"

Brinkman kept his eyes on him. If he'd ever heard the name before, he was either a hell of an actor or she meant nothing to him. He went for broke. "She was found murdered a few days before," he shouted. "Before the car blew up, I mean."

Brinkman watched Harmon Shaw stare out at his lawn and wished he could take it back. He'd just fucking accused the guy point-blank.

"What might that have to do with my boy Bedford's car? You think this Earla Armstrong was in on it?"

"I don't know," said Brinkman, trying to keep his tone ingenuous in spite of his volume. "It's just a name that kept cropping up. I just wondered if you'd come across it."

Shaw shrugged, as if a man of his position couldn't be expected to remember every last person who walked in the door. He turned abruptly to gesture out at the expanse of featureless green surrounding them. "And God said, Let the earth bring forth *grass,* the herb yielding seed." He bent over and grabbed a handful of grass, then straightened up, holding it tight in his fist. "Genesis, one: eleven." He smiled at it, his knuckles hairy as an ape's. "This here's the hardiest, thriftiest, most adaptable, best-looking grass you can buy." He opened his fist and a gust of wind dissipated it in an instant.

Shaw had yet to look at him, and Brinkman realized he wasn't going to. The interview, such as it was, was over. Maybe his boy had done it after all, but Brinkman wasn't so sure, and right now he didn't care. The wind had increased to the point where it was hard to stand up straight, hard to even breathe.

Harmon Shaw paid no attention. "I grow the stock seed up in Oregon, guaranteed uncontaminated," he said, "the purest seed there is. You help it along with water and fertilizer, it'll grow anywhere." Shaw's small, deep-set eyes surveyed the ground around him, and he dropped suddenly to his knees. He plucked out a little broad-leafed plant with serrated edges and stood up.

Brinkman's panic deepened; there was something drastically wrong in the man's lack of concern. *Grass?* Who could give a shit? Behind Shaw two of the dark tendrils that had been off in the distance a few seconds before were now much closer. Now they'd thickened to gyrating columns under the boiling darkness, menacing as guard towers. Brinkman leaned into the wind, ready to bolt.

"Contaminants," Harmon Shaw said, "multiply beyond reason and without purpose, except to hinder the survival of pure seed." He opened his hand and let the wind rip the dandelion away, then looked straight into Brinkman's face.

Brinkman's scalp lifted as he looked into something as old as the Stone Age. Ancestral disbelief coursed through him, the dormant dread come to life like a virulent bacterium. This was how it felt, this was how it had always felt. "You fucking *Nazi,*" he said.

"Wade?" Without shifting his gaze, Harmon Shaw gave a weary nod to the body guard. The man produced a cannon from under his windbreaker and aimed it at Brinkman.

"The face of evil takes every human form," Shaw said. "Pray to your Satan, false Jew." He watched the reporter fall to his knees, then turned and started walking back to his mower.

After years of disuse, the Hebrew School words came halting at first, then strong and clear. Eyes open, George Brinkman prayed to his God for deliverance, the gunman facing him from a few feet away, staring down in openmouthed fascination. Brinkman prayed, then suddenly saw motion in the far distance, a hurtling object that materialized from behind the house.

His eyes widening, Bri
straight line like an avengi
wind. He became a believ
second head fake and a ha
mow him down.

Harmon Shaw kept wal
glance and immediately r
jitterbugging across the ne
he took it as a sign. *Praise (*
Storms pass by the rightec

He barely heard the *cra*
followed not more than a

He snapped around. Hi
understand at first. The Z
was in two parts, his upp
smeared grass, his lower tc
feet beyond.

It was not at all the way
rapture but with the inc
seemed to have leapt fr
swirled and shot upward i
him, then disappeared. *Th*
catching a last glimpse of
the true storm upon then

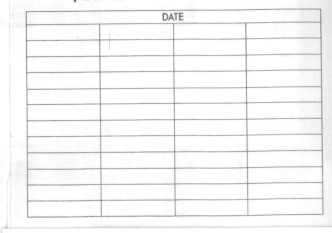